Islam in the Middle East

To my daughter Katerina

ISLAM
in the Middle East

A LIVING TRADITION

G.P. Makris

Blackwell Publishing

BLACKWELL PUBLISHING
350 Main Street, Malden, MA 02148-5020, USA
9600 Garsington Road, Oxford OX4 2DQ, UK
550 Swanston Street, Carlton, Victoria 3053, Australia

First published 2007 by Blackwell Publishing Ltd

1 2007

Library of Congress Cataloging-in-Publication Data

Makris, G.P.
Islam in the Middle East : a living tradition / G.P. Makris.
p. cm.
Includes bibliographical references and index.
ISBN-13: 978-1-4051-1602-2 (alk. paper)
ISBN-13: 978-1-4051-1603-9 (pbk. : alk. paper)
ISBN-10: 1-4051-1602-1 (alk. paper)
ISBN-10: 1-4051-1603-X (pbk. : alk. paper) 1. Islam—Middle East—History. 2. Religious awakening—Islam. I. Title.

BP63.A35M35 2006
297.0956—dc22

2005057245

A catalogue record for this title is available from the British Library.

Set in 11.5/13.5 pt Bembo
by Graphicraft Limited, Hong Kong
Printed and bound in Singapore
by COS Printers Pte Ltd

The publisher's policy is to use permanent paper from mills that operate a sustainable forestry policy, and which has been manufactured from pulp processed using acid-free and elementary chlorine-free practices. Furthermore, the publisher ensures that the text paper and cover board used have met acceptable environmental accreditation standards.

For further information on
Blackwell Publishing, visit our website:
www.blackwellpublishing.com

Contents

Preface

Some years ago a colleague teaching anthropology at the University of London asked me "Is there any textbook that a non-Islam specialist may read to get a general idea about this tradition?"

I realized that despite the wealth of writings on Islam there was no one introductory volume to Islam that offered an entry to the Islamic tradition and included specific ethnographic examples, not from the entire Muslim world but at least from a sufficiently extensive and recognizable region such as the Middle East. Instructors from a wide range of courses needed a book for students that celebrated Islam's living tradition – in other words an introduction to the transcultural similarities and universal aspirations of Islam as a major world religion, as well as to the wealth of its local interpretations. To fill that gap I wrote this book gathering information found mostly in specialized volumes on Islamic theology and politics and enlivened by ethnographic descriptions from a number of Muslim societies in the Middle East. By bringing together these disparate materials, the book offers non-specialists a rounded, albeit by definition incomplete, picture of Islam in the region. An anthropologist might say self-deprecatingly, all ethnographic descriptions are partial.

The book differs from other textbooks in that it offers students detailed descriptions of cultural practices and discusses their multiple interpretations across different societies but also within each one of them. In this way, it goes beyond the norm and brings forward local meanings in all their complexity. In contrast to other studies, there is an emphasis on spirit-possession cults as an integral part of Islamic tradition and it introduces politics and current affairs as key elements in understanding contemporary Islamic discourse. Unlike the multitude of conventional studies by political scientists and international relations specialists, this text takes an informed anthropological look at Islam that is critical, reflective and continually changing. What the book argues in the end is that "orthodoxy", what is considered to be "correct" and traditionally acceptable, is always in the making, the unsteady and ever-changing result of an eminently political process.

Islam in the Middle East will form the ideal core textbook for courses on Islam across cultures or courses on the Middle East. For anthropology courses it will provide a key central text that can be enriched by adding several full-length ethnographies. Whatever its application, I hope that it provides students and instructors with a rich alternative to some of the less multi-faceted portraits of Islam that have proliferated in recent years.

The reader is kindly requested to keep in mind the political situation in the Middle East which is and always has been fluid. By the time he or she reads this book it would not be at all surprising if events had overtaken the narrative.

G.P. Makris

Acknowledgments

The following individuals have given me valuable criticisms and suggestions regarding the structure of the study and the various arguments discussed in it: D. Gefou Madianou, C. Papadakis, A. Athanasiou, T. Geros, D. Arkadas, S. Roussos, A. Kannas, G. Clonos, D. Bekridakis, D. Oulis, L. Papoutsis, B. Magna, Artemis Sotiropoulou. To all these friends and colleagues I am greatly indebted. I should also thank my students in the Department of Social Anthropology at Panteion University, Athens, for their penetrating comments and questions during my lectures on the anthropology of the Middle East. Naturally, it goes without saying that all responsibility rests with myself alone. My gratitude and sincere thanks to Jane Huber, Emily Martin and Sue Leigh from Blackwell. They not only acted as really professional editors, but as the project evolved they also proved to be trusted advisers and friends. Finally, I should thank my wife Mary for her patience and emotional support during a difficult period for our family, when older members passed away and our little daughter Katerina made her first steps in the world.

Transliteration and Abbreviations

Arabic terms have been italicized. Arabic names, titles, and words have been transliterated according to the norm of the *Journal Sudanic Africa*. For Turkish and Persian words the appropriate spelling has been used. Anglicized words such as caliph or sultan, as well as names of modern well-known politicians or organizations such as Anwar Sadat, Hosni Mubarak, HAMAS, or Islamic Jihad have been treated as English words. Place names are spelt in the way they appear on modern maps, except Saudi Arabian Madīna in order to indicate the city's special character in Muslim history. Inconsistencies may appear with authors' names which have been variously transliterated in international bibliographies, for example Hassan Turabi/Ḥasan al-Turābī. In such cases, correct Arabic transliteration has been invariably employed throughout the text, although in the bibliographical notes and the References, I have reverted to the spelling as published. As there are no surnames in Arabic, I have followed international bibliography and my instinct. For example, "Mawlānā Abū 'l-Aʿlā Mawdūdī" is called in the text "Mawdūdī," but in the References he is found under "Maududi, Mawlana Abul A'la." In such cases, the "personal names" are given in full after the surnames. The articles *al-* and *el-* are ignored in the alphabetical positioning of names in the References. I have used two abbreviations: *EI* (*Encyclopedia of Islam*) and *OED* (*Oxford English Dictionary*).

Introduction

Islam is the religion of more than one billion people in Asia and Africa, and of a growing number of immigrants in Europe and North America. During the last few years it has become more visible in the context of the political situation in the "Middle East" and Central Asia and in association with accusations of global terrorism.[1]

The present study is an effort to open up the field and present the wealth and variety of Islamic tradition, which Geertz has very aptly called "a supposedly single creed,"[2] as this can be found in the "Middle East" and North Africa, without denying the violence among fringe groups of self-styled religious fighters. In the chapters that follow I try to portray Islam as a unified tradition possessing a global vision that aspires to go beyond cultural and other specificities, but at the same time as a dynamic tradition that is locally shaped and continually reinterpreted in terms of specific idioms grounded on history. As Eickelman has argued,

> [t]he main challenge for the study of Islam is to describe how its universalistic and abstract principles have been realized in various social and historical contexts without representing Islam as a seamless essence on the one hand or as a plastic congeries [*sic*] of beliefs and practices on the other.[3]

To do this I have employed the concept of "discursive tradition" which has been variously developed by several scholars, including the moral philosopher Alasdair MacIntyre and anthropologists Abdel Hamid el-Zein and Talal Asad. As the latter argues, "[a]n Islamic discursive tradition is simply a tradition of Muslim discourse that addresses itself to conceptions of the Islamic past and future, with reference to a particular Islamic practice in the present."[4] This allows for both continuity and change, firmness and plasticity, agreements and disagreements, within historically informed social contexts. Especially in the context of the present study, the concept of "discursive tradition" enables me to discuss the multiple interpretations of doctrines and practices with all the contradictions they may present in terms of locality and of the identity of those involved.

Such positions are squarely situated within the tradition of social anthropology. This is important because anthropologists make every effort to eschew essentialism and to go beyond the terms set by elite conceptions of social reality, always questioning the normative status that certain beliefs and practices may assume. Likewise, they contextualize seemingly fringe ideologies and patterns of behavior, taking into account the specificity of local conditions and the possibilities afforded on each occasion by the historical conjunction. In this way, anthropologists bring forward something of the complexity, inner contradictions and multiple levels of signification of local discourses, as well as their historical constructedness and their positioning within, and engagement with other, discursive frameworks. Thus being critical of themselves and of their subject matter,[5] anthropologists can minimize the danger of falling victims to both cultural imperialism – that portrays a "Western" *Weltanschauung* as a universal constant – and orientalism – that portrays the Other as ultimately different to, if not the opposite of, "Western" man.

An anthropological introduction to Islam, then, allows me to examine Islamic tradition at two levels simultaneously. First, at the level of a world religion with a well-defined doctrinal framework and body of ritual practices, and second, at the local level where doctrines and practices take shape in the context of particular societies at particular historical conjunctions. To put it differently, I study Islam as a living tradition, however defined, of specific people(s) who are living their lives at the very moment you are reading this page, without disregarding Islam's claims to universality and its appeal to a universal Community of Believers, the Muslim *umma*.

Following the logic of the anthropological project, the present study approaches critically the manners in which doctrines and practices acquire their locally recognized canonical status. In practical terms, that leads to an inquiry into what Asad calls the production of "orthodoxy," a process close to the heart of the previously mentioned understanding of Islam as a "discursive tradition." This entails an analysis of the political terms that allow particular interpretations to become dominant in historically specific social contexts. Or, to paraphrase Gilsenan, who thinks along very similar lines, it involves the study of ways in which

> [i]n the name of tradition many traditions are born and come into opposition with others . . . [and how tradition] becomes a language, a weapon against internal and external enemies, a refuge, an evasion, or part of the entitlement to domination and authority over others.[6]

This, then, is the red line that goes through the eight chapters of this book. The "orthodox" character that doctrines and practices assume locally or translocally is duly acknowledged as such, but always as the tentative result of continuous negotiations.[7] Here, I believe, lies the importance of the whole project; that "orthodoxy" is never a given or a predetermined fact. It is always challenged to the degree that the relational position of those involved in each case is transformed. This can be clearly seen in chapter 3, where I consider the *'ulamā'* religious scholars-jurisconsults in relation to the production of Islamic "orthodoxy," then in chapter 5, where I discuss mystical Islam, and in the last three chapters of the study, where I discuss different approaches to Islamic tradition by Muslim reformists and Islamists. But even in the cases of doctrinally seemingly "unassailable" notions and practices, such as *ijtihād* (independent reasoning), orality, the ritual prayer, or the pilgrimage, which are discussed in chapters 2, 3, and 4, every effort is made to contextualize interpretations and to situate them within wider discussions among Muslims about the "straight way" (*al-ṣiraṭ al-mustaqīm*). This is, after all, what all Muslims pray for when they recite *al-Fātiḥa*, the seven-verse introduction to the *Qur'ān* that constitutes an integral part of prayers and other everyday formulaic expressions.

> Thee do we worship,
> And Thine aid we seek.
> Show us the straight way,
> The Way of those on whom
> Thou has bestowed Thy Grace,
> Those whose (portion)
> is not wrath.
> And who go not astray.[8]

Following this line, the present study of Islamic discourse has consciously attempted to avoid the pitfall of the Great/Little tradition thesis, that juxtaposes an allegedly scriptural "orthodoxy" of the learned religious scholars and jurisconsults with local popular practices associated with the uneducated masses; as well as the pitfall of the many-*islams* thesis, which alludes "to an essentialist, a-historical core" and neglects the politics of "orthodoxy" production both in the local context and in that of the universal imagined Community of Believers (*umma*).[9]

Does the present study constitute an *anthropology of Islam*, then? I am not sure it does. If an anthropology of Islam seeks "to understand the historical conditions that enable the production and maintenance of specific discursive traditions, or their transformation – and the efforts of practitioners to achieve coherence,"[10] I am afraid that what follows deals with such issues to a rather limited extent. As it is, the present volume is but an introduction to a living and apparently thriving world religion, the only such tradition that has been trenchantly assumed, for better or worse, to be flying in the face of a deceptively secular globalizing world. Based on ethnographic material from the "Middle East" and on concepts from the anthropological theoretical armory, my aim is to present a more or less coherent picture of: (i) its guiding doctrinal principles and the way these affect society through a process of continuous reinterpretation; (ii) its normative practices, including those related to mysticism, which provide locally held templates that regulate admission to the *umma*; (iii) some of its major intellectual and political trends which articulate dimensions of contemporary Muslim experience and practice. By definition, then, the present study is not and cannot be complete. The constant reformulation of doctrines and practices makes this an impossibility.

If this makes sense at a theoretical level, where "orthodoxy" is always in the making as a product of a never-ending process of negotiation among Muslims, it also constitutes a strategy of anthropological interpretation that works well in the present context of political turmoil and violence in the Muslim world and beyond. The gist of the argument is not that people do what they like in the name of their understanding of Islam, but that within the space delineated by binding first principles, there are a lot of paths that claim to be straight – and up to a point they may very well be. To examine such claims is a worthwhile endeavor. To know that such an examination cannot but remain incomplete is what in the last analysis keeps the project aligned with the realities of social change and the bitterness of political struggle. From this point of view, the undoing of stereotypes and the unraveling of emerging essentialist discourses on the "Muslim Other" that serve rather shortsighted political goals acquire a degree of urgency which was not there before.

LIMITS

Having said that, I should add a sober note concerning the current state of the anthropological study of Islam and Muslim societies. Although many respected anthropologists, such as Michael Gilsenan, Dale Eickelman, Richard Antoun, Ernest Gellner, Lila Abu-Lughod, Clifford Geertz, and Talal Asad, have written extensively on Islam and on Muslim societies, a closer look reveals that wide areas of the Islamic tradition – like prayer, the Ramaḍān fast, the pilgrimage, the ideas of Muslim reformers, Islamist groups, Islamic economics, and so on – are represented in anthropological literature by only a handful of articles or the occasional book. More recently, anthropologists such as Patrick Gaffney, Brinkley Messick, Charles Hirschkind, and Saba Mahmood, have somehow ameliorated this situation by producing a string of high-quality studies on subjects close to the center of contemporary Islamic discourse, like prayer, preaching, and law. Still, there is much to be done to cover, first, those areas which have not yet received the attention they deserve, like doctrinal issues (long held to be the province of orientalists), and Islamism, a field dominated by political scientists;[11] and, second, to produce truly comparative works.[12]

The presence of such lacunae in the study of Islamic tradition in the "Middle East" and North Africa is such that on many occasions I have found myself working with almost exclusively non-anthropological material. In itself this is not problematic if the material is employed critically. Where the problem lies is with the fact that on many issues of great interest to both academia and the public, say the Islamist movement, for which thousands of pages of political analysis are available, existing analytical frameworks and epistemological assumptions are erroneously seen as the only possible ones.

Clearly, the learned discussions on Islamism by Olivier Roy, John Esposito, Emmanuel Sivan, Fred Halliday, Nazih Ayubi, Sami Zubaida, Beverly Milton-Edwards, Shaul Mishal, Avraham Sela, and other political scientists, sociologists, and international relations scientists do offer great insights and function as correctives to the shortsightedness and prejudice that often characterize such approaches to Muslim societies.[13] It is only rarely, however, that in such discussions one comes across an ethnographically charged "view from below" which the anthropological "fieldwork mode of production" can generate.[14] As a result, certain dimensions of social reality remain unexplored and misconceptions or widely held assumptions half-hidden.

I do not wish to appear presumptuous and unduly critical toward non-anthropologists who study Islam. I am not arguing that an anthropological view would invalidate currently reached conclusions of research based on political science or sociological models and theoretical assumptions. But certainly, it would enrich and modify them considerably and, indirectly, may even make the need for alternative political options more strongly felt and more vigorously theorized. As Ernest Gellner argued – rather abrasively, I admit – on the occasion of the 150th anniversary of the establishment of the British *Royal Anthropological Society*, "in a world where the political scientists and the economists have been unable to deliver, perhaps it is time to let the anthropologists have a hearing."[15] More emolliently, in a recent article on the 9/11 attacks entitled "The Roots of the Conflict," Umberto Eco has asked outright for a more robust engagement of anthropologists in international organizations and the institutional structures of decision-taking.[16] Certainly, the public role of anthropologists and their cooperation with other social scientists is something that needs to be seriously discussed, but this cannot happen here.

DEFINITIONS

Moving to this line of anthropological critical tradition and reflexivity, I would now like to consider briefly the terms "West," "Middle East," "globalization," and "secularization" as they are constitutive of the framework within which my analysis operates. The term "West," especially, is often projected among many Muslims as the non-Muslim "Other," which through "globalization" – here understood as "Westernization" – is bent on impairing the Muslim vision of the world and on subjugating Muslim societies. Seen from another perspective, equally essentialist and alarmist, many in the "West" feel that the project of secular modernity and its baggage – rationalism, liberty of sovereign subjects, democracy, economic prosperity – are in danger from a pre-modern form of religious fanaticism. Given the tenacity of such views, it is advisable to describe the framework within which the terms acquire their meanings before embarking on the main project of the book. The discussion of the term "Middle East" is included in this section in order: (i) to clarify from which societies I draw the necessary ethnographic material and why; (ii) to dispel ideas concerning the perceived homogeneity and uniqueness of the region and its inhabitants in terms of social structures and political processes, especially in its metonymic association with Islam. All four terms are considered in an abridged manner and only as far as they relate to the present study.

The "West"

Neither a monolithic entity outside history nor a coherent project without internal contradictions, the "West" – and "Western" discourse – should be understood as a historical and cultural construct;[17] in other words, as a project under continuous construction/execution, part of a political landscape whose elites try to overcome, ignore, or brave many of the particularities of its constituent parts in order to secure global hegemony. From this point of view, the term "West" appears to acquire an almost autonomous existence as *discursive potentiality*, which in turn directly affects, and is affected by, social praxis at the level of population at large.[18]

This open and dynamic understanding of the "West" is totally different from that of Huntington (1993) who, as Halliday has cogently argued, refers to "blocs of culture and/or religion . . . [and] assumes that such entities exist as coherent, historical givens, and that international forces can be mobilized around them."[19] However, in denouncing Huntington's crass essentialism one should not underestimate the practical consequences of the "West's" "almost autonomous" existence as discursive potentiality mentioned above. That is, one should not overlook the fact that for hundreds of millions of people both in the "West" and elsewhere, Huntington's views are considered accurate descriptions of reality based on real structures of economic exploitation and ideological hegemony.[20]

The "Middle East"

A brief and to the point anthropological discussion of the term "Middle East" can be found in Eickelman's *The Middle East: An Anthropological Approach* (1989). As we read there, the term "originated with nineteenth-century European military strategists and thus is unabashedly Euro-centered."[21] Still, it is better than any other term as a description of the vast region stretching from Mauritania and Morocco in the Atlantic to Afghanistan and Pakistan in Asia via North Africa – the Sudan included – and Turkey.[22]

It would not be inaccurate to say that, like the West, the "Middle East" too has been made objective through discourse – although its symbolic load differs from that of the West at the level of both political action and ideological commitment. To unravel this and strip the term from its quotation marks, four points should be noted. First, the Middle East is not exclusively Muslim. It includes Christians and Jews, although the vast majority of its 300 million inhabitants are Muslim.[23] Second, it is not exclusively Arab. It includes three other distinct cultural traditions, those of Turkey, Iran, and Israel.[24] Third, the Middle East is not the "heartland" of Islam. World religions may appear in certain areas and gravitate around them for some time, but they soon cease to be tied to them. Fourth, the Middle East is not exceptional in terms of politics. Although at the forefront of publicity for half a century due to the Palestinian issue, its vast oil reserves, and the rise of Islamism, the Middle East presents many of the traits that characterize other regions of what international relations scientists call the Third World.[25] Still, the Middle East does exhibit important cultural and historical continuities at many levels, which allow us to make anthropologically valid generalizations.[26] Finally, the occasional use of the phrase "the Middle East and North Africa" does not invalidate what has been said above; it is used either for rhetorical purposes or because it makes the discussion clearer in the particular context.

These clarifications are deemed necessary because in the present study the Middle East provides the ethnographic grounds upon which I base my discussion of Islamic discourse. However, I should emphasize that this is not a book about the Middle East, nor is Islam approached as one of "the dominant 'theoretical metonyms' by means of which this vast and complex area is grasped."[27] Irrespective of how well researched, detailed and comprehensive an anthropologically inflected analysis of Islamic discourse might be, it should never be equated with a study of the Middle East or any other predominantly Muslim region – say Southeast Asia or sub-Saharan Africa – or, indeed, any single Muslim society. Religion and society do not coincide.[28] At the same time, it is impossible to study Islam without reference to a sociocultural context and to a particular set of historical conditions which shape, and are themselves shaped by, a domain of possibilities within which tentative forms of "orthodoxy" are articulated. If, then, I had chosen to focus my research on sub-Saharan Africa, Central or Southeast Asia, I would have produced another book in terms of tone, emphasis, color, and, possibly content.

My choice of the Middle East as the ethnographic ground for the present discussion rests on my own ethnographic experience in the Sudan and on geographical proximity. Istanbul, Amman, and Cairo are less than a two-hour direct flight from home in Athens and historically closer than other regions of the Islamic world or, indeed, of certain experiential dimensions of the West through the prism of modern Greek history. At a more personal level, my wife and I belong to expatriate Greek families from Egypt and the Sudan, which we still visit regularly.

Finally, my choice of the Middle East has precluded the study of Muslim immigrants in Europe and elsewhere. This is because such a study would amount to entering an entirely new research area, both in terms of theory and in terms of ethnography. For better or worse, I did not see how I could deal with this mass of new material. Thus, I refer to Muslim minorities only to the extent that this improves the presentation of certain issues discussed in the volume.[29]

Globalization

As was argued more than a decade ago, globalization should not be seen as a one-way process which leads to a more harmonious and integrated world,[30] but as "a process of uneven development that fragments as it coordinates."[31]

From an anthropological point of view, globalization is understood in a way that brings forward the fluidity which characterizes the notions of culture and society, as well as the interconnections between the local and the global in the study of society. From this angle, "[e]thnic and cultural fragmentation and modernist homogenization are not two arguments, two opposing views of what is happening in the world today, but two constitutive trends of global reality."[32] In this context it would be wrong to maintain that the globalization process results in the abrogation of the local and in the cultural homogenization of the world, although "globalization involves the use of a variety of instruments of homogenization."[33] On the contrary, as Hannerz has written, "[t]he world system, rather than creating massive cultural homogeneity on a global scale, is replacing one diversity with another; and the new diversity is based relatively more on interrelations and less on autonomy."[34] In other words, what we have is an ongoing conversation between cultures, which leads to, and at the same time takes place in, a space of creolization of the world. "In the end, it seems, we are all creolised."[35]

In a later publication (1992), Hannerz offered a rather more downbeat version of the creolization process than the one discussed in his 1987 paper. As he argued, "desirable as one might find it to be able to speak of world culture in terms of more equal exchange, the conclusion can at present hardly be avoided that asymmetry rules."[36] In other words, globalization is conceptualized as a complex project wherein we can discern strands of *engagement* between different traditions. These strands are articulated within particular structures of possibilities which in turn are overdetermined by specific historical asymmetries – i.e. what can happen, given the relative position and capabilities of those involved.[37]

Hannerz's historical asymmetry is directly associated with the West, not in the sense of Westernization, but in terms of Western hegemony in defining the structures of possibilities. As Featherstone argues,

> [i]t becomes impossible to talk about a common culture in the fuller sense without talking about who is defining it, within which set of interdependencies and power balances, for what purposes, and with reference to which outside culture(s) have to be discarded, rejected or demonified in order to generate the sense of cultural identity . . . We are slowly becoming aware that the West is both a particular in itself and also constitutes the universal point of reference in relation to which others recognise themselves as particularities.[38]

This point should be kept in mind throughout the present work, especially in relation to chapters 6 to 8 where I discuss Muslim reformism and Islamism.

Secularization

The term "secularization" has been widely discussed among social scientists as far as its genealogy, content, and domain of application are concerned.[39] For the purposes of the present work, I adopt a definition proposed by Alexander Schmemann:

> Secularism, I submit, is above all a negation of worship [of God]. I stress: – not of God's existence, not of some kind of transcendence and therefore of some kind of religion . . . It is the negation of man as a worshiping being, as *homo adorans*: the one for whom worship is the essential act which both "posits" his humanity and fulfills it . . . [T]he real cause of secularism . . . is ultimately nothing else but the affirmation of the world's autonomy, of its self-sufficiency in terms of reason, knowledge, and action.[40]

A priest of the Eastern Orthodox Church, Schmemann sees secularization as a historical development which is foreign to the eschatological truth of Christianity.[41] For him, Christianity is primarily God's revelation to mankind; secularization is a by-product of its historical course, that is, the result of specific sociocultural changes. Initially, these changes took place in Western Europe and led to reformulations of the Christian tradition in its Roman Catholic and Protestant versions. At a later stage, these processes were extended to the Eastern Orthodox societies in the context of globalization. From this point of view, the acceptance of a secular domain outside God's providence for the world is a heresy, and one not about God, but about man in history. As such, the secular cannot but coexist in a dialectical relation with the revelatory – and, in the case of Christianity, eschatological – nature of religion, as both unravel new manifestations in their historical course.

Though not strictly sociological, this understanding of secularization and the secular does not radically depart from Asad's conception of it. As he argues:

> [t]he secular . . . is neither continuous with the religious that supposedly preceded it (that is, not the latest phase of a sacred origin) nor a simple break from it (that is, it is not the opposite, an essence that excludes the sacred). I take the secular to be a concept that brings together certain behaviors, knowledges, and sensibilities in modern life.[42]

And again:

> [i]n the discourse of modernity "the secular" presents itself as the ground from which theological discourse was generated (as a form of false consciousness) and from which it gradually emancipated itself in its march to freedom. On that ground humans appear as the self-conscious makers of History . . . and as the unshakable foundation of universally valid knowledge about nature and society. The human as agent is now responsible – answerable – not only for acts he or she has performed (or refrains from performing). Responsibility is now held for events he or she was unaware of – or falsely conscious of.[43]

This is what allows me to use the concept of secularization in the context of Islamic tradition as discussed in the present work. Like Christianity, Islam is a revelatory religion of the Abrahamic tradition which (i) rests on the negation of the world's autonomy and (ii) presupposes the existential truth of *homo adorans* (worshiping man), regulating its social implications through prescriptive ritual worship (*ʿibadāt*) and mysticism.[44]

But does secularization hail exclusively from the West? Is it historically related solely to Western modernity and the accompanying notions of democracy and liberalism? Is it impossible to think of it in the aforementioned terms as a development from within historically specific forms of Islamic discourse as well? There are no easy answers to these questions. Studying Asad's chapter on law and ethics reconfigurations in colonial Egypt in relation to his general discussion of the secular, we read that "the modern idea of a secular society include[s] a distinctive relationship between state law and personal morality."[45] This did not seem to exist in pre-colonial Egypt. It was only in late nineteenth- and early twentieth-century Egypt under British colonial rule that we saw the creation of

> some of the basic preconditions for secular modernity. These involved the legal constitution of fundamental social spaces in which governance could be secured through (1) the political authority of the nation-state, (2) the freedom of market exchange, and (3) the moral authority of the family.[46]

These were the conditions that made possible the emergence in Egypt of the autonomous sovereign subject, as well as the reformulation of Islamic law and, more generally, of Islamic tradition in a manner compatible with this new framework. As will be seen later in the book, this can be discerned in the efforts of Muslim reformers to articulate a persuasive version of Islamic discourse in conversation with European modernity and in the restrictive conception of the Islamic law held by modern Islamists as a closed body of rules which should be ideally administered by the state, rather than as principles delineating the domain within which the Community of Believers (*umma*) should operate.

In contrast with Schmemann, most European and American analysts, such as those mentioned in note 1, see secularism as a fundamental condition for the flowering of Western-type democracy.[47] As for secularized religion, they see nothing wrong with it; on the contrary, religion should become a matter of private faith. Indeed, this is a central theoretical position in their view of Islamism as a grave impediment in the "democratization" and "modernization" of Islamic societies along Western lines. How this can be achieved is still debated, but no one among such intellectuals and policy-planners disagrees that it is an imperative. As Zakaria argues in relation to the Middle East, "[n]o one can make democracy, liberalism, or secularism take root in these societies without their own search, efforts, and achievements. But the Western world in general, and the United States in particular, can help enormously."[48] In a more ornate but decisive manner, replete with biblical imagery, President G.W. Bush's 2005 inauguration speech followed the same logic. This determination is what makes all debate about secularism in Islam part of the present analysis. For the author, all this is not a matter of developing a political agenda apropos of this book, but of inviting political realities to inform the analysis.

PLAN OF THE BOOK

I conclude this introduction with a description of the individual chapters that follow. The first chapter offers an overview of the history of Islam in the Middle East and North Africa. It starts with a short reference to pre-Islamic Arabia and then introduces Prophet Muḥammad and his mission. It moves quickly to the discussion of the four caliphs and the Umayyad and ʿAbbāsid historical periods and then describes the loss of unity of the Muslim world. Out of the three major empires – Mogul, Safavid and Ottoman – the analysis focuses on the last one, which more than the other two shaped the Islamic societies of the Middle East and North Africa. This is used as a device to bring into the picture European colonialism and the struggle for independence, this time in the name of nationalism. The late and post-colonial periods are considered rather briefly, as I return to them in the last three chapters of the book through the discussion of Islamic reformism and Islamism. Chapter 1 concludes with a short discussion of the *sunnī–shīʿa* distinction.

The second chapter is divided into two parts. In the first part I introduce the doctrinal sources or foundations of Islamic tradition, that is the *Qur'ān*, the Prophetic traditions (*sunna*, *ḥadīth*), the consensus of the community (*ijmā'*) and the methodological principle of analogic reasoning (*qiyās* or *ijtihād*). In the second part of the chapter I discuss the *umma* (the Community of Believers) as a concept that connects the universal vision of Islam with the local understandings of it. *Umma* and society, *umma* and the nation-state, *umma* and "orthodoxy" are among the subjects I consider. The main point is that the discourse about the unity of the *umma* is very important among Muslims today and should be recognized as a powerful political tool, as well as a part of a unifying Muslim vision that may shape local realities. At the same time, though, the *umma* should not be essentialized and removed from the realm of history. The chapter concludes with a discussion of those mechanisms that bring together distinct communities of Muslims as members of the universal *umma*, either in the context of international Islamic organizations or through the development of transnational channels of "Islamic" aid.

The third chapter introduces the religious scholars and interpreters of Islamic literary tradition, the *'ulamā'*. The chapter begins with a discussion of Islamic education and Islamic schools (*madrasa*). The analysis touches upon the nature of religious knowledge and the ways it has been traditionally disseminated. It then continues by showing how the colonization of the Middle East and Islamic Africa led to the diminishing of the power of the *madrasa* in favor of Western-type education.

I then proceed to discuss the traditional world of the *'ulamā'* and the changes that the establishment of national states brought to it. The idea is that today, in the context of "orthodoxy" production, the state itself functions as the most authoritative interpreter of Islamic tradition using for this purpose the system of national education. At the same time, I describe how the role of the *'ulamā'* has been further transformed through the appearance of "lay" interpreters of Islamic doctrine and practices, the Islamists. The chapter concludes with an analysis of the role of orality in the interpretation of Islam's textual tradition. Despite the fact that Islam is often called one of the "religions of the book," I endeavor to show that to an extent it is the oral that determines the power of the text and that the present use of audiovisual material for calling people to God (*da'wa*) has important consequences for both the articulation of the Islamic message and its political implications.

The fourth chapter presents the five pillars of Islam: the confession of faith (*shahāda*), the ritual prayer (*ṣalāt*), alms-giving (*zakāt*), the Ramaḍān fast (*al-ṣawm*), and the pilgrimage to Mecca (*ḥajj*). The five pillars of Islam consitute templates for practice which shape Muslim subjects and through which Islam is presented as something more than a religion in the Western sense of the word, which nowadays has a ring of privacy. In contrast to this, the five pillars organize the framework within which Muslims can act as members of the *umma* despite the differences which characterize individual Muslim societies and despite the different interpretations offered. Here again the elusive nature of "orthodoxy" plays a prominent role. Additionally, with an eye to the political implications adhering to the prescribed duties associated with the five pillars, special attention is given to the political and civic elements of *zakāt* and the *ḥajj* as ways of organizing and articulating the vision of the universal *umma*.

The fifth chapter deals with Islamic mysticism and functions as a counterweight to the previous one. Indeed, mysticism is intricately associated with Muslim theological and legal discourse as two dimensions of Islamic experience. In the first part of the chapter I discuss the notion of generalized blessing (*baraka*) and the role of Muslim "saints" in relation to the organization of the *ṣūfī* brotherhoods. I then discuss several examples of sufism from Egypt, the Sudan, Algeria, and elsewhere. In the second part of the chapter I consider the world of the spirits and their cult. As a rule, the discussion of spirit-possession cults does not constitute part of scholarly accounts of Islamic tradition; they are somehow seen as rustic local "traditions" of a rather "un-orthodox" character. This is wrong, as the cults are often central in the self-identification of local populations as "good" Muslim persons. After a short discussion of the notion of "syncretism," I discuss cases of spirit-possession cults from North Africa.

In chapters 6, 7, and 8 I discuss what I call modes of action or of being in the world, namely Islamic reformism and Islamism. I treat these modes of action as ideal types which enable us to codify the responses that many Muslims give to themselves and the world around them concerning Islamic discourse. In chapter 6 I introduce the political history of Islamic reformism through discussion of the Ottoman *Tanẓīmāt* and the views of Jamāl al-Dīn al-Afghānī, Muḥammad ʿAbduh, Muḥammad Rashīd Riḍā, and some of the more recent reformists in Egypt and Syria. The chapter is not meant to present a comprehensive history of Islamic reformism, but an overview of a movement which, although it never acquired a popular character, has nonetheless been influential in the manner in which Muslim intellectuals and political actors see Western discourse and employ notions they initially discovered in colonially imposed forms of Western modernity. The chapter concludes with a critical discussion of Islamic reformism as a political movement and as an ideological trend within the wider Islamic discourse. Although the notion of "orthodoxy" production is present in the analysis, chapter 6 is the least anthropological one of the book – if I may put it thus – because its subject matter is removed from what I called earlier the "ethnographic mode of production."

In the last two chapters I consider Islamism. Chapter 7 starts with a brief discussion concerning the terminology (fundamentalism, political Islam, Islamic resurgence, etc.), which I relate to some of the underlying assumptions concerning Islamism, and an overview of Islamist discourse and its relation to Western modernity. I then present Islamism as a polycentric movement which brings together political parties, organizations, groups, and single individuals who exhibit a number of common characteristics and more or less share the same Islamic vision. This enables me to avoid both oversimplified conceptions of Islamism as a single monolithic religio-political trend and those that see each group or organization operating in its own separate universe. Instead, I approach Islamism at two levels. First, in chapter 7, I consider five ideological positions which I believe characterize all Islamist groups. Then, in chapter 8, I single out five other ideological points of view which distinguish between them.

These ten points of similarity and difference between Islamist groups are not exhaustive. To a certain extent, they have been selected in an idiosyncratic way. Nonetheless, considering Islamism through the analytical framework they construct enables us to discern some kind of order. All this gives me the opportunity to discuss several important issues, such as the Islamists' views of the West, their views on polygyny, female employment, and the nuclear family, their understanding of democracy and pluralism, and, most importantly, their indirect connection with a general trend of conservatism that characterizes many sectors of the lower and middle classes in many Muslim societies. In that sense, chapters 7 and 8 aspire to destroy stereotypes and go beyond demonization, thus enriching our understanding of a trend in Islam that is currently seeking to acquire a hegemonic role in the process of "orthodoxy" production.

1

The Islamic Community through History

For many Muslims today important events of the past continue to influence the way in which they perceive themselves within the world. Terms, such as "sunnis" and "shiites" which came into being in the eighth and ninth centuries, as well as events such as the battle of Badr (AD 624), the battle of Karbalāʾ (AD 680), the eleventh- and twelfth-century crusades, the Mongol attacks (AD 1258), the destruction of Spanish-Arabic lands, European colonization, and the establishment of the state of Israel in 1948 retain particular gravity within the framework of Islamic discourse.

My reference, therefore, to the past is not meant as a mere presentation of historical facts. It is more an attempt to refer to the emergence and initial formation of certain basic notions and processes of Islamic tradition which are still operational. In the context of a religious tradition with a sacred history the "past" does not signify something that simply "happened" or "was," but something that was "fullfilled" or "accomplished."[1] From this point of view, it is hoped that this attempt at sketching Islamic history, however inadequate and partial, will help readers achieve a greater understanding of what follows in later chapters, mainly in relation to the mechanisms of production of Islamic "orthodoxy." By this I mean those interpretations of Islamic tradition which in particular historical conjunctions achieve political dominance.

Within this framework, it is important to remember that traditionally the history of Islam has been connected with the existence of some sort of Islamic political entity or entities, similar to what is today called an "Islamic state." Excluding the case of Muslim minorities in Europe and elsewhere, it is difficult to speak of an Islamic tradition without bearing in mind the existence, even an imagined one, of geographically defined areas governed by Islamic law (*sharīʿa*) – in spite of disagreements between Muslims as to its nature, content, and application.

Indeed, with the appearance of the first Islamic polity in seventh-century Madīna – which is rhetorically used as the prototype for modern-day efforts at the formation of Islamic states – Islam spread *both* as a religious faith and as a political order, creating during the course of its history an Islamic civilization. In other words, what one would call "religion" seems to have been the dominant political idiom of Muslim societies for centuries – claiming a particularly active role during the twentieth century – without this making us blind to the existence of conflicts and disagreements when other idioms, like ethnicity or nationalism, also claimed a role in the historical process.

According to this vision, and its partial applications in different historical periods, the believers in their entirety make up a single religious, cultural, and (occasionally) political entity *vis-à-vis* the non-Muslims, not only in terms of a well-designated area, but also in terms of "a complex of social relations" informed by Islamic discourse.[2] Even within the framework of the very real diversity that characterizes Middle Eastern and North African Muslim societies, belief in the Islamic vision together with important common cultural ties originating from a common Arabic heritage guaranteed, and for many still does, a deeply felt unity for significant numbers of people, certainly without ignoring important differentiating elements. In other words, what has been achieved throughout Islamic history, sometimes more and sometimes less successfully, has been a dynamic composition, not always harmonious, but also conflictual. The unity to which I refer, then, is not synonymous with homogeneity; it does not dispense with the local or support the existence of only *one* interpretation of Islamic discourse. Its imagined character and the fact that it has nearly always been a cherished goal, a noble quest, a dream to be fullfilled, a project to be completed, may have been its greatest source of power.[3]

In terms of Islamic discourse, until the onslaught of European colonialism this imagined unity implied a division of the world into two separate houses, estates, abodes, states of being, or kingdoms: the "land of Islam" (*dār al-Islām*) and the "land of war" (*dār al-ḥarb*). The former was inhabited by Muslims, allegedly irrespective of race, color, or language. The latter was inhabited by non-Muslims also irrespective of race, color, or language.[4] Both states were under the leadership of some person or persons and the best relationship existing between them at the level of doctrine was a non-attack agreement rather than an agreement based on friendship and cooperation – although this idea was pursued in the realm of law. This surely neither excluded economic cooperation and diplomatic relations between believers and infidels, nor hostilities between Muslims. It is however important to remember that diplomatic relations as well as hostilities were conceptualized and legitimized in terms of Islamic law, as the economic, political, or other motives at their base were often conceived or expressed in terms of Islamic discourse.

As it were, historical developments over the centuries brought both Muslim and Western societies face to face with continually transforming policies and economic conditions. These required new ways of perceiving reality and new interpretations of religious/cultural ideas. Obviously, the division of the world in two spheres according to religious allegiance could not remain static. In due time, prompted by real changes in the world surrounding them which demanded the continuation and extension of political and economic relations, Muslim societies responded to the challenge. This neither happened everywhere at the same time nor in the same manner. It was a long process which is still evolving. Perhaps the only constant one could easily observe is the growing overdetermination by Europe, or nowadays the West.

It is therefore obvious that the imagined unity of the Community of Believers and the division of the world into "land of Islam" and the "land of war" should be seen as constructs, as open-ended templates always open to interpretations which at all times support, and are supported by, the prevailing historical conditions. Therefore, for Muslims in modern-day Egypt, Jordan, Indonesia, Pakistan, Bahrain, Turkey, Senegal, or Nigeria – to take a few random examples – the meaning of the terms is continually changing in relation both to the historical experience of their own societies and the way in which the subjects perceive Islam, in other words in relation to the position which this tradition holds in their lives and in the life of their communities. Possibly for some, Islam lies at the center of their world; for others, it could be an old tradition which has now been overtaken by events. For some others, it could represent the basis of one of many identities which, depending on the case and circumstances, serves as a medium for self-expression. Similarly, for others, it could be combined with a common Arabic cultural heritage which characterizes the whole of the Middle East and North Africa. And of course, there would be some for whom Islam might never have been of importance. Since the past is rendered meaningful in the present, all meanings of Islamic tradition are constantly in a historic process of redefinition and contestation.

The historical trajectory attempted in this chapter takes us from pre-Islamic Arabia to the emergence of the modern Middle East and North Africa. It should be read in conjunction with chapters 6, 7, and 8, where the discussion of the modern period is extended to the present and certain themes and practices of Islamic traditions are considered in detail.

FROM PRE-ISLAMIC ARABIA TO THE ARABIA OF PROPHET MUḤAMMAD

Islam appeared in the Arabian Peninsula in the seventh century; it therefore has a history of approximately thirteen centuries. The largest part of Arabia, roughly equal to a third of the area of contemporary Western Europe, is desert and steppe. Agriculture is only possible in some small areas, mainly close to the coasts of the Red Sea and the Indian Ocean.

The inhabitants of seventh-century Arabia were Bedouin. The Bedouin tribes had a nomadic lifestyle, moving from oasis to oasis in search of water and pastures for their camels and their few goats and sheep. The leader of every tribe was called "*shaykh*" and headed a council of elders made up of the heads of the tribe's clans. The council, however, did not have the legal power to impose its opinions on its members. Thus, the basic institution of the Bedouin political structure was the feud in an environment of continuous hostilities. Within this climate, the institution of patrilineal descent and the law of revenge were the only protection which an individual had when faced with the threat of murder.

The main towns of the area were Mecca and Yathrib. Both were important commercial centers and Mecca in particular was a junction in the caravan routes. In the dialect of the Ṣābi'ans, a local "group of tolerated monotheists,"[5] the word "Mecca" (*Makkah*) means "asylum" or "refuge."[6] This indicates that long before the birth of Prophet Muḥammad in the sixth century, the city had some religious significance apart from its wealth. Mecca lies 48 miles from the Red Sea in a rocky valley of southern Ḥijāz that is unsuitable for cultivation. From this position, it dominated the caravan routes which connected the north with the south and the east with the west. As a result, from early on, the city had become a principal trading station between the Mediterranean port of Gaza and Marib in the Ṣābi'an country. In this way, Mecca connected the Indian Ocean with Syria and the areas of present-day Iraq, and Iran and Central Asia with East Africa.

Mecca was therefore the most important city in Arabia and was under the domination of one particular Bedouin tribe, the Quraysh. The dominant position of the Quraysh in the political life of Mecca as well as of the surrounding area was directly related to the distance of the city from the main political and cultural forces of the area: the Zoroastrian empire of the Sāsānid Persians and the Christian Byzantine Empire, which reached as far as Syria and Palestine, from which the Jewish cultural tradition had diffused around the surrounding area. At the same time, Mecca was far enough from Yemen, which at that time dominated the southern tip of the Arabian Peninsula, and it could, if local geography had allowed it, pose as a rival political and economic power. The role of the Quraysh was to maintain Mecca's political, economic, and cultural independence against all those other powers and at the same time, continue their leadership over the neighboring desert Bedouin tribes.

In this undertaking they were aided not only by the great distances from the political giants surrounding them, but also by the economic prosperity of the city. Also of help was the elevation of Mecca by the Quraysh to a sacred site, where pagan Bedouin worship could be expressed through a commonly accepted symbol, the rock of *Ka'ba*. With this aim, the Quraysh had imposed a four-month truce period, which allowed thousands of pilgrims each year to visit the city to celebrate in the temple of *Ka'ba*, which housed 360 tribal idols.

At the same time, the Quraysh and the other Bedouin knew quite well the basic tenets of the surrounding monotheistic traditions, i.e. Christianity, Judaism, and Zoroastrianism, while they themselves believed in the existence of *Allāh*, the one and only God and Creator of all things. Therefore, in the seventh century, when the Muslim Prophet Muḥammad ibn ʿAbd Allāh preached the absolute monotheism of Islam and spoke of paradise, hell, and final judgment, his listeners could easily understand the terms he used and the meaning of his words. However, the socio-political implications of Muḥammad's preaching were, at the very least, revolutionary for the establishment of the Quraysh and their allies.

More than one billion Muslims all over the world enunciate, whisper, pray to, sing, or simply hear the names of God and Prophet Muḥammad every day.[7] Let's take, for example, the calling to prayer five times a day from the minarets of the mosques in all the cities and villages in Islamic societies. In this call, the believers are emphatically reminded that there is one God and his Prophet is Muḥammad.

But apart from that, one does not have to be a believer and to pray in order to pronounce the names of God and the Prophet. All that is required is to speak one of the basic languages of Islam – Arabic, Persian, Urdu[8] – or more simply to use in the course of daily speech standard expressions of Arabic origin which a person hears whether in Lahore in Pakistan, Cairo in Egypt, Damascus in Syria, Kano in Nigeria, or Kuala Lumpur in Malaysia.

The basic facts of the Prophet's life are known to all Muslims. They are taught in schools, are woven into the daily lives of the believers, and, depending on the circumstances, are used as living examples of action and codes of behavior, becoming the object of speeches on radio and television and commented on in countless publications which are to be found in bookshops, open-air markets, outside mosques, or in bazaars and fairs. Indeed, separate studies could be carried out into the position the name of Prophet Muḥammad holds in the collective imagination of Muslims worldwide.

Muḥammad ibn ʿAbd Allāh was born in AD 570–1 in Mecca. He belonged to the Quraysh tribe and was the son of ʿAbd Allāh and Amīna. He lost his parents very early and was raised by his paternal uncle, Abū Ṭālib. Muḥammad was involved in trade and took part in many caravans, thus coming in contact with Byzantines, Jews, and Persians. At the age of 25, he married Khadīja, a wealthy widow, the owner of the business for which Muḥammad had worked for some time. They stayed married for fifteen years. All of their children died young except for their daughter Fāṭima, who was to play an important role in Islamic history.

Although illiterate,[9] Muḥammad was considered by the society of Mecca to be a fair, honorable, and intelligent person. As tradition has it, he would often leave the city for short periods of time and wander in the desert, contemplating his life and the suffering he saw around him, the injustice of the traders, and the misery of the poor. During one such night, Muḥammad had the first revelation of God's word, thus being admitted into the ranks of the Semitic prophets.

For the first 10 years, the society of Mecca was opposed to the words and teachings of the new Prophet, who professed a strict monotheistic worship and condemned economic exploitation, thus appearing totally opposed to the existing political order. The main center of opposition was the Umayyad clan of the Quraysh. However, in 620 the situation changed fundamentally. The Prophet was invited by the inhabitants of Yathrib, a fertile oasis town 300 miles to the north of Mecca, to come as an arbitrator in a vendetta between the tribes there. From July to September 622, Muḥammad and his followers gradually left Mecca in secret, their lives in danger. Soon after their establishment in Yathrib, the local population converted to Islam and the first Community of Believers (*umma*) was established.[10] From then on, Yathrib was called *madīnat al-nabī*, meaning "the city of the Prophet" or simply al-Madīna. The move or emigration of the Muslims to Madīna was called *hijra* and has become the beginning of the Muslim calendar.

For Muḥammad, settling in Madīna was an opportunity to establish a community based exclusively on the message of Islam regarding not only the personal life of its members but also its very social structure. In the previous years it had become clear that Islam was something more than a personal code of conduct which allowed the believer to follow God's path. More than that, Islam provided society with a law which informed all social practices and values, transforming them into something fundamentally different from what had existed up to that point.[11]

Islam was not limited to the pious reformation of the individual; it sought the reformation of the whole of society. It is here that the historic meaning of the Madīnan polity is to be found for many Muslims: the matrix organization of the Islamic state and the organizing principle for Islam as "a total way of life."[12] The Islamic polity of Madīna was a regime, a social order of things, as well as a personal and social vision completely interwoven with Islam as a religious tradition, as a political practice, and as a social command, with the Prophet of God as the religious, political, and military leader of the Community of Believers.

Once in Madīna, Muḥammad went to war with Mecca and the pagan tribes of the desert Bedouin. One of the most significant battles, which is still evoked, was the battle of Badr (624), in which the Muslims under the leadership of the Prophet defeated a much larger army from Mecca.[13] Finally, in the spring of 632, the whole of Arabia was unified under the flag of Islam. The Prophet died three months later in June 632 and was buried in Madīna.

For the Muslims, Muḥammad did not establish a new religion. Just as other prophets before him, he came as a reformer of the Semitic monotheistic religion of Abraham, Moses, and Jesus, all of them earlier prophets of the same God in an unbroken Abrahamic tradition. God's final prophet was an exemplary yet ordinary man, Muḥammad – although one later provided with an Abrahamic genealogical connection.[14] His revelation came to Muḥammad gradually. After the latter's death, the revelation was written down so that it would not be lost with the death of the men who knew it by heart. Thus, the *Qur'ān* (translated as *Recitation*) came into being as a holy book.

THE PERIOD OF THE CALIPHATE

Given the central role of the Prophet, his death could have proved fatal for the unity of the Community, since he had not appointed a successor. The Prophet's comrades, an informal but powerful group of believers, who had followed Muḥammad from the beginning of his mission and who had distinguished themselves as much for their devotion to him as for their strategic and other abilities, hastened to reassure believers and elect his successor – a difficult job, certainly, but one they carried out with minimum strife.

Be that as it may, the death of the Prophet caused rifts in the Community. The period which I shall describe briefly in the following pages is called the period of the caliphate and is divided into three separate periods: the period of the rightly guided caliphs (632–61), the dynastic period of the Umayyads (661–750), and the dynastic period of the ʿAbbāsids (750–1258).

The Period of the Rightly Guided Caliphs (632–661)

This period includes the governing of the Islamic community by four *khalīfa*s (successors; hence the anglicized "caliph[s]"), all of whom were numbered among the initial and faithful followers of the Prophet. During the leadership of the first three the great expansion of Islam began. All of Arabia, Palestine, Syria, Jordan, Iraq, Persia, and Egypt fell into the hands of Arab Muslims. Huge areas of the Byzantine Empire and the Persian Empire of the Sāsānids became Islamic colonies with a strong Arabic character,[15] functioning as an impetus for the Islamization of the local populations. This large expansion brought great profits to the families of big merchants in Mecca and Madīna, thus sowing the first seeds of internal strife. In 656, the third caliph, ʿUthmān, was murdered and his place was taken by the son-in-law of the Prophet, ʿAlī ibn Abī Ṭālib. ʿAlī is one of the most important figures in Islamic tradition because he was at the epicenter of the separation between the *sunnī* and *shīʿa* Muslims, which is discussed on pp. 29–34.

ʿAlī was one of the first converts to Islam and a charismatic personality. With Fāṭima, the only living child of Muḥammad and Khadīja, he had two children, Ḥasan and Ḥusayn. After the Prophet's death, many Muslims believed that the leadership of the Community of Believers should remain with his family, and specifically with ʿAlī who was his closest paternal male relative. The supporters of ʿAlī, who were later called *shīʿa*, believed that he should have become the first caliph and not Abū Bakr. For this reason, even today, the *shīʿa* consider the first three caliphs as illegitimate.

During ʿAlī's reign, two armed conflicts broke out between Muslims, which are remembered to this day as a period of great trial and strife (*al-fitna al-kubrā*). Both conflicts were related to the stance taken by ʿAlī against those who had murdered ʿUthmān. In the first conflict, ʿAlī defeated the army of the youngest of the Prophet's wives, ʿĀ'isha, who sought revenge for the death of ʿUthmān and accused ʿAlī of having been elected by those who had murdered the previous caliph. In the second conflict, ʿAlī fought against the army of Muʿāwiya, the governor of Syria, nephew of ʿUthmān and brother-in-law of the Prophet, who refused to obey ʿAlī's orders to relinquish power. These wars have been very important for Islamic tradition and their consequences are still felt today since they led indirectly to the murder of ʿAlī and directly to the death of his son Ḥusayn in the battle of Karbalā' (680), the two events which make up the basis of *shīʿa* Islam.

In an effort to achieve political dominance, ʿAlī and Muʿāwiya's armies confronted each other in Syria in 657. To solve the problem they entered into peaceful negotiations, but ʿAlī rejected the results and continued fighting. Before that, though, he had to find a solution to a more pressing problem. ʿAlī's decision to embark on negotiations for his legal ascent to the position of caliph made some of his supporters abandon him. Known as Khārijites ("seceders" or "rebels"), these extremists quickly increased in number while their intransigent dogmatic positions placed in jeopardy the legitimacy of ʿAlī in the eyes of the Arab Muslims of the wider area. Then in 658, after unsuccessful intermediary efforts, ʿAlī slaughtered a large number of Khārijites, an act which was morally condemned by nearly all believers. In this climate, highly unfavorable for ʿAlī, Muʿāwiya continued governing Syria and managed to extend his control over Egypt. Finally, in 661, ʿAlī was murdered by a Khārijite. This development allowed Muʿāwiya to become caliph, establishing the Umayyad dynasty and transforming the caliphate into a monarchy with Damascus as its capital.

The Dynastic Period of the Umayyads (661–750)

In many respects, the Umayyad dynasty was really an Arab kingdom. Society was based on an Arab military aristocracy, which was transformed into a hereditary caste. The heart of the defense of the Umayyad polity, which also included many non-Arab Muslims, was composed of Syrian Arab forces under the direct orders of the caliph. Since these constituted the guarantee of his remaining in power, they were well rewarded with booty from various campaigns. The Arab Muslims, as well, received better treatment than the non-Arabs and paid less tax.

The state was imperialist in character. Arab bureaucracy appropriated the more developed elements of Greek and Byzantine legislation. Arabic became the lingua franca of the Umayyad polity, laying the foundation of an Arab-Islamic vision of unity which still prevails in the Middle East and North Africa.[16] However, the incorporation of non-Islamic elements and ideas came gradually into indirect conflict with Islam as an ideology which legalized the existing political power. Nowhere is this more obvious than in the issue of Islamic law.

The customary rights of the provinces, the decisions of the caliph, and the laws issued by the judges created a situation of pronounced subjectivity, where the purportedly one and only law of God could not be exactly defined. This situation led to the development of a legal science and other theological sciences since the intellectuals of the state tried to find solutions. As time passed, what became known as Islamic law (*sharīʿa*) was created, without, however, being considered by all Muslims as a complete and clear set of rules. As we shall see, the *sharīʿa* has always maintained a degree of ambiguity and a dynamism which allowed it to define and reflect Islamic "truth" in societies and times quite different from each other, depending on the existing socio-political conditions.

On the other hand, ruling-class excesses, political competition, and palace intrigues, as well as the corruption of the bureaucracy, led to the development of mysticism or sufism which, initially, had more the characteristics of a personal quest for God and the truth rather than that of an organized social movement.[17]

The Dynastic Period of the ʿAbbāsids (750–1258)

The difficulties encountered during the Umayyad period gave rise to factors which finally led to the disintegration of their dynasty. Among the many disenchanted groups were the *shīʿa*, other Islamic factions, non-Arab Muslims, and the rich families of Mecca and Madīna who envied the wealth of the Syrian ruling class, as well as many devoted believers who disagreed with the violation of moral rules and what they saw as the alienation of society from Islamic principles. Amongst them was Abū al-ʿAbbās, a descendant of the Prophet's uncle al-ʿAbbās, who became caliph and moved the capital to the newly established city of Baghdad. Thus, the center of the Islamic polity was moved from Syria to Iraq.

Even though the new political order relied on the *sunnī* and crushed the *shīʿa* and other sects, it had Islamic legitimacy. The ruling class took care to develop Islamic discourse and became protector of a new ascending group of intellectuals and law students, the religious scholars-jurisconsults (*ʿulamāʾ*).[18] Islamic teaching was specifically encouraged by the building of mosques and the establishment of schools. The arts, as well as theology and law, were developed to a great extent. The appearance of a comprehensive theory for the *sharīʿa* is a product of this period.[19] In addition, Islamic philosophy served as the conduit through which Greek philosophy, mainly Platonism and Neo-Platonism, became known in Europe of the Middle Ages. The ʿAbbāsids were also influenced by Persian culture. Bureaucracy and the army ceased to be regarded as the occupation of the aristocrats. Soldiers were paid as civil servants, and a large number of Persians were promoted to high ranks.

'Abbāsid prosperity was based on trade, industry, and agriculture. At the same time, Islam spread to a large part of the then known world, including the whole of North Africa and Spain in the west, and Iran and the uplands of Central Asia in the east.

THE PARTITIONING OF THE ISLAMIC WORLD (*AL-'ALAM AL-ISLĀMĪ*)

For the Christian populations of Europe, Muslim power was initially an unknown factor with which they had to learn how to come to terms.[20] On the one hand, Muslims rejected the divinity of Jesus, which was the basis of Church power, as well as the perfection of the Christian teaching; on the other hand, their communities were continually spreading, placing under their control huge areas and Islamizing thousands upon thousands of Christians. Those who were not Islamized were Arabized to a great extent. Just at the time when Christian Europe was going through the Middle Ages, with all its ideological and cultural rigidity, Islam glowed with life and energy. Considering the Muslims as enemies at the gate, the Christian-European response to Islam was, except in a few cases, negative, hostile, and uncompromising. Muḥammad was considered to be the archetype of evil, the apocalyptic figure of anti-Christ. Even Dante, in his *Divine Comedy* placed Muḥammad in the lowest level of hell.[21]

In the fifth AH/eleventh AD century[22] European societies reacted. In a series of battles, Spain and those areas of Italy that had been under partial Arab occupation were recaptured, while 1095 saw the beginning of the crusades, which peaked in 1204.[23] Gradually, the 'Abbāsid state lost its unity and was transformed into a commonwealth of semi-autonomous sultanates, such as the North African provinces of the *shī'a* Fāṭimids, the *sunnī* Ayyūbid sultanates in the lands of present-day Syria, Iraq, Ḥijāz, Yemen, and Egypt, and the *sunnī* sultanate of the Saljuq Turks in Asia Minor.

In the thirteenth century Ginghiz Khan and his descendants invaded the Muslim lands of western Asia, defeated the Saljuqs, and established a Mongol presence that came to be known as the Il-Khans. Despite their notorious ferocity, the Il-Khans were Islamized relatively quickly and melted into the Middle East, thus rendering their distinction from the Turks irrelevant. At the same time, Egypt managed to remain outside the sphere of the Mongols' influence and was ruled by the Mamlūk sultans of Turkish descent for 300 years until 1517. Still, in spite of internal conflicts and the crumbling of the Islamic world in areas administered mainly by military leaders, the fourteenth and fifteenth centuries were periods when ideas flourished and during which many of the basic tenets of Islamic law, theology, and philosophy were formed.[24]

In the fifteenth to early sixteenth centuries there were three Muslim empires: the Ottoman, the Persian Safavid, and the Mogul of the Indian subcontinent. Here I shall refer to the Ottomans, since the other two, despite their importance, did not play a direct role in the Islamic Middle East and south Mediterranean order of things on which I am focusing my interest.

The thirteenth-century Mongol invasions had led to a westwards migration of the Anatolian Muslim Turkic nomads. Among these groups, a number of small independent political entities developed with clear orientation towards expansionist activity within the framework of a holy war against the local Christian populations and often against each other. Of all these groups of holy Muslim warriors (*ghāzī*), the most successful was that of the Osmanli family.

Under capable military leaders (*begs*), the Osmanli or Ottomans, as they were called in Europe, attracted large numbers of Muslim warriors and landless local peasants, and advanced on the rich lands of neighboring Byzantium. In the course of 100 years, the Ottomans established a powerful empire with Constantinople/Istanbul as its capital. The new imperial order set the collective imagination of the wider Islamic world on fire. Although adopting pre-existing Byzantine models, all administrative practices were clearly within an Islamic interpretative framework. The Ottoman Empire was a fully fledged Muslim polity.

This is well demonstrated in the political philosophy upon which imperial authority was based, especially during the sixteenth century, as well as in the prominent position of Islamic law and the *ʿulamāʾ*. Concerning the former, the spread and consolidation of the empire, and mainly the occupation of Constantinople, allowed Ottoman sultans to claim that the *amīr*, i.e. the Muslim leader, was a natural necessity and that he governed according to Islamic law. That made him indeed the Prophet's caliph (successor).[25] Accordingly, the whole imperial government and the administrative staff formed the army of Islam (*ʿaskerī*) which, together with the whole of society and its wealth, were at the disposal of the leader.[26] This political philosophy was dominant during the particularly important (also on a symbolic level) expansion of the Ottomans into the Muslim lands of Egypt and Arabia (1517).

Concerning the law and the *ʿulamāʾ*, it is true that in all Islamic societies, Islamic law has always had an important role as an idiom of social cohesion and as a code of cultural practices and dispositions. Apart from this, though, in the case under consideration the *sharīʿa* came to legitimize the political commands of central power and the mission of the state itself. This gave the *ʿulamāʾ* significant power and allowed them to identify their interests and expectations with those of the empire as a whole, despite the lack of administrative self-sufficiency.[27] Therefore, particularly after the occupation of the Arab lands, the Ottoman *ʿulamāʾ* were asked to express, on an ideological level, the will and aspirations of the Islamic world as a whole. Correspondingly, Islamic law formed the basis of state legislation, with well-educated judges holding important positions in the bureaucracy. This led to the further codification of the *sharīʿa* and state jurisprudence, which was often independent of the former concerning the content, but drew from it its legality.[28]

During the sixteenth and seventeenth centuries the pace of Ottoman expansion was checked. Although it included much of the Balkans, today's Middle East and North Africa, and counted sizeable numbers of Christians among its subjects, the empire showed signs of political slothfulness and passivity. Political power passed to the grand vizier and the aristocracy, the famous Janissary slave-soldiers, traditionally the backbone of the imperial armies, lost their effectiveness, and political intrigue and corruption became rampant. The situation worsened in the eighteenth century, though there were areas of social life, especially in the big urban centers, which showed some dynamism. A mismanaged polity suffering from a deep economic and political crisis, the Ottoman Empire exhibited very clearly the structurally limited capabilities of an agrarian society.[29] The encounter with the ascending power of European imperialism further aggravated this.

The nineteenth century showed the culmination of these trends. One after the other, Ottoman provinces such as Egypt, Algeria, Tunis, Cyprus, Bessarabia, and large areas of eastern Anatolia came gradually under British, French, and Russian control, while other areas such as Serbia, Montenegro, Greece, Bulgaria, and Romania eventually gained their independence. What remained of the empire held itself together under the watchful eye of the three competing European empires, the British, the French, and the Russian, and gave rise to the so-called Eastern Question, i.e. how to settle Ottoman territorial disintegration without Russia gaining excessively.[30]

Certainly, the Ottoman sultans did not sit idle watching their world crumble. Perceiving the demise of the Ottoman imperial order as a technical problem, they initiated a number of modernizing reforms (*Tanẓīmāt*) in a last effort to avoid the unavoidable. However, due to their autocratic and bureaucratic character, the reforms were rejected by society; whatever their other qualities, they were really half-baked measures dictated by the political elites who wanted to retain some vestiges of power.[31] Moreover, seeing them as a Trojan horse for the secularization of society made many prominent Muslim intellectuals view the nineteenth-century imperial reforms critically, if not with actual hostility. Both in Turkish and in other provinces, movements like the New Ottomans of Nāmīq Kemāl came into being, and intellectuals such as Sayyid Jamāl al-Dīn al-Afghānī (1838–97), Muḥammad ʿAbduh (1849–1905), and Muḥammad Rashīd Riḍā (1865–1935) voiced their concern and articulated alternative policies. These intellectuals were the fathers of Islamic modernization who criticized the *Tanẓīmāt* and palace totalitarianism, while at the same time warning of the danger of European imperialism and calling Muslims to keep the Community of Believers (*umma*) united. As we shall see in greater detail in chapter 6, in their effort to achieve this, Muslim modernizers also castigated *'ulamā'* conservatism, preaching the need to open Islamic tradition to everything creative, even if that came from infidel Europe.[32]

In 1908 the regime of Sultan 'Abd al-Ḥamīd fell with the revolution of the Young Turks, who remained in power until 1918, the end of World War I, in which the Ottomans were allies of imperial Germany. The defeat really meant the end of the empire, and after the war, the political scene changed dramatically with the emergence of Turkish nationalism under Mustafa Kemal Atatürk. Offically, the state of Turkey was born on October 29, 1923. By 1927 a series of measures had wiped out many elements of the centuries-long Ottoman regime and put Islamic practices aside, sometimes with surprising ferocity.[33]

Obviously, the establishment of a strong secular, or even anti-religious, republican state did not bring about the full and complete obliteration of all Islamic elements from modern Turkish reality. It was, nevertheless, a manifestation of the end of centuries of *Islamic* history. Let us not forget that the Ottoman sultan/caliph maintained that his power originated from that of the 'Abbāsid caliphs (750–1258). Certainly, it is clear that in its various historically defined versions Islamic discourse was *part* of Ottoman tradition and contributed to Ottoman reality together with other ideas, movements, concepts, and practices. However, it cannot be doubted that this multiracial empire at many levels was understood as an Islamic political order, even when provinces asked for or demanded autonomy, or when the authority of the sultan/caliph was questioned by other poles of Islamic legitimation – from the eighteenth- and nineteenth-century revivalist movements discussed in Karpat 2001, such as the Arabian Wahhābīs, the Sudanese Mahdiyya, the Turkic *Naqshbāndiyya*, and the North African Sanūsiyya, to the Arab revolt of the early twentieth century and the emergence of *sharīfīan* monarchies. It is possible, then, that as time passed the notion lost some of its luster, but it never completely disappeared, nor did it become completely alien to the unfolding of history.

THE BEGINNING OF THE LONG TWENTIETH CENTURY

As we have seen, from the nineteenth century until the fall of the Ottoman Empire and the emergence of the Turkish nation-state early in the twentieth century, European colonialism was at its zenith. With the end of World War I the Arab-Islamic ecumene came to a violent end and new political entities were constructed along lines dictated by the colonial powers. Geographically, some of them coincided with Ottoman administrative units, while others were the result of negotiations between European empires. Legally, some of these new lands took the form of colonies, while others became mandates, condominiums, or protected territories. Thus, Palestine, Greater Jordan, Iraq, the Arab Emirates,

Oman, Aden, Egypt, the Sudan, and the northern part of present-day Somalia, became parts of the British Empire. Southern Somalia and Libya became Italian territories, while the rest of North Africa, along with Syria and Lebanon came under French control. Soon Muslims realized, to quote Umberto Eco, "that the world was composed of alien architectures."

What had happened? Many wondered how could anyone come to terms with such a calamity. From an Islamic point of view, a series of questions emerged. Had God forsaken His faithful? Or, had the faithful abandoned their God and He reacted by exacting such a terrible punishment? As Said S. Samatar argues,[34] since all Muslims have the assurance that God protects them if they live according to the tenets of Islam, the cataclysmic subjugation to the Europeans could only be interpreted as a sign that their society had distanced itself from Islamic tradition – in the various forms that they perceived it at that historical junction – and that they no longer followed God's law. What other explanation could there be *in the context of Islamic discourse* besides this for the Community of Believers? We must bear these kinds of questions in mind because important clues will emerge in our analysis of Islamic modernization and of Islamism in chapters 6, 7, and 8 respectively.

Today, the Middle East and North Africa, two regions which are in the media almost daily either as hotbeds of terrorism or as exotic tourist destinations, are still scarred by their colonial legacy. Let us remember that the "Middle East," a veritable political construct poignantly called by Eickelman "unabashedly Eurocentered,"[35] is perceived as oriental or as a geographically eastern destination because it lies to the east of London and Paris, which by definition are in the West (with a capital w). Secondly, as already suggested, today's borders in this area were defined by the Great Powers without consulting the local populations and without taking their history into account.

Thus, we come face to face with a situation where the Middle Eastern and North African Muslim societies, notwithstanding their shared Arab-Islamic cultural heritage, struggled for the establishment of *independent nation-states*, which for many demonstrates an acceptance on their part of allegedly Western-style concepts such as "nation-state" and "democracy" which were not present in their pre-colonial history. Then, after the end of the colonial era most Arab governments in the 1950s and 1960s promoted secular ideologies, such as those of Arab socialism or pan-Arabism, which shelved most references to Islam. That does not mean that for the communities to which I am referring Islamic tradition ceased to be important. Not at all.

Even in the heyday of nationalism, Arab socialism, and pan-Arabism, Islam remained present in people's everyday life and was an important element in the formation of group identities in a myriad ways. However, at least directly, Islamic discourse was absent not only from the arena of mass politics, but also from the sphere of intellectual production of theory that could reach a wider public. This situation began to change in the 1970s, a decade marked by the

1973 Arab–Israeli war, the 1979 Islamic revolution in Iran, and the emergence of successor situations to the first Arab nationalist governments, entering into increasingly treacherous sociocultural and financial straits from which they have yet to emerge. In a double act, Islamic discourse has made again its appearance as an ideological tool in the hands both of weary governments opening their economies to the West and of progressively more defiant Islamist groups operating against the West, just as against local governments, under the banner "Islam is the solution." It is perhaps not a coincidence that the most significant non-state perpetrated terrorist act of modern history was committed by those considered by many in the Muslim world as "holy warriors" against the USA, the epitome of Western political and cultural global hegemony.

Many of these issues will be revisited in the last three chapters of the book in relation to Islamic modernism and Islamism, thus compensating for the brief manner in which historical events in post-colonial Islamic societies have been treated here.[36] For the time being, I hope that this short presentation of some historical themes will be helpful in the consideration of the content, processes, and practices of Islamic discourse that follows in the succeeding chapters.

THE DISTINCTION BETWEEN *SUNNĪ* AND *SHĪʿA* ISLAM

Another significant historical element of Islamic tradition which has to be discussed here is the distinction between *sunnī* and *shīʿa* Islam, which has already been briefly referred to. The term *sunnī* refers to the form *ahl al-sunna wa al-jamāʿa* (the people of the tradition and community), that is, those who accepted the continuity and essential unity of the community established by the Prophet. The word *shīʿa* can be translated as "the people of. . ." or "the followers of. . . ," and in this case it refers to the cousin and son-in-law of Prophet Muḥammad, ʿAlī Abī Ṭālib.[37] The majority of *shīʿa* Muslims currently live in Iran, southern Iraq, Lebanon, and the Gulf States. Although appearing in the seventh century, the distinction between *sunnī* and *shīʿa* is still relevant, based as it is on differences concerning the nature of Islamic political and religious authority, as well as the not always friendly relations between the two communities in the context of the post-colonial nation-states.[38]

The rise of Abū Bakr to the position of caliph after the Prophet's death in 632 demonstrated the dominance of the Quraysh vis-à-vis the other Bedouin tribes. It also signified the setting aside of the principle of blood relation as a precondition for succession in office, as it bypassed the cousin and son-in-law of the Prophet, ʿAlī. The same applies for ʿUmar, Abū Bakr's successor, and ʿUthmān, the successor of ʿUmar.

With the murder of the third caliph, the election and murder of ʿAlī, and the rise of Muʿāwiya to the position of first caliph of the Umayyad dynasty, which dominated until 750, everything changed significantly. The *sunnī* and the *shīʿa* gradually evolved into two quite distinct political entities and cultural camps possessing different principles of political philosophy.

In the turmoil of these developments, three basic viewpoints were formulated regarding the leadership of the Community of Believers. For the majority, later named *sunnī*, the legitimate line of the first four *imāms* (Muslim religious and political leaders) to follow the Prophet coincides with the first four caliphs.[39]

For the Khārijites, who initially had helped ʿAlī to claim the caliphate, but then abandoned him when they considered that he had distanced himself from their positions, every attempt to impose the human will on the election of the *imām* rendered it invalid and required his dethronement, by violence if necessary. In fact, the deposed *imām* and his followers were even considered infidels. Thus, the Khārijites considered that both ʿUthmān and ʿAlī had become for different reasons infidel, even though they maintained that their original choice of ʿAlī as caliph-*imām* was correct. The Khārijites also believed that Muslims should be ruled by a single *imām* even if he were the son of a slave. For them, the only criterion was the man's sincere belief in Islam.

Finally, for *shīʿa* Muslims, the first legitimate *imām* of Islam was considered to be ʿAlī, the fourth of the four orthodox caliphs. This viewpoint promoted the creation of a different concept for the role of the *imām* in Islam and the meaning and importance of the imamate, which even today distinguishes the *shīʿa* from the majority of Muslims, i.e. the *sunnī*, who developed the historical meaning of the caliphate.

If we were to describe, in brief, the *sunnī* understanding of the caliphate, we would say that the caliph/*imām* is considered to be the chosen successor of the Prophet. He has political and military power but he is not a prophet. He is considered to be the leader of the Muslims in a way which does not clearly separate religion from politics.

In later years, mainly from the tenth century onwards, the role of the caliph changed. New political developments resulted in the division of the leadership of the Community of Believers among two politico-religious figures, the sultan and the caliph. At the same time, independent political formations emerged in various parts of the Islamic world, resulting in the de facto political separation of the allegedly united and homogenous Islamic Community of Believers into independent entities, although the idea of the imagined unity in the name of Islam continued to exist on an ideological level.

These socio-political changes in the now immense and internally divided Muslim world were reflected in the different approaches to the issue of the caliphate and the unity of the *umma* by the *sunnī* intellectuals. It seems that the fundamental principle uppermost in their thoughts was the maintenance of legality with respect to the application of Islamic law, as well as the need for smooth governance of the Islamic community, even by leaders who were below the required level of perfection on moral issues and theological knowledge, which was supposed to characterize the Muslim leader.

Thus, a clear distinction emerged between the period of the first four caliphs and that of the later state of affairs, which basically had all the characteristics of a hereditary monarchy with the sultan as a monarch appointing the caliph as a high civil servant. The *sunnī* intellectuals and law teachers considered that since the kingship belonged to the sultan who held the position based on military power there was no point in insisting that the caliph be appointed strictly according to traditional criteria established during the period of the orthodox caliphs. According to their line of reasoning, the traditional doctrine was in no case reinterpreted; it simply lay inactive.

The *shīʿa* practice was markedly different. From the moment they appeared as a politically coordinated group up until today, the *shīʿa* have been claiming that the religious and political leadership of the Community of Believers belongs to the *imām*, who, although not a prophet, is considered to be a man inspired by God, both sinless and faultless. In practice, however, his authority has to be in harmony with the collective opinion of the Community of Believers, as it is expressed by the religious law teachers. Both *sunnī* and *shīʿa* versions of political theory have certainly developed throughout the centuries, but they have not gone far from the principles discussed here. In fact, amongst the *sunnī* the notion of the caliphate has been put aside, except in the case of certain Islamist groups, while amongst the *shīʿa* the office of the *imām* and its executive powers have been additionally boosted in the spirit of Ayatollah Ruhollah Khomeini and the 1979 Islamic revolution in Iran.[40]

Without going into too much detail, it is worthwhile to mention that the *shīʿa* fall into three subcategories: the Zaydiyya, the Ismāʿīliyya, and the Imāmiyya. A basic difference between them is the proper succession of *imāms* after ʿAlī's death. For the Zaydiyya, every patrilineal descendant of ʿAlī – and not just descendants of ʿAlī and Fāṭima – could be proclaimed *imām*. The Zaydiyya founded an imamate in 893 in Yemen and governed the country according to this precept until 1963.

For the Ismāʿīliyya, the *Qur'ān* has an inner meaning that was revealed only to ʿAlī and through a special process of initiation to his representatives and missionaries.[41] All the elects constitute a religious elite which should spread the message even by force, if that becomes necessary. The high point of the Ismāʿīliyya was the establishment of the Fāṭimid dynasty in tenth-century Egypt, which was destroyed by Ṣalāḥ al-Dīn 200 years later. A contemporary offshoot of the Ismāʿīliyya are the Druze of Syria and Lebanon, a closed, secretive, and hierarchically organized community with their own scriptures and rituals.[42] Here we should also mention the Alevi, or ʿAlawī, of eastern Turkey, northern Iraq, Syria, and Lebanon who are often considered by other Muslims as infidels. Their ritual life is very different from that of both *sunnī* and *shīʿa* Muslim (for example, their praying cycle is structured differently, they fast for twelve days in the month of Muḥarram rather than in Ramaḍān, and consider the pilgrimage to Mecca unnecessary). Although held politically suspect by other

Muslims, the ʿAlawī in Syria have retained a prominent position in the political system due to the ʿAlawī descent of former and current presidents Ḥāfidh and Bashār al-Asad.[43]

The main *shīʿa* sect, the Imāmiyya, claim that the imamate is based on the rational need of the Community of Believers for leadership, as well as the eternal need of mankind for guidance by a spiritually faultless leader. The Imāmiyya believe that the proper succession of *imāms* continued until 874, when the twelfth *imām*, Muḥammad al-Muntaẓar, "disappeared." The dilemma of the way and timing of the succession was solved theologically through the dogma of the hidden *imām*. According to that dogma, the *imām* of the Community of Believers has hidden himself in a metaphysical way and will reappear at the end of the world in the guise of the messianic figure of the *Mahdī*, meaning "the Awaited One."[44] Then he will lead the Muslims in their final victory against Evil, and Goodness will reign in the world. Up until that time, the *shīʿa* Muslim community shall be administered by a government of religious scholars-jurisconsults (*ʿulamāʾ*/*mullah*s) who will interpret Islamic law.[45]

The rejection of ʿAlī by the majority of Muslims, his murder, and the death of his son Ḥusayn have a great symbolic meaning for the *shīʿa* because they show how Good was conquered by Evil and how subsequently the Muslims were split and finally defeated at the hands of the infidels. According to Akbar Ahmed,[46] this allows the *shīʿa* to see themselves and their community, and even their *imām* who is guided by God and in turn is a guide for them, as heroes in the eternal battle between Good and Evil, which must in no circumstances be lost again.

In modern times, the *shīʿa* model of governance has become the dominant model of socio-political organization in Iran after the 1979 Islamic revolution. Indeed, for many *shīʿa* the twelfth *imām* was Ayatollah Khomeini, even if he himself never accepted the title.[47]

One of the most thorough analyses of the *imām*'s role in modern Iran is that of Ernest Gellner (1987). In this analysis of the *sunnī* and *shīʿa* views on legality and sanctity in the framework of Weber's pattern of a charismatic and bureaucratic authority, Gellner offers an interesting anthropological interpretation, exploring the contrast between God's transcendence and the governance by the legally minded religious scholars-jurisconsults, which is one of the basic tenets of the modern Iranian political system. His analysis seems to refer almost exclusively to the *shīʿa* of Iran, even though it is presented as if it applied to all *shīʿa* Muslims.

According to Gellner,[48] if *sunnī* Islam is a compromise between the power of the word of the *Qurʾān* and the Prophetic traditions on the one hand and the unanimity of the religious scholars-jurisconsults on the other, then *shīʿa* Islam gives priority to the leadership of the holy *imām* at the expense of unanimity. This priority in many cases even surpasses the authority of the text itself. In addition, *shīʿa* Islam emphasizes protest, martyrdom, retribution, the logic of dissimulation (i.e. the hiding of one's religious conviction when in danger), and recognizes the executive authority of the religious scholars-jurisconsults, who for the first time in our era rule Iran without the help or the consent of tribal leaders within a framework of a "*vilayeti-i-faqi*" (clerical democracy). The latter, however, as an element of political theory has been added by Ayatollah Khomeini; it is not part of the classical *shī'a* tradition.[49] Nonetheless, this direct involvement of the *shī'a* "clerics" in politics has become the norm wherever there are *shī'a* minorities. The best-known examples are those of the Lebanese Ḥizb Allāh movement, whose spiritual guide is Muḥammad Ḥusayn Faḍl Allāh, and of the Iraqi *shī'a* resistance to the US occupation under Muktaḍar al-Ṣaḍr – who nonetheless bowed to the demands of Ayatollah 'Alī Sistānī, the higher *shī'a* "cleric" in the region, for a more peaceful solution.

At a cultural level, *shī'a* religious practice is steeped in the drama of 'Alī and Ḥusayn, as well as the pain their unjust loss caused in the world. A brief ethnographic description by Eickelman of a holiday pageant on the anniversary of the battle of Karbalā' shows us how the ceremony of mourning Ḥusayn's death gives the *shī'a* community hope of rebirth and celebrates the victory of life over death.[50] In another description from a village in Iran in the 1960s, Fischer and Abedi describe similar scenes from the ritual dramatization of Ḥusayn's death. We see how the central roles were distributed and follow through the elaborate preparations of the stage. Like Eickelman, the two anthropologists stress the psychological burden articulated in the ritual enactment of Ḥusayn's murder and the almost transcendental grief of his victimized community. Such is the intensity of feelings, Fischer and Abedi write, that when Shemr, "the evil general of the Sunni Syrian army,"[51] gallops center stage calling for Ḥusayn to show himself, he announces to the audience:

> "I'm not Shemr, nor is this the land of Karbala; I'm just playing the role." This formula was partly used to fend off the danger that the onlookers would become so enraged at his killing of their beloved Imām that they would kill him.[52]

From a similar point of view, another anthropologist, Michael Gilsenan, describes how the re-enactment of the Ḥusayn drama in the *shī'a* villages of Lebanon is directly related to the local ruling socio-political order of things and can be understood on two levels: as a nostalgic memory and a cry of agony by simple people who are at the mercy of those more powerful than themselves, and also as a battle cry of the victims of history which serves as a call to action.[53] It is here that 'Alī and his wife and daughter of the Prophet, Fāṭima, are elevated into male and female religious and moral prototypes. Beyond this, if we bear in mind the emotional and passionate involvement of the audience during these re-enactments, it would be no exaggeration to suggest that Ḥusayn's martyred death at the hands of the Syrian soldiers resembles the sacrifice of Christ for the redemption of mankind – but without the element of God's grace. Often, this passion is interpreted by external observers as a sign of religious fanaticism; at least this is the predominant image that the world has formed of *shīʿa* Iran after the 1979 revolution and because of the war between Iran and Iraq, as well as the activities of *shīʿa* Islamist groups such as Ḥizb Allāh in Lebanon. But, at a deeper level, it expresses a strongly felt existential agony ingrained in *shīʿa* theology. This is what gives martyrdom its unique political power, which has been deftly employed by states and political organizations, especially since the 1980s war between Iran and Iraq when the former's soldiers were portrayed as martyrs for the Good Cause.[54]

Finally, *shīʿa* Islam also places a great deal of importance on the role of the saints and martyrs who characterize the *shīʿa* theological universe and ritual practices: the saints because of the absence of the *imām*, and the martyrs on account of the tragic nature of the *shīʿa* community, which has always been at a disadvantage compared with those more powerful in the world. In a way which resembles Christianity, the meanings of pain and mercy, but not, as I said, that of God's grace, martyrdom and sacrifice, atonement and redemption are present in the *shīʿa* notion of salvation.

Thus, as opposed to notions of intercession found in *sunnī* legal tradition, though not in popular practice, the *shīʿa* believe that blessings, pleas for mercy, and prayers of and to the *imāms* and their other saints are a necessary element of faith. For this reason, in addition to the anniversaries of the births and deaths of the members of the Prophet's family, they also celebrate anniversaries of all the saints' deaths at their tombs and at other places associated with *shīʿa* history.

2

The Foundations of Islamic Doctrine and the Community of Believers

In the first part of this chapter I consider the four doctrinal foundations of Islam: the *Qur'ān*, the Prophetic tradition (*sunna, ḥadīth*), the consensus among Muslims (*ijmā'*), and the principle of reasoning by analogy (*qiyās or ijtihād*). In principle the Islamic law (*sharī'a*) is derived from and developed through them in an unceasing process of continuous reformulation and reinterpretation. The people who confess to the divine truth of this doctrinal and legal framework as it is experienced through time call themselves Muslims and constitute the worldwide Community of Believers (*umma*), a concept I discuss in the second part of the chapter.

DOCTRINAL FOUNDATIONS

The presentation of the doctrinal foundations of Islam and the sources of Islamic law will allow us to understand why today, more than a thousand years after the initial formulation of certain normative principles, a debate is still going on among many Muslims about their exact content and scope in ways that shape current political affairs and activism.[1] For example, debates about the relationship between the Muslim world and the West, about the establishment of Islamic states in Algeria, Egypt, Iran, Afghanistan, and elsewhere, or about the Israeli occupation of Arab Palestine and the employment of suicide bombers are deeply affected by particular and historically bounded understandings of these doctrinal foundations and the attendant interpretations of Islamic law. As a living tradition, then, Islam does not "issue," so to speak, from doctrine in a theologically exact and sociologically predictable way. Rather it develops and exists within history through the multitude of ways in which doctrine is impregnated with life through everyday practice.

Additionally, the present discussion will offer a glance at the wealth of Islamic theological and ethical discourse, dispensing with the erroneous assumption that Islam is more concerned with "orthopraxy" (emphasis on commonly observed ritual practices) than with "orthodoxy" (concern about doctrine) as supposedly Christianity is.[2]

Be that as it may, a comprehensive analysis of this doctrinal and legal framework in all its theological complexity and socio-political interpretative intricacy is beyond the scope of the present work, the abilities of the author, and, indeed, the knowledge and interests of the vast majority of Muslims around the globe. I shall thus offer a general presentation, laying emphasis on elements of anthropological interest intimately related to everyday practices. Such an emphasis is significant if one wishes to avoid the traps of neo-orientalism, which considers Islamic tradition to be static and approaches Islamic law as a relic of the past.

The *Qur'ān*

The holy book of Islam was revealed to Prophet Muḥammad over 20 years. The term "*Qur'ān*" is included in the text and can be translated as "recitation." Indeed, in terms of syntax and style the *Qur'ān* is to be recited rather than read. In that sense, it differs considerably from the Bible or the Torah and is closer to ancient epics (e.g. the *Iliad*) which were recited by heart.

The *Qur'ān* is divided in 114 *sūra*s whose length varies from three to 286 verses. The first *sūra* is called *al-Fātiḥa* (the Opening, or Introduction) and is repeated during prayer sessions and in many other everyday occasions. The last two *sūra*s are short psalms reminiscent of magical spells. With a very few exceptions, no *sūra* treats any single particular theme. Many of them are comprised of sections connected to one another in a very loose way. Also, apart from the very short *al-Fātiḥa*, all other *sūra*s are arranged according to their length, starting with the longest one. So the *sūra*s are not chapters and the *Qur'ān* is not a book that narrates a single story. One may start reading it from the beginning, the middle, or the end without necessarily losing anything.

The *sūra*s are divided into those revealed to the Prophet when he was still in Mecca and those revealed after the emigration (*hijra*) to Madīna. The first ones are often short and poetic referring to God's manifestations in nature and to His benevolence, to prophetic stories and descriptions of life in paradise and in hell, as well as to the tribulations awaiting the unbelievers. In contrast, the Madīna *sūra*s reflect the increasing socio-political power of the Prophet and the *umma*. It should also be added that the *Qur'ān* includes a quantity of legal material which is utilized in Islamic law, such as legally enforceable injunctions, but it cannot be described as a legal text.

For Muslims, the *Qur'ān* is the actual words of God faithfully repeated by a messenger, Muḥammad – in contrast to the Bible which is a book about God written by spiritually guided humans. This is an important point, because Muslims see the *Qur'ān* as part of the Abrahamic tradition in the course of which the same single God revealed himself through the prophets to the Jews and through Jesus to the Christians and, by extension, to the whole world. But, according to Islam, the biblical message was corrupted right from the beginning: Christ was just another prophet, not the son of God; that would have compromised His singleness. So the one and only God decided once more to reveal himself to the world through the *Qur'ān*, this time not through prophets speaking on His behalf, but through a Prophet who would repeat His exact words. This occasion is considered to be final and concluding. In that sense, the *Qur'ānic* revelation represents for Muslims the crowning stage in a long discussion between God and the world which started at the beginning of the creation. So, the *Qur'ān* is not a new revelation, but a rectification of those mistakes that humans supposedly made in interpreting God's will as revealed to all prophets prior to Muḥammad.[3]

Soon after the death of Prophet Muḥammad, his successors collected all those parts of the *Qur'ān* which until then had been orally transmitted, as well as those parts which had been written on papyrus, animal skins, etc. The motive behind this was to secure the knowledge of the *Qur'ān* after the death of those who knew it by heart[4] and to agree on a text which would serve as the basis for legal reasoning. The results of this process were the codification of the Arabic language and the articulation of legal theory which gradually led to the development of Islamic law.[5] Here, I shall concentrate on the former. The "mystical" relationship between the *Qur'ān* and the Arabic language is implied in the idea that it wants non-Arab Muslims to study Arabic in order to read the *Qur'ān* in the original and in the practice of listening to *Qur'ānic* recitations almost exclusively in Arabic. But there is something more.

Never being the language of everyday life, *Qur'ānic* Arabic is a formal language that obeys complex grammatical rules and follows an elaborate syntax. Most probably, it represents a Meccan variant of an artificial literary language,[6] which today is little understood by the great mass of believers. As Bloch has shown, this formalism characterizes most types of religious language – both sacred texts and rituals – and in a way expresses and legitimizes its authority and that of officiants, be they elders, priests, or lay preachers.[7] In the case of the *Qur'ān*, then, its recitation or its study as a sacred text does not invite believers to approach it critically and to engage in dialogue on what it stands for, but to accept it without reservations as the true Word of God. No interpretation can question this.

The exalted position of the *Qur'ān* in Islam has greatly influenced many areas of social life. One of them is the arts. On the one hand, *Qur'ān* forbids all types of iconic representation of God, man, and nature as forms of idolatry. On the other hand, the *Qur'ān* attests to the power of the word and to the divine beauty of the language. Taken together, these two factors are to a large extent responsible for the virtual absence from the Muslim world of painting and sculpture as art forms and for the corresponding impressive development of calligraphy and text ornamentation.[8] This type of artistic expression has been further expanded to decorative designs (arabesque) which adorn mosques and many palaces and public buildings.

Another area of social life concerns the development of a particular conception of religious knowledge and its communication among the faithful. As Eickelman argues, in Muslim societies "[t]he cultural idea of religious knowledge has remained remarkably constant over time,"[9] stressing the memorization of fixed texts. Often, these texts are written in rhyme and exhibit a "poetic" rhythm, just like the *Qur'ān*, which is the archetypal text and the very first which those studying in religious or *Qur'ānic* schools should memorize, usually in part, before turning their attention elsewhere. Although in this process mnemonic rotation appears to be valued higher than critical thinking and deconstruction, the assumed rigidity and immobility of the tradition pertains more to its form and style than to its content.[10] As we shall see, even the most conservative religious scholars do enrich the Islamic tradition they strive to preserve by the interpretations they produce laying emphasis on *taqlīd*, i.e. the unquestioning acceptance of existing doctrines. Muslim modernists as well as Islamists of all shades start with the *Qur'ān* and, though they advertise their close reading of the text and their interpretative conservatism, they reach starkly different conclusions from each other. This is not something peculiarly Muslim, of course, but a constitutive trait of all interpretations, particularly when these relate to texts which are somehow seen as foundational. Eastern Orthodox, Roman Catholic, High Anglican, and Evangelical Christians all invoke the same Bible, but their views on, say, the creation, the Trinity dogma, the ordination of women, or the practice of abortion differ dramatically. It is all part of what Asad has called the "production of orthodoxy" process, that is the establishment of dominant versions of religious tradition in specific historical conjunctions through a discursive process that extends in time and space.

Lastly, no discussion of the *Qur'ān*, and indeed of Islam as a whole, can be completed without reference to *Qur'ānic* recitation. However, the significance of *Qur'ānic* recitation can be more fully understood within the context of a wider discussion of orality in Islamic tradition and of what Charles Hirschkind (2001a) has called "ethics of listening." These issues I consider in detail in chapter 3. For this reason, here I shall simply draw the readers' attention to the ubiquity of *Qur'ānic* recitation throughout the Middle East and North Africa.

One can hear the *Qur'ān* recited not only during religious feasts, like the *Ramaḍān*, or during the prayer sessions in the mosque, but practically anywhere at anytime. For example, there are radio and television programs which offer hours of *Qur'ānic* recitation daily and can be heard at home or in the workplace, sometimes forming a sort of "background music" which inundates the whole atmosphere of the place with a particular aura. Similarly, recitations of the holy book can be found on audiotapes, often played in taxis and private cars, on videotapes watched by family members and groups of friends, and, for the most technologically advanced, on DVDs and on the Internet. Beggars, too, may recite the *Qur'ān* while standing in the market waiting for the charity of the faithful, while travelers to the Middle East can listen to *Qur'ānic* recitation during their flight with a Middle Eastern airline.

The *sunna*

Although the Prophet was an ordinary man, he is considered by Muslims as a perfect human being. That is why all acts and sayings of Muḥammad have acquired an exemplary character.[11] The term "*sunna*" refers to the paradigmatic acts and utterances of the Prophet themselves, and the term "the *ḥadīth*" (*al-ḥadīth*) to the reports of the Prophet's *sunna* as they have been handed down to posterity. In practice though, the two terms are often used interchangeably and can be translated as "Prophetic tradition." Together with the *Qur'ān*, the tradition of the Prophet constitutes the material from which the Islamic law derives.

In the Muslim world there are a number of *ḥadīth* compilations, each running to several volumes. Among the most important ones are those of Muḥammad bin Isma'īl al-Bukhārī and Muslim bin al-Ḥijāj al-Qushayrī of the third century AH/ninth century AD. Given their significance, the subject of authentication has always remained crucial. So certain criteria have been agreed upon by the religious scholars, pronouncing some of the *ḥadīth* listed therein as more satisfactory than others.[12] These criteria distinguish between sound and less sound, even forged, *ḥadīth* on account of the number and kind of persons who transmitted them historically, certain specific traits that they exhibit, and their relationship with other generally accepted or rejected *ḥadīth*.[13] In any case, the "authentic" character of the *ḥadīth* should not be confused with claims on my part or that of most analysts outside the Islamic theological fold to historical authenticity. The emergence of the Prophetic *sunna* was a creative process up to the third century AH/ninth century AD, with religious scholars and legists attributing to the Prophet local administrative and legal practices, as well as doctrinal views they themselves or the various local communities held, thus endowing them with authority.[14] This was done in the context of a growing need for the development of clear legal and administrative principles based on God's revelation. The whole process is often called "sciences of the *ḥadīth*."

The importance of the *ḥadīth* as explanatory propositions employed in *Qur'ānic* studies reveals what Fischer and Abedi see as hegemony of the oral over the textual in Islamic tradition.[15] This may be related to certain traits of the early Community of Believers, especially the significance ascribed to the face-to-face dialogic discourse; hence the importance attributed to the chain of transmittance through time: the oral endows the text with authority, not vice versa. I shall return to this in chapter 3.

Even though criteria concerning the authenticity of the *ḥadīth* have been more or less agreed upon, their interpretation can differ widely among those religious scholars who belong to distinct theological traditions and legal schools and are – sometimes by default – associated with particular socio-political orders. This implies that from very early on the political implications of *ḥadīth* interpretation were particularly important. The very term *sunnī* Muslims (in contrast with *shī'a*) is related to the specific ways in which this fold, who came to be called *ahl al-sunna wal-jamā'a*, approached the *Qur'ān* and the Prophetic tradition and agreed upon "a set of principles and tenets in the form of consensus (*ijmā'*), to uphold as the distinguishing mark of their identity."[16] Even today all those who speak in the name of Islam or put their message across in Islamic terms, be they conservatives, modernists, or Islamists, use the *ḥadīth* eclectically and color their interpretations in ways that further their political objectives. We shall see examples of this in the following chapter.

Ijmā'

Technically, *ijmā'* is defined as

> a sanctioning instrument whereby the creative jurists, the *mujtahids*, representing the community at large, are considered to have reached an agreement . . . on a technical ruling . . . as conclusive and as epistemologically certain as any verse of the Quran and the Sunna of the Prophet.[17]

The term refers to the consensus among Muslims on matters concerning the Community of Believers. It reflects the emphasis that the *ahl al-sunna wal-jamā'a* placed on the homogeneity of the Community, something that has led some analysts to a poor and legalistic understanding of Islam in terms of "orthopraxy" rather than "orthodoxy."

As Hodgson argues,[18] the Community of Believers that the Prophet had established in Madīna shared many common traits with the existing Jewish and Zoroastrian monotheistic communities and less with the Christian. This he attributes to the fact that the Christians had elected to live alongside non-Christians, thus accepting non-Christian social and political commitments. According to Hodgson, the only completely Christian policy vis-à-vis the world at large was that of monastic life.[19] This option did not exist for Jews and Zoroastrians who rejected monasticism. Instead, both traditions offered their members the opportunity to live in polities socially and personally regulated by their respective sacred laws at all levels. The difference between the two was the presence of a strong clerical hierarchy in Zoroastrianism and its absence from Judaism.[20]

Islam developed along the lines of the Jewish model, perhaps because among the first Muslims many were of Jewish origin. Islam stressed the absolute equality among all believers, not allowing for the emergence of a clerical aristocracy. There was a difference, though, from Judaism in that Islam was a proselytizing religion offering a comprehensive practical guide that everyone could embrace, whereas Judaism presented the Jews as the "chosen people."

Islam's cosmopolitan attitude was fully endorsed by the *ahl al-sunna* who, in the end, were those who shaped the doctrinal basis of *sunnī* Islam and Islamic law. For them, every person is individually accountable to God, and there is no room for clerical mediation. Equally impossible is considered to be the existence of any other form of allegiance besides that owned to the Community of Believers.

Based on the early Muslim polity in Madīna led by the Prophet himself, this model has always been regarded as an ideal towards which all Muslims should strive and is distinguished by two characteristics. It provides an ideal model for the relationship between the individual and the community, where face-to-face contact is considered the norm, and an ideal model of sociocultural homogeneity, protecting the absolute nature of societal orientation towards God and safeguarding the rejection of any other alternative.

This vision, such as it is, of sociocultural homogeneity that characterizes the imagined Community of Believers is based on the Madīnan Arab traditions as these were reshaped by the Prophet. It is from here that the importance attributed to *ijmāʿ* springs: the principle of consensus of the Community of Believers – which cannot err since it is guided by God – presupposes and preserves, at least at the theological level, this coveted sociocultural homogeneity ideal.[21]

It is not certain if this homogeneity was in place during those early days of Islam. In a sense, it does not matter since for those concerned *it is* a historical fact. What is more clear is what started happening soon after the death of the Prophet, complicating immensely the practicalities and the theological and legal underpinnings of *ijmāʿ*.

With the spread of Islam outside the small Madīnan community to the wider Arabian Peninsula and gradually to non-Arab Africans and Asians, relationships between the individual and the community became increasingly complex. Forms of positive law had to be developed with revelation and local practice in all its vast variety cohabiting a legal and social universe organized by and rendered meaningful through human reasoning. That was not easy. Even a cursory reading of the history of Islamic societies reveals the existence of alternative idioms of belonging, such as tribal or racial considerations, which functioned as distinct poles for the articulation of complex, ever-changing Islamic identities. Although the religious scholars could banish history from the era of the Prophet and his immediate successors, the "Golden Age" of Islam, they now had to bow to its realities which were often tarnished by wars between Muslims and by doctrinal disputes.

As a result, reaching a consensus according to the principle of *ijmāʿ* was transformed into a technical issue. Accepting the primacy of revelation and seeking to determine the way in which reason can work its way through it so as to offer binding solutions to the ever-emerging new situations that Muslims found themselves in was something that only the religious scholars and jurists could do. They were the ones who knew well the interpretation of the *Qur'ān* and the *sunna* and who possessed a methodology enabling them to produce therefrom theologically sound reasonings. This methodology became known as *qiyās* or *ijtihād*.

Qiyās or *ijtihād*

So if the *Qur'ān* and the *sunna* are the sources from where the law is derived, at least in the cases mentioned, and *ijmā'* is a sanctioning instrument then "[t]he processes of reasoning involved therein" are what we call *qiyās*,[22] later to be identified with *ijtihād*, i.e. the exercise of one's "utmost effort in extracting a rule from the subject matter of revelation while following the principles and procedures established in legal theory."[23]

The adventure of *ijtihād* started during the early days of Islam with the need to promulgate laws in order to administer the emerging Muslim polity. But how was subjectivism to be avoided? How could anyone ensure that the actual rulings would reflect God's will as they should? The principle of *ijmā'* moved towards that direction; but in itself that was not enough. The existing forms of reasoning known in a still rather inarticulate manner as *ra'y*, *ijtihād*, or *qiyās* had to be rethought and reshaped. In this context, *ra'y*, which really referred to "free human reasoning based on practical considerations and bound by no authoritative text . . . [or] based on such a text but motivated by practical considerations,"[24] was restricted and later abandoned, while *ijtihād* was deemed a separate activity and was identified with *qiyās*, i.e. with the systematic analogical reasoning that was based on revelation.[25]

After a long period of gestation these views became dominant in *sunnī* Islam mostly through the work of Muḥammad ibn Idrīs al-Shāfi'ī (d. 204/820), which represented the middle way between rationalism and traditionalism. But a real synthesis between the two was achieved later in the third century AH/ninth century AD, though it would not be inaccurate to say that after that period traditionalism gradually got the upper hand.

This happened as the principles of Islamic law were formulated in an increasingly systematic manner[26] and the question "Who can exercise *ijtihād*?", that is "Who can be a *mujtāhid*?" arose, probably for practical rather than theoretical reasons.[27] As it were, the response to this question and to all the others that stemmed from it was not clear and cannot be discussed here but in an oversimplified manner.

In as much as *ijtihād* was involved in the political process, it appears that in the fifth century AH/eleventh century AD the consensus was that if the caliphs were incapable of exercising it, then someone else should do it for them. For example, *Imām* al-Ḥaramayn al-Juwaynī (d. 478/1085), an acknowledged *mujtāhid* himself, listed the ability to exercise *ijtihād* among the necessary characteristics of the ideal *imām*, but if he were incapable of fulfilling the role the task could be transferred to the religious scholars who would advise him; after all they were "the real sovereigns" and "the leaders and masters of the community."[28] Similar views were held by his famous student, Abū Ḥāmid al-Ghazālī (d. 505/1111), renowned *mujtāhid* and renovator of the faith (*mujāddid*).[29] But very quickly a new problem arose: "Are there any *mujtāhid*s any more?" or, more generally, "Can one envisage an era with no *mujtāhid*s?"

From this point onwards, scholarship itself differs. The dominant approach on the issue that has been taken by most Western scholars of Islam is very precise: the overall answer that was given to all these questions sometime around the fourth century AH/tenth century AD was that only the important religious scholars and jurists of the past could exercise *ijtihād*; the younger generations can only follow them. This privileging of a particular reading/interpretation of the tradition and its endowment with paramount authority and authenticity led to what became known as "the closing of the gate of *ijtihād*" or as "the adoption of *taqlīd*," i.e. the unquestionable acceptance of the existing doctrines.[30]

Who closed "the gate of *ijtihād*" according to these scholars is not clear. The whole issue is somehow entangled in a cyclical argument where an assumed sociocultural recession and political fragmentation that came after the initial three-century thrust of Islam is discussed here as the cause and there as the result of the purported "closing" which in itself is directly associated with theological stagnation, philosophical poverty, and sterile imitation. To be sure, the view that, as Muslims were moving further from the "Golden Age" of the Prophet and his immediate successors, things were going into decline was entertained by many in the fifth century AH/eleventh century AD. But this had to do more with the disintegration of political institutions rather than with the decline of legal standards.

According to Hallaq, who represents an alternative approach that does not accept "the closing of the gate of *ijtihād*," the careful study of Islamic legal history shows clearly that contrary to our common belief "the sophistication of technical legal thought was in fact achieved . . . during the fifth/eleventh and sixth/twelfth centuries"[31] and not during the so-called "Golden Age" of Islam. He also argues that the Muslims themselves never reached in a technical sense a consensus concerning the existence or the absence of *mujtāhid*s and, charting the debate all the way through the tenth century AH/sixteenth century AD, shows that famous jurists from the various schools of law did in fact exercise *ijtihād* "without [this] being recognised under its proper name."[32]

I have dwelt upon these issues in some detail because "the closing of the gate" debate soon erupted in a way whose repercussions are still with us, especially in the guise of the debates between pro-*ijtihād* Islamists and conservative religious authorities in the various Muslim societies. Especially after the events of 9/11 we read about these issues in the papers or listen to learned analyses on radio and television, but without recognizing it for what it is.

As both Hallaq and the adherents of the dominant school argue, from the eighteenth century onwards a growing number of *taqlīd* opponents mounted a ferocious attack against those who questioned the significance of *ijtihād* or the existence of capable *mujtāhid*s. Among those mentioned by Hallaq the best-known are Ibn ʿAbd al-Wahhāb (d. 1202/1787) and Ibn ʿAlī al-Sanūsī (d. 1313/1895), the leaders of revivalist movements in Arabia and Cyrenaica respectively. Although such men and their adherents espoused the return to a pristine form of primitive Islam, they were unanimous in proclaiming the right to exercise *ijtihād*.[33]

But the biggest challenge for the opponents of *ijtihād*, in the sense that it was widespread, persistent, and of a greater scope than anything mounted before, came at the turn of the twentieth century from the so-called Muslim reformers or modernizers. These scholars and religious activists argued that the abandoning of the principle of *ijtihād* had deprived Islam of the dynamism of the first three or four centuries of its history, transforming it into a theory that could not stand up to the intellectual and political power of the West which at the time had colonized the entire Muslim world. As will be discussed in detail in chapter 6, the Muslim reformers believed that the exercise of *ijtihād* would allow Muslims to renegotiate the principles of Islamic law and to adopt new concepts and methodological tools from the West. That would result in the reinvigoration of Muslim societies and in the transformation of Islam into an important force for modernization, on a par with Western ideologies. Such views still hold sway among liberal Muslim intellectuals, as well as those Muslims who do not feel threatened by the West.

Lastly, as will be seen in chapters 7 and 8, since the closing decades of the twentieth century the various types of Islamist movements have joined this chorus of criticism championing the free and vigorous exercise of *ijtihād*, this time in order to combat what they perceive as the Westernization of the Muslim world. To a considerable degree, such views have been influenced by the historical experience of the eighteenth- and nineteenth-century revivalist Islamic movements such as those mentioned earlier, as well as by the theories of even older religious scholars-jurisconsults, such as Taqī al-Dīn ibn Taymiyya (1263–1328), whose work has taken today a place similar to that of the Marxist canon among the 1960s student activists in Europe.

THE COMMUNITY OF BELIEVERS

The Community of Believers (*umma*) includes all Muslims. It can also refer to local socio-political units, such as the Sudanese or Egyptian *umma*, without refuting their members' participation in the wider Muslim *umma*. During the Prophet's lifetime, the term referred originally to the Madīna community (Muslims, pagans, and Jews) under his leadership, but it was later restricted to

Muslims only. In classical Islamic literature, the religious and tribal-cum-social dimensions of *umma* were initially intertwined, though progressively the term came to indicate an undivided community of Muslims juxtaposed to the *umma* of, say, the Franks or the Slavs. It is only since the late medieval period that the term ceased to be associated with distinct social or other population groups, although it has occasionally been used to describe the "Arab nation."

Despite the sociocultural differences between Islamic societies, for centuries the religious and socio-political unity of the *umma*, especially in the Middle East and North Africa, was realized through the caliphate and, later, the sultanate. Although religious interpretations never managed to harmonize Islamic law with politics, the political theory produced by religious scholars legitimated existing political arrangements, even when there was more than one Islamic polity and these were often fighting against each other. Thus, religious imagination and political expediency could sustain visions of what, in any case, had always been imagined.

Things changed with the colonization of the Muslim world in the eighteenth century. If in the context of Western modernity history has evolved around certain forms of nationalism, in the context of Islamic discourse recent Muslim history centers around the "loss" of unity in the hands of the West. Even when the Muslim societies got their formal independence in the mid-twentieth century, that happened in the name of nationalism – which was embraced by the masses and, as will be argued in the next section, proved to be perfectly compatible with local Islamic and other traditions.

But when the Islamic world (*al-ʿalam al-Islāmī*) as such becomes the subject of contemplation and the context wherein identities are constructed according to widely shared norms and principles, the emphasis shifts. Nationalist allegiances and sociocultural differences recede into the background, without ever disappearing, and what most probably never existed in a definable and historically extended form, the united *umma*, appears at the center of popular imagination. This is especially true after the conflicts in Iraq, Bosnia, Kashmir, and Afghanistan. It was not accidental that in a message on October 7, 2001 addressed mainly to Muslims Ussāma bin Lāden talked about 80 years of humiliation and shame. For most Westerners that allusion remained obscure, but for many Muslims it was clear that it referred to the 1922 abolition of the Ottoman caliphate. That institution symbolized the uninterrupted unity of the *umma* since the days of the Prophet. This, at least, is what many history books say and what the *al-Jazīra* television station announced to the millions of its viewers in the Arab world and beyond. Whatever the historical truth of such claims, the fact that they do capture public imagination suggests that we should approach this shadowy, elusive, even quixotic, term "*umma*" very carefully.

As Asad argues, "[t]he *umma* is the concept of a religio-political space – divinely sanctioned and eternally valid – within which rational discussion and criticism can be conducted. It is also a space of power and of punishment."[34] And elsewhere:

> The Islamic *umma* in the classical theological view is thus not an imagined community on a par with the Arab nation waiting to be politically unified but a theologically defined space enabling Muslims to practice the disciplines of *din* [religion] in the world.[35]

At one level, it appears that the *umma* cannot be transformed by the historical processes that Western modernity has set in motion. However, this is not so, as the terms "power" and "punishment" imply.

As has been suggested in the previous chapter, Islamic discourse loses much of its meaning if it is not somehow associated with a specific geographical area which ideally should concern all Muslims, i.e. the *umma*. If, accepting Asad,[36] we define Islam as a discursive tradition, a discussion between Muslims that is extended in space as well as in time, and if, following the premises of this tradition, we accept Islam as a revealed Truth, then the *umma* can be seen as that trans-historical subject towards which this Truth is addressed, creating it out of nothing.[37] This subject is obliged to transform this Truth into lived experience, each time according to the exigencies of the particular historical conditions.

Simultaneously, then, in the context of Islamic discourse the *umma* is beyond history and its transformative power, but also present in history through the purposeful action of man. Understanding this relationship between the eternal nature and the historical energies of the Community of Believers, as reflected in the imagined character of its unity and singleness ("my community cannot agree in error"), we may be able to understand better what brings together a Mauritanian Muslim with a Syrian, an Egyptian, or a Pakistani, despite the importance each one of them may attach to his or her particular cultural tradition.

There are no ethnographies focusing on local understandings of the *umma*. However, there are some in which the term might have been employed productively and others where the term is mentioned but not fully discussed. Among the former is Barth's 1983 ethnography of Sohar (*Sohar: Culture and Society in an Omani Town*). Barth describes the society of Sohar and its environs as a disordered system, a concept fully explored in a later work,[38] because he sees no other way to study its population which, besides the non-Muslims, consists of five different ethnic and language groups symbolically connected to different centers – Mecca, Cairo, Tehran, Qom in Iran – for their religious dogmas or their moral, cultural, and political outlook. It would have been interesting if the term *umma* could have been employed analytically to provide an overarching framework for such disparate social categories and religious outlooks that would make sense to its own members.

Among the ethnographies where the term *umma* can be found is Combs-Schilling's 1989 study of the Moroccan monarchy and specifically her discussion of the royal sacrifice at the celebration of *'id al-kabīr*, the Feast of the Great Sacrifice. As she argues, the *'id* sacrifice constitutes the most significant symbol of legitimation of the Moroccan royal family.[39] Whereas during the preceding ritual prayer the king is considered one among the faithful, he approaches the nearby sacrificial ground as leader of the kingdom and of the Community of Believers, the "symbolic incarnation of the political whole."[40]

The sacrifice is theoretically attended by all male members of the *umma*. As this is impossible in practical terms, community sacrifices are performed all over Morocco. The author shows how the royal sacrifice is offered in the name of the *umma* and how each community sacrifice is seen as the realization of this vision at the local level. Indicative that each male member of the kingdom is personally transformed through the royal ritual is that he returns home following a different route.[41]

Another ethnographic example comes from my own fieldwork in the Sudan. As I have discussed elsewhere,[42] the Northern Sudanese tribes, a product of intermarriage between local populations and Arab immigrants who have moved to the Sudan since the ninth century AD, claim an Arab-Muslim identity. They speak Arabic, are *sunnī* Muslims, and exhibit social and cultural traits similar to the rest of the Arab world. Additionally, they believe that their ancestors, long-practicing slave-traders amongst the animistic African tribes of the southern Sudan, were in reality engaged in the spreading of Islam and its civilization among the unbelievers.

The contemporary Northern Sudanese see themselves as members of the Islamic *umma* and as citizens of the Sudanese state – where a strict version of Islamic law has been in effect since 1983. Interestingly, the many times prime minister and now exile, Sāḍiq al-Mahdī, is a descendant of the nineteenth-century messianic figure of Muḥammad Aḥmad al-Mahdī, originally a leader of the Samāniyya *ṣūfī* order.[43] Sāḍiq is also the long-standing head of the *Anṣār*, a Mahdist religious sect-cum-*ṣūfī* order, and of the *Umma* Party, one of the most important Sudanese nationalist political parties, whose name alludes to both the wider Community of Believers and to the Sudanese nationalist struggle. Impossible as it is to distinguish between the *Umma* and the *Anṣār*, one is forced to concede that the party's nationalism is shaped by its Islamic Mahdist tradition, rather than the other way round. This has been painfully demonstrated through the party's stance in the long-running civil war between the Arab-Muslim Northern Sudanese-dominated government and the non-Muslim African rebels from the South. Faithfully following the traditions of the North, Sāḍiq's followers portray the Southerners, as well as most non-riverain Northern Arab Sudanese, as descendants of slaves or enslaveable peoples, irrespective of their embracing of Islam for many generations now.[44]

But if the *Umma* Party is presented as a point of convergence between the Islamic and the (Northern Arab) Sudanese *umma*, a more credible, at least for some, socio-political bloc in that respect is that of the Islamists who took power in 1989. Two of the Islamists' most important moves were the organization in Khartoum of the *Panislamic Conference* in the mid-1990s and their association with Ussāma bin Lāden until 1996. On the home front, as expected, the Islamists followed the same path of violence towards the Southerners and the other peripheral people of the Sudan as had all previous governments. The Dār Fūr genocide is part of this policy, where religious chauvinism articulates socio-economic considerations and long-term ethnic conflicts.[45] In that sense, it is ironic that the Sudanese Islamists immersed themselves in discussions on the breadth of Muslim *umma*, and on its wonderful inclusiveness with everybody except their own non-Arab kin. Forgetting that their own Arabness is really part of an imagined identity, they seem to pose Arab descent as a requirement for admission to the *umma* for all those living in sub-Saharan Africa.

Indeed, in the contemporary Islamic world the concept of *umma* is widely discussed, partly because Islamist groups have made it part of their political vocabulary in more ways than one. But this has not made it more precise. It is more than certain that were we to expand the present work to include African and Asian Muslim societies, the concept of *umma* would be seriously revised. It may be that in the Middle East and North Africa, a common Arabic heritage has made the discussion of *umma* somewhat easier, hiding or ignoring the colossal leaps of imagination that such a discourse demands. Especially today, when a heightened Islamic awareness appears to characterize several Asian societies, any anthropological contribution on the local understandings of the term would be valuable.

Umma and Nation-state

For some analysts, *umma* and nation-state are antagonistic concepts.[46] For example, Vatikiotis argues that the nation-state was a concept introduced to the Muslim world by European colonialism.[47] Until then the Muslim political entities were based on networks of allegiance and kinship, on patron–client relations and on the importance of honor, descent, and wealth.[48] Even after independence, most Islamic societies were not transformed into nation-states, but continued to exhibit dynastic characteristics. Indeed for Vatikiotis, Middle Eastern and North African nationalism failed as the very invocation of the past (necessary for the construction of a national identity for the newly-emergent post-colonial states) brought to the present the Islamic character of Arab history, thus demonstrating exactly the opposite: the lack of membership criteria in connection to the soil, language, common ethnic identity, and political legitimation.[49] True, the Middle Eastern and North African states have survived, but without being transformed into nation-states in the Western sense of the term. The numerous references to their common Arab descent, the rhetoric surrounding the significance of the Arab League, as well as the intolerance toward many ethnic and religious minorities,[50] and the high level of human rights violations are indicative of this.[51]

Contrary to Vatikiotis, Gellner maintains that Islamic tradition has such characteristics that have enabled it to move along with the notion of nationalism without becoming subservient to it and without losing its vision of a transnational *umma*. Gellner's argument has been developed in his *Nations and Nationalism* (1993b), but has its roots in his *Muslim Society* (1985). There Gellner distinguishes between High Islam, a scriptural, puritanical, transcultural, and urban egalitarian tradition expressed by the religious scholars who acted as guardians and interpreters of the sacred texts, and Low, or folk, Islam, an often ecstatic and occasionally revolutionary tradition that put emphasis on the holiness and superhuman powers of particular persons or descent groups and on the ritual practices performed around sacred places outside the urban centers. For Gellner, the two traditions are interlocked in a pattern of replacing each other periodically in a manner that preserves the overall system through cyclical changes of political leadership. This is known as the "pendulum theory."[52]

With the advent of colonialism and nationalism, things changed drastically. The rise of nationalistic ideology signaled the replacement of the variety of Low – and by definition local – cultural traditions with "standardized, formalized and codified, literacy-carried high cultures."[53] But according to Gellner, that was not a problem because Islam was already equipped with a unified literate tradition, High Islam. This enabled its carriers, the urban middle classes, to embrace the identity of the nation-state citizen without many problems. The reformist movement of early twentieth-century Islamic modernism played a prominent role in this process.[54] In this way, High Islam managed to keep its hegemonic position within the new nationalist order without losing its universalistic and transhistorical revelatory character.

Gellner's distinction between High and Low Islam has been criticized by many anthropologists because it mistakenly identifies High tradition with the puritanical "orthodoxy" of the learned religious scholars and Low tradition with the mystical practices of the illiterate rural masses.[55] Such distinctions are erroneous and a-historical because of "the tendency to insulate different tiers or segments [of society] in ways that preclude the examination of their vertical or horizontal interconnections."[56] Other critical points concern Gellner's use of the term "tribe," the employment of different theories when defining the concepts he uses, and his silence concerning women and the peasants, the relationship between Islam and Europe, and the existence of other forms of Islamic discourse.[57]

What Gellner seems to suggest is that Islam, High Islam, and the reformist movement of Islamic modernism more or less refer to the same thing. This methodological "ploy" allows him to characterize Islam as reformation *ex perpetua causa* and to associate High Islam with the Protestant Reformation.[58] This is not a useful suggestion. The Christian Reformation was directly related to the rise of individualism and the process of secularization of European – and later Western – societies. Contrary to this, Islamic modernism of the turn of the twentieth century, which Gellner associates with nationalism, emerged for different reasons and functioned in conditions far removed from those existing in Reformation Europe. Notwithstanding its relationship to nationalism, Islamic modernism promoted the awakening of a comprehensive Islamic consciousness that would tap the reserves of the transnational Islamic tradition and would advance the interests of the worldwide *umma*.[59]

Even in the case of Pakistan, which has been often described as the first nation-state that was established on the basis of Islamic tradition, the situation is much more complex. As Hobsbawm writes,

> It is by no means evident that Pakistan was the product of a national movement among the Muslim of the then Indian Empire . . . it is quite certain that the bulk of ordinary Muslims thought in terms of communal and not in national terms, and would not have understood the concept of national self-determination as something which could apply to belief in Allah and His Prophet.[60]

Most Pakistanis, the author continues, saw the establishment of Pakistan in religious rather than national terms, forming an Islamic nationalism.

In the end, what makes Gellner's thesis untenable are three assumptions situated at the basis of his entire theoretical edifice on nationalism and Islam. The first concerns his reluctance to accept that Islam in the era of nationalism differs from Islam in previous historical periods. He is trapped in the static distinction between a High and a Low Islam and the identification of the former with an allegedly real archetypical Islam. Contrary to this, the very question "Is Islam compatible with nationalism?" or indeed with "democracy," "human rights," "feminism," and what not is the wrong type of question. Islam is not an object, it is a discursive tradition, i.e. a tradition in constant movement within the flow of history as this is concretized in particular societies at particular times. Instead of an essentialist approach, ethnographic and other case studies can illuminate us more about how specific understandings of Islamic tradition can be implicated in the construction of national identities.

The second assumption concerns the other term of Gellner's rhetorical question, nationalism. In their introduction to a series of articles on nationalism and the colonial legacy in the Middle East and Central Asia Cole and Kandiyoti argue that "[m]any authors [Gellner included] speak as though 'nationalism' is a unitary set of practices and beliefs", whereas in reality it "changes according to whether it is a metropolitan phenomenon or a colonial one" and indeed its "making and conceiving . . . continue in the post-colonial period, throwing up new forces and perspectives that challenge previous formulations of it."[61] It is in this sense that Sami Zubaida's adoption of Chatterjee's term "fragments"

– simultaneously referring to "a multiplicity of shifting groupings and forces . . . [with] conflicting interests and sentiments . . . [who speak] the language of patriotism, the nation, and representation and constitutions, albeit in the context of vague and shifting spheres of reference,"[62] and to the vague and shifting spheres of reference themselves – can be usefully employed in the study of Middle Eastern nationalisms. In the article just mentioned Zubaida discusses early Iraqi nationalism showing how the *efendiyya* (Ottoman officials), the *shīʿa ʿulamāʾ*, and the tribes reacted in the 1920 uprising against British occupation and how they positioned themselves in the emerging nationalist Iraq after the 1921 declaration of the "British-sponsored and -protected Iraqi Arab kingdom under Faysal."[63] Nationalism, tribalism, Arabism, Islam, Ottoman Islam, and Arabian Islam are some of the spheres of reference considered by Zubaida.

Lastly, the third assumption underlying Gellner's view of nationalism is its purported direct connection to modernity and the move to industrial society, which most examples from the Muslim world prove to be spurious. More precisely, as Cole and Kandiyoti maintain in the previously mentioned article, an alleged shifting to a capitalist mode of production, even in the form of agrarian capitalism, and the reorganization of family patterns along lines characteristic of industrial societies, were totally absent in most Middle Eastern and Central Asian countries when nationalist movements made their appearance. Moreover "national identity in most individual Arab states, such as Egypt and Syria, really congealed with solidity only in the period from 1920 forward."[64] If anything, states create nations rather than vice versa. This takes the form of a continuous process that is still very much evident in post-colonial situations where sometimes earlier-achieved forms of unity and internal cohesion appear to falter as significant markers – race, ethnic identity, language, religion – are reinterpreted.

In the aforementioned case study of early Iraqi nationalism, Zubaida approaches the nation as

> a territorial, economic, and social reality . . . buttressed by a highly totalitarian and, for a while, very wealthy state . . . a fact or "facticity" compelling on the cognition and imagination of its members (much like Durkheim's constraining "social facts as things"), yet not necessarily of their sentiments of solidarity or loyalty.[65]

Another example comes from Zubaida's study of contemporary *Baʿthist* Syria. Dismissing essentialism, Zubaida starts his analysis in terms of Anderson's 1992 theory of imagined communities. As he argues,

> this idea of the conception or imagination of the nation does not necessarily entail political commitment to this entity: pan-Arab, pan-Islamic as well as narrow ethnic commitments are clearly beyond that of the nation state, but the conception of the nation becomes the field and the model in terms of which to think of these other commitments and loyalties.[66]

In the case of *Baʿthist* Syria, the state distributive mechanism has resulted in the reinforcement of the interdependence between the various regions of the state, making even distant desert populations aware of their economic dependence on the state mechanism. This has not made them more devoted to the central government, but has reinforced their belief that their economic situation and political position are very much determined at "national level." Does this make them feel less Muslim? Zubaida finds the question meaningless. The specific conditions that gave birth to the Syrian state and the form that that state has taken "have produced mutual interests in the territorial state" which, in the last analysis, has come to constitute the working concept for all economic and political agents.[67] And Zubaida concludes by wryly observing that all challenges to the modern state have sprang not from the loins of a curiously everlasting and unchanging Islamic tradition, but from the studies of modern Muslim intellectuals who have worked from within the premises of the territorial state.[68]

Similar conclusions can be reached from Zubaida's case study on Iran. The contemporary Islamic Republic of Iran, he argues, is the result of particular forces which operated in a specific historical framework and not "the inevitable product of the will of an Islamic people who understand or accept no other form of ideology or government."[69] What we see in this state is a mixture of modern bureaucratic and Islamic elements, especially a fully Islamized political field which, nonetheless, works decisively within the context of the Iranian nation-state. These, and the fact that it is a field surprisingly open with "ideologically based organisations contesting 'class' issues among others,"[70] brings it closer to the type of political fields we find in non-Islamic societies. Also, and this is of great theoretical importance for Zubaida, in Iran the state is not external to society,[71] a point that goes against those who see nationalism as a foreign implant in the Muslim world.[72]

Umma and "Orthodoxy"

The semantic ambivalence surrounding the term *umma* points toward a tension characterizing the dialectical relationship between the global vision of the worldwide imagined Community of Believers and the ways in which this is translated in specific Islamic societies, informing and being informed by local idioms and worldviews. Practically, the value of fine-grain ethnographic studies of specific societies is certainly acknowledged, if not prioritized, but in a manner that does not overshadow that more ethereal and encompassing vision of Islam that the term *umma* alludes to.

Such thoughts are not new. Already in 1982, Eickelman had emphasized the importance of studying Islamic tradition in local contexts so as to avoid approaching it as if it were an object outside history, while at the same time he called attention to Islam's claims to universality and their enunciation in terms of the specificity of the local. In two other works, the same author has brought forward the dynamic character of Islamic tradition, first within a single society, Morocco (1982b), and then in the context of the Islamist movement more generally (1987). This latter article is in a volume edited by Roff where a more general theme is discussed: the *political economy of meaning* in Islam, i.e. the material and other conditions of the continuously refashioned Islamic tradition and their importance in the emergence of dominant versions of Islam.

In a similar manner, Asad (1986) has criticized the use of all types of dichotomies in the study of Islam, such as central versus peripheral (i.e. local) practices or High versus Low or folk, as an essentializing strategy that implicates the analyst in the process of defining "orthodoxy" as on the side of the dominant actors, be they the state, the urban elites, the religious scholars, or men versus society, rural populations or uneducated masses, the *ṣūfī* mystics, or women respectively. Instead, Asad argues, a practice is "orthodox" because it is regarded as such in the context of Islamic tradition and because it is taught as such to Muslims in a particular place at a particular time. The dominant form that is considered to represent the "correct" or "orthodox" Islam is what Muslims at a certain time regard as such in every historical conjunction.

It is only in such a politically informed and sociologically agile manner that the imagined Community of Believers can be conceptualized in its universality and in its particularity at the same time. "Orthodoxy" is produced in the context of a grand negotiation process that is utterly political, and which takes place incessantly everywhere in the Muslim world, implicating all sorts of actors in a myriad ways and with no predetermined outcome.

Such an understanding of "orthodoxy" is not based on any abstract and high-minded theory advanced by liberal anthropologists who like to be open-minded, all-embracing, and inclusive. This otherwise worthy intellectual stance and these thoughtful and generous attitudes are meaningful within the intellectual framework of Western secularism and not in the context of a living Islamic discourse – or, for that matter, a Christian, Buddhist, Hindu, or whichever religious tradition. There, difference is conceptualized differently, variation is laden with theological considerations, plurality is negotiated in the teeth of eternity and in extra-temporal terms which are nonetheless realized in history, and change, however inevitable, is accepted or exorcised with prayer and/or divinely sanctioned bloodshed. This does not imply the absence of pragmatism or the shunning of strategic options based on strictly political and economic realities. Rather, it implies the presence of something more than that: it affirms the coloring of these realities by religious considerations. This we often see in communal or liberation politics, say in Palestine. Even when abandoning negotiations and opting for the most extreme form of retribution against allegedly erring co-religionists or foreign occupation forces, the situation is still conceptualized in terms internal to the corresponding religious tradition – without this precluding the use of other adjectives issuing from external and equally important discourses, such as "terrorist." We shall return to these issues time and again in the following chapters. But presently, I would like to discuss some forms of transnational Islamic cooperation or association operating in the contemporary environment at a level of assumed doctrinal likeness that is inattentive to the harsh realities of the production of "orthodoxy" process. Indeed, one is tempted to say that the simplistic formula "one God, one Prophet, one Book" plus "one People" works miraculously well here – at least at the level of rhetoric if not of concrete action.

Organizing the *Umma*

As several anthropologists have suggested since the early 1990s, the notion of an "assumed isomorphism of space, place, and culture" does not hold any more – if it ever did;[73] locality is not necessarily a basis for identity formation processes. On the contrary, as Appadurai has argued, the current disjuncture between economy, culture, and politics has led to the appearence of entire "imagined worlds" inhabited by increasing numbers of people, where the concept of nation-state is challenged – while new forms of constructed primordialism make their appearance – against a background of emerging diasporic public spheres.[74]

For Eickelman and Piscatori, this disjunction between locality and identity formation has two important consequences for the Muslim Community of Believers.[75] First, believers become aware of the existence of an infinite variety of social, cultural, political, and economic relationships among Muslims worldwide. As a result, they realize that the Islamic world has no single center of gravity or, to put it from the perspective of the Middle East and North Africa, that the Arab world is not the center of the Islamic world. The whole idea of Islamic "heartlands" is questioned, as the Islamic world takes the form of a polycentric system, where "centers" of Islamic discourse and activism include Pakistan, Indonesia, Afghanistan, Egypt, and Nigeria, but also Britain and France where large Muslim minorities reside.[76]

Second, the actual and conceptual reduction of physical distance that the relative ease of traveling and the new electronic media have brought about has given the opportunity to groups or single individuals with minority views, which often challenge hegemonic ideologies, to acquire a transnational organizational base for the dissemination and practice of their ideas. This new political geography may assist in the emergence of new forms of Islamic pluralism which could undermine the closed political character of many contemporary Islamic societies.

Eickelman and Piscatori focus on two organizational forms which today promote such a pluralistic vision of *umma*: those transnational Islamic organizations that function in parallel with the United Nations, the International Monetary

Fund, the World Bank, and other international bodies effectively "controlled" by the West; and those Islamic organizations which work in more than one country, supporting and encouraging the broadening of *umma*-consciousness throughout the Islamic world. After a brief account of these two forms, I shall conclude the chapter with a short reference to Islam on the Internet, drawing from the work of Jon Anderson and his articles with Eickelman.

Among the most important transnational Islamic organizations is the Organization of the Islamic Conference (OIC).[77] Established in 1969 after the Arab–Israeli 1967 war, the OIC has 52 members. Its main aim is to promote solidarity amongst its members without endangering their sovereignty through favoring more Islamic forms of government. To a large extent, OIC recommendations have not been put to practice. Discord between its member states during the Cold War era, differences between the rich oil-producing states and the less developed sub-Saharan Islamic societies, as well as OIC's inability to reach viable solutions during the 1980s Iran–Iraq war, the early 1990s Gulf War, the Bosnia crisis, and the more recent wars in Afghanistan and Iraq testify to the organization's political weakness.[78] Still, as Eickelman and Piscatori show, there have been instances of success, especially at the economic level. Among the examples they cite is the organization's attempts to draw attention to Afghanistan's struggle against Soviet occupation (a cause that did not antagonize Western interests) and its substantial economic and humanitarian assistance through the Islamic Solidarity Fund and Islamic Development Bank to many developing African and Asian countries.

Referring to the organizations whose mission is the heightening of *umma*-consciousness, Eickelman and Piscatori focus on what they call "non-state actors [which] promote *da'wa*, the 'call' to Islam."[79] First, the two authors discuss briefly the *ṣūfī* brotherhoods, with special reference to the Ottoman/Turkish *Bektāshiyya*, the *Qādiriyya*, *Tijāniyya* and *Khatmiyya* of the Sudanic belt, and the *Naqshbāndiyya* of the Iran, Iraq, and Turkey border regions. In all cases, Eickelman and Piscatori point out how the brotherhoods function as translocal and transclass organizations linking populations from distinct ethnic groups, states, and classes in a dynamic network of political, religious, and economic affiliations and transactions.

Then Eickelman and Piscatori consider more directly political organizations, such as the Muslim World League, the *Da'wa* Society, and the General Muslim Congress, describing how they use their extensive publication networks, their access to communication technologies, and their dispensing of financial assistance to a variety of Islamic causes in order to facilitate the establishment and development of communities of like-minded individuals totally beyond state control.

Such practices have succeeded in focusing Muslim and world attention on a number of issues presented as "Muslim" issues. Among them are the Bosnian, Afghanistan, and Iraq wars, the Indian–Pakistani dispute on Kashmir, the problems of Muslim minorities in the West, and, of course, the Palestinian struggle. Some of these issues, especially the Palestinian struggle against Israeli occupation, have acquired a symbolic and emblematic character in what has come to be called "Islamic politics." In this context, we have seen significant numbers of Muslims fighting as volunteers against non-Muslim adversaries, thus assuming the moniker of "holy warriors" (*mujāhidūn*), as well as several of the more fanatical amongst them swelling the ranks of international terrorist groups, such as *al-Qāʿida*. Interestingly, in most cases where UN troops are to be involved, an effort is made to include as many Muslim soldiers as possible.

Recently, the *mujāhidūn* phenomenon has had some rather adverse repercussions on the way Muslim minorities in the West are perceived, as some of their members were caught in Afghanistan fighting with the *Ṭālibān* forces. Such cases, rare though they are, highlight some of the differences between younger and older generations of migrants, although the situation is much more complicated than that. For example, in Britain when a small number of British citizens were found among the foreign *mujāhidūn* in Afghanistan, many older members of local Muslim communities as well as several journalists promoted a picture of traditional law-abiding communities that somehow went wrong, bemoaning the "loss of control" by the community "elders" to more extremist elements.

Such differences are not novel. Rather, they express the dilemma that Muslim migrants in the West have always faced. As Eickelman and Piscatori argue, the normative Islamic view on migration to the land of unbelief is negative. Many Muslim intellectuals maintain that it is acceptable only if it is part of a *daʿwa* strategy, which should then include some proselytization on behalf of Islam; others go a step further in accepting migration if it is for the acquisition of technical knowledge, for example through postgraduate studies, which could then be used for the improvement of the *umma*.

This being the case, and taking into account the atrocious terrorist acts of the last few years which may have been initially organized in Europe, the issue of Muslim migrant communities in the West has become almost by definition part of the political discourse of the Islamic societies, especially those which see themselves as "furthering the Muslim cause," whatever that is, such as Saudi Arabia and Iran. For example, Saudi Arabia attempts to come in contact with Muslim diasporic populations through the broadcasting of religious and other satellite television programs under the authority of the Ministry of *Āwkāf, Daʿwa* and Guidance.[80] Similar efforts to provide satellite television facilities are also made by most other countries in the region, thus keeping alive a channel of communication not only with their own nationals, but with the rest of the Arab world since the broadcasting language is Arabic. Some of these attempts are directly goverment-controlled whereas others, such as the well-known *al-Jazīra* television station, retain a considerable degree of autonomy.[81]

I shall now turn to the Internet, the other major technology that connects people, and I shall start with the work of Jon Anderson.

Anderson focuses mainly on the use of the Internet by individual Muslims and Muslim organizations – student societies, educational and other institutions, political groups and factions – all over the world. A great and ever-increasing number of sites has been launched, providing material that ranges from practical information concerning prayer times in Bradford, Britain, or where to find *halāl* meat in Tucson, Arizona, to *Qur'ānic* recitations on-line, English translations of the *ḥadīth*, or guides for performing the pilgrimage to Mecca according to the tradition. Popular preachers post their sermons, exegeses, and *fatwā*s where they become public knowledge and subject to continuous – and often irreverent by "traditional" standards – reviews, criticism, and discussion.

Anderson argues that this trend is not new in Islam in the sense that "intermediate communities have frequently arisen between the spiritually minded and the scripturalists," but cyberspace is different in the way it transcends physical distance.[82] He also reminds us that this development is working hand in hand with what Eickelman has called "Islamic Reformation," i.e. the opening up of a discussion among increasing numbers of believers on what it means to be a Muslim in the modern world.[83] Both Eickelman and Anderson have explored many of the issues involved in all this in earlier publications (1997, 1999) that focused on new and more accessible forms of print. Islam-in-the-net, then, is really presented as one more step down the road opened by technological innovations in the print and media industries and the ensuing more open participation in the process of a widening public that includes Appadurai's "emerging diasporic public spheres" as well as those believers who lead a more sedentary life in Islamic societies. What is implied by all this is that an *umma* connected or wired together is on its way towards the creation of a (Western-type?) civil society.

I would not disagree that Internet Islam does indeed bring many believers closer together, fostering forms of relatively uninhibited dialogue and thus stimulating a high degree of openness. I myself have experienced that when I followed a *Sudan List* dialogue group where the mainly Sudanese participants discussed the civil war and the Islamist dictatorship in that country. However, just as I argue in chapter 3 that the invention of printing did not in itself foster critical thought, here too I would like to tread cautiously for similar reasons.

First, some of the articles posted on the net concerning various aspects of Islamic tradition may transform it into a much more coherent and exact set of dogmas and practices than it really is, thus robbing it of its polyphony and its essentially open-ended character. "How to fast" guides or "What the Prophet said on marriage" may lead many to more "cohesive" and at the same time "intolerant" forms of reasoning.[84] Second, speaking about intolerance, we must not forget that the Internet has been assiduously used by extremists to propagate their views and by terrorists to plan their actions, transfer funds, and evade state security agencies. So Islam-on-the-net is not only a force of democratization, whatever that means; it may well be the opposite too. Finally, what is the number of Internet users in the Middle East and North Africa? Is it correct to see the Internet in the same light as the airwaves when every family has a radio whereas very few own or know how to operate a computer?[85]

3

Authority and Knowledge

The processes concerning the formal study of Islamic tradition have been traditionally in the hands of the religious scholars-jurisconsults (*'ulamā'*, sing. *'ālim*). Even today, when Western-style formal education structures are predominant in most Muslim societies, the role of the *'ulamā'* as master instructors of Islamic tradition remains significant.

The knowledge the *'ulamā'* possess (*'ilm*) refers to the knowledge of the *Qur'ān* and the *sunna* of the Prophet, as well as to the theories and methodology of its interpretation and application in everyday life. This applies not only to their erudition on theology and ethics, as one would expect, but also to the mastery of the intricacies of Islamic law and, at least in previous historical periods, of the so-called "Islamic sciences," ranging from politics and economics to mathematics, medicine and areas of Islamic mysticism.[1] As a theoretical expression of Islamic discourse and as the epistemological substratum for its application in public and domestic spheres, this knowledge constitutes one of the foundations of political authority, conferring on its guardians and interpreters undoubted political significance and a central role in the process of production of "orthodoxy." Nonetheless, the *'ulamā'* have never been alone in this process. As we shall see in the following pages, their intellectual preeminence and their "semi-institutional" position – in the sense that there is no well-defined and all-inclusive "clerical" hierarchy in the *sunnī* world (in contrast with the *shī'a*) – has always been challenged by many contestants ranging from mystics and Islamist activists to the state itself. This makes it difficult to define the outer limits of the term *'ulamā'*.

The first part of the chapter deals with the formal study of Islamic tradition in pre-colonial and colonial times. The second part presents the world of the *'ulamā'*, concentrating more on the present so as to situate these guardians and interpreters of Islamic tradition within the current socio-political framework. Lastly, the third part of the chapter discusses orality in the context of Islamic discourse.

THE FORMAL STUDY OF ISLAMIC TRADITION

In the pre-colonial Muslim Middle East and North Africa, formal education was synonymous with the acquisition of knowledge pertaining to Islam and its applications in everyday life. In a basically non-literate world,[2] formal education concerned very few believers, always male, and was organized within the premises of mosques and other Islamic institutions.[3] Schooling constituted an initial stage of training in which students were given the knowledge that could turn them into *ʿulamāʾ*, that is knowledgeable persons who could follow a diversity of professional paths. In reality, from this student body only a small minority would "graduate" with full qualifications; the majority would learn basic reading, writing, and arithmetic, and would be able to recite by heart parts of the *Qurʾān*.

The *Qurʾānic* "School" or *Madrasa*

Since the Middle Ages, the development of systematic theology, jurisprudence, and the sciences of the *ḥadīth* was followed by the progressive development all over the Muslim world of a more specialized form of educational institution, the *madrasa*.[4] Still, there was no clear-cut distinction between mosque and *madrasa*, as the latter remained an educational institution *and* mosque at the same time. In the relevant literature the *madrasa* is often called *Qurʾānic* "school."[5]

Initially, *madrasa* was the name of the area within a mosque used for teaching, but from the thirteenth century we observe the building of huge complexes which, besides a mosque, also included lecture halls, teachers' quarters, students' dormitories, and libraries, as well as kitchens, storage rooms, and bath houses. This type of structure related to those Islamic educational institutions in the big urban centers which could be called Islamic "universities," and not to the smaller and much more numerous rural and urban *Qurʾānic* "schools" where, as a rule, younger students learned the rudiments of reading and writing under the tutelage of an instructor (*shaykh*) with the assistance of the *Qurʾānic* text.

As Eickelman and Mitchell point out for Morocco and Egypt respectively, until the mid-nineteenth century the student body of the *Qurʾānic* "schools" and "universities" comprised a heterogenous assemblage spanning all age groups and social classes. Even the distinction between instructors and students was often blurred, with advanced students acting as instructors of those at the lower levels.[6]

The structural fluidity that such a system implied became more pronounced in the absence of common bureaucratic structures and timetables, comparable curricula and reading material (besides the ubiquitous *Qurʾān*), and a standardized system of examination and accreditation. Usually, after an indeterminate period – which varied between different establishments or students, as some would be in today's parlance "full-time," while others would interrupt their studies to assist in family business or for other reasons – students would receive reference letters from their instructors verifying the length and content of study for each particular subject, testifying to their abilities, and allowing them to continue with their studies at a higher level or to teach somewhere else.[7]

This fluidity was highly beneficial for the system and for the development of Islamic discourse at many levels. For example, in the province of the *sharīʿa*, the flexibility and decentralization that characterized the formal production of Islamic knowledge, as well as the cooperation between the best-known Islamic "universities" and the authorities in different locales of the Muslim world, with the aim of solving problems and putting into practice the principles of the law, discouraged the development of a rigid system of legal rulings and fostered the notion that the *sharīʿa* constituted at the same time God's unalterable law *and* an adaptable set of principles interpreted according to the problem at hand.[8]

For the students, the structural plasticity of pre-colonial Islamic education and the absence of entrance examinations and tuition fees advanced social mobility, especially at the higher educational levels, as it facilitated contact with intellectual elites and with the higher echelons of state bureaucracy. In that sense, it would not be inappropriate to consider Islamic educational institutions as a first stage of training in a professional field, as a type of vocational studies which in turn created intellectual kinship between different generations of teachers and instructors. It is not rare to read that such and such famous *ʿālim* was a former student of x famous teacher who had been a student of y who had been instructed by z, and so on. Such chains of intellectual, indeed academic, kinship were important as markers of excellence and as proof of one's intellectual abilities and of the soundness of one's professed theoretical argumentation and legal rulings.

It goes without saying that, as in all paths of life, those excelling in their field are always a minority. Among *madrasa* teachers, too, there were those few who really made their mark intellectually and the majority who had mustered enough knowledge to pass to their students something they could usefully apply to their everyday lives. In the same manner, one should not try to locate what was right, i.e. "orthodox," in this process of imparting knowledge. That was, and still is, a quality extended to certain interpretations of Islamic tradition and denied to others within a wider socio-political framework.[9] Fluidity there was, but always within limits set by the prevailing conditions. This dialectic is what allowed certain theological interpretations and political theory lines of argument to develop further than others which were deemed to be unduly critical of the status quo and potentially disruptive to social order.

In this environment the Islamic *madrasa*s supported themselves through grants from local rulers or the government and through pious endowments (*waqf*) offered by believers in the form of arable land or buildings for commercial use. There were no fees as such, although in smaller *madrasas* the students' families collectively shouldered the responsibility for the teachers' well-being, especially in rural areas.

Moving towards more centralized political forms, which in the pre-nationalist era culminated in the formation of the Ottoman Empire, the *waqf* system became more extended and elaborate. As it conferred rights on both founders and beneficiaries, a considerable body of legal rulings defining their statutory positions had to be developed. With the gradual establishment of nation-states, things got further complicated after the introduction of land registries and modern taxation – from which *waqf* was, and to an extent still is, exempted – and the early post-independence nationalization fever. All this robbed Islamic educational establishments of a significant source of revenue. I shall return to this in the following section.[10] Here it suffices to say that today many Muslim societies, such as Egypt, the Sudan, Jordan, Saudi Arabia, and the United Arab Emirates, have *waqf* ministries or special administrative departments that deal with the whole issue, mainly with taxation and expropriation of *waqf* lands and the reorganization of the relevant inheritance laws.[11]

The Content of Islamic Education

The institutional expansion of *madrasas* to "university" level offering a much wider Islamic curriculum than small local *Qur'ānic* "schools," was accompanied, already since medieval times, with the emergence of new subjects and scientific fields studied by the *ʿulamā'* as intrinsic parts of Islamic discourse and as knowledge necessary for the creation of well-rounded professionals, be they jurists, bureaucrats, doctors, engineers, or astronomers. This development did not take place everywhere at the same pace and did not follow well-defined linear lines of progress. Still, the basic principles concerning the nature of Islamic knowledge remained more or less constant until the introduction of Western educational systems, especially in the Arabian Peninsula and sub-Saharan Africa.

Progressively, the so-called "Islamic sciences" came to include practically all fields of knowledge, from linguistics, rhetoric, Arab and Persian philology, history and philosophy to politics, economics, logic, mathematics, astronomy, and medicine. As part of Islamic tradition and as expressions of Islamic discourse, these fields were gradually transformed into relatively well-defined "scientific subjects" which were approached in different ways by the four schools of law (*madhhab*) that in the meanwhile had been crystalized in *sunnī* Islam, as well as by the *shīʿa* tradition. For this reason, we often come across bibliographical references to this or that *madrasa* belonging to a specific school of law, as many of the most well-known establishments were named after the most important professor (*ʿālim*) who taught there.

In all cases, the knowledge imparted in the *madrasas* was conceptualized as immutable and unalterable by human intellect, whose powers of reason could perhaps investigate its content and enlarge its scope of applications, but should bow to the completeness of Prophetic revelation that was taken to be its ultimate source. However, as Eickelman argues, this immobility was apparent rather than real, as it constituted an element of a particular style of language, a trope of realizing divine will, a trait of a deeply internalized set of archetypical linguistic and cognitive structures which promoted mnemonic rotation.[12] In reality, Islamic discourse as formally organized and imparted by the *madrasas* was always associated with the wider society, in the sense of being able to formulate socially relevant responses to specific problems.

This can be seen in the case of Islamic law. As Mitchell suggests, in turn-of-the-nineteenth-century Egypt the *sharīʿa* was seen not as an abstract and well-bounded legal code that determined proper behavior, but as a commentary on particular practices, a set of comments upon comments.[13] Brown (1997), too, reaches similar conclusions in his study of the relations between *sharīʿa* and state authority in Egypt in the same period, while Messick, who works in Yemen, describes *sharīʿa* as a "'total' discourse" and stresses its political character, arguing that it constituted the basic idiom of pre-national political discourse in the Muslim world.[14] Despite appearances of opacity and blessed immobility, then, the range and scope of possible interpretations of reality in terms of *sharīʿa* and the Islamic sciences, as well as their practical applications and political repercussions, have always been linked to prevailing socio-political conditions.

At the same time, it should be acknowledged that as Middle Eastern and North African societies moved from a period of political expansion and intellectual efflorescence towards one of fragmentation and political antagonisms with increasingly more muscular European powers, those scientific fields which were based on deductive methodology – mathematics, logic, philosophy – were marginalized in favor of those based on revelation – theology, the study of the *Qur'ān*, and the *ḥadīth*.[15]

In reality, the decline was more general, especially where European economic and military antagonism from the fifteenth century onwards was felt more acutely. Though the "gate of *ijtihād*" was never properly closed, there was a relative regression in the formal study of Islamic tradition, a lack of creative imagination and an absence of impact on society of whatever theoretical advances were attempted. For example, though in eighteenth-century Egypt there were around twenty urban centers with one to seven *madrasas* each – Cairo's famous al-Azhar Islamic "university" included – their curricula were outdated and intellectually limited and the instructors were not engaged in new research. Gamal el-Din el-Shayyal[16] writes that the main reasons behind this were Egypt's isolation from Europe due to Ottoman suzerainty, the gradual delegitimization of the Mamlūk regime and its unpopular policies, as well as an increase in the number of Muslim mystics and in their influence that allegedly fostered resignation and intellectual apathy. Still, one wonders if such a simple cause–effect relation can explain a very complex situation whose political repercussions were of immense significance. As will be seen in chapter 6, this decline in the production of Islamic knowledge, real or imaginary, was considered by the Muslim modernists of the late nineteenth and early twentieth century as one of the main causes of colonial subjugation of the Muslim world, although the opposite could be argued as well: that the political and economic arrival of imperial Europe arrested some developments in the Muslim world.

Islamic Education and Colonialism

In the course of the nineteenth century the socio-political and economic structures of the Middle Eastern and North African societies were indeed dramatically transformed by European imperialism. This transformation affected both the economic base as well as the role of Islamic educational establishments, especially of the prestigious Islamic "universities." Egypt is a case in point.

Though not under direct colonial control until the 1880s,[17] Egypt suffered from a protracted economic crisis caused by political opportunism, unwise economic planning, administrative corruption, and involvement in a world order increasingly dominated by European imperialism. Set in a course of modernization alongside lines dictated by the constraints of colonialism, the country found itself under the tutelage of European banks and – by extension – governments.[18] Inherent in the modernization process was the restructuring of the legal status that governed until then the position of Islamic "universities," the dilution of their privileges, and the expropriation of their considerable land holdings which were in the form of tax-exempted *waqfs*. But more than that, administrations compliant with colonial logic, willingly or under compulsion, further eroded the status of Islamic education through the introduction of a Western-style national system of education.

In this context, the educational process was physically removed from the mosque and was confined within the framework of a new institution – the school and its classrooms – and among a homogeneous age group – the children – who as pupils were further divided into grades which were all insulated from the class of instructors. In this way, education became a well-defined sector of social policy, allowing the state to present itself as the single authority that defined school curricula and textbooks and controlled the examination process and the conferring of degrees at a national level.

As a result, education attained an autonomous existence outside the encompassing framework of Islamic tradition. It was thus severed from conventions and practices which until then had belonged to a single discursive universe: the daily prayer regime or the Ramaḍān fast – which traditionally structured the time-table of instruction – the fluidity and informality that governed the relations between students and *'ulamā'* instructors, and the undifferentiated quality of Islamic instruction as a preamble for admission to the bureaucracy and the legal profession.

Clearly then, Western-type education became one of the most important mechanisms for the modernization of Egyptian society in accordance with the principles of the colonial authorities and the interests of local elites. Both of these wished Egypt to be transformed into a new type of society which would fit well in the colonial order of things. And this could not happen without the emergence of a new type of subject: the modern, educated Egyptian citizen who would have internalized European ideals and patterns of behavior. A similar policy was followed in most European colonies.

For the Islamic educational establishments, these developments had deleterious results. Not only was their financial position adversely affected, to the degree that they could not afford any more to offer the same level of service to their students (many of whom where full-boarders) nor to attract the highest calibre of instructors, but a growing percentage of their students from the upper and middle classes deserted them in favor of state schools. These promised immediate access to the new type of bureaucracy and the armed forces of which the modern state of Egypt was now in need. Degrees in accounting or English became more important than knowledge of *Qur'ānic* interpretation and logic.

In this way it came about that the majority of those who continued their studies in the Islamic educational system were now from the lower middle classes. The smaller *Qur'ānic* "schools" were not affected that badly, but that was because the newly introduced national system of education soon proved to be incapable of being fully extended to the periphery, as well as relatively expensive in terms of textbooks, occasional fees, and cost of transportation to and fro. Nonetheless, in the process Islamic education came to be identified by governments, elites, and the aspiring middle classes of most late-colonial Middle Eastern societies with "traditional" stagnation and cultural regression vis-à-vis the alleged sparkling and much-promising modernity of the national education. As will be seen in the following section, that impression remained strong during the post-colonial period as well.

That, of course, was not the end of Islamic education, which remained dominant in several Middle Eastern and North African societies – in Morocco until the beginning of the 1930s, in Yemen and Oman until the 1950s. Even today, *madrasas* and Islamic "universities" have remained open throughout the Middle East and North and sub-Saharan Africa, as well as in Iran, Afghanistan, Pakistan, Indonesia, and elsewhere. However, their internal structure and the ways in which they approach knowledge and instruction have passed into the hands of the state which, as I shall argue, now seeks to define Islamic "orthodoxy" sometimes in cooperation with and sometimes in defiance of the *'ulamā'*. In that sense, the post-colonial state cannot be seen to be far removed from the logic of its colonial predecessor. But before moving there, we should first discuss the evolving identity and institutional position of the *'ulamā'* who man the system of religious education, but do not run it as they used to in the past.

THE WORLD OF THE *'ULAMĀ'*

The *'ulamā'* are seen as the guardians and interpreters of the holy texts of the classical Islamic textual tradition. They should not be mistaken for a priestly caste, because they are not priests. They may hold official positions, act as preachers or jurisconsults, conduct weddings, and bury the dead, but they do not officiate in sacraments like those of the Roman Catholic and the Eastern Orthodox churches, and they cannot threaten anyone with excommunication. No such things exist in Islam.

So what exactly do the *'ulamā'* do? The answer is: the collection, systematization, and interpretation of the *Qur'ān* and the *ḥadīth*; the definition of categorical forms and principles of argumentation and interpretation in the manner of *ijmā'* and *ijtihād*; the construction of an epistemological framework for the *sharī'a*, its interpretations, and practical applications; the establishment of the basic principles of Islamic political theory; the distinction between four basic (*sunnī*) schools of law; the planning and establishment of an Islamic legal system in cooperation with a variety of political administrations; the formal instruction in all the fields of knowledge and academic subjects that formally belong to Islamic discourse; and the drafting of legal rulings (*fatwā*s) for thousands upon thousands of issues ranging from inheritance problems and marital disputes to current affairs comments, company law, banking and accounting methodologies, human rights deliberations, and critical reviews of government policies; these are all work of the *'ulamā'*. To this we should add the political pronouncements and execution of policies that fall into the purview of the *shī'a 'ulamā'*, who have a much more directly political role than their *sunnī* counterparts.[19]

Having said that, it becomes obvious that one should not confine the work of the *'ulamā'* to the realm of theology and dogmatics, thus implying that, more or less, this work belongs to the past (as the dogmatic basis of Islamic tradition has been settled once and for all centuries ago), or that their theological discourse is just that, *theological* in an academic sense and in terms defined by pre-existing discursive principles which do not spill outside theology to other areas of human praxis. Even the most conservative amongst the contemporary *'ulamā'*, who may wholeheartedly adopt the "closing of the gate of *ijtihād*," are obliged to respond to those who comment on their work, be it in theological or other matters, if only to answer to their criticisms and to point out what they see as their misconceptions. In this way they do produce new work and continue to enrich Islamic tradition, even while they themselves may conceptualize it as a well-bounded whole, perfect in its ideal stillness. Even pure conservation – if such a thing exists – is a dynamic process in which believers and infidels of all kinds are implicated in the production of new interpretations of "orthodoxy." In practical terms, which will be further considered in the last three chapters of the present work, this means that the continual emergence of new interpretations leads of necessity to reformulations of "orthodoxy." When this does not happen, then a tradition is simply dead.

This dynamism suggests that the body of treatises and commentaries produced by the *'ulamā'* cannot make up a monolithic set of theoretical propositions. Despite the fact that they are all products of a more or less well-defined, however fluid, system of Islamic education, make use of the same body of academic literature, and formulate their arguments according to the logic and premises of formally recognized schools of law, the *'ulamā'* can and do reach different conclusions on a variety of issues. In that sense, as a scholarly class operating within ever-transforming social conditions, the *'ulamā'* do present internal differences and follow a variety of intellectual trajectories with diverse political implications, even when we consider them within the limits of their respective national traditions – a sensible distinction in terms of practicality, but a questionable proposition theoretically.

The Limits of the "Orthodox" Vision: Textual Inundation and Ways Out

Before delving into the internal differences of the *'ulamā'* social category, more should be said about them as a relatively distinct category of guardians and interpreters of the Islamic tradition. More precisely, it is important to note at this point that *as a body of specialists* the *'ulamā'* perceive themselves, and are perceived by society at large, as having *the* leading role in the process of "orthodoxy" production – however inappropriate and undeserved this might seem to many. This trait is attributed to them *collectively* because of their history in the formulation of Islamic doctrines, their institutional position throughout Islamic history, and their central role in most ceremonial moments of every Muslim man and woman – as officiants or administrative officers in legal cases, prayer sessions, and all sorts of religious celebrations, as well as in circumcisions, weddings, divorces, funerals, *zakāt* committees, school councils, and what not. Even their harsher detractors have to consider their own views in relation to those of the *'ulamā'* versions of Islam.

But how relevant is the *'ulamā'* version of Islam to society – because if it is not relevant then how can it retain its "orthodox" credentials except by inertia or indifference? This is an altogether different issue from the previous one – ascribing to the *'ulamā'* a leading role in the process of defining Islamic "orthodoxy" – because it attempts to capture the political potentialities of the *'ulamā'* position in relation to those of other actors, such as the various Islamists and the state itself. We are confronted then with a curious and even contradictory situation: the *in principle* ascription of "orthodox" credentials to a particular class of religious specialists and the simultaneous questioning of the social relevance these credentials may have vis-à-vis those ascribed to other competing actors.

At the level of sociological observation this is relevant to the fact that if any quality truly distinguishes human behavior, this is the human ability to envision and put into practice unending series of dialectic combinations, often at the same time, irrespective of their mutual consonance – a trait that to an uncharitable mind devoid of imagination and self-reflection may be condemned as inconsistency. If that is correct, then it is easy to see how in our case people can believe *practically* in the *'ulamā'* versions of "orthodoxy" (that is, they can act as if nothing worries them in relation to this issue), while at the same time they may be skeptical about them and resort to other competing actors *as well* – such as other members of the *'ulamā'* category, mystics, or Islamists of all sorts – in the process of experiencing/producing/sustaining "orthodoxy" in their everyday lives.[20]

The way this particular type of dialectic, acceptance, and skepticism can be approached is with reference to the textuality that dominates the *'ulamā'* versions of Islamic "orthodoxy" and the manner in which this is reflected on their traditional institutional positions within the Islamic discursive universe.

Textual Inundation . . .

In the process of producing Islamic "orthodoxy" the *'ulamā'* guard and creatively reproduce God's will in the form of *text*.[21] As text, God's will is subjected to interpretation in the service of humanity without losing its transcendental timelessness and immutability. According to this view, however enmeshed in particularistic understandings related to local conceptualizations, historical peculiarities, differing legal traditions, and idiosyncratic characteristics, *'ulamā'* textual interpretations elucidate divine will, clarify obscurities, and present the faithful with intelligible "orthodox" guidelines that ensure doctrinal conformity and consistency of practice at the level of the *umma*. Or do they?

From another point of view, there is a danger lurking in this interpretative process, a danger inherent in all interpretative processes which assume a *telos*, either in the Aristotelian or in the positivistic sense of the term. As textual comments multiply, taking the form of interpretative texts commenting on earlier generations of commentaries, the "true" meaning and context of the original, unadulterated, and simple will of God – whose existence cannot be doubted or the whole thing would be meaningless – can be easily lost. Then both those directly involved in this never-ending project of interpreting this eternal but ultimately recoverable divine will (the *'ulamā'*, and those indirectly implicated in it (the Community of Believers – who after all are supposed to be the beneficiaries of all this) are faced with a strange situation. The very overprofusion of textual interpretations, which in theory would have made God's will easily understood and readily accessible to everybody, has produced exactly the opposite: a spiritual labyrinth in which the faithful are trapped and from which, it appears, only the *ʿulamāʾ* specialists can liberate them, that is the very same people who have originally created this confusion.[22]

This situation appears to be directly associated with the abstract nature of the *ʿulamāʾ*'s spiritual authority, which, suprisingly, is a by-product of Islam's "equality of believers." In a legally over-determined framework that has been worked out by the early heads and doyens of the law schools and dutifully refined by subsequent generations of *ʿulamāʾ*, each *ʿālim* is theoretically an integral part of an interpretation project occurring within an allegedly neutral and objective academic framework and wherein the comprehension of God's will depends solely upon objectively observed individual capabilities.

Taking into consideration the high degree of institutionalization and its immense discursive potency, it is evident that such a framework has always supported ideologically the socio-political system that allows it to flourish (even when that system simply tolerates it by overlooking its excesses), providing it with Islamic legitimacy,[23] while at the same time it safeguards the exalted status of its own carriers, the *ʿulamāʾ*.

It is these two elements – the complexity of the *ʿulamāʾ* interpretations and their conservative political views – which estrange them from society at large, as several studies describe especially in relation to the emergence of Islamism, which is often analyzed as an alternative to *ʿulamāʾ* Islam. Indeed, what we have in this image is *a retreat of the faithful* in the face of *ʿulamāʾ* Islam in search of alternative sources of religious and political inspiration. Amongst such sources, one can identify various types of mystics, who may offer the faithful the opportunity to develop a personal relation to God, and the previously mentioned Islamist intellectuals and political activists, whose knowledge of Islamic tradition has not been formally acquired, but is the product of an individual quest with strong political overtones that has been honed in the conditions of post-colonialism.

Still, such a *retreat of the faithful* from *ʿulamāʾ* Islam in search of alternative sources of religious and political inspiration can never be complete and irrevocable. If our previous discussion of the dialectic between acceptance and skepticism is correct, the *ʿulamāʾ* cannot be wholly dismissed as irrelevant.

This can be approached at two levels. First, as has already been suggested, the canonical framework of Islamic tradition formally organized and exposed by the *ʿulamāʾ* is deeply ingrained in the everyday life of hundreds of millions of Muslims, shaping their dispositions, moral choices, and actual behavior. Given the deep-seated institutional roots of the *ʿulamāʾ*, *structurally* they are the most eligible to provide this service. Indicative of their tenacity is the popularity of radio and television programs offering religiously inflected advice on a number of issues, from marital difficulties to lifestyle and business advice, the consumption of audio- and videotapes containing sermons given by famous *ʿulamāʾ*, and finally the lively attendance by huge crowds at the Friday noon sermons in the mosques. To that extent, *the retreat of the faithful* from the *ʿulamāʾ*, however plausible theoretically, may be exaggerated or, to put it more correctly, it should be adressed in a directly political manner if we want to understand better its nature and its dynamics.

At a second level, a closer discussion of what I have called "sources of religious and political inspiration alternative to the *ʿulamāʾ*" proves them significantly less discursively independent from them than one may have thought initially. What matter here are overt political considerations rather than canonical matters and a concern with ceremonials. Here is the point at which one should stop talking about the *ʿulamāʾ* collectively, as we did until now for analytic reasons, and delve into their internal differences. To do this more profitably, the *ʿulamāʾ* should be discussed in relation to other participants in the process of defining Islamic "orthodoxy."

. . . and Ways Out

As far as the mystics are concerned, some of them are members of the *ʿulamāʾ* social category who have studied across the range of formal Islamic education and have a deep understanding of Islamic law. True, certain types of mysticism are far from the *ʿulamāʾ* *sharīʿa*-centered Islam and from the type of piety it fosters, but, as will be argued in chapter 5, mystical Islam and the textual tradition of the *ʿulamāʾ* do not oppose each other. On the contrary, they constitute two complementary – albeit not always institutionally symmetrical – dimensions of Muslim experience which are difficult to separate without doing violence to the completeness and unity of Islamic discourse.

As for the Islamists, here too things are far from clear. Although most Islamist intellectuals and political activists have not received a formal Islamic education – a trait until now attributed only to the *ʿulamāʾ*, whom the Islamists accuse of having turned Islam into an ossified tradition precisely because of their formalism – they do not operate in an intellectual vacuum. Their diatribes are based on the work of famous *ʿulamāʾ* of the past, whose vision was politically robust and doctrinally intolerant towards those they perceived as enemies of the faith.

But more than that, as I argue in chapter 7, the Islamist trend has acquired so much strength because it has managed to radicalize the most conservative elements among both the *ʿulamāʾ* and the general public. That means that in the battle lines drawn by the Islamists in order to save society from what they identify as the pernicious influence of secularism and the onslaught of the imperialist West, their battle-cry, "Islam is the solution," has been taken up by many of the more radical *'ulamā'* who do not flinch from chiding governments and local elites for ungodly behavior and from cursing the West and Israel as agents of evil and enemies of Islam.

Indeed, and despite the absence of detailed ethnographic data from different Islamic societies which would allow comparison, it seems that the emergence of contemporary Islamism in the political landscape of Muslim societies since the late 1970s has indirectly benefited the *'ulamā'*. Zeghal (1999) and, to a lesser extent, Moustafa (2000) show how this came about in the 1950s–90s Egypt, the seat of the famous al-Azhar Islamic university. We are told how the Nasserist state limited the independence of al-Azhar by nationalizing its *waqf* lands in 1952, abolishing all *sharī'a* courts in 1955, and finally, in 1961, by placing the university under the formal jurisdiction of the Ministry of Endowments. At the same time, al-Azhar received large sums of money which allowed it to double its student intake and increase its foreign missions throughout the Muslim world. Despite the fact then that many (though not all) *Azharī 'ulamā'* went on praising government policies, thus harming the university's status as an independent Islamic establishment, on the whole al-Azhar gained the status of an official body and part of the state bureaucracy which could, in the proper conditions and under the right guidance, articulate a message that all Egypt would hear.

Albeit partial in terms of success, this process commenced in the 1970s when Anwar Sadat eased restrictions on religious discourse as he moved away from Arab socialism. In that context, many *Azharī 'ulamā'* participated in the government-supported anti-left campaign and offered legitimacy to government policies, just as others had done 10 years earlier with Nasser. However, this time things were different, largely because of the emergence of the still nascent but vigorous Islamist trend. This presented the *'ulamā'* with a God-sent opportunity of playing the role of the moderator, decrying Islamist violence and blind state repression while simultaneously preaching their own *sharī'a*-centered programme of gradual Islamization of society as the only way forward. The 1977 assassination of the endowments minister (see note 11 on p. 266) and the 1981 assassination of the Egyptian president by Islamic militants, as well as the ferocious state repression that followed and the renewal of Islamist violence in the second half of the 1980s, brought the *'ulamā'* to the political limelight demanding from them a voice, the articulation of a position.

It was in that climate that a rift between what Zeghal calls "central" *'ulamā'*, who actively supported the government, and "peripheral" *'ulamā'*, who did not associate themselves with the government's anti-Islamist campaign and other policies, became particularly noticeable.[24] There are many examples from the political activity of Zeghal's "peripheral" *'ulamā'* that could be cited and many names of famous scholars whom we will meet in chapters 7 and 8 when I discuss Islamism. The following were results of this: the late 1980s effort by *'ulamā'* Members of Parliament in collaboration with the newly elected Islamist MPs of the Muslim Brotherhood, to strengthen the position of the *sharī'a* in national legislation; the early 1990s organization of *Nadwa al-'Ulamā'* (*'Ulamā'* Conference) against secularism; the condemnation for apostasy of certain liberal Egyptian intellectuals, such as Naṣr Ḥamid Abū Zayd and Faraj Fūda (who was later assassinated by Islamists); the action against the positions taken by the 1994 United Nations International Conference on Population and Development on abortion and premarital relations; the offical recognition of al-Azhar as the only authority that may grant or refuse a license for audio and audiovisual productions with Islamic content; and the movement of the so-called "third party" (*al-ṭā'ifa al-thālitha*), where *'ulamā'* of the stature of Muḥammad Mitwāllī al-Sha'rāwī and Muḥammad al-Ghazālī organized themselves into a "Mediation Committee" aiming to bring together the state and the Islamists.[25]

Yet, the political scene is so volatile that one should be ready to recognize reverses and the emergence of new alliances. With the 1996 appointment as head of al-Azhar of *shaykh* Muḥammad Sayyid al-Tantāwī (the former Grand *Muftī* who had refused to recognize Palestinian suicide bombers as martyrs), the continuation of repressive policies towards Islamists, and the geopolitical considerations dictated by the "War on Terror," the Egyptian government seems to be making a great effort to (re-) accommodate the *'ulamā'* vis-à-vis the demonized Islamists.

This being the case, I am prepared to argue once more that *the retreat of the faithful* from the legally minded *'ulamā'* is partly true. Surely, there are *'ulamā'* who are not as popular as others either because they have lost contact with society and its everyday problems or because they are interested in issues which by definition are technical and obscure. But this does not mean that one can talk of a well-defined scriptural Islam promoted exclusively by *the 'ulamā'* and discounted by *the people* due to its complexity (or, by the same token, the latter's ignorance) in favor of different versions of Islam promoted by other actors participating in the process of defining Islamic "orthodoxy."

Bricoleurs and Their Religious Goods

Instead, we should first look more closely at the new discursive tropes that some of the *'ulamā'* have developed during their prolonged brush with the state and because of the strengthening of the Islamist movement. Second, we should ask if the newly found empowerment of those called "peripheral" has affected the *'ulamā'* as a whole in the new conditions that Islamism has helped to bring about in the wider region.

The first issue is addressed by Zeghal in her previously mentioned article through the employment – and reworking – of Roy's concept of "bricolage." Noting that most Islamist political activists and intellectuals have a science background and have received only a scant religious education, Roy criticizes their discourse as "disparate and fragmentary," a bricolage of "open and fragmented intellectual constructions" of dubious value.[26] For Roy,

> The new [Islamist] intellectual is a tinkerer; he creates a montage, as his personal itinerary guides him, of segments of knowledge, using methods that come from a different conceptual universe than the segments he recombines, creating a totality that is more imaginary than theoretical.[27]

On her part, Zeghal extends this notion of bricolage to the younger generations of (*Azharī*) *ʿulamāʾ*. Reminding us al-Azhar's de facto transformation into a "modern"-type university through its post-1961 administrative reorganization according to national education system principles and through the introduction of new subjects such as medicine, engineering, public administration, and pharmacy,[28] Zaghal maintains that the conceptual universe of the younger *Azharī ʿulamāʾ* was opened up. That gave the *ʿulamāʾ*

> the opportunity to enter the world of bricolage, by mixing religious and modern knowledge. The transformation of their educational background transformed the religious scholars into intellectuals who had the same references and vocabulary as their Islamist colleagues educated in modern universities. This phenomenon brought about, among the ulema of al-Azhar, the emergence of Islamist tendencies that became socially and politically visible in the 1980s.[29]

The above quotation suggests that Zeghal's understanding of bricolage differs from that of Roy. For the latter, bricolage is a negative attribute signifying amateurism and intellectual confusion and presupposing another closed, self-sufficient, "traditional" and in the end static type of knowledge historically attributed to the *ʿulamāʾ* – a contentious proposition of the neo-orientalist type. For Zeghal, bricolage indicates an opening up to society which enables its proponents, in our case the "peripheral" *ʿulamāʾ*, to join the battle for the definition of Islamic "orthodoxy" with renewed vigor. Indeed, Zeghal moves in the right direction when she connects these developments with the relative liberalization of the Egyptian political arena by Sadat in the 1970s and his "deregulation" of the market in "religious goods."[30] On the one hand, this made al-Azhar once more a crucial player in the process of producing "orthodoxy"; on the other, it pushed its *ʿulamāʾ* to work hard in order to maintain this position in the face of the Islamist discursive strength. This is why, Zaghal argues, "the shaykhs of al-Azhar never really tried to destroy the peripheral ulema, who helped diversify the ideas produced within al-Azhar."[31]

The second issue, how the newly found empowerment of those called "peripheral" has affected the social category of the *ʿulamāʾ* as a whole, is discussed by Zaman in his previously mentioned study of the Pakistani and other

ʿulamāʾ. Zaman is building his case on Wickham's concept of "parallel Islamic sector," i.e. "a community sustained by ties between the lower-middle-class (*shaʿbī*) neighborhoods and the university graduates, as well as by private mosques, private voluntary organizations, independent preachers, and the wide dissemination of Islamic literature." The members of this "parallel Islamic sector," many of whom have access to the remittances of expatriate labor from the Gulf States, "maintain close connections with business and other economic interests and with the state bureaucracy."[32] For Zaman, this mass of people is important because it

> represents new opportunities for the expansion of the ʿulama's influence. Even though most of those associated with this sector are lay people – for example, university graduates – rather than ʿulama, and the most popular preachers in contemporary Egypt are not associated with the Azhar or with government-controlled mosques, the effort to deepen and enhance people's religious commitments at the grass roots may arguably extend, at least potentially, the reach of the ʿulama's discourses.[33]

So here is the big picture as far as Egypt is concerned, although it can be reproduced for other Middle Eastern societies with some modifications: in an effort to manipulate the *ʿulamāʾ and* to curb Islamism, the Egyptian government gave the former the opportunity to improve their position in the process of defining Islamic "orthodoxy." The price was to offer Islamic legitimation to government decisions. The price was paid, but not always and not fully. Basking in the limelight, some of the *ʿulamāʾ* allied themselves to the more moderate Islamists, while some others kept pressing the government into accepting their own agenda concerning the "proper" Islamization of society. Taking into account the enormity of the issues involved and the shifting ground of political life, all tendencies intermingled, sometimes in the very same person.

Given the emergence or invigoration of a conservative trend since the 1980s among the lower middle classes, whose religious ideology has managed to incorporate the vision of university graduates and other middle-class professionals with Islamic tendencies, the *ʿulamāʾ* agitation has found a receptive audience that could accommodate a variety of views, from the conservative to the most radical ones. This synergy has secured the upgrading of the *ʿulamāʾ* position in the process of producing Islamic "orthodoxy."

On top of these factors, which relate to the national scene for each individual country, Zaman adds two international factors that make the picture even more dynamic. The first is the international patronage that many *ʿulamāʾ* associations have been receiving from mainly Saudi-sponsored international bodies and rich individuals. The second is the impact of the Iranian revolution, which has made available a workable model of an *ʿulamāʾ* government.

Though strange to the *sunnī* world, the idea has not left the faithful there totally unimpressed. I return to this issue in chapter 8.

Who or What are the *ʿUlamāʾ*?

This being the case, it is reasonable to argue that, if anything, claims and counter-claims to Islamic "orthodoxy" demonstrate how thin the lines separating the *ʿulamāʾ*, the Islamists, and the mystics are, although they never totally disappear; institutionally, the body of the *ʿulamāʾ* does occupy a different position within the discursive domain of Islamic tradition from the Islamists. In the same manner, one should refrain from classifying the *ʿulamāʾ* themselves in clear-cut categories except for analytical purposes. In both cases, blurring of lines and internal differentiation should be openly acknowledged. Four points could be made in particular.

First, all *ʿulamāʾ* employ concepts and propositions that stem from the same pool of Islamic religious literature and political philosophy. Some may do it more elegantly than others and attract popular attention or may concentrate on subjects which are closer to the heart of current affairs. In this case, the whole issue becomes one of individual taste and/or personal capability.

Secondly, as will be seen in chapters 6 and 7, the same scholar may hold what are locally conceived as "conservative" views on a number of issues and more "liberal" ones on others, thus appealing to different audiences at the same time. Equally, the local idioms in which Islamic discourse is articulated and the specific sense of local history foster distinct versions of political discourse and public debate that often make comparison between different Islamic countries, or even between different areas within the same country, a difficult, but not impossible, issue – since in all cases we will be situated within the parameters of Islamic discursive tradition creatively interpreted.

For example, political discourse in Saudi Arabia and the Sudan should be compared only in the light of the very different histories of what is considered to be official Islamic doctrine in each country and how this should be implemented. In Saudi Arabia there has been a well-established body of *ʿulamāʾ* which has traditionally given Islamic legitimacy to the ruling royal house. At the same time, the latter pursues policies which are in fair agreement with the *ʿulamāʾ* "orthodoxy." All criticism of the government that is voiced by members of this body should be seen in the light of this understanding. On the contrary, in the Sudan there has never been an indigenous body of *ʿulamāʾ* with strong popular support. Sudanese Islam and national political life have always developed along *ṣūfī* sectarian lines until the emergence of Islamists in the second half of the twentieth century, and especially after the 1990 Islamist coup. It is the latter who have assumed the role of the *ʿulamāʾ* today. But contrary to the conservative Saudi *ʿulamāʾ*, who uphold the *taqlīd*, the Sudanese Islamist intellectuals-turned-*ʿulamāʾ* are assiduous proponents of *ijtihād*. As a result, their political language presents a curious affinity with Muslim modernism that is totally absent from Saudi Arabia. Examples like this suggest that all previous discussion on the *'ulamā'* should be treated as a general framework within which only detailed ethnographic descriptions can produce fine-grain studies for individual societies.

Thirdly, drawing firm lines of classification between *'ulamā'* whose positions are closer to that of the government or of its Islamist critics implies taking sides in a sensitive and politically charged public debate, itself a part of the production of "orthodoxy" process and the continuous battle between competing interpretations of Islamic tradition. The case of Yūsuf al-Qaradāwī, a prominent Egyptian intellectual and head of the *Sharī'a* Faculty at the University of Qatar, is instructive. al-Qaradāwī is a very popular preacher whose political views on a number of issues are close to those of Islamist activists. For example, he has repeatedly expressed sympathy for Palestinian suicide bombers, but has never condoned the views of Ussāma bin Lāden. Also, he has repeatedly criticized Arab governments on a number of issues, but has never gone as far as advocating their violent overthrow. In this way, al-Qaradāwī has made himself unpopular with the Egyptian government, but has secured a top academic position in Qatar. Equally, he was refused entry to the USA on grounds of his alleged extremism – though he was tolerated in the UK – but he is admired by millions of Muslims worldwide.[34]

Finally and most importantly, what the previous discussion has demonstrated is the vagueness that characterizes the term *'ālim* itself. If we approach the term at the level of those who have completed some unit of studies in an Islamic educational establishment – the conservative way – the identity of the *'ulamā'* emerges in a more or less definite way. But if we approach the term at the level of those who are popularly regarded by large numbers amongst the faithful as possessors of a deep understanding of Islam allegedly based on a profound knowledge of its extended textual tradition and of its applications on both private affairs and public life, then a large percentage of mystics and Islamist activists can qualify as *'ulamā'* in everything but the title. Such an expanded definition can accommodate side by side staunch traditionalists and the leaders of the big Islamist groups like the Muslim Brothers, HAMAS, and Jihād al-Islāmiyya, who, admittedly, have spent years over the *Qur'ān* and other Islamic texts and have written volumes of textual commentaries. And if unduly stretched, for die-hard supporters of *al-Qā'ida* the term may even accommodate Ussāma bin Lāden himself, a public works contractor by trade and self-identified holy warrior by choice.[35] Ussāma's well-known photograph where he poses sitting on a bench with an AK-47 between his knees and row after row of books stacked in bookshelves in the background is the modern image of the self-acclaimed warrior-*'ālim*.

Without losing sight of the conservative definition, which is useful for the study of formal structures and traditional institutions, I would opt for the extended one in order to admit as many as possible protagonists in the process of "orthodoxy" production, although not Ussāma and his like. And perhaps the most important protagonist of all is the state itself.

The State as "Collective *ʿĀlim*"

Indeed, even a casual look demonstrates the central role of the state in the process of "orthodoxy" production. The case of Egypt, which presents itself as the center of the Arab world, is once more revealing.

In the country that houses one of the most revered institutes of Islamic knowledge, al-Azhar University, the *ʿulamāʾ* had for centuries been an influential social category, whose political feelings and convictions could not be easily dismissed. In the nineteenth century this changed.

The last political "victory" of the Egyptian *ʿulamāʾ* took place in 1805. Interceding with the Ottoman authorities on behalf of the people,[36] the religious scholars-jurisconsults played an important role in the popular revolution against the Mamlūk rulers.[37] Soon however, the *ʿulamāʾ* saw their political power decline when their erstwhile ally Muḥammad ʿAlī, now viceroy of Egypt, expropriated huge tracts of their *waqf* land holdings, thus fatally undermining their economic independence.[38] The decline of the *ʿulamāʾ* continued throughout the century, compounded as we saw earlier by the introduction of Western-type education, so when successive Egyptian governments failed to address the country's mounting economic problems and to repel European imperialism, the *ʿulamāʾ* themselves proved incapable of organizing any sort of popular resistance. Unable to offer any alternative to the lopsided modernization that was enforced by the Europeans and the local elites, they soon found themselves severely criticized both by Muslim reformers and by the emerging nationalists who led the anti-colonial struggle.

With the advent of independence and the progress of Nasserism, the position of the *ʿulamāʾ* was further undermined as society came under the sway of Arab socialism and pan-Arabism. Islam itself retreated to the background, and Egypt entered a period of massive reconstruction and modernization dictated by the logic of the Cold War and the ideological exigencies of the Arab–Israeli conflict, as well as by a real desire, indeed need, to improve its economic indices, if not actual standards of living. Things changed with the end of the Nasserist period and the readmission of Islam into the cultural scene by the end of the 1970s and more so in the 1980s. This transformation allowed the Egyptian *ʿulamāʾ* once more to influence public life in the way described in the previous pages, but this time in competition with the Islamists, who saw very few allies amongst the class of religious scholars.

Still, as I shall presently argue, the biggest adversary of the *ʿulamāʾ* proved to be the state, which elevated itself in the position of what could be seen as a "collective *ʿālim*," who alone would define the content and the limits of Islamic "orthodoxy."

One of the most significant ways of promoting a state-approved, or state-constructed, version of Islamic tradition is the national system of education. As Starrett writes, in contemporary Egypt the school has taken the place of the mosque as the "house of God"[39] for two reasons. First, education is compulsory for all Egyptian citizens, thus making the school an ideal laboratory for social reproduction, especially if the knowledge it imparts to the pupils reaches also their parents. But more than that, Starrett continues, the school represents the nation itself and "the idea of national social, economic, and technical progress."[40] Second, the school is surrounded by strong emotions on the part of the pupils and their families because it is considered to be one of the "primary rationers of social status" through the grading system. In that sense, the school is seen as a mechanism for social advancement.[41]

Especially for Islam, the introduction of a national educational system has transformed the state into a constitutionally recognized agent responsible for the imparting of Islamic tradition to the younger generations of Egyptian citizens. In practice, that means that Islam has to be approached in a manner that would enable its utilization as a political instrument.[42]

In this project, Starrett identifies two complementary processes that have been also discussed by Eickelman.[43] The first one is the process of "objectification" of Islam. Through this, people are invited to see Islam as something objective, as a closed and well-bounded set of beliefs and practices, as a total way of being in the world which colors all aspects of private and public life. This process has two important consequences. First, in the form of a subject to be taught in school, Islam is transformed into something that the teacher has to "explain" and the student to comprehend.[44] Second, most differences between the four main schools of law that dominate *sunnī* Islam, as well as the entire existence of alternative interpretative frameworks advanced by a variety of *sunnī* and *shīʿa* organizations and movements, are completely overlooked by the teachers, if not for anything else, but for brevity and precision in the context of primary and secondary schooling. The end result is the presentation of a single, unidimensional Islam instead of an introduction into a rich, dynamic, multi-layered, and ever-changing Islamic discourse.[45] And this is not limited to religion classes offered by public and private schools, but more generally concerns the way in which Islam is presented in all subjects offered in the context of the national system of education,[46] as well as in that of the *Qur'ānic* schools, the majority of which are under state supervision.

The second process that Starrett identifies in this transformation of Islam into a subject that can be taught in the context of a state-determined educational system, is that of "functionalization."[47] There Islam is presented as a tradition characterized by social usefulness. The functionalization of Islam can be seen at three levels.

At the level of institutions, the independent character of instruction characteristic of traditional Islamic education ceases to exist and its place is taken by a state-defined process that applies equally to the whole nation. At the organizational level, all school curricula are determined by bureaucrats in a centrally designed manner without necessarily taking into account the real needs and interests of the students. At the philosophical level, beliefs and practices are reinterpreted in a manner conducive to the aims of the government and in the general context of specially useful concepts such as modernization, public health, productivity, and public order.

These two processes, objectification and functionalization, are still running, since the project of national education in which they are embedded is and will remain an ongoing concern for the Egyptian state. So what could be called a state "orthodox" Islamic tradition should not be conceptualized as a finished product offered to consumers in a monopolistic market. On the contrary, it is always in the process of continual transformation, as the state is continuously fighting other agents of Islamic "orthodoxy," ranging from conservative or recalcitrant *ʿulamāʾ* and the traditional Islamic educational establishments to all sorts of Islamist preachers and political activists.[48] In other words, the state may occupy a hegemonic position in the wider process of producing Islamic "orthodoxy," but to win over an often distrusting public requires continuous effort at all levels. This can be attested by the state's attempt to control as closely as possible the remaining Islamic "schools" and by the efforts of the Islamic educational establishments to retain some degree of autonomy. A most recent episode in this struggle concerns the summer 2004 decision of the Governors Council to turn more than 6,000 Islamic "schools" run by al-Azhar into regular public schools. Among other things,

> The decision means that affected schools will experience a significant drop in the amount of religious education provided to students. Instead of a curriculum featuring up to a dozen religious subjects only one – the same religious education class provided in public schools – will be taught.[49]

Then, one should also take into account that the state itself should not be seen as a monolithic and homogenous actor, a view tacitly implied by Starrett's analysis. As our previous discussion of the *ʿulamāʾ* has demonstrated, a considerable, and inherently fluid, percentage of the religious jurisconsults have developed a working relationship with the state, either directly or indirectly, just as many others are exhibiting sympathy for the Islamist activists. Institutionally, this can go further than that. As Hirschkind suggests with reference to contemporary Egypt,

> [m]any of the state-administered religious organizations include sizable factions sympathetic to the same religious arguments that their own institutions have been called on to officially denounce and combat. Indeed, many of the faculty members and students at the government-administered al-Azhar University . . . also

> participated actively in the affairs of independent Islamic institutions associated with Islamist currents. Not surprisingly, the use of such state institutions to enact policy decisions is frequently unsuccessful.[50]

The extent to which such tendencies have developed in Middle Eastern societies other than Egypt can only be guessed at, since the very detailed ethnographic studies that could shed some light on the issue are virtually non-existent. The political stakes, too, of such eventualities, real or assumed, are very high indeed, given security concerns in the region and abroad; rather than seeing in such debates and multivocality the flowering of what Hirschkind calls civic virtues, such concerns unfortunately, often take the form of doomsday scenarios of the type "Ossama and Saudi princes bent on destroying the 'Free World!'" Still, in all cases, acknowledging the state's heterogeneity in Hirschkind's terms does not invalidate Starrett's argument, as it does not question the state's hegemonic position in relation to other actors shaping the process of producing Islamic "orthodoxy."

Finally, it could be argued that *grosso mondo* there has always been a competition between the state and the *ʿulamāʾ* in Islamic societies. However, the elevation of the state to the position of a "collective *ʿālim*" is a new and qualitatively different development from what went on in the past, not only in Egypt, but practically everywhere in the Muslim world, with the possible exception of Saudi Arabia, where the ruling house of Saʿūd continues to derive its legitimacy from the Wahhābī interpretation of Islam, the only one that is freely available in the country.[51] Irrespective of the relations between the *ʿulamāʾ* and the state, which, as we have seen, could be cordial or antagonistic, in pre-colonial times and in the early colonial period the visions of the *ʿulamāʾ* and the state, in so far as they were distinct and relatively cohesive, emanated from a single discursive universe and were governed by similar epistemological presuppositions. This is not so any more as the state "orthodox" Islam has incorporated to a great extent the logic of modernization, while the Islamic tradition served by the *ʿulamāʾ* retains a number of "traditional" traits, which are nonetheless inevitably comprehended through the prism of some kind of modernity. But in any case, the fact remains that in the eyes of the public this modernity-inflected "traditionality" is less accessible intellectually than the state "orthodoxy" and its self-evident "authenticity"; hence *the retreat of the faithful* mentioned earlier.

ORALITY IN THE CONTEXT OF ISLAMIC TRADITION

The impression that many in the West have of Islam and the other two cognate Abrahamic monotheisms, Judaism and Christianity, is that all three put particular emphasis on the written text to the detriment of orally transmitted traditions. It is no coincidence that all three religions are called "scriptural," that is religions in which God had His will communicated to humanity in a written form – the Jewish Torah, the Christian Bible, and the *Qur'ān*. Especially for those raised or working in countries with a Protestant tradition, such views come almost naturally, irrespective of personal religious beliefs. The use of the term "Islamic fundamentalism," too, however inaccurate as will be seen in chapter 7, betrays a preoccupation with literalism that is projected onto Muslims in line with biblical evangelical literalism. But even outside such religiously inflected presuppositions, it is undeniable that textuality rather than orality is at the center of those social systems which occupy a hegemonic position in the globalization process. Lastly, and in apparent agreement with the previous discussion on the *'ulamā'*, Muslims themselves seem to stress that at the center of their religion is "one God, one Prophet, one Book."

This, however, is only part of the picture. To understand Islamic discourse better, we must also take into account the significance of orality. In this section I discuss these issues from an anthropological perspective in relation to the *Qur'ān* and the *ḥadīth*, as well as the position of charisma in Islamic tradition as a whole. Similar considerations can be found in the chapters that follow, especially in relation to preaching (chapter 4) and Islamic mysticism (chapter 5).

Textuality and the Techniques of Writing

The relationship between writing and orality has been much studied by anthropologists, mainly out of an interest in questions related to cognition, and because professionally we anthropologists are close to small-scale, non-literate societies. The work of Jack Goody (1977) and Jonathan Parry (1985) offers a good introduction to this complex debate that will be briefly sketched here in so far as it is related to our purposes.

Echoing Parsons' query "Why was the decisive step towards modernization not taken by any of the High Eastern civilizations?,"[52] Goody argues that most classical anthropological studies presuppose a binary opposition between Western and non-Western societies, thus exhibiting traces of a Levy-Bruhl (1926) type of social evolutionism. Equally guilty, Goody continues, is Lévi-Straussian structuralism. Though the latter's *Savage Mind* (1966) advances in terms of an a-historical continuum, Goody argues that Lévi-Strauss proposes a historically situated dichotomy between a savage mind associated with the Neolithic period and its modern domesticated counterpart.

For Goody, such attempts to understand human society in all its variety are futile. Instead of presupposing a distinction between "us and them" the way forward is the careful study of the history and social function of the different types of communication between human beings.

Concentrating on the analysis of literacy, Goody suggests that it effects transformations in the mode of human thought itself. Dismissing Horton's 1967 claim concerning the absence of skepticism from traditional modes of thought, Goody maintains that skepticism has always been present in African thought, but because literacy was absent it could not be registered, stored, and eventually reproduced. When literacy was introduced, oral statements could be checked much more easily than before, something that could bring forward otherwise undetected internal contradictions. Moreover, literacy assisted the development of complex lines of argument and was instrumental in the administration of increasingly large areas, the emergence of more elaborate and impersonal bureaucracies, and finally in the strengthening of individualism.

From his point of view, Parry finds Goody's argument unconvincing because, just like Horton's and Lévi Strauss's, it is based on a dichotomous categorization of societies, this time in terms of the absence or presence of literacy. Instead, Parry argues that literate and non-literate societies share numerous characteristics and, additionally, in literate societies the "magic of the book" can often enhance social conservatism, as it can be used by the dominant ideology for political purposes. This being the case, it is printing technology and not literacy that is critical in the discussion. But even this is not enough by itself to make a difference.

Distinguishing between "scribal" societies and those possessing printing technologies, Parry insists that this does not correspond to a distinction between traditional and modern forms of society. What is important for any form of modernization is the incorporation of printing technologies into a democratization process that includes the establishment of a mass education system. Otherwise, printing technology, just like all technologies, can become a tool of oppression in the hands of an elite or clerical establishment, thus stifling all traces of modernization.[53]

The Oral Reconfirmation of Textual Truth

Parry's analysis allows us to raise some important points regarding orality in Islamic tradition, especially in relation to the *Qur'ān*. A first point concerns the preservation in literate societies of elements of their non-literate past that confirm the truth of their holy texts.[54] This conclusion is supported by ethnographic data from the holy city of Benares (Varanasi), India, which, according to Hinduism, is an auspicious place to cremate the dead. Though not monotheistic, Hinduism shares many traits with Islam as far as the apparent supremacy of the written text is concerned.

As Parry writes, Hindus distinguish between a written and an oral religious tradition. The written tradition makes use of the ancient language of Sanskrit, which, as with Arabic in Islam, is considered to be divine and a manifestation of civilization. In a manner similar to the *Qur'ān*, the holy texts of this tradition are regarded as the only source of real knowledge. Any other type of knowledge is considered to be inferior because it comes from the illusory world of everyday appearances.[55]

But just as the *Qur'ān* is God's word, so the written Brahmanical tradition is an oral revelation that the gods sent to humanity. Even the Vedas reached humanity orally. For this reason, their study cannot be done exclusively through the use of texts. The presence of a teacher who will orally explicate their truth is imperative. Futhermore, just like the *Qur'ān*, most texts of the Brahmanical tradition are written in verse and their correct recitation – again just as in Islam – is of paramount importance.[56]

In the course of Islamic history, the importance of the *Qur'ān*'s oral character has come to the fore in many instances. During the Prophet's lifetime, the *Qur'ān* was never fully written down, its recitation being associated with its thaumaturgical character. According to the tradition, Abū Sa'īd al-Khūdrī, one of the Companions of the Prophet, asked his permission to write it down, but Muḥammad refused. 'Abd Allāh ibn 'Abbās, an important early commentator on the *Qur'ān*, claimed that, according to a *ḥadīth*, the destruction of the pre-Islamic civilizations was partly related to the use of writing.[57] Lastly, we hear God himself stating in the *Qur'ān*, "[i]f We had sent unto thee a written (message) on parchment, so that they could touch it with their hands, the unbelievers would have been sure to say: 'this is nothing but obvious magic!' "[58]

According to Watt and Bell,[59] after the Prophet's death the process of collecting and recording in writing the various pieces of *Qur'ānic* revelation was resisted by the first caliph, Abū Bakr, who allegedly claimed that he had not received such an order from Muḥammad, who was himself most probably illiterate. Later, when the *Qur'ān* was recorded in writing, the issue of orality and the importance of *Qur'ānic* recitation were not forgotten. On the contrary, in the third century AH/tenth century AD, after much debate among Muslim scholars, it was decided to accept officially seven versions of *Qur'ānic* recitation. This decision was based on the studies of the renowned *'ālim* Ibn Mujāhid (859–935) and is still valid today throughout the world.[60]

Politically too, the oral dimension of the *Qur'ān* was duly acknowledged. When at the battle of Ṣiffīn (657) 'Alī's followers retreated at the sight of the *Qur'ān*s that Mu'āwiyya's soldiers had put on the tips of their lances so as to avoid bloodshed between Muslims, 'Alī shouted, "What you see on the lances is but paper and ink; I am the living Qur'an, the speaking Qur'an."[61] And on another occasion he allegedly said that "[h]e who obtains knowledge orally from a master, he is safe from being misled and from misreadings. But he who obtains knowledge from books, his knowledge is nil according to those who know."[62] Lastly, lest it be suggested that this emphasis on orality is a *shī'a* phenomenon, I should quote Muḥammad Ibn Idrīs al-Shāfi'ī, the famous *sunnī* jurist of the second century AH/ninth century AD, who argued that "it is a mistake to take the written page as your mentor . . . he who learns jurisprudence from the book alone loses sight of the law."[63]

This brief discussion of the oral character of the *Qur'ān* may now help us understand why it is so important for the faithful throughout the Muslim world to recite the *Qur'ān* in Arabic, even when they are not native speakers and, as often as not, have only limited knowledge of that language. The revelation of the *Qur'ān* gave the Arabic language an exalted status. After all, the development of the Arabic alphabet, the use of diacritics and the systematization of its grammar and syntax were prompted to enable the most precise textual representation of the oral *Qur'ān*.[64] As a Sudanese friend and informant well versed in *Qur'ānic* interpretation told me when I was doing fieldwork in the Sudan, when I learn perfect Arabic, I will become a Muslim. Neither of these has happened.

Lastly, the above discussion allows us to appreciate why in Muslim societies the recitation of the *Qur'ān* is not confined to the mosque or to the context of religious festivals. As has been mentioned in chapter 2, throughout the year certain television and radio stations offer 24 hours per day *Qur'ānic* recitation, on top of similar programs offered by regular broadcasters. On the Internet, too, numerous sites offer *Qur'ānic* recitation, a service that does not apply to holy "texts" of other religious traditions. Likewise, hundreds of audio- and videotapes of *Qur'ānic* recitation are sold in shops, in open-air markets, outside mosques, and other Islamic establishments, even in the duty-free shops of some airports. Additionally, passengers on national air carriers of some Muslim countries, such as Egypt Air and Emirates, can listen to the *Qur'ān* in-flight alongside other programs on the aircraft's radio.

Verbal Analysis and Interpretation of Holy Texts

Orality should also be considered in relation to the Prophetic traditions and to the devotional literature that abounds in all Muslim societies. As far as the former is concerned, the most extensive anthropological treatment of the subject is that of Fischer and Abedi (1990).[65] In an ethnographically rich description we can follow one of the most famous contemporary guides on Islamic tradition, Ayatollah Khomeini, interpreting certain *Qur'ānic* verses in the light of sixteen *ḥadīth*. Khomeini did this in an effort to formulate the foundations of *vilayeti-i-faqi*, his theory on the political administration of the state by *shī'a 'ulamā'*. The discussion took place in the presence of a number of students in the Iraqi town of Najāf a few years before the 1979 Islamic revolution in Iran, which gave Khomeini the opportunity to apply his theory.[66]

The whole event was conducted in the form of a debate called *ishkāl* (criticism or question), which permits the use of four types of data: the *Qur'ān*, the *sunna* of the Prophet and of 'Alī, the traditions of the *shī'a imāms* who followed 'Alī, and the formulation of rational arguments in order to reach some form of final conclusion. The structure of the debate includes the exposition of the argument, the discussion of questions from the audience-participants, and the subsequent reformulation of the argument. Perfect knowledge of theology and oratorical skills are a key element in the whole process, as well as the personality of the speaker, his assumed piety and knowledge, and in many cases his history of independent thinking and political views. It would not be inaccurate to say that the significance attributed to the content of a homily, explication, or debate is directly related to the identity of those involved and to their rhetorical skills.

Fischer and Abedi's ethnographic example makes this perfectly clear. To an observer, much of the discussion appears to revolve around methodological issues concerning the content and authenticity of certain *ḥadīth*, a task that requires perfect knowledge of Arabic grammar and syntax. However, what is really debated are the principles one can tease out of the material and the way these should guide social practice, having as the ultimate aim the realization of a particular Islamic vision, in this case the establishment of an Islamic state in Iran. Indeed, with the benefit of hindsight, we now recognize these Najāf dialogues as seminal moments in the intellectual process that led Khomeini to crystalize the principles governing Iran.[67]

Turning to Islamic devotional literature, we find that the picture gets more complicated. Although it is difficult to define its exact boundaries, this rich constellation of disparate works stands alongside the voluminous theological, philosophical, and legal treatises which comprise the "officially" designated "academic" textual tradition of Islam produced by the *'ulamā'*. Thus, the devotional literature I refer to includes *Qur'ānic* commentaries of an esoteric nature, which are accessible to only a few illuminati, "unauthorized" biographies of Prophet Muḥammad and his companions, lives of popular saints and *ṣūfī* mystics, books on magic, astrology, numerology, the esoteric properties of personal names, traditional medicine, spells, charms and divination, the numerous manuals on ecstatic enlightenment and popularized interpretations of theological treatises, as well as a multitude of "How to . . ." instruction guides concerning prayer, pilgrimage, fasting, sexual continence, correct ways of dressing, inventories of Islamic phrases and proverbs in Arabic for non-Arab Muslims, child-rearing methods, family matters, and so on.[68] This rich and composite picture is what prompted Ioan Lewis to dismiss the classical dictum describing Islam as the paradigmatic scriptural religion of the Book and, tongue in cheek, to portray it as the "religion of the books."[69]

Lewis's observation is of particular significance for two reasons. First, it rectifies the erroneous impression of Islam as a dry, austere, and legalistic religion. Second, it debunks often prevalent orientalistic and essentialist approaches to Islam which effectively ignore what they deem to be outside the boundaries of a high textual tradition, thus robbing the tradition of its vitality and of the richness of its local manifestations.

However, Lewis's insight is only partly correct – for two reasons. First, a sizeable part of the devotional literature can be seen not so much as religious *texts*, but as *mnemonic devices* which allow people to remember what to do in order to come closer to God or what to say or do when they want to succeed in this or that endeavor. This does not detract from the importance of devotional literature *qua* religious literature; on the contrary, it adds new layers of meaning and enriches the field of its application. In this sense, it is legitimate to talk about the magic of the book and the power of words.

Second, a large percentage of the devotional literature discussed here cannot serve its purpose properly, that is to develop a "correct" relationship between believers and God, if its study is pursued in an individualistic manner independent of the directions of an appropriate teacher. I have already indicated in chapter 2 how important it is for Muslims to establish a definite chain of transmission that proves the "authenticity" of each tradition.[70] It is on the strength of such chains of clearly identifiable persons that the *ḥadīth* receive their status. At another level, this too is the meaning of *ijmāʿ* which prioritizes the community as a whole at the expense of the individual.[71] For the same reason, emphasis is given to the study of the holy texts of Islam, be they the *Qurʾān* or the various *ḥadīth* collections, theoretical treatises, and *ʿulamāʾ* commentaries, as well as all sorts of devotional manuals *under the supervision of a qualified teacher or spiritual guide* – a *shaykh*, as he is usually called in the Arab world. Only when the student sits by the teacher, will he or she be able to comprehend the "inner" meaning of Islam. This happens gradually as the teacher pours into the student's soul the wisdom of his own teachers, which is often not to be found in books, but has been passed on to him verbally or absorbed in an unmediated experiential manner that goes beyond intellectual effort.[72] Depending on the circumstances, such teachers can be seen as more or less knowledgeable or illuminated, sometimes even holy. In Weber's terms they all possess charisma,[73] thus blurring the line between charismatic and traditional authority, and in all cases seen as indispensable. I personally came across this view more than once during my fieldwork in the Sudan. As I was told, "*huwa mā ʿendū shaykh, shaykhu Shayṭān*" (the one who has no guide, has Satan as his guide).[74] Given the indeterminacy of the term *shaykh* (tribal or religious leader, *ʿālim*, saint, *walī* or friend of God, mystic, officiant in a *ṣūfī* order or a spirit possession cult, divine, *darwīsh* mendicant, *faqī* traditional medicine practitioner, or simply bearer of a honorific describing high status, professional reputation, or advanced age), I could think of scores of different people whom I had met during my fieldwork and who could be validly described as charismatic personalities, possessors of God's blessing, and masters of some sort of Islamic knowledge which they could impart to those who sought it.

This being the case, orality refers to something more than a contrast to literacy. It could be likened to an enabling analytical tool that highlights issues ranging from the positioning of social actors implicated in the production/consumption of "oral forms" – most significantly, this includes audiences as well, thus divesting the term from its presumed passivity – to the mystical entwining of words, utterances, and selves. Through the prism of orality one can see Islam coming alive in relation to individual persons who authorize the Truth through their own recitation, speech, statements, narration, exposition of arguments, pronouncement of theoretical assumptions, facial expressions, gestures, and oratorical techniques, in other words with all their body.[75] Moving our discussion of orality in Islam a final step further, we can better understand this by considering a special form of preaching, the *da'wa* movement.

The Call to God

Anthropologist Charles Hirschkind has written extensively on *da'wa* and the *du'āt* (those who undertake *da'wa*), focusing on contemporary Cairo. At a general level, *da'wa* "refers to God's invitation, addressed to humankind and transmitted through the prophets, to live in accordance with God's will."[76] More specifically, in today's Egypt *da'wa* refers to a "mode of action by which moral and political reform" can be brought about and is "understood as an ethical form of speech and action aimed at improving the moral conduct of one's fellow community members."[77] Individually undertaken or situated in more institutionalized contexts, *da'wa* is conducted orally, in written form, and audiovisually (mostly by means of cassettes and videotapes), taking the sermon as its paradigmatic rhetorical form.

For Hirschkind, "[v]irtuous conduct . . . is seen by the [*da'wa*] movement both as an end in itself and as a means internal to the dialogic process by which the reform of society is secured."[78] Concerning the former, that is the inculcation of individual virtuous conduct, the *dā'iya* (sing. of *du'āt*) "must be an active and concerned citizen" who could set him- or herself up as an example that fellow Muslims would like to emulate. His or her speech should be characterized by friendliness, temperateness, and gentleness that emanate from sincerety (*ikhlās*), humility (*khushū'*), and fear of God (*taqwa*, *khaūf*). Moreover, those practicing *da'wa* should exhibit courage (*shajā'a*) because after all they have elected "to speak the truth in the face of the quite real danger of arrest and torture by the Egyptian state,"[79] which is not always friendly towards those preaching an Islamic vision critical of the government.

Turning to the target audience for *da'wa* practices, Hirschkind writes that to be properly responsive and to make the best out of it, one should exhibit "[a] properly disposed heart," something that goes beyond a simple cognitive orientation to a real "act of submission and resignation to God."[80] More specifically, concerning proper sermon audition, Hirschkind shows how this "demands a particular affective-volitional responsiveness from the listener . . . a condition for 'understanding' sermon speech, while simultaneously deepening an individual's capacity to hear in this manner."[81]

Though it is not entirely clear if the young men Hirschkind was working with in Cairo comprised some particular type of congregation or "piety group,"[82] it is clear that they viewed the audition of sermon tapes "as a means by which a range of Islamic virtues could be sedimented in their characters, enabling them to live more piously and avoid moral transgressions."[83] The manner in which this was effected involved a kind of moral physiology, with the subjects employing a variety of medical expressions to describe how their bodies were permeated with faith (*imān*) through the evocation of a particular set of ethical responses which are defined in classical textual Islamic tradition.

For Hirschkind, the invocation of an open heart as a precondition for the generation of such emotions prioritizes forms of "embodied capacities of gesture, feeling, and speech" rather than "obedience to rules or belief in doctrine."[84] This implies the existence of *normative standards* that define "proper" audition as a means of, and tool for, putting the subjects in a course progressing "from fear, to regret, to asking for forgiveness, to repentance."[85] The existence of such normative standards was in effect directly explicated by Hirschkind's informants, who distinguished between the common act of hearing (*sam*ʿ) and that of inclining one's ear toward or paying close attention to (*anṣat*), and being silent in order to listen (*aṣghā*). From this point of view, the whole body of the listener participates in a performance, which is nothing less than a dialogue with God that demands the attention of total man – rather than man's total attention.

Concerning the reformation of society, *daʿwa* practices should be conceived as an exemplary form of activity aiming at what has been called "Islamization from below." As I show in detail in chapters 7 and 8, this is a process which centers on a critical understanding of culture as a dimension of lived religion and as a political tool employed in order to achieve the gradual Islamization of society. As a preacher engaged in *daʿwa* activities told Hirschkind, "[t]he enemies of Islam use *fann*, *adab*, *thaqāfa*, and *mūda* [art, literature, culture, and fashion] to attack Islam,"[86] a comment alleging the Western and secular genealogy of these concepts and their attendant practices. "What is at stake here," the anthropologist suggests, "is not simply a case of political criticisms being deflected onto the safer realm of culture,"[87] but the transformation of the latter into the very battleground where *daʿwa* activists go after the hearts and minds of the people.

Besides "proper" preaching, to do this the proponents of *daʿwa* have developed and encouraged the use of alternative "Islamic diversions" – "Islamic" songs, "Islamic" children's summer camps, "Islamic" theater, "Islamic" literature – which color appropriately the everyday experience of believers, thus contextualizing, and further enhancing, the Islamic virtues inculcated in the manner discussed earlier. The ultimate aim of this project is the (re)constitution of proper Muslim subjects who will actively implicate themselves in the strengthening of Islamic society and promote the gradual establishment of an Islamic state. It is not in the service of personal reformation or regeneration *per se*, but in that of the moral, social, and political restructuring of society as an integral part and a living cell of the *umma*, the Community of Believers. Only within such a context, and only under the protection afforded by an Islamic law properly administered by the courts, can a (re)constituted Muslim subject flourish and lead a socially meaningful life.

Having said that and in agreement with what has been said earlier about the state as a collective *ʿālim*, "Islamization from below" as a whole, and *daʿwa* practices in particular, should not be approached as a process outside or opposite the state on behalf of society – or at least the Islamist and conservative circles that pursue such activities. Hirschkind makes this abundantly clear when he argues that the Islamic counterpublic articulated through and in *daʿwa* practices in contemporary Egypt

> does not . . . play a mediatory role between *state* and *society* . . . daʿwa does not take place within, or serve to uphold, that domain of associational life referred to as civil society. Rather, the dāʿiya's narrative locates itself within the temporal frame of an Islamic umma and in relation to the succession of events that characterizes its mode of historicity.[88]

And he concludes,

> [m]y argument here is that in Egypt, over the course of the last century, [*daʿwa*] has been elaborated in such a way so as to define a mode of public life, one founded on argumentation and debate about the orthodoxy of current practices. The aim of this discursive activity is not "public policy" but the formation of Islamic public virtues. In articulating itself against the modernizing programs of the Egyptian state, the daʿwa movement has drawn on the universalistic discourses of the Islamic tradition to create a form of community and identity that transverses the moral and geographic boundaries of the nation.[89]

The same holds true for other Muslim societies as well, although the exact manner in which *daʿwa* activities are organized and institutionally supported or undermined – sometimes simultaneously, an indication of the state's ultimate ambivalence in the project for "orthodoxy" production – differs accordingly.

Lastly, it is important to stress that despite the arsenal of classical terms and concepts implicated in these ethics of listening, which are often expounded or insinuated by preachers and other informants, the whole complex procedure analyzed by Hirschkind does not rest upon a return to some "traditional" practice or proper way of doing things. As he writes,

> [t]he perceptual capacities listeners seek to cultivate are mediated . . . by functional possibilities of cassette technology . . . [and] by the discursive conventions of the modern print and tele-visual based public sphere . . . What makes the practice of cassette-sermon audition part of an Islamic tradition is not its exact conformity to a fixed model, but the fact that, in its contemporary organization, assessment, and performance, the practice relies on authoritative discourses and historical exemplars embedded in that tradition.[90]

In this manner, the spurious bi-polarity of the "modern" and the "traditional" is destroyed and, following Asad, Hirschkind speaks of the former as an enabling condition of the latter within a process of "orthodoxy" production, the red line that I am using throughout the present volume in an effort to understand Islam in "local contexts"[91] without losing sight of the greater totality that the vision of the imagined universal Community of Believers aspires to. This is what transforms the simple but tremendously profound act of listening to a taped sermon in one's Cairo apartment in the company of friends into a means toward, and the possibility of, realizing the Islamic vision in the world. For Hirschkind, here rests *daʿwa*'s modernity or contemporaneity, and, I would add, its claim to universalism. As he writes,

> Although the notion that Muslims have a duty to speak in the face of moral error for the sake of the umma has clear precedents within earlier Islamic societies, the contemporary nationalization of this notion owes considerably to the idea and experience of national citizenship and the notions of civic responsibility implied in that status . . . [However], it would be wrong to understand the practices of public sociability articulated around the concept of daʿwa in Egypt as nationalism cast in an Islamic idiom. Although the views and attitudes cultivated within this domain sometimes find application in the public sphere of the nation . . . the concerns, loyalties, sentiments, and practices that daʿwa has given rise to presuppose a form of community for which the nation is a contigent but not essential component.[92]

In the wider context of our discussion on the identity of contemporary *ʿulamāʾ* and on the significance of orality in the production, formulation, and distribution of Islamic "orthodoxy," the new techniques described above and the novel types of dialogue and communication they promote (close to what Ong has called "secondary orality"[93] and to what Starrett understands as "postmodern knowledge"[94]) have enhanced the importance of orality in Islam, while at the same time have indirectly subverted other more traditional forms of orality and textuality. Claims similar to those of ʿAlī ("I am the living *Qurʾān*") are enunciated by countless lips and blinking on countless computer screens. Screams, whispers, casual talk, chit-chat, or carefully manicured exposés, all these utterances voiced by millions in mosques, universities, study groups, cafés, central squares, avenues, back streets, courtyards, and living-rooms, as well as in thousands of constantly updated sites, lists, and chat rooms concerning the "real" meaning of Islam, make an unending flood of melody and noise that can be only inadequately expressed in textual forms,[95] and that allows us to revise, again, the previously mentioned dictum and declare Islam to be the "religion of books and words."

Stories, Story-Tellers and Audiences

If this is so, the theoretical importance of anthropological writings, which for some time now have shifted "their attentions from the stories people tell to those who tell the stories and to the act of telling stories,"[96] may prove to be of crucial importance in accounting for and interpreting this multitude of voices, as well as in probing deeper into the production of Islamic "orthodoxy" in local contexts.

Some of these issues can be considered in terms of Tonkin's discussion of the social construction of oral history. Strictly speaking, the oral expositions of themes from Islamic tradition, be they directly associated with the *Qur'ān* and the *ḥadīth* or with *da'wa* practices, differ from Tonkin's "narrations or representations of pastness." From this point of view, then, her theoretical insights can be used in the present context mainly as examples/opportunities of creatively approaching the issue of orality. From another point of view, though, such oral expositions by members of the various Muslim publics can be seen as sets of propositions informing the structuring of a common topos of memories and bodily hexes which infuse the subjects' present with what is at a particular time locally conceived as Islamic ethos. For example, what the Prophet did or did not do or say in a particular case in seventh-century Arabia is looked upon as exemplary behavior which should be emulated *in the present.* In that sense, the continuous study of the *ḥadīth* and the interpretation of religious texts take place in the context of a *sacred* history, where the past does not refer to something that was or simply happened, but primarily to something which was accomplished or realized in accordance with God's providence.[97] With this in mind, Tonkin's insights on history and narration can be usefully employed in our consideration of orality in Islam.

From the outset, Tonkin is clear that "[o]ne cannot detach the oral representation of pastness from the relationship of teller and audience in which it was occasioned."[98] In the issue under discussion, this suggests that the oral expositions offered by the *'ulamā'*, the mystics, or the various types of Islamist preachers cannot be divorced from the social relationship networks that bind them together with their audience(s) in each particular historical moment. We have already glanced at the way that this may have worked when discussing earlier the content and social positioning of the various types or groups of Egyptian *'ulamā'* vis-à-vis the state and the national education bureaucracy. The themes explored by the various protagonists prioritized specific readings of Islamic tradition and of past practices in Egypt, invoked particular arrays of memories and sought to awaken well-orchestrated responses from the audience(s). This is something we shall also see in the discussion of mosque preachings and in the local expressions of Islamism examined in chapters 4 and 8 respectively.

But if oral representations of pastness and expositions of tradition should be seen in the context of specific relationships rather than divested of their social referents, Tonkin also reminds us that "accounts of pastness are socially constructed through the intervening power of genre."[99] This is of great importance from an anthropological perspective because it leads researchers to consider the message *through* the means in which it is delivered and in relation to the identities of all who are implicated in the process. It encourages them to study the manners in which local communities structure lines of argumentation – oral or written – and types of accounts, as well as the techniques by which they deliver them, aiming for the highest degree of persuasion and acceptance through the invocation of the audience's sense of logic and/or the arousal of its sentiments. Hence, it would be difficult to understand what went on in Najāf (see above pp. 84–5) if we discounted the identities of the interlocutors and the structural principles underlying the debate or to appreciate the importance of *daʿwa* practices without the consideration of their sermon-like attributes and what they presume as ethical audition.

Significantly, too, this is something that concerns not only expositions of a strictly defined religious nature competing against each other within the premise of an "orthodoxy" production process, but whole areas of social practice. As Caton maintains in his account of oral poetry in Yemen, "politics and poetics are inseparable,"[100] and he reminds us that in Middle Eastern tribal societies power should be reconceptualized in terms of persuasion rather than in terms of force.

> Each side uses all the rhetorical weapons at its disposal to present its position in the best possible light, and the intermediaries attempt by the same means to induce the two opponents to stop fighting and start negotiating . . . Issuing a poem as a challenge *invites* a response and thus begins a dialogue by which mediation has a chance of succeeding. The dialogue gives voice to each side and thus assures balance and fairness.[101]

In a similar manner, religious argumentation cannot be approached but as constitutive of social relations in the form of a dialogue between contesting voices that takes place in the arena of everyday life and within parameters locally accepted as internal of Islamic discursive tradition. Rather than ascribing to religious discourse a privileged position within a well-defined sphere of activities, we should strive each time to integrate it within the wider socio-cultural discursive universe of the actors, thus localizing it in a manner that does not conceal its translocal characteristics as the idiom of the worldwide imagined Community of Believers.

Lastly, to return to Tonkin, it is in this manner that the author is able to assert that "authenticity is a claim embodied in the narrative."[102] This can be addressed in two ways. First, as a comment on "orthodoxy" production through the employment of an "authenticity" idiom: an interpretation is regarded to be correct, i.e. "orthodox," because it is "more authentic" historically or objectively. In the most clear-cut way Tonkin rejects such a proposition, questioning the claim that oral narratives do contain some core data which are of historical value in a positivist sense and which researchers can actually "discover" in a stripping-away process of extraneous material that was added while the tradition was carried through time.[103] Still, this does not make a narrative or oral exposition non- or less historical. Advancing claims to authenticity, hence orthodoxy, is the essence of the whole exercise. Indeed, as Barber has shown in her discussion of West African Yoruba "praise poetry," *oríkì* texts are "intrinsically and profoundly historical . . . They represent the 'past in the present,' the way the knowledge of the past makes itself felt stubbornly and often contradictorily today. They represent a way not just of looking at the past, but of re-experiencing it and reintegrating it in their present."[104] Is it not the same with accounts among Muslims, be they *ʿulamāʾ* or illiterate tribesmen who strive to define "orthodoxy" in the context of Islamic discourse?

Second, asserting that "authenticity is a claim embodied in the narrative" should be seen in relation to the formalism that characterizes ritual and oratorical language, such as *ʿulamāʾ* oral expositions, preaching, and *daʿwa* activities. As Bloch has argued, formalized language is the language of traditional authority, a particularly impoverished form of language which "dramatically restricts what can be said, so the speech acts are either all alike or all of a kind and thus if this mode of communication is adopted there is hardly any choice of what can be said."[105] At its extreme, ritual language takes the form of intoning or singing – and I would add, reciting. The significance of this observation is that in such cases

> no argument or reasoning can be communicated, no adaptation to the reality of the situation is possible. *You cannot argue with a song*. It is because religion uses forms of communication which do not have propositional force . . . that to extract an argument from what is being said and what is being done in ritual is, in a sense, a denial of the nature of religion . . . Religion is the last place to find anything "explained" because . . . religious communication rules out the very tools of explanation.[106]

In other words, explications of the *Qurʾānic* message and the Prophetic *ḥadīth*, as well as *daʿwa* sermon-like preaching are not arguments and cannot invite discussion in terms outside those governing Islamic discourse itself. Rather, they are propositions built on specific principles intrinsic to the tradition which they set out, demonstrating a particular vision of the world which cannot be questioned. It can be accepted or rejected, but cannot be discursively approached outside its own referents which are themselves accepted by faith.[107] As Bloch writes, formalization not only removes "what is being said from a particular time and a particular place," it also removes it "from the actual speaker," thus creating a supernatural being or God which the speaker "is slowly becoming or speaks from."[108] Significantly, Bloch extends his argument to dance, which he describes as "typical of religion," as "formalization of the body movement" amounts to the acceptance of a code wherein communication ceases from being dialectic and becomes generative of "fixed, repeated, fused messages."[109]

The same argument is advanced by Connerton in his discussion of the commemorative ceremonies. For him, ritual language is performative and formalized. "The utterance of the performative itself constitutes an action of some kind."[110] In a manner reminiscent of Hirschkind, Connerton argues "that act takes place in and through the enunciation. Such verbs [to ask, to pray, to give thanks] do not describe or indicate the existence of attitudes: they effectively bring those attitudes into existence by virtue of the illocutionary act."[111] Moreover, Connerton maintains, the formalism of ritual language or, as he phrases it, the "economy of formalization" which is extended in ritualized posture, gesture, and movement is what allows it to work "so powerfully as a mnemonic device."[112] Both he and Bloch, then, and indeed Tonkin herself, situate their analyses within the wider framework of embodiment, just as Hirschkind does for *da'wa* and Mahmood for prayer in the following chapter.

4

The Five Pillars

In the words of Prophet Muḥammad, "Islam is based on five pillars."[1] These are: believing in one God and in his Prophet (*shahāda*), praying five times a day (*ṣalāt*), giving alms to the poor (*zakāt*), fasting during the month of Ramaḍān (*al-ṣawm*), and undertaking the pilgrimage to Mecca at least once in one's lifetime (*ḥajj*).

The five pillars of Islam constitute intricate templates for practice which present Islam to both Muslims and non-Muslims not as a religion in the strict sense of the word, but as a dynamic and all-encompassing cultural tradition which cannot be dissociated from the political realities of the world. Through the five pillars the imagined Community of Believers can come together despite the differences which characterize individual Muslim societies.

SHAHĀDA: THE CONFESSION OF FAITH

Recited by all Muslims in the world, the confession of faith declares: "There is no (other) god except (the one and only) God (*Allāh*), and Muḥammad is the messenger of *Allāh*." This concise sentence accurately describes the very essence of Islamic monotheism.

Allāh existed in pre-Islamic Arabia for many centuries[2] and was regarded as creator among other deities and lesser spirits.[3] In Islam *Allāh* is the creator and protector of everything that is. He is omnipotent, omnipresent, and infinitely wise. Reminding us of the Old Testament God, *Allāh* has no son, daughter, or companions.[4] To press this point, when the Prophet subdued the opponents of Islam and returned to Mecca in 632, he destroyed all the idols of the neighboring Arab tribes. At the symbolic level, Islamic monotheism prohibits all iconic representations of *Allāh*, a ban that came to include all types of human representations too. Lastly, the relation between *Allāh* and man resembles that between master and servant or, as Asad argues, master and slave.[5]

In his absolute power over man and the creation, *Allāh* is presented as both merciful and compassionate, two attributes of His stressed in the *basmāla* (*bismillāhi al-raḥmān al-raḥīm*/in the name of *Allāh*, most Gracious, most Merciful) which precedes all *Qur'ānic sūra*s and often official talks, radio and television news bulletins, and university lectures, as well as numerous printed texts and personal correspondence.

Indeed, for the faithful the mercy of *Allāh* animates the whole cosmos and is revealed through the *Qur'ān* which, like the New Testament, is considered to be *Allāh*'s gift to humanity. For those who do not elect to follow the *Qur'ān*, punishment on the Day of Judgment will be swift and terrible.

In the *shahāda*, Muḥammad is called *rasūl* (messenger), a notion close to that of the Christian apostle. In the *Qur'ān* the title has been given to many persons before Muḥammad, making the latter part of a long tradition pre-dating Islam. In this way, the "new" religion of seventh-century Arabia is depicted as a continuation, indeed affirmation and perfection, of Abraham's religion and not as something novel without solid foundations.

Besides *rasūl*, in the *Qur'ān* Muḥammad is also called *bashīr* (announcer), *nadhīr* (warner), and *mudhakkar* (reminder). All three titles describe Muḥammad as an ordinary person without foreknowledge of the future or any other superhuman power. In that, Muḥammad was not different from all the previous messengers of God. When the term *nabī* (prophet) is introduced, the picture becomes more dynamic. Most probably, the term first appeared after the *hijra*, suggesting that the Muslims adopted it after coming in contact with the Madīnan Jews.[6] Muḥammad is called in the *Qur'ān* "*khātam al-nabīyyūn*" (the seal of the prophets [of the Abrahamic tradition]),[7] something that can be translated as "the last of the prophets."

The actual text of the *shahāda* can be found twice in the *Qur'ān*. It should be seen as the basic principle of the distinction between the "land of Islam" (*dār al-Islām*) and the "land of war" (*dār al-ḥarb*), defining the governance of the former as submission (*Islām*) to the will of God. Uttering the *shahāda*, one declares oneself *mū'min* (believer), *muslim* (submitted to the will of God), and member of the universal *umma*; denouncing the *shahāda* one becomes *mushrik* (polytheist) and *kāfir* (infidel). That is why the *shahāda* is also seen as a Muslim "war-cry" which, in the hands of extremists, rejects all sorts of relativism that contemplates the equality of different cultural traditions.[8]

ṢALĀT: THE RITUAL PRAYER[9]

The second pillar of Islam concerns the five institutionalized daily prayers (*ṣalāt*) that all Muslims should ideally perform at dawn, noon, in the afternoon, in the evening, and late at night. As with all ideals, this too is never fully realized, so we should not imagine all the inhabitants of a Middle Eastern city or village interrupting whatever they are doing in order to pray at the appointed time of the day. All the same, in many shops and offices prayer-mats are kept to hand for those staff members and customers who would like to pray on the spot. Similarly, many public buildings, educational institutions, airports, and bus and train stations have special rooms for praying in. Furthermore, in certain countries inter-city buses do interrupt their journeys to let passengers off in order to pray, and friendly gatherings and formal meetings can easily be interrupted with some of the participants retiring to the next room, only to return after they have completed their prayers and resume the conversation from the point at which it had been broken off. When experienced from the outside, such events may seem odd, but in reality they are very well integrated into the flow of everyday activity.

For example, during my fieldwork in the Sudan the most impressive observation of prayer took place in the summer of 1989, while I was returning to Port Sudan from a nearby village on a local mini-bus. Just before sunset, the bus pulled over to the side of the road that was covered by sand. The few passengers got off and started preparing themselves for the prayer session. They "washed" their feet with the fine sand of the desert and then spread the prayer-mats which the bus always carries for such occasions. After that, they formed two neat rows with the women standing behind the men. The prayer leader was a middle-aged man. As far as I could see, nothing singled him out from the rest of the passengers. After the short prayer, people smoked or ate something light and then we continued our journey.

The daily prayers I refer to in this chapter are part of the *ʿibādāt*, the religious duties of all Muslims. Besides the *ṣalāt*, there are other collective or individual prayers to which I shall refer only in passing.[10]

The Basic Characteristics of Prayer

In accordance with the *Qur'ānic* vision, there is no religion without prayer. The importance attributed to prayer is suggested by the fact that the first *sūra* of the *Qur'ān* is regarded as part of the daily prayers and is recited by every believer in the first person plural, thus including all members of the *umma*. This is particularly significant, if we keep in mind that 33 out of the 67 times the term *ṣalāt* is mentioned in the *Qur'ān* can be found in *sūra*s 2, 4, 5, 9, and 24, which belong to the period when the Prophet had established himself in Madīna as the head of the first Community of Believers. This shows that the institutionalization of *ṣalāt* as one of the religious duties of the faithful follows that of Islam as an emerging religious creed and political reality.

The *ṣalāt* had been given to the Prophet as a personal duty toward God. Gradually other Muslims started praying, forming rows next to him, thus transforming *ṣalāt* into one of the most important collective obligations for the entire *umma*. This can be attested by many *Qur'ānic sūras*[11] and Prophetic traditions. There we read that a collective prayer is of equal value to 25 prayers one may perform alone. Also, as a precaution against Satan's intrusion, it is written that the Prophet encouraged Muslims not to allow empty space between them when they pray, but to touch those next in the row on the shoulder, the thigh and the ankle.[12] Finally, we also read that the Prophet wondered whether to burn the houses of those who prayed alone and did not join the congregation in the mosque, the focus of the Islamic vision.[13] In anthropological parlance, we could say that being a good Muslim is a quality to be performed routinely and publicly in the context of the *umma*. I shall return to this issue later in the chapter.

The basic principles governing *ṣalāt* concern its institutionalized character and its daily compulsory practice by all adult Muslims (except those who suffer from insanity) in Arabic, especially for the recitation of the *Qur'ānic* verses, its carrying out in an atmosphere of sobriety and calmness, and the adoption of particular body postures.

The prayer is always performed in the direction of Mecca (*qibla*). Praying toward a particular direction had long been practiced by both Jews and Christians,[14] from whom the Prophet adopted the practice after the *hijra*. The initial direction of the *ṣalāt* was toward Jerusalem. This is not odd if we consider that Islam was presented as the culmination of the Abrahamic tradition and not as a new religion. Similarly, it is not odd that a few months after settling in Madīna, the Prophet changed the *qibla*, this time toward the *Ka'ba* which historically constituted part of the Arab tribal symbolic universe. This decision shows that the Prophet had reconsidered his relations with the Jewish clans of the town after their rejection of Islam. In that decision, accompanied by an appropriate *Qur'ānic* injunction[15] and the expulsion of the Jews from Madīna, we can observe the transformation of Islam into a specifically Arab interpretation of Abrahamic monotheism.

Description of the Prayer

The ritual of the prayer process starts with the *mu'adhdhin*, an employee of the mosque, performing the call to prayer (*adhān*) on the minaret of the building. The first *mu'adhdhin* of Islam was Bilāl, an Ethiopian slave among the first followers of the Prophet. That a black slave was calling the Arabs to prayer is of great symbolic significance. And even today his name is mentioned in the context of spirit-possession cults among black Africans who are themselves slave descendants or members of the lower classes.[16]

The *adhān* text, unchanged since the Prophet's era, is as follows:

> God is most great [thrice]. I witness that there is no God but *Allāh* (the God) [twice]. I witness that Muḥammad is his messenger [twice]. Come to prayer [twice], come to prosperity [twice]. God is most great [twice]. There is no God but *Allāh*.

As Delaney has suggested in her ethnography of a Turkish Anatolian village, the daily repetition of the *adhān* throughout one's life transforms it into a kind of embodied knowledge which cannot be ignored.[17] She also points out that the intervals between the prayers become steadily shorter as the day draws to its end. For Delaney, the long interval between the first and the second call to prayer stands for the innocence of childhood. Then, the following two calls close to midday symbolize adulthood, when temptations are many and people have to pray frequently. Finally, the last two calls, very close to each other, remind believers that as they come close to the end of their life they should remember God more often.[18]

With the call to prayer, those who will pray assemble in the local mosque or, alternatively, in private houses, shops, and offices. They usually form small groups, although many may pray alone, a habit that is rather discouraged as we have seen. Thus gathered, the faithful perform their ablutions, i.e. the ritual cleansing with water of the face, the hands, and the feet. For this reason, in many public places there are rows of taps where people can wash. In places with no running water, small plastic containers are used for the same purpose. Thus ritually cleansed, the barefooted believers step onto their prayer-mats forming straight lines (*ṣufūf*) behind the *imām*.

Strictly speaking, the term *imām* refers to the prayer leader of a group of people, a man of upright character, good reputation, and some (not necessarily formal) education. More generally, it refers to the leader of the Muslim *umma* in charge of all its affairs. For some, like the *shī'a* Muslims, the *imām* is the Prophet's successor and is responsible for the preservation and spreading of Islamic tradition. In the context of the mosque, it is the mosque preacher who serves as *imām*. This is usually a member of the *'ulamā'* social category with some "professional" knowledge of the Islamic tradition and often enough, in case of public mosques, he has the status of civil servant. Otherwise, when people pray impromptu in offices, shops, houses, or public areas, the above-mentioned criteria are applied in a somewhat ad hoc manner to whomever is chosen to function as *imām*.

As prayer leader, the *imām* stands in front of the congregation who follow his movements and repeat, almost simultaneously, his utterances. Everybody can function as *imām* and in no way should the *imām* be seen as the representative, deputy, or delegate of the congregation; thus he cannot be compared with the Christian clergy.

The structure of the prayer is always the same. Initially, the praying person touches his ears lightly with the tip of the fingers uttering *Allāhu akbar* (God is most great). After this he or she rests the palms at the lower part of the chest and offers a prayer praising God and asking for protection from Satan. Then the first *rak'a* is performed.

The term *rak'a* denotes a well-defined set of ritual utterances and body postures. During each prayer session, a *rak'a* is performed twice or four times in the following manner: the first *rakʿa* finds the praying person reciting the *fātiḥa* and other *Qur'ānic* verses standing with the palms against the lower part of the chest. Then, the praying person utters *Allāhu akbar* and, bending over, rests the hands on the knees proffering blessings to God thrice. Standing up again, the praying person offers blessings to God using once more standard expressions and then performs the first prostration. With the forehead touching the ground, the praying person glorifies God and then, staying in the kneeling position, shifts the body's weight onto the toes and brings the hands to rest on the thighs. In this position, the believer asks God for forgiveness and then touches once more the ground with the forehead offering more benedictions. Finally, the praying person stands up. The first *rakʿa* has been completed and the second one follows without a pause.

At the end of the second *rakʿa*, instead of standing up, the kneeling praying person sits back on the heels and, with the hands resting on the thighs, recites the *tashahhud*, the profession of God's oneness. After this, the third and fourth *rakʿa*s may be performed. When this does not happen and the prayer session is concluded, at the end of the second *rakʿa* the *tashahhud* is recited once more and a benediction is offered to the Prophet and his family. Then the faithful turn to each other saying "May peace be with you and the mercy and blessings of God."

The Collective Character of Prayer

Besides its external characteristics, the Muslim ritual prayer exhibits many internal traits which allow us to include it in a wider complex of techniques whose purpose is to cultivate the "proper" relationship between man and God, always within the overarching context of the Muslim *umma* and according to the principles of the normative Islamic tradition. One of the few anthropological studies of prayer in Islam, that of Saba Mahmood (2001), focuses on these issues.

Mahmood studied a pietist group which belongs to the women's mosque movement in Cairo. For the members of the group, a dominant feature of contemporary social life is the marginalization of religious knowledge and experience. This secularization (*ʿalamanā*) or Westernization (*taghrīb*) has transformed Islamic discourse into an abstract system of beliefs divorced from people's quotidian experience.[19]

To remedy this, the members of the group argue that neither the study and intellectual understanding of theological texts nor the popular forms of mysticism offer a way forward. What is needed is the application of specific strategies, an economy of discipline, as Mahmood writes, through which Islam will return to the center of one's experiential world.

Mahmood's analysis shows how by practicing *ṣalāt* the group members form themselves into subjects embodying certain qualities that classical Muslim piety cherishes, such as sincerity (*ikhlāṣ*), humility (*khushūʿ*), and fear of God (*taqwā*). What makes Mahmood's article interesting is that she approaches *ṣalāt* as part of a discipline regime that combines what she calls "pragmatic action," i.e. everyday activities organized by the group, with specifically formalized types of behavior which are part of a historical armory of normative Islamic tradition.

Through participating in group organized activities, such as informal gatherings, study groups, sermons and "scientific" discussions on the importance of prayer, praying regularly every day, and conforming to the moral and spiritual standards of Islamic pietism, these women seek to transform their everyday life in two ways. First, they try to suspend all emotions and behavior that run counter to what is considered to be "orthodox" Islamic discourse, not only at the level of action, but at the very level of intention. Second, they try to cultivate the appearance and strengthening of those emotional states which they see as characteristic of a "good Muslim." In other words, regular participation in the prayer routine, with all its well-defined sets of ritualized utterances, body postures, and expressions, allows for the cultivation and acquisition of genuinely *spontaneous rehearsed emotions* whose presence can gradually take shape in one's consciousness and whose nature can be honed through constant training in the prayer routine.[20]

Mahmood goes beyond the polarities of ritual versus pragmatic action and of spontaneous expression of emotions versus their rehearsed performance in ritualized contexts that a number of anthropological studies of ritual assume (Bloch 1974, 1975; Evans-Pritchard 1965; Leach 1964; Tambiah 1985; Turner 1976). Instead, she employs Asad's study of the genealogy of the anthropological category of "ritual" (1993) and Starrett's analysis of the concept of "bodily hexis" (1995a) in order to examine the manner in which her informants use the praying body "not so much as a signifying medium to which different ideological meanings are ascribed, but more as a tool or developable means through which certain kinds of ethical and moral capacities are attained."[21] In this context any "disparity between one's intention and bodily gestures is not interpreted as a disjunction between outward social performance and one's 'genuine' inner feelings," but as a sign of inadequate training of the self, something that can be ameliorated through more strenuous efforts and devotion to regular prayer and to the other activities that the mosque movement's discipline regime prescribes.[22] One can "learn" to feel, nay, to *be*, pious.

At the end of her analysis Mahmood advises caution, arguing that anthropologists should not attribute cross-culturally the same meaning, indeed the same significance, to emotions that arise during ritual performances. Regarding emotions as historically and socially constructed, she stresses the importance of ethnography as the only means to understand how individualized feelings and emotional expressions are related to specific economies of discipline.

Before continuing our analysis of the *ṣalāt*, it should be pointed out that Mahmood's analysis is interesting for one more reason; namely it demonstrates the central position that women can occupy in the context of everyday Muslim devotional life. It must be admitted that, almost inadvertently, one can form an exclusively male mental picture when thinking of praying Muslims, from which women are totally absent. Mahmood's analysis comes as a corrective to this bias, reminding us, as Tapper and Tapper put it, that "women too practise the central day-to-day rites of Islam" and that very often their performances "may carry a religious load . . . of greater importance to the community than that borne by men."[23] In their article Tapper and Tapper discuss the women's celebrations of the Prophet's birthday in a Turkish market town, showing how they "create and confirm the promise of individual salvation which is offered to all Muslims."[24] It is true that Mahmood does not follow her group of women outside the mosque, but we are permitted, I suggest, to imagine them as members of individual families and kin networks, and as workers and members of wider communities. There they may act as agents and exemplars of relatively well-defined modes of religiosity and piety alongside men who may perform their religious duties in a phenomenologically more visible way.

The Ritual Prayer in Society

Mahmood's hesitation concerning cross-cultural understanding of a particular quality of the *ṣalāt* – its use as the locus wherein Islamic spontaneity is rehearsed in the quest to mold "good" Muslim selves – can be further explored at a more elemental sociological level. As has been argued, through participation in the ritual prayer each individual believer shares in the experience of the universal imagined Community of Believers, especially when praying in the mosque. In a Durkheimian manner the *ṣalāt* appears to dissolve individuality and to allow believers to visualize themselves as members of the undivided and indivisible *umma*. But is it? A number of ethnographic examples suggest that the imagined unity of the Community of Believers is often a figment, not a present that is but a future to be. The political order is taxing the dogmatic principles although it does not annul them.

A first example comes from a northern Lebanese village where Gilsenan conducted fieldwork. Space conceptualization, Gilsenan writes (1990), is influenced by a running vendetta between certain descent groups and the dividing of the population in two broad categories: the big land-owners and the landless peasants.

There are two mosques in the village. One, a small rectangular building with no minaret, is situated close to a big tree in whose shadow the villagers pass their time with small talk. Nearby there is a spring used for the prayer ablutions and a plain table where the dead are washed. In other words, the mosque and its immediate surroundings constitute the public space around which much of the community's social life evolves.

There are, however, two features which transform this picture considerably. The first concerns the women – or rather their absence. The public space in front of the mosque is really restricted to men. For the women, the well outside the village serves as a meeting point. So the public character of the mosque and its environs serves only half of the faithful.

The second feature, Gilsenan continues, concerns another exclusion. Being the space for prayer *par excellence*, the mosque ought to be open to everybody, but it is not. A vendetta between two families does not allow their members to pray at the same time, as they should then acknowledge one another in a manner they might find disagreeable. That means that the two dimensions of the mosque, as "a sacred space and as socially central space, and the requirements of these two dimensions are sometimes in tension."[25]

The situation gets more complex when we consider the second mosque of the village, on the hill near the cemetery. Built in marble and stone, it is much larger than the other and its minaret rises above the whole village. However, it does not constitute a focal point of the community's social life. Built under the aegis of one of the most powerful local lords, who is now buried next to it, it serves only members of the land-owning families; the landless peasants and laborers are not to be seen in it.

Sponsoring the construction of mosques has traditionally been one of the privileges of the elite. Its purpose has not been so much to provide the space necessary for the *umma* to communicate with God (although this should not be automatically excluded as personal piety has always been part of it) but rather to be seen as a manifestation of worldly power and, in our case, as a means for the legitimation of the landlord's power over the peasants. The egalitarian character of the *umma* is certainly not disputed, but the differences in wealth and status are duly recognized as if they belong to a sphere of activities whose importance is transient and of little interest to God and His Prophet.

Our second ethnographic example concerning the practice of *ṣalāt* in society comes from the Sudan. As I have shown in chapter 2, the Arabized Muslim Northern Sudanese look down upon the animistic and Christian Africans of the Southern Sudan and, until the beginning of the twentieth century, had enslaved them in great numbers. During the colonial period (1898–1956) slavery was almost eradicated, but racial tensions remained alive, fanned by efforts to exploit the South and other peripheral regions economically for the benefit of the North. As a result, as soon as the country became independent a civil war broke out between the North and the South. After a period of relative peace in the 1970s, the situation got increasingly nasty with the 1983 imposition of Islamic law and the 1990s discovery of oil in the northern part of the South.

Due to the long practice of slave trading during the nineteenth century, a considerable part of the population in the North is of slave descent. This populous social category has adopted a great many traits of the Arab Sudanese Islamic culture in terms of habitat, language, dress, religion, customs, mores, and behavior. Indeed, most of them do claim an Arab ancestry, sometimes in parallel with, but contradicting, the half-hidden view of themselves as the original African inhabitants of the land, brushing off the painful reality of a not-so-distant slave past. However, along with certain tell-tale practices they may participate in, part of a fast-disappearing slave cultural milieu, the greater obstacle to their integration is their dark skin color, which condemns them to remain second-class citizens, along with the hunderds of thousands of more recent impoverished refugees and migrants from the South to the big urban centers of the North.

One would be inclined to think that this inequality, painfully obvious in the context of everyday transactions, should be obliterated or at least politely ignored in the context of *ṣalāt*. Sadly, it is there that it is more viciously manifested. As I had the chance to observe in many mosques of the wider area of the Sudanese capital, which is situated in the Northern Sudan and is the heart of the Arab Islamic elite, these "black Muslims" often form rows at the back of the mosque during the communal ritual prayer sessions. Certainly, there is no rule for this, but everybody understands that any other arrangement would be problematic.

The victims of this slight interpret it in a way that questions the hegemonic ideology of the North. As they argue, they themselves are the "real" Muslims and not the Northern Arabs because the "real" Islam does not permit any distinction between the members of the *umma*. Being racist, the Northern Arab Sudanese are accused of betraying the "true" nature of the egalitarian Islamic message.

For their part, the Northern Arabs maintain that the beliefs of their darker compatriots are confounded because they are based on an imperfect understanding of the Prophet's message. However, a closer reading of such claims reveals that for the Northern Sudanese it is Arab descent that has been elevated to being the mark of a "true" and deep understanding of Islam; after all, the Prophet himself was an Arab and the *Qur'ān* was revealed in Arabic. Such ideological positions are common enough in many Islamic societies in Africa among those groups who claim descent from the Arabs who proselytized the indigenous populations between the tenth and the eighteenth centuries.[26] It is thus ironic that when many of the self-proclaimed Arabs from the Sudan and elsewhere in Africa visit the Arab countries, especially Saudi Arabia and the Gulf States, they experience forms of racism at the hands of the locals.

It would be wrong, however, if ethnographic examples like those presented above made us ignore the collective and transnational character of Islamic discourse, especially within the area of the Middle East and North Africa which forms the focus of the present work, and more specifically the collective character of the ritual prayer. As I have argued elsewhere,[27] the adoption of Islam by the indigenous African populations was intimately connected with both political and economic considerations, as well as with a conviction that

Islamic beliefs and Islamic culture, dominated as they were by the Arabs, could offer viable solutions to problems of adaptation that large populations encountered when their "traditional" environment was assailed by the incoming Arabs. As I.M. Lewis has cogently argued, "[a] critical consideration here is the scope that Islam offers as a viable personal and universalistic group identity when socioeconomic changes are expanding social and experiential horizons."[28] What exactly Islam meant in each case was, as it is today, a matter of negotiation – as a rule between unequal partners – expressed in the maxim about the production of "orthodoxy" that is at the center of our understanding of Islamic tradition throughout the present work.[29]

The Friday Prayer

Without forgetting the complexities of reality as they emerge from the ethnographic studies, let me confine myself here to the analysis of the dissolution of the barriers between the person and the *umma* in the context of the Friday noon prayer, the *ṣalāt al-jumʿa*, whose very name refers to the collectivity as the corresponding verb root is *jamaʿa*: to gather, collect, unite, bring together.

The Friday prayer is specifically mentioned in the *Qur'ān*,[30] in a *sūra* revealed to the Prophet after the establishment of the Madīnan polity. This implies a period when the newly formulated Islamic institutions were in a process of consolidation and the concept of the Islamic *umma* was taking shape as a religio-political reality. This *Qur'ānic* endorsement makes *ṣalāt al-jumʿa* obligatory for every adult Muslim. Interestingly, *ṣalāt al-jumʿa* should "not be performed in the open air, or in tents or outside the town; but inside the town or village, in a mosque or a decent prayer house."[31] If anything, *ṣalāt al-jumʿa* is an urban practice bringing together under one roof all the members of the local community of believers, both men and women, although they pray separately.

The Friday noon prayer includes a sermon (*khuṭba*) consisting of two parts and a two-*rakʿa* prayer. The *khuṭba* is delivered by the *khaṭīb* before the actual prayer. Just like the ordinary daily prayer, the *ṣalāt al-jumʿa* has its roots in a tradition which depicts Prophet Muḥammad performing it in the courtyard of his house in Madīna. The practice continued after his death in the army camps of the advancing Arab armies and even later in the villages and cities of the Muslim polities.

During the Friday noon prayer each member of the congregation performs a personal prayer of two *rakʿa*s before the commencement of the actual ritual prayer session.[32] After the call of the *mu'adhdhin*, when most of the faithful are already in the mosque performing their personal prayer, the *khaṭīb* climbs up into the pulpit and delivers his double sermon standing. The two parts are distinguished by a short pause when the *khaṭīb* remains seated. After the conclusion of the *khuṭba*, the *khaṭīb* takes his position as *imām*, leading the faithful through the ritual prayer session.

The *khuṭba* has its origins in the pre-Islamic Arab formal speeches by judges or elders of an assembled descent group.[33] The Prophet's *sunna* includes many references to opportunities when Muḥammad used the *khuṭba* in order to announce his decisions concerning a vast array of issues, not necessarily related to Islam. This means, that right from the beginning the *khuṭba* was employed as a discursive domain where the political and religious dimensions of Islamic discourse worked together. Indeed, as Gaffney argues in his study of Islamic preaching in Upper Egypt, the *khuṭba* was the moment when the governor communicated with his subjects, announced his decisions, "sought to mobilise opinion on issues of general political, social, economic, and military relevance," listened to their reactions, tried to fathom their intents and forestall their designs. Naturally, the same was true on the side of the subjects as well.[34]

Gaffney's study analyzes in particular some of these dimensions of the Friday noon prayers in contemporary Upper Egypt. As he maintains, today the quality of the *khaṭībs*' rhetoric is much lower than in the past. Their power, too, to influence public opinion has been weakened. However, Islam is still a potent medium for official and popular mobilization and the *khuṭba* an efficient way of communicating with the masses, on one condition, though: its employment "within a virtually indefinable range that nonetheless prompts recognition as the charisma of the Prophet."[35]

That means that not every message is amenable to the strictures of the *khuṭba* form. The *khaṭīb* has to follow certain rules and to comply with particular traditions. For this, of interest is the case of the well-known Saudi Arabian *khaṭīb* al-Zaʿīr discussed by Asad,[36] because there we can discern the way in which specific technical terms of Islamic discourse can be used as weapons of political criticism, protecting at the same time the person who is wielding them from being accused of deviating from the Islamic path by charging the authorities of the country with un-Islamic conduct.

ZAKĀT: ALMS-GIVING

The third pillar of Islam, *zakāt* or *ṣadaqa*, concerns a tax imposed on certain forms of private property, which, despite this, is fully respected and legally protected in Islamic tradition. The revenue is then distributed among eight categories of the population at the bottom of the social hierarchy. *Zakāt* is often translated by Muslim analysts as "purity"; hence its association with *ṣalāt*. Other researchers argue that the Prophet adopted the term from the Hebrew-Aramaic *zakut* which referred to the offering of material wealth for the sake of paradise.

Before the *hijra*, the few Meccan Muslims offered assistance to the needy ones amongst them as a sign of solidarity and piety, but when they were established in Madīna this took a more institutionalized form. Several of those who emigrated from Mecca had left behind their property and lacked the means of subsistence. At the same time, through military campaigns the new polity became progressively more self-sufficient. A system was devised then for distributing part of the wealth to its most impoverished members. Perhaps, the actual form of this system was also influenced by the practice of pious alms-giving among the Jewish population of the town, but on the whole *zakāt* remained relatively fluid during the lifetime of the Prophet. In the *Qur'ān*, 9: 58–60 appears to refer to some disagreement over the manner in which Muḥammad used some *zakāt* proceeds. Then, after the Prophet's death, *zakāt* became a bone of contention between certain Bedouin tribes and the Community of Believers. It was only when Abū Bakr became caliph that *zakāt* became obligatory for all Muslims.

The *Qur'ānic* and *ḥadīth* rules concerning *zakāt*, which still underlie contemporary legislation, are particularly complicated and cannot be reproduced here except in a sketchy manner.[37]

To start with, *zakāt* is paid only by Muslims to Muslims. Non-Muslims are exempted, although they are liable to other forms of taxation. The *zakāt* tax covers particular categories of products and wealth such as fruit, domestic animals, gold, silver, and merchandise, but in all cases the government cannot tax wealth that is not freely declared by the individual. The eight categories among which the *zakāt* revenue is distributed are defined by the *Qur'ān* in 9: 60, but without clarity. The two problems which arise concern "those whose hearts have been (recently) reconciled (to truth)" and those who are dedicated "in the cause of God." It seems that the former include recent converts to Islam, something that has been used to accuse Muslims of spiritually motivated bribery.[38] The latter includes the *'ulamā'*, something that may lead to accusations against the religious scholars of endorsing interpretations advantageous to their own class.[39]

In any case, in itself the doctrinal framework governing *zakāt* reveals little about the role it plays in contemporary societies. There *zakāt* is associated with or incorporated into the welfare system, and its collection and administration are regulated through the (not always amicable) coordination of the state and the non-governmental sector. At this level *zakāt* is discussed within the framework of what is called Islamic economics, in conjunction with other technical issues of fiscal policy. As it would be difficult to reproduce this complex discussion here, I shall instead present some general points concerning the relationship between *zakāt* and social welfare in certain Middle Eastern societies. After this I shall consider three short ethnographic studies. It is only through the analysis of such case studies, which can then be used for comparative purposes, that one can hope for the emergence of a more complete picture of *zakāt* that goes beyond the deliberations of economists and political scientists.

Zakāt and Social Welfare

As Weiss argues, scholars agree that in the modern period most, if not all, economies of Muslim societies are run along secular lines dictated by global capitalism. The only way to put forward programs of comprehensive Islamization that would lead to the establishment of Islamic states is on the basis of principles deriving from the *Qur'ān* and the *sunna* of the Prophet. From this perspective, the very concept of an Islamic state, as employed by Islamists and other Muslim activists today, is a modern idea put forward "as an alternative to the failure of the various secular nation-states in the Middle East during the twentieth century."[40] Equally modern is the idea of Islamic economics which, according to Pfeifer, aims "to recapture the original moral and political authority of the anti-colonial movements that gave rise to state capitalism, but without the latter's domineering centralism and bureaucratic rigidities . . . Generally hostile to socialism, both for its atheism and its stress on material (rather than spiritual) growth . . .[41] as well as to capitalism for its deification of profits and its philosophical foundation on the model of *homo economicus*, Islamic economics thinkers present their ideas as "variations on a 'third way'."[42]

More precisely, Islamic economics puts at the center of its rationale the individual, but under the moral supervision of the *umma*; there is no autonomous individual as such. Secondly, according to this vision Islamic economics prohibits the payment of interest and future speculation on fluctuating market prices, as value cannot be generated out of non-materially productive activities.[43] Lastly, Islamic economics promotes the practice of *zakāt* and the reformulation of inheritance laws according to Islamic principles as ways of ensuring a baseline of decent living standards which would allow the faithful to fulfill their social and religious duties unencumbered. With this ends all agreement between economists. In all cases, it is difficult to argue that the motley assortment of Islamic economic institutions do comprise an Islamic economy or an Islamic sector.[44]

Returning to *zakāt*, Weiss identifies the major difference between Muslim economists on its allegedly compulsory or voluntary character.[45] Those arguing for the latter stress that *zakāt* should be seen as a form of temporary financial assistance loosely associated with the state and not as the basis of a comprehensive welfare system. Those arguing for the former, see *zakāt* as a paramount responsibility of the government. Inherent in this disagreement are two opposing views on the very nature of an Islamic economic system. Those who see *zakāt* as a government responsibility tend to support the "minimisation of the distributive gap . . . [as] the major social goal of an Islamic state."[46] Those who see *zakāt* as *temporary* financial assistance argue that "an Islamic economic system does not seem to strive for a total eradication of poverty – poverty as such is as much the target as it is in fact a crucial and much needed component of the whole system."[47] In no case, however, do Islamic economics thinkers accept a class analysis of society.[48]

Complex as this picture may be, it becomes more so when we admit into it the various *ʿulamāʾ* who treat *zakāt* as part of Islamic jurisprudence rather than economics. Here the central issue is the relationship between *zakāt* and other forms of taxation, as well as that with the revenues of the *bayt al-māl* (public treasury). Though interesting, the *ʿulamāʾ* deliberations on the issue are removed from everyday life as they disregard the fiscal and economic realities of contemporary Muslim societies.[49]

There are, though, some exceptions to this, as some amongst the *ʿulamāʾ*, in collaboration with other interested parties, have begun since the 1980s to call for the reformulation of the rules of *zakāt* and for a major reassessment of the role of the state vis-à-vis that of the burgeoning non-governmental organizations (NGOs) sector.[50] After a careful consideration of a number of recent *fatwā*s, Weiss stresses the following four points that should govern both state and NGO practices. First, Islamic governments should establish special bureaucratic mechanisms for the collection and distribution of *zakāt* under the inspection of the *ʿulamāʾ*. Second, the payment of taxes should not replace the payment of *zakāt*. Third, national, and when needed local, conditions should regulate both the collection and the administration of *zakāt* funds. Fourth, it is permissible to transfer *zakāt* funds to other locations as a means of achieving a legal target.[51]

This is then, in a highly formulaic manner, the legal framework that governs the practice of *zakāt* in most Islamic societies today. It provides a number of common principles which supposedly derive from Islamic law, while it allows for governments, local authorities, and NGOs to proceed according to local conditions. Most significantly, too, it puts *zakāt* in the service of Muslim solidarity worldwide through its administration by international Islamic bodies, such as those discussed in chapter 2.

Using specific examples, Weiss first discusses Kuwait, Bahrain, and the United Arab Emirates. In all three, the collection of *zakāt* is voluntary, that is, not legally enforced, and is administered by official or semi-official bodies which work in a way similar to Western NGOs, but are under government supervision, usually the Ministries of Endowments and Islamic Affairs or the Ministry of Labour (in Dubai). Moving from the Arab Gulf, Weiss briefly considers Morocco. There the debate centers on whether *zakāt* should become an obligatory tax. Discussions have taken place for a long time but have been effectively stalled due to technical and logistical difficulties, but above all due to popular mistrust of a state-supervised collection and administration of *zakāt* funds.[52]

Finally, Weiss moves to Muslim NGOs. Among the issues he raises is that in non-Muslim societies, Muslim NGOs have managed to cater for the growing population of local Muslims, thus functioning within the premises of Western civil society. However, in an Islamic context their position is controversial, as they can be seen as replacing the state itself in providing welfare services. This is problematic because most authorities, especially those associated with the *'ulamā'* and with state bureaucracy, maintain that only an Islamic state can legitimately collect and administer *zakāt*. The whole issue becomes more complex when one considers that both in Western and in Muslim societies, Muslim NGOs are using modern technology extensively – think, for example, of online collection of *zakāt* – which makes monitoring even more problematic.

Zakāt, Modernity and Civil Society

Weiss's article is not the kind of specific case study that would help us see through the contemporary politics of *zakāt* at the local level, despite its wealth of information and the use of examples. For this, one should turn to ethnographic studies of which there are but few. However, Weiss's analysis is useful because it demonstrates three important points that underlie all contemporary debates on *zakāt*. First, it places all discussion within the premises of an Islamic modernity. *Zakāt* is not seen as a traditional practice that has to be honored in a modern context. It is understood as a practice governed by principles enshrined in Islamic tradition, which should be followed as part of a wider project that calls for the Islamization of modernity as a way of establishing a vibrant Muslim vision in the framework of globalization. The full import of this will be seen in chapters 6, 7, and 8 where I discuss Islamic modernism and Islamism.

Second, the discussion concerning the reformulation of *zakāt* rules and the relationship between the state and the NGOs as institutionalized channels for the collection and administration of *zakāt* points toward the ongoing battle for the definition of Islamic "orthodoxy." Indeed, it is of crucial importance whether one accepts that only the state can collect and administer the *zakāt* or whether the NGOs too can be admitted to the process. In the first case, the state, any state, can garb itself with Islamic legitimacy, maintaining that it does everything appropriate towards the impecunious members of the community, all in perfect accord with the injunctions of Islamic law. In the second case, as shown in detail in chapters 7 and 8, Islamist NGOs effectively replace the (as a rule) financially weak state as main providers of welfare services to the faithful. This allows them to accuse the government of mismanagement, corruption, and in the end un-Islamic behavior and to demand the establishment of a "true" Islamic state.

Third, this brings to the fore the issue of Islamic "civil society." A very brief introduction is in order. Contrary to the ethnocentric view that recognizes civil society only in formal associations and, consequently, stresses its absence from the Muslim world,[53] anthropologists suggest an alternative approach. As Hann argues, we should refrain from perceiving civil society *negatively*, as referring "to a wide range of associational activity outside of, and usually opposed to, the state," and approach it *positively*, "in the context of ideas and practices through which cooperation and trust are established in social life."[54] This approach has the advantage of situating state and society in the same "seamless field of moral interaction"[55] and shifting the emphasis from elite groups to the grass-roots through "the study of the social and cultural framework of trust and cooperation."[56]

Following this line, another anthropologist, Richard Antoun, finds a vibrant civil society in a Jordanian village that has been "traditionally" expressed through the tribal principles governing conflict resolution. But this is only part of the picture. Through successive visits spanning three decades, Antoun shows how this model of civil society has been transformed or perhaps enriched. The village of Kufr al-Ma has grown both in size and wealth, mainly due to migration to Saudi Arabia, as well as the extension and improvement of local amenities and transportation. These changes opened up the village to a new worldview and ethos "that is more critical of government policy, more entrepreneurial, and more revisionary of kinship norms."[57] Antoun encountered these sentiments among many of his informants, but also in the context of newly established formal associations.

However, "one should not be hasty in concluding that civil society in the Western sense is about to prevail," nor should one relate directly what one encountered in the field to any notion of general political liberalization. The few voluntary associations do not dominate the community's life or social structure, and "vociferous critics of government programs and policies . . . are still a distinct minority."[58] Overall, Antoun concludes, yesterday's close kinship and neighborly relations are fondly remembered and the new individualistic ethos is criticized. "[T]he assumptions and mechanisms of tribal process remain part of pan-Jordanian social and political life."[59]

From an anthropologist's point of view, then, civil society can emerge in or through a combination of socially and culturally appropriate frameworks of trust and cooperation working along lines of tribal or other locally meaningful principles and through formal associations that may come close to Western models of social action. It is in this highly dynamic field that the previously mentioned Muslim NGOs operate, a field that to a large extent is constructed in terms of Islamic discourse and according to the dictates of the "orthodoxy" definition process, although other considerations and modes of concerted action, such as the trade unions, should not be excluded.[60]

That is why one should be careful with comparisons. External similarities between Muslim and Western NGOs are certainly important in themselves or even indicative of a convergence that may go beyond structural necessities and logistic considerations. But this should not blind us to the existence of equally important dissimilarities between the two that arise from the Islamic conceptual framework which informs the former's action in the wider community and their relationship to the state. Providing financial assistance to the less affluent members of the community in the name of Islam or, to put it more blandly, exercising a principle enshrined in the *Qur'ān*, a legal obligation that stems from the claim that man is only a guardian of God's wealth, never the owner, is significantly different from the humanist concerns of the Red Cross, Oxfam or Save the Children that operate in a different universe as far as human rights and human dignity are concerned. Similarly, questioning the state's ability to provide welfare services in terms of casting doubts on its "real" Islamic character – and thus denying the legitimacy of its existence – is qualitatively different from questioning government accountability or the wisdom or popularity of a policy in terms of budgetary constraints, asking for more efficiency, proposing parliamentary debate and supervision of the relevant civil service departments, or, as a last resort, demanding elections to save the country from incompetence.[61]

Lastly, the fourth point raised by Weiss's analysis concerns the introduction of Western concepts or tropes relevant to the organization of *zakāt* collection and distribution mechanisms in the public sector and in the private sector of the NGOs. This is akin to the previous two points as it is related not only to the structures and procedures that should be established and monitored for the whole process to function smoothly, but also to the social and moral characteristics attributed to those who are deemed recipients of *zakāt* financial assistance. The Moroccan popular distrust of a state-supervised *zakāt* collection, mentioned earlier, is one side of the coin. The other is provided by Wiktorowicz, whose work is discussed in some detail below. Wiktorowicz writes about the efforts of the Jordanian Muslim Brotherhood to garner support among Palestinian refugees by manipulating the local *zakāt* committee. In the end, the complaints about "unbalanced" and selective practices were so loud that the government removed the Brotherhood members from the committee altogether. Beyond the obvious point, concerning political manipulation and the exercise of patronage, assuming that all practices become the object of discursive analysis and political evaluation means that in our examples the Moroccan government and the Jordanian Muslim Brothers would have to put forward rationales that would legitimate their behavior. Such examples also demonstrate that the nature of poverty may become the arena for contested interpretations similar to those existing in the West.

Three Case Studies

Let me now briefly consider two short case studies by Benthall (1999, 2002) concerning Jordan and the Gaza Strip and one by Seesemann (2002) concerning the Sudan. Arguing that *zakāt* constitutes a kind of "financial worship," Benthall writes that contemporary Muslim governments use a variety of ways for the collection of *zakāt*. Thus, in Pakistan, Saudi Arabia, and the Sudan *zakāt* collection is fully controlled by the state, while in Morocco and Oman it is left to the faithful with the assistance of NGOs. Between these two poles, Benthall focuses on the Jordanian and Gaza Strip cases where the state and NGOs are working in unison.

Benthall's articles stress three important points. The first concerns the role of non-religious charities such as the Jordanian General Union of Voluntary Societies. This is a secular organization which handles substantial amounts of money, mainly some of the proceeds of the national lottery. Among the union's activities are the financing of nurseries and youth clubs for low-income families, care for the handicapped and orphans, and support for women's education in "traditional" arts.[62]

Besides the union, Benthall refers also to those voluntary organizations supported by the royal family, such as the Queen Alia Fund for Social Development, established in 1977, and the Noor al-Hussain Foundation, established in 1985. Both organizations have structures similar to the ones of their European counterparts and receive significant support from governments and international bodies. Without doubting their importance, Benthall wonders if such organizations attract more attention than they deserve, thus putting at a disadvantage smaller but more efficient schemes.[63]

The secular character of such institutions does not preclude direct references to Islam, which is anyway the official religion in Jordan. Especially in the case of the royal institutions, all references to Islam are made in a way that promotes a humanistic version of religion combined with the dominant state ideology concerning Jordanian national identity. As it were, the authorities try to balance their duties toward the transnational Islamic *umma* and those toward Jordanian citizens, some of whom are Christian.[64]

Secondly, turning to Islamic charity, Benthall maintains that *zakāt* represents the "first system of social security."[65] He also mentions Sayyid Quṭb, the Islamist intellectual and political activist, who claimed that the concept of *zakāt* is higher than that of Western charity and regarded it as "the outstanding social pillar of Islam." According to Sayyid Quṭb, *zakāt* should not be conceptualized as an unreciprocated gift because, as Benthall, following Mauss, suggests, such a gift hurts the recipient. On the contrary, *zakāt* has no such effect because it simply reminds people that human wealth ultimately belongs to God.[66]

Especially in occupied Palestine, Islamist groups such as HAMAS, and Ḥizb Allāh in those areas of Lebanon that were under Israeli occupation, have developed well-organized *zakāt* networks based on the vision of an Islamic community whose boundaries are larger than those of the occupied land. As Benthall writes, HAMAS experiences the occupation as a contemporary form of crusade against Muslims and turns the rhetoric of the Israeli political program, as well as all religious ideology on Greater Israel and its association with the Jewish biblical lands, on its head by declaring Palestine a *waqf*, i.e. a religious foundation to the end of time. In this manner, Benthall argues, *zakāt* acquires a specific political character.[67]

Lastly, another point made by Benthall concerns the connection between *zakāt* collection and the "Islamic aid" offered by international Islamic organizations, such as the International Islamic Relief Organisation and Islamic Relief.[68] The recipients could be people who have suffered from natural disasters or who wish to perform the *ḥajj*, the poor who are fed during the Ramaḍān, poor students who need scholarships, and Muslim populations who are persecuted such as Chechens, Iraqi Kurds, and Afghans during the Soviet occupation. It thus becomes evident how *zakāt* can foster unity at the level of the Community of Believers as a whole, a point also mentioned by Weiss in his discussion of recent *fatwā*s regarding *zakāt* practices.

Seesemann's article on the Sudan does not concentrate on *zakāt*, which it mentions only in relation to the suspicious appropriation of it by the Islamist government for the funding of its alleged "holy war" against Southern rebels, but on the charitable activities of two *ṣūfī* leaders. Still, the reason I consider it here is because it reveals how NGO-like humanitarian projects are inspired by religious injunctions. The first case concerns a program for the social rehabilitation of street children that is run by the *Tijāniyya ṣūfī* order in the capital of Dār Fūr province. In 1979, *shaykh* Ibrāhīm Sīdī established a *Qur'ānic* "school" next to a *Tijāniyya* mosque. Soon the school attracted a large number of street boys aged 6 to 18 years old, many of whom had an addiction problem. In time, the facilities improved and came to include dormitories and a complementary school, where children with learning disabilities were helped to catch up with their public school education. But most important was the vocational study program that the center offered, which included carpentry and metal workshops, as well as the center's "art" classes, where the children were encouraged to express themselves through music, theater, or painting.[69]

The motive spurring *shaykh* Ibrāhīm, a former teacher, into action was his conviction that the country's obvious socio-economic decline was the fault of the invasion of alien cultural principles (mainly from the West) and the devastating early 1980s drought, and the decline could be reversed only through the social rehabilitation of youth according to the principles of Islam. That is why the core of *shaykh* Ibrāhīm's efforts has always remained the memorization of the *Qur'ān* and the daily performance of the five prayers.[70] Even the methods of discipline, which included the chaining of recalcitrant pupils, allegedly followed the traditions of Sudanese Islam.

At the same time – and here lies the study's significance – parallel to *shaykh* Ibrāhīm's religious justification for the project, which he recorded in book form full of *Qur'ānic* and *ḥadīth* quotations, Seesemann notes important humanitarian considerations as well. As he writes, the *shaykh* "also borrows from the rhetoric of humanitarian aid by presenting his work for the youth as a contribution to the world wide fight against drug addiction and as part of the struggle for a better future on the planet."[71]

The second case considered by Seesemann concerns the huge Charity Hospital that *shaykh* al-Ḥajj Ḥamad Muḥammad al-Jaʿalī of the *Qādiriyya ṣūfī* order established in 1997 in Kadabas in the Berber region. There are three interesting points in this case. First, the construction of the hospital was undertaken by a civil association founded by *shaykh* al-Ḥajj specifically for the purpose of promoting social welfare: the Shaykh al-Jaʿalī Charity Society.[72] That enabled the *shaykh* to realize his project, which was on a far larger scale than *shaykh* Ibrāhīm's center considered above. However, the hospital's executive committee describe themselves in strictly religious terms according to the following *ḥadīth*:

> God has chosen some of his [*sic*] servants for the task of responding to the needs of the people. He loves them for their good deeds, and He endows them with His grace. They are secure from God's punishment on the Day of Judgement.[73]

The members of the executive committee see the hospital as part of a much bigger project at the center of which is the *Qur'ānic* school of Kadabas. In that sense, the concern with public health is seen as an almost automatic emanation from the members' activities in the wider field of religious education.

Shaykh al-Ḥajj was initially renowned as a "traditional" healer who treated patients with amulets, supplicatory prayers, and the bestowing of *baraka*. Now, without abandoning these activities, he is also an executive board member of a hospital with departments for surgery, internal medicine, gynecology, and neurology, as well as an eye clinic and a children's clinic, and with an impressive annual budget that is partly financed by Sudanese migrants to Saudi Arabia and the Gulf States and by the Saudi government itself.

The foregoing discussion of *zakāt* and its relation to social welfare and charity and the brief digression concerning the nature of "civil society" in a number of contemporary Muslim societies have demonstrated the importance of this pillar of Islam in the life of the Community of Believers as a whole and in all its local refractions. Compliance with the spirit of *zakāt* can be seen at two interconnected levels. The first is the level of rules which have to be worked out, interpreted, reformulated, redrafted in a manner that, from the point of view of those who are implicated in the process, allows its "traditional" meaning to pervade its modern applications. The second is the level of planning, logistics, and applications that flesh out the abstract rules and legal frameworks in order to produce real effects at the local and translocal level.

In accordance with what has been argued so far, seen as an integrated whole, this is a creative process that molds (one is tempted to say reformats) the past in terms of the present and informs the present with its past "traditional" bearings. Equally, it is a deeply political process, as it purports to be constitutive of Islamic "orthodoxy" that brings together different classes of actors: the *ʿulamāʾ*, the government and state bureaucracy, the various NGOs, and the recipients. The political character of the process is further accentuated by three factors. First is the association of *zakāt* with social welfare and taxation, which, together with pensions, are the most explosive issues politically. Second is its connection to Islamic aid transnationally as a comprehensive proof of solidarity across the Community of Believers. It may range from the innocuous form of help for victims of natural catastrophes or the financing of school building to the more politically charged assistance to separatist groups or militant movements. Third is the elevation of *zakāt* into a policy issue in the framework of civil society, an area where different conceptions of an Islamic public field of action is continuously redefined and where state prerogatives are continuously contested.

AL-ṢAWM: THE RAMAḌĀN FAST

The ninth month in the Muslim lunar calendar is Ramaḍān. During the twenty-seventh night of this month, the "Night of Power," God revealed to Prophet Muḥammad the *Qur'ān*.[74] According to a *ḥadīth* recorded by Muḥammad bin Isma'īl al-Bukhārī, with the coming of Ramaḍān the gates of paradise are swung open and those of hell are locked and the demons are chained.[75] Those who spend the Night of Power in prayer will have their sins forgiven. Also, in another *ḥadīth* compilation we read that during this night "God makes a decision and writes down who shall participate in the coming pilgrimage to Mecca."[76]

Ramaḍān is a month of fasting. The Arabic term which is used is *al-ṣawm* and refers to abstinence from food, all kinds of beverages including water, smoking, sexual relations, and a lot more. The Ramaḍān fast lasts every day from sunrise to sunset. Just before daybreak, a meal called *suḥūr* is eaten. After this, the fast runs until sunset, when people conduct their evening prayers and partake in a rather celebratory meal called *ifṭār* which is followed by a more substantial and festive meal later in the night, sometimes around midnight. Throughout the month, a feeling of intense religiosity can be detected in all aspects of social life, especially during evenings when many people may visit the mosque or participate in communal readings of the *Qur'ān*. Restaurants and coffee shops remain closed during the day, while people pray in the mosque rather than individually much more than at any other time. This atmosphere of religious alacrity is significantly heightened on every Friday of the month, especially on the last Friday of Ramaḍān. At the same time, Ramaḍān is a month of joyous celebrations and family reunions. In that respect, especially in urban environments throughout the Middle East, it has come to remind us of Christmas. However that may be, the religious importance of the fast is not allowed to wither. In many countries the Ramaḍān fast is legally obligatory.[77]

The Rules for the Fast

The Ramaḍān fast is mentioned in the *Qur'ān*.[78] Verse 183 of *sūra* 2 makes it clear that fasting is not a novel divine demand, but follows the example of the pre-existing Judeo-Christian tradition.[79] What perhaps is novel with the Ramaḍān fast is its absolutely collective character and a return to a form of legal stipulation that reminds us more of the Old Testament books of Leviticus and Deuteronomy (especially the former)[80] rather than the Christian doctrines on fasting. Besides this, fasting is recommended in a number of Prophetic *ḥadīth*.[81]

The precise rules governing the Ramaḍān fast are complex and, almost certainly, not known to the majority of people. The following examples are only indicative.

As Ramaḍān is a lunar month, its exact beginning and end are not always the same, as in the case of the date of Christian Easter. Thus, it is essential for all Muslims to find out exactly the date and time of the onset of Ramaḍān so as to prepare themselves, spiritually as well as practically, for the ensuing fast. As Buitelaar shows for Morocco, such preparations start during the previous month of Shaʿabān. Besides cleaning the house, these include a purification of the body through visits to public baths, bloodletting, and the end of possible alcohol consumption, as well as the "purification of the psyche" [*sic*] through participation in spirit-possession ceremonies (which are suspended throughout the holy month as spirits are considered to be chained in hell).[82]

Today, information on the timing of Ramaḍān is easily available through the mass media and the Internet.[83] In previous times that was not the case, especially for areas removed from the big urban centers. Of course, most people could see the new moon rising in the sky, but the necessary precision was not always there. As Fischer and Abedi write, the latter's grandfather was the first to possess a pocket watch so naturally he served as "the village timekeeper" and would wake up the villagers for the fast by singing hymns to the first *shīʿa imām*. Alternatively, people started their fast with the rooster's crow; roosters who were unlucky enough to crow untimely were considered a bad omen and had their throats cut.[84]

Before modern technology became widely available, the advent of Ramaḍān was everywhere declared by the state astronomers in cooperation with the religious scholars. Usually, announcements were made through the local mosques and the sending-out of emissaries. Gunshots punctuated the beginning and the end of each day of the fast. Today, the onset of the holy month is announced by city sirens and the media. Still, many people believe that the best way to learn when to start fasting is through a reliable person, someone whom they know to be a good Muslim. When told, one is obliged to start the fast.

According to Islamic law, all adult Muslims who are in good physical and mental health are obliged to fast. Those who do not fast are the psychologically disturbed, children, the elderly, and the chronically ill for whom fasting would cause undue strain. Pregnant or menstruating women, as well as those who are ill or traveling outside the city limits, defer their fasting until a more suitable time. Apart from the fact that such injunctions publicly proclaim the onset of menstruation, which in most cases is kept a private matter, they can also be seen as containing several obscure points. For example who should be considered to be adult or who is really a traveler? Such points have been elaborately discussed by religious scholars, sometimes to a degree which for some may look almost ludicrous.[85] But there is something more here. It seems that the rules concerning the fast were laid down with a different society in mind. Traveling by camel was the fastest way to get around, while city limits constituted a social and geographical boundary that was connected to the rhythm of everyday life in a much more straightforward manner than today. Today, many people travel on a daily basis, if only to go to work, and many live outside the "city limits."

Similar obscurities concern the actual content of the fast. Thus, a large number of practices have been singled out by commentators discussing what is and what is not permissible. It seems to me that there are two guiding principles behind the selection. First, the fasting person is considered to be totally obligated, except when medical problems need to be taken into consideration. Second, the fasting person is given the opportunity to experience tenderness and love, but not to the point of full sexual satisfaction.

Starting with the medical practices, orally taken medication, injections of nourishing substances, blood transfusions, and kidney dialysis break the fast and should be postponed until after the evening prayer. Dental fillings, asthma puffers, eye- and ear-drops, tablets placed under the tongue, oxygen, medication absorbed through the skin, gastroscopy, laparoscopy, taking samples for biopsy, catheters, medical tools inserted into the vagina do not break the fast.[86] For affection and love, the rule is that kissing, embracing, and foreplay are permissible. However, if a person cannot control himself,[87] then even such practices should be avoided as what may lead to forbidden acts should be itself forbidden.[88]

Where does all this leave us? Having discussed the fast of Ramaḍān with friends and others and having observed how people practice it in Egypt and the Sudan, I observed that most people do follow the general rules of fasting in a sincere manner, with not much attention to details. People continue working, albeit at a much slower rhythm than usual and maintain their everyday contacts. They meet, discuss how they fare personally with the rigor of the fast, occasionally joke about it, persevere, and more or less take their cue from each other. Mild rebukes may be expected as a matter of course, directed especially by older people toward the young, but these may concern more the latter's general attitude and an allegedly unseemly demeanor rather than specific acts, except in the case of not regularly attending prayer sessions.

Fasting and Feasting in Different Ethnographic Contexts

Muslims are enjoined to fast in Ramaḍān in order to develop a sense of "piety" and to enhance their feeling of "fear of God" (*taqwā*).[89] This is the standard explanation of the fast. Indeed, it is repeated in all the relevant studies

I have consulted, whether in printed form or on the Internet,[90] and has been confirmed by all my informants. Because of this, religious scholars argue that fasting should be accompanied by abstinence from all types of immoral behavior and thoughts.

In addition to this, *shaykh* Muḥammad Ṣāliḥ al-Munājjib maintains that the Ramaḍān fast offers important moral services to every individual Muslim, but also to the community as a whole.[91] At the individual level, when one feels hungry, one is less inclined to commit sins. So fasting is a powerful weapon against Satan and the evil spirits, as well as a tool used for exercising human will and steeling self-discipline.[92] At the social level, the feeling of hunger can make one more responsive to the needs of the poorer members of the community. Indeed, this has not gone unnoticed by Muslim theologians and other religious scholars who have theorized about *zakāt al-fiṭr*, a special type of *zakāt* collected at the end of the Ramaḍān. Lastly, a further point made by *shaykh* Muḥammad is that Ramaḍān allows believers to act in a way that will provide the community with living examples of true Muslim deportment and character.[93] It seems, then, that the most significant dimension of Ramaḍān's social importance is its confirming of the community's inner unity and single-mindedness.

A "Return to Tradition"

Indeed, all these elements can be found in Buitelaar's study of Ramaḍān in the Moroccan towns of Berkane and Marrakech, the only anthropological full-length study of the Ramaḍān fast. While at the surface Buitelaar's informants maintain that they fast in order to be Muslim, to learn to be patient, to become healthy and strong, or in order for rich and poor people to be equal,[94] at a deeper level they seem to be concerned with their positioning of themselves as Muslims and as members of Moroccan society. Buitelaar analyzes this in terms of three notions: *umma* (Community of Believers), indicating "the capacity of the fast to unite all Muslims"; *ṭahāra* (purity), referring to the importance of purity in the Moroccan ethos; and *ajr* (religious merit), referring to the gaining of merit through fasting and through the performance of good deeds occasioned through fasting.[95]

What springs from Buitelaar's rich ethnographic description is that Ramaḍān festivities construct a framework allowing for the temporary "restoration" of many Moroccan traditions. At a superficial level this seems to concern simple practices, like the use of "traditional" cooking methods for the preparation of "traditional" dishes, especially the *ḥrīra* Ramaḍān soup.[96] However, the manner in which these dishes are presented and consumed, as well as the activities organized around them, reflects something more. At one level, this traditionality is suffused with the elements of abundance and cleanliness. More food than usual is prepared and of better quality. It is as if people who do their duty to God throughout the day can be rewarded with nothing less than that when they retire to their homes. "It should have been like that every day; this is true and blessed life in God" is the subtext I read beneath the ethnographic description, and also when I hear the congratulatory formulaic remark "*mebrūk* '*lil Remḍān*" (blessings be upon you this Ramaḍān) and the reply "*Allāh ibārak fīk*" (God bless you).

At another level, all this is organized around the privileged notion of the extended family. This acts as a conduit through which Ramaḍān's blessings, its abundance, and holy joy connect each and every individual, thus making everybody a partaker in the holy feast and, by extension, in the feasting community. This is all organized in circles. It starts with the extended family whose members make every effort to meet around the table as often as possible and share the evening breaking of the fast. Next, this sense of communion is extended to friends and neighbors as well, whose presence around the festive family table is believed to accrue *ajr*. Lastly, in a symbolic manner, this sense of communion comes to include all Moroccans, indeed all Muslims, presenting them as one people "breaking the fast by eating the same soup."[97] In a manner of speaking, then, Ramaḍān festivities organize the construction of a traditional template wherein Moroccans find what they seem to lack or to overlook during the rest of the year due to the particularism characteristic of everyday life: piety, joy, and conviviality as members of a single community that can be symbolically extended to include the entire *umma*.

At the same time, Buitelaar notes three important characteristics of Ramaḍān festivities which significantly complicate this picture. The first is the "blurring of, or even challenge to, normal moral standards"[98] that a temporarily more tolerant than usual society allows, such as the semi-open meetings of unmarried couples which are facilitated by the general gaiety and mobility of both sexes under the cover of dark. This Buitelaar finds "typical of the liminal character of Ramadan."[99] I am not certain if that is an adequate interpretation, especially as the author seems to base her argument on impressions from the rich upper-class neighborhood of Gueliz, which is described as Westernized and as totally removed from the old city of Marrakech festivities, while she admits that in the smaller town of Berkane the younger girls were not even allowed to go and pray in the mosque with their brothers.[100] In her discussion of Ramaḍān as a ritual complex, where Buitelaar discusses the notions of *umma*, *ajr*, and *ṭahāra* as expressions of a liminal sacredness, we can see more clearly the liminal traits of the holy month.[101] As she writes, the fact that normal classification patterns fade or are turned upside down during Ramaḍān (for example, social activities are organized around the time of breaking the fast) draws attention to the basic conceptions that underlie the Moroccan worldview. Also, the emphasis on the tradition of collectivity demonstrates the distance between the everyday and the ideal.[102]

The second characteristic is that Ramaḍān festivities, and by implication the manner in which the meaning of the fast is conceptualized, can vary widely with class and locality. I am not referring here to phenomenological differences related to local customs, but to the atmosphere that imbues the occasion. As Buitelaar writes, those belonging to the Europeanized upper classes live in apparent seclusion in their rich neighborhoods and "are not aware of the fact that several of the festive Ramadan traditions are still performed within the old city walls."[103] Although she appears to construct a vision of traditionality that has been lost to or abandoned by the Europeanized elites, a questionable proposition, Buitelaar is correct in her observations concerning the existence of class differences in the way Ramaḍān is perceived.

Lastly, the third characteristic is the gendered character of the Ramaḍān fast. On the one hand, in comparison to other collective rites focusing on the *umma*, women are much more visible during Ramaḍān as they fast alongside and in the same way as men.[104] However, their activities seem to stress the family and the local community rather than the *umma* as a whole. It is they who clean the house and prepare the festive food without dispensing with their "ordinary" household chores, thus preparing the place for the extended family gathering. It is they who distribute bread to the neighborhood children, offer soup to mendicants, and prepare couscous for those men who pray in the mosque. It is they, too, who visit the tombs of the saints and the cemeteries to obtain blessing, as well as the spirit-possession houses at the end of the Ramaḍān to pacify the spirits.[105]

On the other hand, women's activities during Ramaḍān and the value of their fast are considered to be inferior to those of men. If fasting is seen as a source of religious merit, women get less of it because they do not fast during their menses. Then, they are not allowed or encouraged to go to the mosque and, consequently, they are left out of most mosque-centered practices which are more directly associated with the notion of the Islamic *umma* as a whole. Women deal with this slight in a variety of ways, emphasizing among other things the notion of *ṣabr* which can be rendered as patience, endurance, or tenacity. This very important *Qur'ānic* notion, Buitelaar argues, was seen by her informants as a female virtue. As she writes, "[w]omen attribute their superiority in exercising *ṣabr* to the confined space within which they spend their lives. Unlike men, they do not leave the house, seeking distraction out of doors to forget their sorrows."[106] From this point of view, *ṣabr* is paired with *'aql* (reason), which is connected more directly with men, and both are seen as ways of achieving control over passions and desires. So,

> if the core meaning of Ramadan is putting to the test the self-control of Muslims . . . then *ṣabr* may be considered the female counterpart of *'aql*. Therefore, the following rephrasing of Eickelman's argument represents more closely the views of most Moroccans: "The celebration of Ramadan distinguishes men with reason and women with endurance."[107]

A Rather Low-Key Affair

I shall now turn to another ethnographic example of Ramaḍān festivities, this time among the impoverished shanty-town dwellers in the Sudan where I conducted my fieldwork. If anything, the Sudanese case highlights the importance of economic and class considerations – more precisely, ethnicity rather than class, although the two are interconnected – in Ramaḍān practices. In that sense, it questions the idea that wants Ramaḍan to confirm the community's inner unity and cohesion in an almost automatic Durkheimian fashion. The general notion is not denied, but it should be put in perspective in order to be analytically valid.

The first Ramaḍān fast I ever encountered was in Khartoum in 1989. That period was a difficult one for the Sudanese capital which was suffering from prolonged power cuts during the day. Fans, air-conditioning, water-coolers and refrigerators were not functioning while the temperature was above 100°F. In such conditions, not being allowed to drink water forced people to stay at home or to keep their activities to the minimum. All canteens and restaurants in the city were closed, most shops were empty, and very few cars were out on the streets. Both the center and the residential neighborhoods gave off a sense of mild resignation. As it happened, it was the time that I had to renew my visa. When I went to the Ministry of Interior to get my passport stamped, I was shown into a room with two offices. The fan was not working and the customary tea never came. The window was closed just to keep the sun outside. After a while, the two clerks and I were sleeping in our chairs affected by the stultifying heat.

I worked in the outskirts of the capital in Umm Badda Janūb, a shanty-town of several thousand people, especially from the Nuba hills, Dār Fūr, and the Southern Sudan. Except for the latter, who were Christian and tended to live close to each other, the rest were Muslims. Umm Badda Janūb had no electricity or running water. Bus and mini-bus connections were erratic. Most of the mud houses had been significantly damaged by the unprecedented flood of August 1988. In many places there were no roads any more; potholes, rubble, and garbage could be seen everywhere. Many people were living in sacks and makeshift tents made of plastic, wooden planks, and all sorts of junk. The few shops were rather sad places with dusty, empty shelves. Only the fruit and vegetable markets were colorful and busy during the morning, but with Ramaḍān things were not as lively as before. The heat, the tense political atmosphere (which eventually led to an army coup), and the deep economic depression were taking their toll on the people. Things brightened up only in the evenings, but again in no way comparable to Buitelaar's Morocco. Certainly, the situation was different in down-town Omdurman, in the heart of the old city, or near the mausoleum of the Mahdī. But in Umm Badda Janūb only a faint echo of those festivities reached the people there with the evening breeze.

Most people working outside the area had to walk a considerable distance from the main bus stations to their houses, a process that was concluded for the majority in the early evening. The fast was broken with some bread, fruit, and a cup of tea. After that, the evening prayers commenced. In the neighborhood, near the house of one of my hosts, there was a small mosque. It was a simple rectangular shape, a mud construction slightly bigger than the ordinary houses. The gathering crowd consisted entirely of men. I knew several of them. They were Nuba people who had come to the capital as migrants in the late 1970s. Forming neat rows, they performed their evening prayers in a rather hurried way, furtively. The mosque did not attract many people because it was far from the main road and everybody wanted to be home and eat with the family. That mosque never managed to fulfill its role as a community center for neighborhood activities – in contrast to the neighboring house of *shaykha* Nūra al-Nūbawiyya, a spirit-possession group leader.

In individual houses the situation was different. Relations and neighbors gathered together around the *iftār*. Men and women ate separately and the children ate with their mothers or sisters, but young boys sneaked out to join the men who usually sat outside the house. The mood was light, and conversations wandered around many things. What was striking was the quality and quantity of food offered, especially on Fridays. In the beginning, I thought that that was a peculiarity of the people I knew, but very soon realized that most families followed the same pattern. Considering the abject poverty of the people of Umm Badda Janūb, it was extraordinary. Discussing the issue with my informants, I realized that a large percentage of the households' funds went towards this conspicuous Ramaḍān consumption. Moreover, people bought things from the local shops on credit, thus running up a considerable debt. Still, I did not come across the situation described by Susan Kenyon for Sinnār, a town in central Sudan, where during the holy month families refurbished their houses and bought new clothing.[108] Most probably, the main reasons for this difference was that when I did my fieldwork in the Sudan the country was in a desperate economic and political situation and that Kenyon worked with people who could be described as middle-class Sudanese of Arab descent, whereas I worked with poor migrants and descendants of slaves.

So for the people of Umm Badda Janūb, Ramaḍān was a special month, but not one of gratifying festivities or, indeed, of deep religiosity. Only once did I see a gathering of older people sitting outside a canteen on the main road of the neighborhood reciting the *Qur'ān*. On the other hand, when I visited friends in the middle-class neighborhood of Mūraḍa on the River Nile, such occurrences were more common. The same is true for the *ṣalāt al-tarāwīḥ*, the long evening prayers of Ramaḍān. This does not mean that the people of Umm Badda Janūb were less religious; they were simply impoverished migrants living in a state that regarded them as second-class citizens because of their dark color, their traditions, and their religious practices, i.e. for the very fact that they were not Arab.

Significantly, the people I worked with in Umm Badda Janūb celebrated Ramaḍān, or rather the end of it, in their own way, though they certainly participated in the general celebratory climate of the national bank holiday. Being members of *ṭumbura*, a spirit-possession cult that belongs to the *zār* cult complex that is widespread throughout Muslim Africa and in certain areas of the Middle East,[109] they celebrated the end of Ramāḍān with a ritual in the name of *shaykh* ʿAbd al-Qādir al-Jīlānī, the twelfth-century *ṣūfī* founder of the *Qādiriyya* brotherhood, one of the most popular in the Muslim world. Claiming a spiritual kinship with him, many *ṭumbura* people also visited the Qādirī Ramaḍān celebrations at the tomb of *shaykh* Ḥāmid al-Nīl, just outside the southern borders of Umm Badda Janūb. Similar celebrations were held by other *ṣūfī* orders in their headquarters in the Sudanese capital. Having carefully read Buitelaar's previously mentioned account of the Ramaḍān festivities in Morocco, I can now argue that more than anything else my Sudanese material from Umm Badda Janūb reflects her Moroccan informants' preoccupation with the return of the spirits.[110] But even this celebration is rather underrated when compared with the other two annual celebrations of most spirit-possession groups, on the Prophet's birthday and on the twenty-seventh of the month Rajab on which the Prophet's ascent to the heavens is commemorated.

As for a "return to tradition," this is something that cannot readily be applied in the case of Umm Badda Janūb. Being relatively recent migrants from the non-Arab periphery of the country, most inhabitants of Umm Badda Janūb celebrate or participate in practices which they did not necessarily have in their homelands. Certainly, as will be argued in chapter 5, Islamization and Arabization have shaped their lives and the horizon of their expectations to a large degree. However, theirs is a situational identity which allows them to project Arab and non-Arab identification props according to the social context in which they find themselves. This being the case, a question mark is raised over the nature of the community whose unity Ramaḍān *à la Maroquain* celebrates.

As it happens, this is not related to any special conditions or characteristics inherent in Umm Badda Janūb or any other shanty-town. Differences can be identified in all sorts of ethnographic settings. As Bellér-Hann and Hann noticed in Turkish Lazistan when they were conducting fieldwork in 1983, most restaurants in the city of Rize (50,000 inhabitants) were closed during the hours of fast. Surprisingly, that was not the case in the nearby village of Sümer where many people were not observing the fast at all or if they were, they offered a number of explanations such as social reasons or "because it had been 'demonstrated scientifically' that to fast for one month each year is healthy for the body."[111] More than that, they discovered during further field research in the 1990s that the same area exhibited a higher level of religiosity than before, although the eastern regions still remained less zealous.[112] According to the authors, such differences have a long history which it is difficult to reconstruct. But this is not a reason to disregard it in favor of unsubstantiated and simplistic generalizations.

Religious Consumption

This discussion of the Ramaḍān feasting and fasting gives me the opportunity to consider the phenomenon of religious merchandise. This is sold in great quantities throughout the year, but especially on festive religious occasions, Starrett's "seasons of demand,"[113] such as Ramaḍān or the birthday of the Prophet, when an air of religiosity animates a socially sanctioned urge to consume – hence its treatment in this section. Religious consumerism is present in all the so-called "world religions," but in Islam one may wonder at it, since it is known for its rather austere religious practices, its simplicity, and its alleged propensity toward scripturalism. This picture is not accurate. A stroll in the markets and fairs of the big cities in the Middle East and outside the major mosques reveals a variety of religious wares sold to the pious and the tourists: *Qur'ānic* inscriptions embroidered in gold against black velvet, colorful reflecting stickers of similar content for cars, shop windows, and private houses, photographs of the *ḥajj* or important mosques, prayer beads, traditional "Islamic" medicines, amulets (*ḥigāb*), green skullcaps and various types of veils and headscarves, prayer-mats, clocks with the *fāṭiḥa* in the background, *Qur'āns* in all shapes and sizes, CDs, audio- and videotapes with *Qur'ānic* recitations and *khuṭbas*, computer programs concerning the calculation of prayer times or the advent of Ramaḍān, and hundreds of books on every conceivable issue related to Islamic law, astrology, divination methods, and so on are bought by the faithful all over the Muslim world. To all these, we must also add the various local delicacies – sweets, main dishes, and beverages – sold during religious celebrations.

The only study of religious merchandise in Islam that I know of is that of Gregory Starrett (1995). Discussing the concept of religious consumption in Cairo, Starrett describes in detail the various items and the manner in which they are sold, examines the way these are associated with or bring about a feeling of piety, and analyzes the apprehension which many Muslims feel about their consumption when they try to connect the phenomenon with the textual tradition of Islam. Presenting the ways in which the contemporary economic system "produces" the consumer of religious merchandise, Starrett defines three areas which future anthropological analysis should cover. The first one concerns the study of religious books and pamphlets, the drawings and comic strips in the press, as well as the computer programs with an Islamic content. The second area concerns an in-depth study of the very emergence of religious merchandise in a tradition that has been particularly hostile towards all types of iconic representation. Lastly, in the third area of study an effort should be made to reach comparative conclusions concerning Islam, Judaism, Christianity, Hinduism, and Buddhism. For Starrett, this is particularly important because it will give us the opportunity to understand how these traditions have been influenced by capitalism.[114]

Such a connection, one of many, can indeed be glimpsed in the following description of a recent book fair in Cairo, where religious consumption can be thought of in the context of a more inclusive domain of lifestyle strategies orchestrated by consumerism. Galal Amin writes:

> The overwhelming majority of books were religious, for this is the type of books middle Egypt likes best. The publishers, regardless of their intellectual leanings, had to display such books as visibly as possible, to attract buyers.
>
> Consider the names of the bookshops exhibiting in the fair: *Taqwa* (Piety), *Nur* (Light), *I'tisam* (Sanctuary), *Yaqin* (Conviction), *Wafa'* (Loyalty), *Fadila* (Virtue), *Iman* (Faith). The list is long. I even saw a bookshop called *Maktabat Al-Thaqafah Al-Diniyah* (Religious Culture Bookshop), as if the point needed stressing. Even publishing houses with a long history of secularism now place religious, or religiously-related, books at the front of their stalls, hoping to lure buyers inside. The loudspeakers – all on high volume – relayed recitations of the Qur'an, or announced the latest editions of one or another exegesis, now available on computer disk.[115]

But this lucid description of religious consumerism is only one part of a more composite picture. Following Galal Amin we see that the visiting crowd – mostly veiled women and bearded men – who showed a marked interest in the religious ware displayed in front of them in abundance was also attracted by another seemingly different type of merchandise. Let me quote Galal Amin at some length.

> I came across an amazing bookshop, one I never knew before. The Gareer Bookshop publishes and sells books of high printing and design quality, almost all of which are about material success. Among those books was one that came out in the 1940s when American culture, and everything American, was just beginning to permeate our lives: *How to Win Friends and Influence People*, by Dale Carnegie. At the time, we knew that this book was a great success all over the world and had sold millions of copies in various languages. Yet, some of us remained dismissive of the book, because of its cynical approach to friendship and success. Now, this book is available, not to the handful of intellectuals who may be sceptical of its value, but to thousands of Egyptians thirsty for this exact kind of knowledge – the very people who have grown accustomed to US television programmes, and who can easily identify with the book's content.
>
> The Gareer Bookshop's further selection included titles such as *How to Abandon Worry and Start Living? Discover the Leader Within* and *Stop Complaining and Start Succeeding*. All are by American authors; all start with the phrase "In the name of

> God, the Compassionate, the Merciful." This attempt to fuse the modern and the traditional, the extraneous and the indigenous, is everywhere. Next to Gareer was another bookshop specialising in computer disks containing educational material of the type that may help the young and motivated acquire marketable skills. Among the displays was a big box, designed in bright colours, bearing the image of a veiled girl with the caption reading: "Nuran learns languages." The bookshop apparently caters to this particular type of clientele, the one partial to such names as Nuran (Two Lights).
>
> It is clear that the new generation of the particular class that frequents the fair is torn between two propensities: one to religious tradition, and the other to the new, to computers and foreign languages. The merchants were the first to identify these two needs, and used their knowledge to make money. Regardless of how far one merchant focuses on one end of the spectrum, because of his leanings or past, he is unlikely to resist adding some titles, or commodities, satisfying the other end.
>
> This was quite evident in the large hall dedicated to computer products. As soon as you got through the door, someone would hand you leaflets detailing the special offers on computer accessories and instalment plans, or suggesting that you buy "the most powerful electronic dictionary" in cash or twelve monthly payments. You also were handed leaflets advertising computer disks containing religious sermons. As this happens, a computer set, placed right at the hall's entrance and emitting loud music, would be showing video clips of scantily-clad women, presumably to market both types of products, traditional and imported. A few steps away from the computer, a veiled young woman was distributing leaflets explaining the instalment plans, with the air of someone embarrassed by having to be so close to a crowd of young men watching partially nude women on the screen.[116]

It seems to me that this sensitive depiction of a behavior that the author considers typical of urban middle-class Egyptians brings forward an important feature of religious consumerism. This I would call the "lifestyle" element, a trait that would allow the classification of religious merchandise in the same category as self-help and personal actualization merchandise, which ranges from guides to spirituality and anti-stress therapies to manuals on *How I Did It!* by self-made millionaires and market gurus. The fact that computer programs and foreign-language learning kits were also included in a display attracting the same people who would buy guides to Islamic rituals may attest to the existence of an inner link between all these outwardly disparate faces of consumption, faces that cater for a deeply felt need to belong, to be grounded in a tradition, and for the necessity to improve within the framework of modernity and according to the logic of its sovereign emblem, the market. It is these two sides of lived experience that inform people's subjectivity. They are not opposed to each other but complementary, though always in a creative tension. In a simplified manner, they could be seen as dimensions of experience locked in a continuous interaction with each other.

Another element of religious consumerism I would like to consider is the immensely popular festive television shows which dominate the religiously inflected sociability of "seasons of demand" like Ramaḍān. Devoid of direct religious connotations, such glitzy shows can be compared with those broadcast by Western television during the Christmas season. Armbrust's article on "The Riddle of Ramaḍān," a television program offering rich prizes to members of the public in various Arab countries for solving the riddles, is a case in point. Armbrust shows that the program, replete with lengthy advertisement intervals, structures the time after the evening prayers, facilitating "a transition from fasting time to 'normal' time."[117] In some versions the show celebrates spectacular illustrations of an imagined community, as in the case of the United Arab Emirates, where the stage represents a "traditional" Bedouin campfire with the addition of a large black Mercedes from which the son of the country's ruler dispenses prize money.[118]

What Armbrust is stressing is that such programs are not "inauthentic." Being instances of an "invented tradition"[119] that promotes specific types of material consumption does not make them false in any way, as one should not assume the previous existence of a non-materialistic and truly spiritual Ramaḍān. Dismissing all forms of piety and "fundamentalist" [*sic*] fuss – though he salutes such interventions as discursive instances of disapproval – Armbrust argues that

> A religious holiday blurs into a ritual of mass consumption. In public culture disseminated by the mass media, the religious obligation of fasting during the month of Ramadan has become the twin of the holiday Ramadan . . . The two aren't exactly the same, but it is becoming increasingly difficult to pull them apart.[120]

At the same time, as the previous examples from Morocco and the Sudan suggested, this "ritual of mass consumption" has very clear class and cultural underpinnings, something that Armbrust's analysis notes only to a degree. In a sense, just like all "religious holidays," Ramaḍān transforms the family and the community into veritable consumption sites, or, more accurately, highlights this structural characteristic of theirs in relation to religious consumption. Participating in Ramaḍān festivities, one could argue, can be seen in terms of "sampling" Islam through the consumption of Islamic "heritage" in a multitude of localized forms of recipes, television shows, new clothing, religious merchandise, the giving of gifts, family reunions, or participation in special religious practices. How far this "sampling" may go and which forms it may finally take depends to a considerable extent on the financial capabilities of the faithful, the prestige that such consumption patterns are endowed with in each particular community, and the standards of piety with which they are popularly associated.

These are important indices of the way in which forms of religiosity are articulated with prevailing socio-economic structures, a fact that calls for more detailed ethnographic studies of Ramaḍān celebrations in different social contexts. To be sure, the previously mentioned Islamic "heritage" is everywhere saluted by those who "consume" it as "authentic" and "orthodox," as Armbrust has rightly noted for the United Arab Emirates Ramaḍān television shows. However, from an anthropological point of view we must always avoid endowing this with an aura of essentialism and approach it as "claims to 'authenticity' and 'orthodoxy'" advanced by local agents who occupy specific social and economic positions in their respective communities.

The Politics of Ramaḍān

The previous discussion should not deter us from recognizing the importance of seeing Ramaḍān in the light of the united imagined Community of Believers. At the level of rhetoric, at least, this is the dominant notion, the lens through which both the faithful and the infidels are invited to understand the holy month. Especially today, many Muslims in the Middle East may need such a confirmation of unity in the face of what they perceive as Western hostility towards Islam. Similarly, this dimension of Ramaḍān is often seen by non-Muslims as an indirect threat to them. In other words, for both Muslims and non-Muslims Ramaḍān has acquired during the last few years an overtly political character.

This view is reflected on the tighter security measures enforced by the Israeli government during Ramaḍān and by the various articles and debates in the mass media concerning the Palestinian struggle and the fighting in Afghanistan and, more recently, in Iraq. Thus, in 2000 the traditional Ramaḍān lamps in Cairo had the shape of the mosque of ʿUmar in Jerusalem. In addition, by pressing a small switch one could listen to the classic song of Fayrūz, a Lebanese diva, lamenting the Israeli occupation of Jerusalem in 1967.[121] The whole device was made in China.[122] On the whole, though, despite the fierce rhetoric, the political symbolism of Ramaḍān in the Arab world has not been transformed into more direct action that would amount to the emergence of a popular movement. Only at the level of urban guerrilla warfare does the holy month occasionally provide an opportunity for covert action, such as the Baghdad blasts that killed 43 people on the first day of Ramaḍān in 2003.[123]

So it is that, through an emphasis on festive materialism seen in the wider context of market mechanisms and the construction of consumer subjects, on personal piety where the fasting subject is made more conscious, at least ideally, of his or her neighbor's needs, and on the politics of the Muslim *umma* and the difficulties its members encounter in hotspots such as Palestine and Kashmir, Ramaḍān acquires a fitting multivocality that justifies the central place it has always had in Muslim social experience.

AL-ḤAJJ: THE PILGRIMAGE TO MECCA

Another of the "five pillars" of Islam which is well known to non-Muslims is the *ḥajj*, the pilgrimage to Mecca – and often to neighboring Madīna as well.[124] According to Islamic Law, the pilgrimage should take place at least once during a believer's lifetime, although more visits to the holy places are certainly considered to be spiritually enhancing.

Pilgrimage Preconditions and the Pilgrims' Identity

The *ḥajj* takes place during the twelfth month of the Islamic calendar, that is the month after Ramaḍān. It always follows exactly the same steps. As the four legal schools of Islamic tradition stipulate, in order to participate in the pilgrimage, one should fulfill the following criteria: being (a) Muslim; (b) adult; (c) free (i.e. not slave); and (d) able to undertake the task. In practice, the majority of pilgrims undertaking the *ḥajj* are men. As for the women pilgrims, these are usually newly-weds on their honeymoon or married women after menopause.[125] In recent decades, it is not uncommon to see whole families undertaking the *ḥajj* together. Interestingly, many of them come from the Muslim communities of Europe.

Especially the last of the four legal points mentioned above is interpreted in different ways by the four schools. The first three schools (those of Muḥammad Ibn Idrīs al-Shāfiʿī, Aḥmad Ibn Ḥanbal, and Abū Ḥanīfa) directly refer to the ability of the believer to collect the funds necessary for the completion of the project. The fourth one (that of Mālik b. Anas) differs in this respect, maintaining that although the *ḥajj* should not be undertaken under conditions which endanger the pilgrim's life, the inability of the believer to collect money before his or her departure to Mecca cannot be seen as an excuse for the postponement of the pilgrimage or the abandonment of the project altogether. For instance, any financial problems could be dealt with through occasional employment during the long journey to Mecca. As for health difficulties, even the blind should go under the care of suitable companions.

Such legal stipulations are of great importance at the practical level. Mālik b. Anass' school of law is predominant in most Western African societies, whose more than two hundred million Muslims are on the whole seriously economically constrained. Making the *ḥajj* means that a great number of West African pilgrims are turned into economic migrants in countries closer to Saudi Arabia, such as the Central African Republic, Chad, and, mainly, the Sudan. In the long run, this has produced significant demographic changes in the host countries, while it has also facilitated the development of a dynamic dialogue between the various local Islamic traditions of Sudanic Africa, that vast belt of sub-Saharan lands extending from the Red Sea to the Atlantic Ocean.[126]

All these issues should be seen as part of the pilgrimage process itself which should not refer exclusively to the actual stay of the pilgrims in Mecca. As a project, the *ḥajj* starts the moment the pilgrim leaves his or her community in order to take part in this wondrous and often difficult journey or even when the first preparations are made.[127] Similarly, the *ḥajj* is concluded with the return of the pilgrim and the subsequent conversations on the subject with other members of the community, many of whom may undertake the journey themselves in the following years. I shall return to this point later in the chapter.

One of the few anthropological studies that deals with some of these not very well-known issues of the *ḥajj* is that of Bawa Yamba (1995). His book is basically concerned with the formation of identity among the populous West African (mainly Hausa) pilgrims who have settled themselves in the Sudan.[128]

An intriguing characteristic of these people is that, although they have been established in the Sudan for decades, have opened up businesses and started families, often with local Sudanese, they still regard themselves as pilgrims. And this despite the fact that they seem to be rather unwilling to conclude their long journey by crossing the Red Sea to Saudi Arabia. It seems that these people have done all the trekking from northern Nigeria only to settle down in the Sudan.

Yamba lays particular emphasis on two issues which he finds central in the process of identity formation among this migrant Western African population: human suffering (in the sense of everyday hardships) and the strength of God's will. According to the author, the pilgrims believe that the difficulties they have encountered through the long, arduous, and often dangerous journey from West Africa to the Sudan – a journey that may last up to two years because of political disturbances, inadequacy of transportation, and lack of money – increase the accumulation of God's blessing, which is the raison d' être of the *ḥajj* process itself.

This conception, Yamba continues,[129] is in congruence with the basic principles of Mālik b. Anas's legal school of Islamic law which, as has been pointed out earlier, is predominant in the pilgrims'/migrants' societies of origin. Indeed, the way in which the pilgrimage process is understood and theorized by the *ʿulamāʾ* of the school gives prominence to the diachronic dimension of its character rather than to the finite nature of its accomplishment.[130]

The second subject discussed by Yamba is God's will in the specific context of the *ḥajj*/migration. God's will is exemplified in and concretized by the formation *inshaʾ Allāh* (God willing!). From this point of view, the pilgrimage is transformed into that paradigmatic experiential terrain where human life is seen as determined by God's providence. What counts in the end is human readiness to comply with God's plan and not the actual result of the project itself.

Description of the *Ḥajj*

The *ḥajj* constitutes a special type of *ʿumra*, i.e. an individual visitation to Mecca that consists of seven circumambulations of the *Kaʿba* and the "walk of Hagar." It can take place at any time of the year, but as a rule most pilgrims arrive in town a few days before the official opening of the *ḥajj* so as to complete the *ʿumra* too. After this, they may rest for a day or two before the beginning of the *ḥajj* itself.

As soon as the pilgrim reaches Mecca, he or she changes into the *iḥrām*, two seamless pieces of white cloth. This symbolizes the departure from society and the effort to approach God.[131] In this condition the pilgrim is called *muḥrim* and is not allowed to cover the head (if he is a man), cut the hair or nails, use perfume, uproot plants, shed blood, kill insects, participate in any debate, or have sexual intercourse. In the case of women, they are additionally not allowed to cover their faces or wear gloves.

Almost upon arrival in Saudi Arabia, the pilgrims start chanting a special prayer called *talbiyya*:

> Here we are God, we are coming!
> You are related to no one.
> Here we are God, we are coming!
> Indeed, To you belongs the kingdom.
> You are related to no one.

Riding in coaches, the chanting pilgrims arrive at their hotels or camping areas in groups led by guides whose job is to complete the paperwork and direct them through the various stages of the whole process.[132] Then, almost immediately after hotel registration, the pilgrims are led by the guides to the central mosque, *al-Masjid al-Ḥarām*.[133] This is a vast complex of 160,000 square yards of floor space and a capacity of more than one million pilgrims. The mosque consists of a rectangular two-storey colonnaded arcade which includes a 500 by 350-foot oval inner courtyard with marble floor. At the center of the courtyard stands the *Kaʿba* and close by the footstep (*maqām*) of Ibrāhīm (Abraham) and the graves of Hagar and Ismāʿīl. The *Kaʿba* is covered by a black, embroidered cloth.

Following the guides, the pilgrims circle the shrine counterclockwise seven times. This is the source of the various well-known photographs of the human river surrounding the huge black shape of *Kaʿba*.[134] This ritual is called *ṭawāf*. The pace of circumambulation is brisk, and each time a circle is completed the pilgrims raise their hands as if saluting the black stone and exclaim *Allāhu akbar*. Reaching the *Kaʿba* in order to touch or kiss it may be impossible for the majority of pilgrims due to the sheer number of people involved. There is a feeling that one does not walk of one's own accord; one is taken round and round by the force of the *umma* itself, the multitude of believers who try to kiss the "touchstone" (literally) of Islam,[135] thus renewing their allegiance (*baʿyat*) to God. As Fischer and Abedi write, "[t]he circumambulation en masse is the primal experience of the *umma*, the maternal spiritual community."[136]

At the end of the final circle, the pilgrims pray two *rakʿa*s near Ibrāhīm's *maqām*, always facing the *Kaʿba*. When this is completed, the pilgrims enter an underground structure where they can drink water from the sacred Zamzam well. According to the tradition, after Hagar and her son had been turned away from the household of Ibrāhīm (Abraham), they took refuge in the desert. As Hagar was desperately searching for water, the archangel Gabriel revealed to her the Zamzam well.[137] Even today, pilgrims collect some of its holy water to take back to their families.[138] There it is used in the event of illness and to anoint the forehead of the dead.

The pilgrims are now ready to walk the distance between the Ṣafā and Marwa hillocks seven times, again in commemoration of Hagar's frantic efforts to discover water. The two hillocks, which are a quarter of a mile apart, are included in the wider complex of the mosque. The walk consists of a two-lane marble mall where the pilgrims walk a total of nearly two miles.

The duration of the *ʿumra* depends considerably on the actual date the ritual takes place. As the time of the *ḥajj* proper approaches, the number of pilgrims rises exponentially. Just a few days before the commencement of the *ḥajj*, it may take more than an hour just to get into the great mosque, let alone to reach the inner courtyard and the *Kaʿba*.

With the completion of the *ʿumra*, the pilgrims can change from the sweat-covered and soiled *iḥrām* – provided they cut a short lock of their hair – and return to their individual attire. They will put the *iḥrām* back on for the rituals of the *ḥajj* proper. In the meantime, they can perform time and again the *ṭawāf* (which stops only during prayer times), read the *Qur'ān*, and participate in communal prayers. On the whole, life is structured along prayer rules, with the call of the *mu'adhdhin* reaching every corner of the city. The only non-religious parameter that affects the pilgrims' activities is the heat which, especially in the summer months, can be unbelievably intense.

The ritual stages for the pilgrimage proper are common for all pilgrims and take place between the eighth and twelfth days of the month of Dhu al-Ḥijja. On the seventh, the pilgrims attend a *khuṭba* in the central mosque of Mecca. There, all the steps of the pilgrimage process are explained in detail. We must not forget that the acts we discuss here are highly formalized and concern people coming from different cultural traditions who often speak languages incomprehensible to each other. That is why the Saudi Arabian government is particularly careful to ensure there are no mistakes, oversights, or misunderstandings.

On the eighth day of Dhu al-Ḥijja the pilgrims do the *niyya*, that is they state to themselves alone their determination to proceed with the *ḥajj*, and then recite the *talbiyya* three times. After this, the hundreds of thousands of pilgrims, both men and women, forming a human river, head toward Mount ʿArafāt, 20 miles east of Mecca. Usually, the pilgrims camp for the night in the uninhabited village of Minā, five miles east of Mecca, although this has no special meaning.

In the past, this procession used to take place either on foot or on camels, while huge numbers of pedlars followed the pilgrims ready to cater for their needs in food and water. Today, multitudes of vehicles carry huge numbers of people, while the Saudi government has established first-aid stations every few miles.

Having spent the larger part of the night in prayer, the pilgrims leave Minā in the morning of the ninth and reach the stony but spacious valley of Mount ʿArafāt where the Hill of Mercy (*jabal al-Raḥma*) lies. Tents are erected there to protect the crowd from the fierce sun. From midday to the early evening the people participate in ritual prayers. A sermon is organized in commemoration of the Prophet's sermon in the same place, but the preacher's voice cannot reach everybody. Water and food are offered free of charge under the aegis of the Saudi government.

The ritual acts performed on the *jabal al-Raḥma* represent the culmination of the *ḥajj*. Many of the pilgrims simply stand, almost in ecstasy, from midday to sunset facing Mecca.[139] Others pray without pause. The place is full with supplications and pleas for mercy. In tears, they ask God to give them and their families health, to drive away problems and difficulties, to bestow paradise upon them. The emotional charge is so great that it could be argued that one could imagine the entire *umma* under the eyes of God.

As sunset approaches, gunfire and loudspeakers inform the pilgrims that they have to leave the Hill of Mercy and return to Minā. However, a few miles before the deserted village the pilgrims stop in Muzdalifa. They pray in the mosque and then they either sleep or continue to Mecca.

The following day, the bulk of the pilgrims reach Minā. As they approach the western exit of the small Minā valley, they reach *jamrat al-ʿaqaba*, an old construction consisting of three pillars. Every pilgrim throws seven small stones at it. According to the tradition, one of the pillars represents Satan who thrice tried to dissuade Ibrāhīm from sacrificing his son following God's orders.[140]

Now, the pilgrims are ready to offer God a ram in commemoration of Ibrāhīm's archetypal sacrifice. On this very day, the head of each family in the Muslim world who can afford it sacrifices a ram, thus connecting the *ḥajj* ritual with each and every member of the *umma* worldwide.[141] In Minā, the sacrificial slaughter takes place in a specially prepared area to avoid hygiene risks. The meat of the sacrificed animals is partly consumed by the pilgrims and the rest is offered to the poor.[142] After the sacrifice the pilgrims can attend to their personal hygiene. Also, in a symbolic act, the men shave their heads and the women cut some of their hair. It is then that the pilgrims return to Mecca where, on the tenth or the eleventh day of Dhu al-Ḥijja, they again circumambulate the *Kaʿba* seven times.

This *ṭawāf* around the *Kaʿba* is the first opportunity for the pilgrims to see the holy structure covered in its new black and golden-rimmed *kiswa*, which will protect it until the next *ḥajj*. When the procession concludes, the pilgrim can rightly call him- or herself *ḥājjī* or *ḥājja* respectively.[143] There is also the opportunity for many pilgrims to do once more Hagar's walk. After this, most of them return to Minā where once again they throw stones at the three pillars and return to Mecca for a final circumambulation of the *Kaʿba*. The following two or three days are devoted to social activities, including visiting the Prophet's tomb in Madīna. This period is also ideal for "pious shopping" for *ḥajj* mementoes like prayer-mats or photographs of the big mosques, etc. Such purchases are deemed to confer a blessing on the buyers.

On their return to their home communities, the pilgrims are regarded with great respect, something that is also reflected on members of their families. However, as Bellér-Hann and Hann argue, this recognition is not automatic. Referring to their own Turkish material from the Black Sea province of Lazistan, they point out that post-pilgrimage lifestyle plays an important role. "If [the pilgrim] refrains from alcohol and gambling and goes regularly to the mosque, the epithet haci [Turkish for *ḥājjī*] will be bestowed, not grudgingly or ironically, but with genuine respect."[144] This is only to be expected from the symbolism caught in the intricate web of meaning of the pilgrimage process. Discussing the stoning of the three pillars/idols associated with Satan, Fischer and Abedi bring forward the person of Cain, not as the archetypal transgressor, but as "a figure of repentance, [just] as the pilgrims are enjoined to repentence (tawba) and rededication to the rules of Islam."[145]

The material of Bellér-Hann and Hann also suggests that the *ḥajj* is a gendered experience. As has been mentioned earlier, the majority of pilgrims undetaking the *ḥajj* are men; as for the women, these are invariably married, except when they are daughters of families undertaking the *ḥajj* en bloc. Bellér-Hann and Hann confirm this picture, situating it in a wider context. As they argue, when the head of a family returns from the *ḥajj*, his enhanced status and accumulated social prestige are extended to his wife. This may account for her reluctance to make the journey herself, even if she has the opportunity. If, however, a woman does decide to undertake the pilgrimage, this can take place only after her husband has completed his and, usually, when they are "past childbearing age [so as] to avoid the possibility of ritual pollution."[146]

Analysis of the *Ḥajj* Process

In 1978 V. and E. Turner distinguished between those pilgrimages established by the founder of a historical religion or his first disciples and those exhibiting elements of syncretism between older and younger religious traditions. The *ḥajj*, they argued, belonged to the first type, although it certainly existed in the pre-Islamic period.[147] More recently, discussing Christian pilgrimage, Eade and Sallnow distinguished between pilgrimages to places regarded as *par excellence* centers of supernatural forces, those made to places which are seen as holy because of their close relationship with a deity or a saint, and those to places whose sacred character is attested by the written texts of a given tradition. Again, the *ḥajj* seems to belong to all three types.[148]

There is a more recent theory by J. Dubish (1995) which I find particularly helpful in our discussion of the *ḥajj*. Analyzing the Eastern Orthodox pilgrimage to the Church of Annunciation on the Greek island of Tinos, Dubish argues that the actual pilgrimage shrine should not be seen as a bounded and well-defined space, but as the center of a wide network of relationships extending over a vast non-contiguous geographical area. This area owes its existence to a sacred geography, i.e. to religious ideas and practices grafted on space.[149] Such ideas and practices do not concern the pilgrims alone, but extend to the mass media, the ecclesiastical authorities, and the governments of the countries involved. This implies that the pilgrimage center is characterized by an air of permanence as far its geographical coordinates are concerned, as well as by important elements of changeability in relation to accumulation of historicity and the meanings it carries through time.[150]

Dubish's deconstruction of the pilgrimage center as a bounded whole is a good starting point for discussing the dialogue between the global and the local in the context of the *ḥajj*. As Eade and Sallnow write, classical anthropology describes pilgrimage as a process through which different local communities and social categories can form wider collectivities.[151] So pilgrimage is understood as a way of spreading the "orthodox" views of the center to the periphery, that is the pilgrims' communities of origin.[152] Pilgrimage, then, functions as a legitimating mechanism that suppresses theological and other dogmatic positions which deviate from the "orthodox" dogma of the official political and religious authorities.

The opposite view has been advanced by V. and E. Turner (1978) who see the pilgrims stepping outside society and being transformed into "liminal beings" fully dedicated to the relevant religious tradition. During this process a sort of energy which society keeps under control through the strictures of social structure is freed in the form of a sense of brotherhood and absolute communication, bringing into being what the Turners call "communitas."[153] From this angle, the pilgrimage experience is opposed to the restrictions of structure and more particularly to those of the ecclesiastical authorities. On the contrary, it strives for the dismantling of boundaries and the disappearance of differences between the pilgrims and, by extension, between all members of the religious tradition.

In our case, what is experienced by the *ḥajj* pilgrims is the very essence of the global imagined Community of Believers, the *umma*. The hundreds of thousands of believers walking around the *Ka'ba* represent the pre-existing and, at the same time, emergent in material form imagined Community of Believers. This is perhaps why a particular photograph from the *ḥajj*, usually shot at very low speed so as to produce white concentric circles of a moving humanity surrounding the black, firm, and immovable mass of the *Ka'ba*, can be seen in many government and business offices, as well as in shops and private houses. It is the best proof of Islamic universalism and of the feeling of brotherhood among believers.

But is this a form of communitas anti-structure? Close though it may seem to be, it is difficult to imagine the Islamic *umma* as a worldwide communitas which is simultaneously structure (based as it is on sacred texts and Islamic law) and anti-structure. I think that the Turners based their analysis of the pilgrimage on their considerable knowledge of Western Christianity. It seems though that their knowledge of Islam was narrower. What they did not take into account was that Western Christianity is characterized by a particularly strong ecclesiastic hierarchy, whereas Islam is not. Hence their conceptualization of *umma* as communitas, a term which refers to the absence of, or the antithesis to, all forms of hierarchy. This is not valid for the *ḥajj*. After all, the *ḥajj* constitutes a legal duty of cardinal importance and, as far as its actual content is concerned, it is one of the most detailed pilgrimage choreographies in the world and one of the most sophisticated cases in logistics management.[154]

Competing Visions

Not being anti-structure does not mean, of course, that the *ḥajj* should be approached as a display of *doctrinal* unanimity and consensus imposed by a center. As will be seen presently, there have been confrontations with the Saudi security forces springing from divergent political views on the very nature and characteristics that the Community of Believers itself should exhibit. The areas where tension is likely to arise are related to the *sunnī–shī'a* distinction, as well as to the messages that Islamist groups may wish to propagate among the mass of pilgrims.

The political situation in Saudi Arabia does not help to keep tensions down. The main causes of friction are the alliance between the Saudi state and the USA, the harsh measures of repression against domestic opposition, especially against those branded as Islamists, and the perceived distance between the Wahhābī ideals which officially govern Saudi society and the self-indulgent lifestyle of members of the royal family.

Thus, in 1980, 1981, and 1982 clashes occurred between *shī'a* pilgrims from Iran and the Saudi security forces. Then, in 1987 things got rougher as 402 pilgrims were killed. More skirmishes followed, when 1,400 pilgrims in 1989 and 1990 were crushed to death in a tunnel. The accident was described by several *shī'a* groups as a "new massacre."[155]

These problems should not be seen outside the more general political context within which the *ḥajj* takes place. As Fischer and Abedi write, the 1987 incident has a prehistory that takes us back to 1964, 1968, and 1971. The first date was when the exiled Ayatollah Khomeini started using the *ḥajj* as an opportunity to send messages to the Iranian pilgrims – while they were beyond the control of the Shah's regime – and to the wider Muslim world. The second date was the year after the Arab defeat in the hands of Israel. In that *ḥajj* the slogans declared that Islam had nothing to do with the defeat; it was the ideology of Arab nationalism that had caused the disaster. Lastly, 1971 was the year that the Shah celebrated the Zoroastrian roots of Iran, disregarding centuries of Islamic history and sweeping away the existing political realities. Khomeini's message to the pilgrims was particularly uncompromising. After the 1979 Islamic revolution, "the Islamic Republic of Iran called for the ḥajj to become the international macrocosm of the weekly Friday sermons of an Islamic government: a communal gathering to discuss the dissemination of the Islamic revolution."[156] And Fischer and Abedi conclude: "the ḥajj itself is a call to institute Islam as a reality: personally, socially, religiously, and politically."[157]

Interestingly, the increase in the popularity of more extreme Islamist views in the period starting with the first Gulf War has found the security forces of the Kingdom much more apprehensive. Similarly, the loyal to the government *ʿulamāʾ* apparatus has used every opportunity during the process to castigate religious fanaticism and violence. For example, in the January 2005 *ḥajj* the state-appointed *imām* of the Grand Mosque in Mecca, ʿAbd al-Raḥmān al-Sudays, told the pilgrims:

> Because Muslims have strayed from moderation, we are now suffering from this dangerous phenomenon of branding people infidels and inciting Muslims to rise against their leaders to cause instability. The reason for this is a delinquent and void interpretation of Islam based on ignorance.[158]

At the same time, new crowd-safety measures have been introduced to the extent of slightly reformulating traditional rules; for example, the stoning of the three pillars now starts earlier than usual to avoid congestion, with the authorities having erected wider and taller pillars and constructed a new pedestrian bridge into the area. Security forces, too, are present throughout the course of the *ḥajj* in greater numbers than before. As a result, until now the *ḥajj* has not been marred by the violence that has repeatedly shaken Saudi society, not only through the bomb explosions and the waves of arrests within the country, but also through the realization that many Saudi nationals are active members of Islamist cells and the implicit accusation that members of the Saudi elite finance Islamist causes worldwide.

In cyberspace, too, the Saudi establishment has become the object of much criticism, especially on the part of *shīʿa* groups. Many of these critical articles focus on the *ḥajj*. Their titles are suggestive: "Time to cleanse the Ka'abah," "Hajj: the Qur'ānic or Saudi Way?" and "Al-Saud: the west's custodians of the Haramain."[159] In the articles, the anonymous writers accuse the government of Saudi Arabia of having transformed the *ḥajj* into a ritual devoid of meaning as they forbid pilgrims to denounce the evil plans of the unbelievers (*mushrikūn*). Such a denunciation, it is maintained, is an integral part of the annual *ḥajj* at the symbolic level because it expresses in the most clear way the unity of the *umma* at the highest moment of its collective "liturgical" life.

Besides such discursive arguments, another area where the variety of views concerning the pilgrimage is noticeable concerns the way the *ḥajj* is narrated in the home communities of the pilgrims. Here ethnographic studies such as those by Delaney of the Turkish villages of Anatolia are important. According to Delaney's informants, the pilgrimage to Mecca constitutes for every pilgrim a significant personal experience as well as a confirmation of Muslim unity. This is so because in essence the *ḥajj* stands for a journey "back home" to a life situation they should experience continuously throughout their life, something that the harsh everyday realities make difficult, almost impossible, to attain. As they kiss the *Ka'ba*, which to them is the House of God, and drink the holy water of Zamzam, which gave life to Hagar and her son, the pilgrims experience paradise, that is, they get a glimpse of the other world, which is the only real world, the world from which one comes down to earth, the world to which (*insha' Allāh*) one will go forever.[160]

This idea of homecoming is also symbolically linked to Prophet Muḥammad himself since for him too the first pilgrimage to Mecca after his victory over the enemies of the new faith represented a return, a journey back to the city where he had started to propagate the new message of God after the first revelation in the desert. The existence of Mecca out there, then, and its identification with the "real" home of the Muslim creates the sense of distance between everyday reality and the Islamic vision. Delaney writes that in the Turkish language this sentiment is called *gurbet*, a word that signifies both the sadness of being away from home and the hope of return, something that can somehow be achieved with the pilgrimage. Interestingly, the same word is used in the context of Turkish migration (mostly) to Europe.[161]

From this point of view, Turkish migration to Europe can be conceptualized as an almost involuntary displacement from the homeland, a process that shares many characteristics with the Muslim *hijra*, i.e. the enforced journey of the first Muslims from Mecca to Madīna. Thus, just like the Prophet returned to Mecca after many years for the first Muslim *ḥajj* in history, in a similar way the Turkish migrants return from time to time to their homeland to enjoy "real" life. We could even go a step further by suggesting that, if Mecca appears in the collective imagination of the pilgrims as an earthly paradise ready to receive them as members of their own local community as well as members of the wider supranational Community of Believers,[162] in the case of Turkish migration Turkey is transformed into an earthly paradise (*cennet gibi*) to which the migrant, *insha' Allāh*, will return forever.

However, the "back home" discourse is contradicted by another set of narratives in which the *ḥajj* returnees focus on the differences between the reality they experienced in Mecca and the expectations they had when they started their journey. The differences they mostly dwell upon are of two types. The first concern the natural environment of the holy places and the second the other pilgrims they found there. As Delaney writes, the latter are especially notable because they reveal the Turkish pilgrims' surprise at the realization that there are Muslims whose language is incomprehensible and whose food is deemed to be unsavory.[163] What alleviates this feeling of initial discomfiture is the white *iḥrām* donned by everybody and the practicing of rituals they know from back home. But even then, the otherness of women pilgrims who do not wear the *iḥrām* and of the various dignitaries who parade in their local dress and the insignia of their office remains visible.[164]

Coming to another ethnographic example concerning the role of pilgrimage narratives in local traditions, I would like to refer to my own material from the Sudan. When I did fieldwork among the members of the *ṭumbura* spirit-possession cult I found out the *ḥajj* was employed as a symbol of their Islamic orthodoxy. As has been mentioned, the members of the cult are mostly African Muslim subalterns of slave descent and poor migrants from the Southern and Western Sudan to the Arabized North. There, they are seen by the majority of the self-proclaimed Arab Muslim Northern Sudanese as inferior.[165] In this context, the very participation in spirit-possession cults such as *ṭumbura* is regarded by the Northerners as proof positive of their inferiority and of their un-Islamic way of life.

For the *ṭumbura* people, reality is the other way around. *Ṭumbura* membership is amongst the credentials of their true Muslim faith. As they assert, the practice itself originates with Bilāl, the first *mu'adhdhin* of Islam, who, significantly, was a black slave,[166] and Prophet Muḥammad himself.[167] And if that were not enough, ʿAbd al-Qādir Kūkū, the blind patriarch of the cult in the area of Greater Khartoum until his death in the beginning of the 1990s, insisted that the *rabāba* lyre, the musical instrument at the center of the cult's symbolic universe, led the *ḥajj* procession in Mecca.

The first *rabāba* was called *Ḥājja Fāṭna* and belonged to Bilāl, I was told by the blind cult leader. He said it can always be seen at the head of the huge procession to the *Kaʿba* on the day when its *kiswa*, the black stone's ceremonial covering cloth, is changed. Behind *Ḥājja Fāṭna*, whose very name proclaims its position as the principal *rabāba* of the *ḥajj*, follow all the *ṭumbura* musicians and the *shaykh*s and *shaykha*s of the cult.[168] Behind them come the Arabs and then the *ṣūfī* brotherhoods with their drums and tambourines. Further behind come the kings and princes of the world, carrying their gifts to the *Kaʿba* and finally, behind this wondrous and marvelous procession, march all the rest of the Muslim faithful (*kullū al-Muslimūn*). And if I didn't believe him, my dear old friend exclaimed, I should go myself and see it with my own eyes.

Of course, ʿAbd al-Qādir had never been to Mecca himself. The son of slaves from the Nuba Hills, he was blind from excessive use of bad-quality *ʿaraqī*, a strong local alcoholic beverage. Surprisingly, perhaps, he was not deterred by this and still drank copiously. A wonderful man in abject poverty, he had never left the shanty-towns of the Sudanese capital, except when he was a soldier in the famous Anglo-Egyptian Sudanese Battalions, which were finally disbanded in the 1920s.[169] Still, ʿAbd al-Qādir knew Mecca and the *ḥajj*. His tales convinced those around him that he could see all these wonders happening in front of his wide-open bleary eyes. If he said so, then it was true: *Ḥājja Fāṭna* was at the head of the *ḥajj* procession. I, too, have never been to Mecca. Still, I knew that such a procession had never taken place, though I never told him so.

Unlike ʿAbd al-Qādir Kūkū, the two most important female *ṭumbura* leaders in the capital, Ḥalīma Bashīr Idrīs Jumaʿh and Nūra al-Nūbawiyya, had both visited Mecca and bore with pride the title of *ḥājja*. The interesting thing, though, was that *ḥājja* Ḥalīma had visited Saudi Arabia not as a pilgrim, but as a cook in the service of a local notable. Nonetheless, the old *shaykha* claims that she did the *ḥajj*, although her description differs from the one offered in the previous pages. I have no doubt that the *shaykha* indeed visited the *Kaʿba* at some point. How and when is not important. What is important, for the cult members and, naturally, for the anthropologist, is the honorific *ḥājja* that functions as a kind of symbolic capital.

The *ḥajj* offers Muslims the opportunity to see themselves as members of that worldwide imagined Community of Believers, the *umma*, and as followers of an Islamic vision of universal aspirations. Within the Islamic discourse that animates this vision the *ḥajj* offers a meeting place, an opportunity for dialogue between many local traditions. Each of these traditions draws life from that vision, but at the same time lends it life. The one and the many coalesce and are made visible through this congregation of the faithful.

The *ḥajj*, then, should be approached not as a process that confirms or opposes the existing social order, neither as a melting-pot nor as a mere shop-window for the display of a startling variety, but as a field within which historically and locally specific Islamic traditions enter into a dialogue without losing their perspective on the vision of Islamic unity or the theoretically problematic but politically demonstrable context of "orthodoxy" that the hegemonic ideology of the Meccan/Saudi pilgrimage center wishes to impose. In this process of producing "orthodoxy" the effects, colors, and configurations cannot be predetermined as the agents involved are unequal. But this is logical. The very idea of Islam as a discursive tradition implies "a history of argument and debate . . . in shared languages and styles of discourse."[170]

5

Islamic Mysticism

In this chapter I shall consider mysticism, a dimension of Islamic experience, equally important and intimately intertwined with what has been described hitherto. Just as in any religious tradition, in Islam we come across different kinds of charismatic personalities who can perform miracles, even after their death. We also find a variety of practices for divining the future, curing disease, combating affliction, appeasing spirits, or bewitching foes, which have been described by Ibn Khaldūn in his *Muqaddimah*, as far back as the fourteenth century AD. Underlying this mystical universe is a desire for a personal relationship with God that complements what is offered by Islamic theology, the five "pillars" included; there is also a need to manage social relationships and everyday occurrences in culturally acceptable ways whose polysemy opens the vista of operative possibilities.

In that sense, Islamic mysticism is inextricably wedded to Islamic theological and legal discourse as two dimensions of the totality of Islamic experience. Crystallized in the specificity of distinct beliefs and practices, these two dimensions are always locked in a creative tension, the uncertain result of a continuous negotiation process between the actors identified with them in particular historical moments.[1]

I say "uncertain result" because on several occasions, some more dramatic than others, the disputed "orthodoxy" of certain practitioners and holy personalities is questioned by those claiming to espouse the spirit of the (Islamic) law and the "orthodoxy" of the mosque, and measures are taken against those branded as doctrinal transgressors. What sort of measures it is difficult to say, as "orthodoxy" is a flexible term that defies the strictures of legality that are often associated with it. For example, in both Saudi Arabia and the Sudan spirit-possession rites are declared un-Islamic, but in the former they are banned while in the latter they are tolerated. However, it seems that a distinction between mystical and scriptural Islam can be made only during specific historical periods and only in relation to specific interpretations of Islamic "orthodoxy" associated with Islamism and certain forms of Muslim reformism, as well as with strict legal traditions such as Ḥanbalism.

Having said that, we can now turn to the presentation of some of the most salient aspects of Islamic mysticism, leaving aside many beliefs and practices that cannot be treated within the limits of space allotted to this chapter. This does not mean that they are of inferior value or less interest, but I think the material presented here covers much of the analytical ground, allowing one to discuss other examples. What I concentrate on is the notion of saintliness in Islam, the role of the *Ṣūfī* orders, and the phenomenon of spirit possession.

THE WORLD OF THE *ṢŪFĪS*

Mystics are the saints of Islam. In Christianity too there are saints, but Muslim saints or holy men are different in four respects. First, while Christian saints attain this status after their death, Muslim saints are elevated to sainthood while they are still alive due to the miraculous power or other traits attributed to them by the faithful. Second, there is no canonization process; elevation to sainthood is rather a matter of public acknowledgment. This means that some saints may be recognized as such only by local populations. Third, sainthood can be transmitted to others. Fourth, sainthood is not directly connected with morality.

Muslim saints are known as *ṣūfī* (from *taṣawwūf*: mysticism),[2] *faqīr* or *darwīsh* (penitent, poor in the eyes of God), and *walī* (friend of God). The *ṣūfī* path (*ṭarīqa al-ṣūfiyya*) is a path of purification through the practice of special techniques which allow one to perceive God directly in an experiential way. "Sufism" is the Anglicized version of *taṣawwūf*.

Sufism appeared relatively early during the long and turbulent era of dynastic Islam and gradually developed into a complex system of intricate beliefs and practices, encompassing aspects of a high literate tradition – theological treatises, Persian poetry, elaborate music – and more popular ecstatic rituals and magic practices. Its emergence was related to the social and intellectual upheavals caused by the expansion of Islam outside its original Arabian context and its dialogue with new ideas, practices, and ways of thought. Enriching though it was, this dialogue led to socio-political and cultural changes which for many diluted the alleged *spirit* of "true" Islam. The perceived decadence of what had become the royal court of a fractious society under the Umayyad (661–750) and ʿAbbāsid (750–1248) dynasties played a special role in the formation of this impression.

Oversimplifying a complex and fluid situation that took a long time to produce more or less stable forms, we may say that sufism was one of the two responses offered by society to these challenges, the other being the emergence of the *ʿulamā'* as a distinct social class and the attendant development of Islamic law.[3]

If the *'ulamā'* were mostly concerned with the development of Islamic law as an autonomous legal structure that could formulate and define the content of faith and the limits of praxis in an ideal Community of Believers, sufism was concerned more with the striving for perfection through a subjective conception of a social reality animated by the spirit of God. This view sprang from the belief that spiritual maturity could be reached by following a particular training regime under the direction of a guide-cum-master with saintly qualities.

Two points are important here. First, although asceticism has always been an aspect of mystical life, the *ṣūfī* saints should not be equated with the Christian monks. Despite spells of retreat, most of them were, and still are, family men with children, animals, fields, and even slaves. Second, the *ṣūfī* saints and the *'ulamā'* should not be seen as two antithetical social groups, but as interactive practitioners of a single multifaceted tradition.

This does not mean that there are no differences between the *ṣūfī* saints and the *'ulamā'*. Especially during the early days, when sufism was more directly oriented against the hegemonic concepts of dynastic Islam, some of its adherents, like the ecstatic mystics Abū Yazīd al-Bisṭāmī (+874) and Manṣūr al-Ḥallāj (+922), clashed with the *'ulamā'*. Soon, though, new people arrived on the scene who tried to reconcile the less extreme forms of asceticism and ecstatic practices with the dominant theological and legal theories, thus situating sufism more securely within the purview of Islamic law. Among the most renowned is Abū Ḥāmid Muḥammad al-Ghazzālī (1058–1111), whose famous treatise *Iḥyā' 'Ulūm al-Dīn* offered an exposition of law and theology that was well within the parameters of *'ulamā'* "orthodoxy" and at the same time was imbued with the spirit of direct religious experience and inner concentration.[4]

Another example is *shaykh* 'Abd al-Qādir al-Jilānī (1077–1166) who spent years studying Islamic theology and the ascetic ritual tradition.[5] When he was 50 he founded his own *madrasa* in Baghdad offering the basic courses taught in most Islamic education establishments of the era. 'Abd al-Qādir's Wednesday and Friday sermons as well as his rulings on legal issues soon became known outside Iraq. After his death, one of his sons took over the *madrasa*, transformed by then into an active *ṣūfī* center where the *shaykh*'s followers gathered to listen to his sermons and participate in the rituals he prescribed. This gave birth to the first *ṣūfī* brotherhood, *ṭarīqa al-Qādiriyya*, which today is considered one of the biggest and most important *ṣūfī* orders. In a similar manner, a large number of other brotherhoods appeared in the Muslim world, each following, at least theoretically, the theological and liturgical precepts of its founder, but all directed towards realizing for its members a mystical union with God.

It should also be noted that many saintly figures did not become founders of *ṣūfī* orders, though they are still remembered and honored. Such saint worship is a local phenomenon, focusing on the tomb of the saint, but on the whole it follows the same general principles that underlie the entire phenomenon of sufism. For this reason, in the following sections I do not distinguish between sufism *per se* and the cult of saints, except when this is analytically required.

The *Ṣūfī* Orders

Organized in brotherhoods since at least the eleventh century, sufism started losing much of its ascetic and elitist character and was gradually transformed into a popular movement characterized by an "essential looseness" that allowed everybody to participate according to their capabilities and needs.[6] For example, following a *ṣūfī* master, believers could apply to their everyday life some of the master's commands as well as some of his prescribed ritual practices, without forsaking family obligations and business interests. A minority would dedicate themselves to their master and change their lives radically. Both ways could be realized within the context of the *ṣūfī* orders. Which way one followed would depend on personal preference and circumstances. However, the brotherhoods' organizational framework had developed along lines that did not easily encourage ecstatic practices and chiliastic convictions, although that was always contingent upon the members' social background.

This picture has remained relatively stable until recently, as the logic of the brotherhoods' internal structure has not been altered much, although their role in society has changed dramatically. This disjunction has not served the brotherhoods well when rival institutions emerged during the colonial and post-colonial periods. But before turning to this, a presentation of the brotherhoods' structure and the principles behind it is in order.

Organizational Framework and the Concept of *Baraka*

In terms of their internal organization, the *ṣūfī* orders are based on the interpersonal relationship between the *ṣūfī* master (*shaykh*, *murshid*, or *pīr*) and the disciple (*murīd*). Ideally, the latter is tied to the former in absolute obedience concerning all his temporal affairs and his spiritual development.[7] In reality, this is not always so because, except in specific instances, a person can be a member of more than one brotherhood. Moreover, as has already been touched on, the degree of one's involvement with a brotherhood may vary considerably, with the majority associating in a rather middle-of-the-road way. In any case, the rationale is that having been thus trained in both the external and the internal aspects of Islamic tradition, the disciple is gradually prepared by his *shaykh* to encounter God through a mystical experience.[8]

The saintly *shaykh* can achieve this for his disciple not so much through the transmittance of exoteric or esoteric knowledge, i.e. through the study of texts, some of which are specific to each brotherhood, and through participation in rituals allegedly designed by the founder, but mainly through the imparting of his own spiritual power which reaches the disciple in the form of a generalized blessing (*baraka*), a concept close to Weber's charisma. In practical terms, for the receiver of *baraka* this is translated into health, prosperity, and moral certainty, blessings which can be further extended to members of his family.

The source of *baraka* is considered to be the founder of the brotherhood who, in turn, had received it from the Prophet to whom it is claimed that he is somehow related. Starting from there, *baraka* is transmitted to subsequent generations, but also to contemporaries of a *shaykh* in two complementary ways which Geertz has called "genealogical" and "miraculous."[9] They apply to *ṣūfī* saints as well as to local saints who are not affiliated with a *ṣūfī* order but are the object of popular veneration.

The "genealogical way" is through patrilineal descent. For example, *shaykh* 'Abd al-Qādir al-Jilānī passed his *baraka* to some of his patrilineal descendants (not necessarily to his sons only; nephews would do as well) who in turn passed it to their descendants, and so on. In this way, a chain of succession is created (*silsila*) which connects the initial founder of the order with each one of the successive leaders of it. In the case of an unaffiliated saint, his *baraka* is also considered to pass to his descendants, some of whom, in their role as custodians of the saint's memory, may themselves become recipients of the affection, even devotion, of believers. As will be seen later, this means that they act as guardians of the saint's tomb. The transmission of *baraka* through patrilineal descent would ideally mean that every leader of the hundreds of *ṣūfī* brotherhood centers currently operating in the Muslim world was indeed a descendant of a brotherhood's original founder. But this is not so.

With the "miraculous" way of transferring *baraka*, it can be passed to literally anybody in all sorts of ways. Every believer can be a recipient of a saint's *baraka* through the laying on of hands or even through casual bodily contact with him or his descendants. Some suggest that just being in the presence of a saint for long periods of time is enough to receive his *baraka*. Also, possessing an object that belongs to a living saint or one of his predecessors may also prove a source of *baraka*. Indeed, the ritual visit (*ziyāra*) to the tomb of a saint who may have died hundreds of years ago or to a tomb of one of his more recent, and perhaps less illustrious, successors is enough for the transmission of *baraka*. Lastly, *baraka* is transmitted through dreams or visions by which a saint offers solutions to problems that trouble the believer.[10]

It becomes evident, then, that the ways in which *baraka* is transmitted are multifarious, if not chaotic. This should not cause alarm nor should it induce one to attempt to impose order where by definition there is none. Let us remember that in Islam there are no central ecclesiastical authorities, that sainthood is often a local phenomenon, and, more importantly, that every aspect of Islamic discourse is the result of a continuous process of negotiation between moral agents, what has been repeatedly called in this work a production of "orthodoxy." Alternatively, an easier way to understand the matter is to consider *baraka* not so much as a thing that one possesses and can give away when certain conditions are met, but as a property or quality of particular persons or even better, following Geertz, as a specific "mode of thinking" about the ways in which the sacred enters the world of everyday life.[11]

Returning to the *ṣūfī* hierarchy succession chain, more often than not a saintly *shaykh* chooses his successor (*khalīfa*) from among his closest and most trusted associates who may very well be members of his family and who definitely share his *baraka* and his saintly qualities. The same is true for those whom he appoints as leaders of the individual lodges that the brotherhood has established locally or further afield. So really, as far as the biggest brotherhoods are concerned, after some time they do look like multinational organizations. This being the case, it is not surprising that some of the most successful local branches of any given brotherhood may acquire semi-independent status from the headquarters in terms of organizational activities, operational services, or personnel development. What keeps them part of the multinational network is doctrinal affiliation and the following of the founder's liturgical and other ritual prescriptions.

Baraka and the Performance of Miracles

The good health, prosperity, and moral certainty that result from the workings of *baraka* often take the form of miracles (*karāmāt*) thought to be performed by a dead saint who could be a founder of a *ṣūfī* brotherhood or just a local saint or his living descendants.[12] For believers, such miracles prove that behind everyday appearances lies another reality governed by God and other supernatural entities, and confirm the saint's closeness (*qarāba*) to God. This is very important because in the case of a *ṣūfī shaykh* and his living descendants it legitimates the functioning of any given order and through this of all *ṣūfī* brotherhoods.[13]

Miracles *are* performed each and every time they are recounted in coffee houses, mosques, houses, or the market-place. The narrator describes to his listeners the wonderful workings of the saint's *baraka* and they shake their heads in admiration, offering blessings to God, His Prophet, and His friends (the saint as *walī*). Having repeatedly participated in such discussions among my Sudanese friends while in the field, I can add to the picture the doubting Thomas whose very presence leads to repeated and more elaborate descriptions of the saint's miracle, whose dramatic effect adds more layers of meaning to what had *really* happened. Such narrations sustain the faith in, and increase the power of, the holy men, but also inform the status of those who have benefited by the miraculous performance. The following example shows this clearly.

Shaykha Ḥalīma Bashīr Idrīs Juma'h, a high officiant of the Sudanese *zār ṭumbura* spirit-possession cult, which its members allege is close to *ṭarīqa al-Qādiriyya*, narrated to me how *shaykh* 'Abd al-Qādir al-Jilānī had restored her sight after she had been bewitched. Lying sleepless on her bed, the old *shaykha* had a vision of *shaykh* ʿAbd al-Qādir, just as he was depicted in the pictures sold outside many Khartoum mosques in the late 1980s: tall, with a long white beard, a white *jallābiyya* and turban, holding a long Y-shaped walking-stick and a decanter for his ablutions. Three times the *shaykh* ordered the blind *shaykha* to stand up and three times she refused, saying that she was blind. He then hit her ferociously in the face. At that moment her sight was restored. The whole household woke up and soon the *ṭumbura* drums were relaying the good tidings to the neighborhood, while the four *ṭumbura* flags – one of them representing the *shaykh* – were hoisted at the eastern side of the courtyard. After a few days, a seven-day thanksgiving ceremony was performed at which a white sheep was sacrificed in the name of the *shaykh*. The whole event proved not only the latter's undisputable power, but also the fact that *ṭumbura* and its people were *indeed* close to the *Qādiriyya* brotherhood. This is sociologically significant because the hierarchy of that respected brotherhood *refuses all ties with ṭumbura*, whose members I have already described as impoverished slum-dwellers, descendants of slaves, and other non-Arab subalterns from the Nuba Hills and Western Sudan. I shall return to this later in the chapter.

A second characteristic of miracles is their dangerous nature which stems from the fact that they suspend the flow of everyday life, thus questioning the authority of those who control it. Indeed, in most traditions, the clergy or the religious scholars, in our case the *ʿulamāʾ*, spare no effort to define the boundaries within which the supernatural and the miraculous *are allowed to* exist. Without dismissing the reality of miracles (how could they?), the custodians of religious tradition are anxious to control the identity of those who perform them, so as to subjugate their wondrous powers to the logic of the "orthodoxy" that they as custodians seek to define and defend and to the demands of its sociopolitical implications.

The *ṣūfī* hierarchy too, realizing the inherent difficulty in controlling the situation, has every reason to be cautious and circumspect towards those popularly proclaimed to work miracles. The reputation of the *ṣūfī* saints needs to be protected from what may prove to be quacks who deceive the masses. They do not want to be accused by the more legally minded *ʿulamāʾ* of encouraging doctrinally questionable practices and so they often repudiate the cults of relatively minor local saints and deny miracles of a flamboyant character. Instead, they promote the *miracle* of a deep understanding of religion, which in one instance allowed the illiterate *shaykh* to silence his educated but pretentious opponents, or that of unsurpassable gentleness and forgiveness.[14] This mechanism, I think, clearly demonstrates the interconnection between what Weber has called charismatic and traditional legitimacy.[15]

Lastly, miracles join two equally *real* levels of existence, that of God and the hidden spiritual powers, and that of the everyday life, thus proving that nothing is accidental. The majority of the saints' followers belong to the middle and lower social classes. With little education and even less money, such people lead precarious lives shaped by powers they cannot control, be they governments, international politics, the climate, and, ultimately, God. He is qualitatively different from the rest in the sense that in His presence all that is accidental or unforeseen is suddenly imbued with meaning; everything, after all, is part of God's providential plan. It is God's providence that appears when it is least expected to bring an order of sorts to the chaos of human existence. This appearance is nothing but a proof of God's power. And the channel through which providence may reach each one of the faithful is the saint and his *baraka*.

*Zāwiyya*s and *Qubba*s

The local organizational center where all liturgical practices and other social activities of a *ṣūfī* order take place is called *zāwiyya*.[16] Each *zāwiyya* may present some structural peculiarities, but they all follow common organizational principles. The central *zāwiyya* of a *ṣūfī* order is usually within, or in proximity to, a settlement and often contains the tomb (*qubba*) of the brotherhood's founder or that of an important former leader of the particular lodge. Obviously, with the proliferation of local *ṣūfī* orders it is impossible for all *zāwiyya*s to have a saint's *qubba*. In this case, the *zāwiyya* keeps contact, when feasible, with a neighboring *qubba* of a local saint who thus becomes associated with the brotherhood by proxy.

In practice, then, besides the *qubba*s of saints who belong to a brotherhood's hierarchical chain of succession, there exist *qubba*s of local saints who do not belong to a particular *ṣūfī* order hierarchically, but have been "appropriated" by them spiritually. And of course there are *qubba*s of saints who are not affiliated with any brotherhood at all. In the first two cases all forms of celebration around a *qubba* are organized by the managing brotherhood, while in the case of an unaffiliated saint they are in the hands of the saint's alleged descendants – themselves recipients of the saint's *baraka*, as we have seen – who also control the upkeep of the tomb. Lastly, in all three cases, all celebrations spill over into the local population and beyond, thus transforming a *qubba* into a pilgrimage center in its own right. Occasionally, this may serve as a *ḥajj* substitute for those who cannot afford the journey to Mecca,[17] though the difference between the *ḥajj* and the *ziyāra* (visiting a *qubba*) is always emphasized. This is true even in places like the Sudan where *ṣūfī* orders and the cult of the saints have been dominant aspects of the country's Islamic tradition as opposed to an *ʿulamā'*-generated discourse, which has never managed to develop fully.[18]

Such visits to the saints' tombs are of great symbolic significance because besides the mosque, where the faithful pray, the *qubba*s and the *ṣūfī zāwiyya*s are the only sacred *topoi* in Islamic tradition where believers can feel closer to God.[19] This closeness is expresssed through the offering of small gifts or sacrifices to the buried saints in exchange for special requests and as tokens of personal piety or thanksgiving. The offerings are of two kinds: those following an annual, or even weekly, cycle of well-defined celebrations and those made on an *ad hoc* basis whenever believers feel they need to contact the saint. The former type usually includes the most important annual celebrations in the Muslim calendar, such as the two *ʿid*s and the Prophet's birthday, as well as the weekly celebrations that a particular *zāwiyya* may organize, based on a near-by *qubba*. These are all collective enterprises and, as far as the annual celebrations are concerned, they may be on a rather grand scale, including sacrifices and the performance of elaborate rituals of remembrance where texts are recited alongside the practicing of ecstatic dances. Such celebrations keep alive the relationship between a saint and his followers, be they brotherhood members or simple believers, ensuring that they will continue to receive his *baraka*.[20]

The *ad hoc* visits are more or less personal and of a contingent character. These are affairs where individual believers ask the saint to grant them a particular wish: to become pregnant or to give birth to a male child, to overcome a disease or some financial difficulties, etc. The exact phenomenology differs with the locality. According to Eickelman, in Morocco visiting women voice their wish and leave by the entrance of the *qubba* a small piece from their dress as a reminder. If their wish is granted a sheep may be sacrificed in the name of the saint or another type of offering made. For Eickelman, this pattern follows a more generally observed North African "ideology of 'obligation' (*ḥaqq*) which informs most other social relationships," such as those between patron and client groups.[21] Indeed, the reputation of a saint seems to depend partly on this granting of favors. Otherwise, his power is questioned.[22]

Besides a *qubba*, which may or may not exist within the premises, a typical *zāwiyya* may include the apartments of the *shaykh* and his family, quarters for a number of resident brotherhood members and guests, reception areas and inner courtyards, a mosque which is open to the general public and where the *shaykh* presides over the Friday noon prayer, storage facilities, and a large kitchen where food is prepared for the residents and visitors, as well as those in need from the wider area. Many important *zāwiyya*s may also include dwellings for patients who visit from distant regions, hoping that the power of the saint and his contemporary successors who operate the *zāwiyya* will deliver them from their illness. Lastly, we must not forget the *Qur'ānic* schools which various *zāwiyya*s subsidize.

The most important *zāwiyya* I visited in the Sudan was that of *shaykh* al-Ṭāyyib in Omdurman, the "old city" opposite Khartoum. My initial visit to this *zāwiyya*, which is formally associated with the *Qādiriyya* brotherhood, took place in February 1989 through the good offices of a friend from the University of Khartoum.[23] Having left behind the paved road and driven along the meandering dirt roads of a lower-middle-class neighborhood, we soon saw the neon-lit minaret of the *zāwiyya*'s mosque. When we entered the central courtyard, the first thing I saw was a group of young pupils squatting around a big fire reciting from the *Qur'ān*. Their teacher, in a long white *jallābiyya* and the *Qādiriyya* green skullcap, was walking around them holding a long whip. This he used, albeit with tenderness, on those who did not perform adequately.

We were soon guided to a reception hall whose three sides were lined with chairs and couches where other visitors were also waiting for the *shaykh*, who was not in the lodge. Tea and cold Pepsi were offered. In the far corner of the room I saw a visitor earnestly discussing something with a brotherhood member whose green headdress was too small for his long, braided rasta hair. At some point, the latter gave the visitor some small plastic bottles with water and received a bundle of banknotes and a kiss on the hand. As I was told, the bottles contained water the *shaykh* had blessed with his *baraka*. I then remembered that I had seen the rastaman some days earlier dancing in front of the *qubba* of *shaykh* Ḥamad al-Nīl in the area of Mūrada. He most probably belonged to the *darwīsh*es of the *Qādiriyya* who practiced their ecstatic dance every Friday evening in front of the *qubba*.

But then shouts and ululation filled the air. The *shaykh* had returned. Another *darwīsh* with braided hair and a long black beard entered the room brandishing a long sword and shouting "*Allāhu akbar, Allāhu akbar.*" Outside a throng of people, including several women and sword-bearing *darwīsh*es, had surrounded the *shaykh*'s Toyota Creseda. Most of the people looked middle-class Sudanese, something that made the appearance of the ten or so armed *darwīsh*es even more startling.

Soon the *shaykh* started seeing his visitors in small groups. Entering the reception hall I saw him sitting on a cushion surrounded by several *darwīsh*es and his secretary. The *shaykh* was old. He was wearing a white *jallābiyya* and turban and had his shoulders covered by a white cotton blanket. He was listening to an old, well-dressed gentleman who was squatting in front of him. Their heads touched. After a while, the *shaykh* took the gentleman's hand in his and started talking to him in a murmur. The other moved his head slowly saying repeatedly "*insha' Allāh, insha' Allāh*" (God willing). When the interview was concluded he kissed the *shaykh*'s hand and took his leave. It was my turn. Squatting in front of the old *shaykh* we held hands and exchanged pleasantries. Then the *shaykh* asked me about my research, the university, and my family. I asked about the *zāwiyya*. When our conversation was over my friend and I were guided to the various parts of the compound by a member of the brotherhood. At all times we were followed by two *darwīsh*es.

I shall mention two important aspects of the *zāwiyya*'s function that I witnessed. The first has to do with the preparation of food. In the kitchen, which was in one corner of the huge compound, I saw the biggest cooking pot I have ever seen in my life. More than two feet high, it was being used to prepare the broad bean salad that is the staple food for most Northern Sudanese. The mushy salad, which contains finely chopped onion, tomato, and strong red pepper, was served with pitta bread twice a day to all the people in the compound, as well as to the impoverished people of the neighborhood. Such generosity is in accordance with the *zakāt* principle discussed in the previous chapter.

Lastly, I should mention the patients' quarters at the other side of the *zāwiyya*, made up of small rooms large enough for two beds. We entered one of these rooms, which was lit by a candle. In the bed lay a man in a white *jallābiyya*. His eyes were glazed and every now and then he moaned as if in pain. He was chained to the wall by his legs. A member of the brotherhood sitting at the edge of the bed was reading to him in a monotonous voice passages from the *Qur'ān*. Every few minutes he struck the chained man gently with a short whip. The room was permeated with the sweet smoke of burning incense. As we were told, the patient was possessed by the *jīnn*, the evil spirit, and had been brought by his family to the *zāwiyya* for treatment. The scene I described is part of the traditional armory of Islamic medicine. Evil spirits like the *jinn* are exorcised by specialists who are often associated with sufism, while other spirits which are deemed not to be evil are accommodated in a symbiotic relationship with the patient.

Dhikr: Remembering God

Besides the aspects of communal service offered by the *zāwiyya* of *shaykh* al-Ṭāyyib, I also had the opportunity to observe much of its ceremonial activities, especially the weekly *dhikr* in the *qubba* of *shaykh* Ḥamad al-Nīl, who was associated with the *Qādiriyya* order.

Dhikr can be glossed as "remembrance of God's name." Constituting the center of the liturgical life of all *ṣūfī* brotherhoods, it refers to a number of dancing and breathing techniques during which performers endlessly repeat the name of God or some praise to God.[24] *Dhikr* is part of a larger regime of training the mind and the body in order to focus on God. It is a collective practice performed independently of the five ritual prayers, although individual disciples will make it part of their own training regime, if they are so instructed by the *shaykh*.

The significance attributed to *dhikr* is based on three *Qur'ānic sūras* which enjoin believers "to remember God."[25] For many *ṣūfīs*, *dhikr* is a means which will lead them to ecstasy, a state they understand as a sign of God's blessing and a fountain of mystical knowledge. Such is the power this state exercises on the imagination that, for some, *dhikr* becomes an end in itself. To avoid this, many *ṣūfī* leaders have written extensively on the meaning of *dhikr*, laying down specific instructions concerning its performance. So every brotherhood trains its members in the precise body movements, carefully timed breathing rhythms, and correct utterance of God's name that constitute part of its received tradition.[26] Still, this emphasis on *dhikr* has gradually resulted in its becoming the main, if not the only, type of spiritual training practiced by members of *ṣūfī* brotherhoods. Indeed, in many of them, music and singing have been added in an effort to concentrate the whole being of the performers on the task at hand: to see, so to speak, God.

In each brotherhood, the collective *dhikr* is performed once or twice a week. Participation varies according to circumstances. A particular *zāwiyya* may boast several hundred members, but, as has already been suggested, few of them would be actively and systematically involved in its liturgical life and even fewer would be proficient in performing the *dhikr*. The majority may perform it every now and then or may sway to and fro together with the main participants. In the case of *shaykh* al-Ṭāyyib's group the most important weekly performance of *dhikr* is that of the early Friday evening in front of the *qubba* of *shaykh* Ḥamad al-Nīl. The event draws a large number of spectators from the surrounding area, as well as the occasional tourist.

The actual *dhikr* lasts between one and two hours. It is preceded by a short ritual in the nearby mosque and the setting up of the electronic equipment for the broadcasting of the accompanying music. The dance is often interspersed with unrehearsed impromptu ecstatic episodes where dancers as well as bystanders may enter into a hightened state of awareness and shake themselves vigorously, shouting the name of God. On the whole, though, *dhikr* choreography is carefully designed and artfully performed by the brotherhood members, to a degree that improvisation appears to be minimal. Forming lines, the dancers perform simultaneously the rhythmical movements of the head, the swaying of the torso up and down, the thumping of the feet, and of course the singing of the brotherhood's special hymn-like pieces. These may consist of the name of God only, sung in specific ways – specified accentuation of a syllable, changing rhythmical bases – or of short praises in the name of God, the Prophet, and the *shaykhs* of the order. As a rule, musical instruments and percussion are not employed on this particular occasion, although there are certain *dhikr* episodes where the dancers use short wooden staffs, swords, or raised flags which they sway in a prearranged manner.

In the beginning the rhythm of dancing is slow, but it gets progressively faster. The movements do not become more complicated; what does change, though, is the breathing pattern. Following the *shaykh*, all dancers breathe audibly, executing several patterns every few minutes. For example, five minutes of two short inhalations and a long exhalation are followed by one long inhalation and three short exhalations. This use of hyperventilation I have also observed among the participants in spirit-possession rituals. It is a powerful technique for guiding the self into ecstasy in particularly designed contexts among people for whom spirits and *ṣūfī* saints are experientially real.

Sufism and Society

Besides their specifically liturgical functions and the offering of educational, social welfare, and health services, discussed in the previous section as well as in chapter 4 in relation to *zakāt*, *ṣūfī* brotherhoods are instrumental in bringing together people from different social, cultural, and ethnic backgrounds.

Morocco and the Sudan

Morocco and the Sudan are good case studies from which to start our discussion. As Eickelman writes, the term "*marabout*", by which the Moroccan saintly figures are known to the wider public, comes from the root *murābiṭ*, meaning the "tied one." Taking us back to a period when North Africa had not been yet fully Islamized (which for vast regions is as recent as the mid-nineteenth century), the term refers to those pious Muslims who traveled into tribal territories converting people to Islam or at least forming the first ties between them and the encroaching world of Islam and Arabism.[27] Such people were often *ṣūfī* or itinerant preachers endowed with an aura of sanctity, but they also operated as militant zealots, political agents, and traders. Their *zāwiyya*s functioned as centers of learning, refuges against the lawlessness of the open countryside, waystations for travelers, and focal points affording protection to the surrounding populations. Especially, in the last capacity, they can be recognized as "a major factor in the reproduction of the North African countryside by a new generation of North Africans too humble to be described by Ibn Khaldūn as a race."[28] Intermarriage was often practiced so the *marabout*s could progressively become founders of saintly lineages which in time could acquire political status as mediators working in parallel with more established lines of authority (chiefly clans). Be that as it may, it would be wrong to see these saintly figures as missionaries, in the strict Christian sense of the term. Although some of them had certainly taken it into their hearts to proselytize the pagans, this was done in conjunction with the furthering of the commercial and political interests of themselves, their families, or their descent groups. We are thus talking about very long processes, the outcome of which was always directly associated with wider political developments.

Knowledge of history, then, is indispensable if things are to be seen in the right perspective. For example, to return to the Sudanese *Qādirī darwīsh*es mentioned earlier, *shaykh* Ḥamad al-Nīl's *qubba* stands just outside a large residential area inhabited mainly by subaltern populations from the Nuba Hills, the Western Sudan, and the South. As I have already observed on pp. 103–4, all these people are considered to be second-class citizens by most Northern Sudanese Arabs who, besides racial prejudice, also exhibit a strong suspicion about their Islamic credentials. In this context, participation in the weekly celebrations at Ḥamad al-Nīl's *qubba*, even as members of the audience, can be seen as part of a process through which such subalterns are accommodated within the Islamic tradition of the Northern Sudan.

Such processes have a long history. Already since the eighteenth century, if not earlier, many *ṣūfī* and itinerant holy men had woven themselves into the socio-political fabric of the non-Arab people of Sinnār in the central Sudan through intermarriage and the foundation of holy lineages.[29] Thus a long Islamization and Arabization process was initiated in the wider area, giving Sudanese Islam a strong *ṣūfī* flavor.[30] Such processes, too, can be clearly discerned among the hundreds of thousands of nineteenth-century African slaves from the Southern and Western Sudan who were transported to the North, and among their descendants and other subaltern populations who live today near the *qubba* of Ḥamad al-Nīl and in other "third-class" residential areas and shanty-towns on the outskirts of the Sudanese capital.[31]

A *ṣūfī* brotherhood affiliation was of great importance. But not all brotherhoods played the same role. Some, like the *Tijāniyya*, became associated with specific tribal areas and acquired a more localized character. Others, like the *Qādiriyya*, had always been more open towards the expanding subaltern populations. This is attested by the large number of ritualistic elements originating with such groups that the brotherhood has accommodated in its liturgical life,[32] but also by the fact that people like the devotees of the subaltern *zār ṭumbura* possession cult see themselves liturgically associated with this rather than with any other order.[33] A further example is the *Khatmiyya* order which fought against the Mahdist regime (1885–98), thus winning the support of many who had been enslaved by it and were freed after its capitulation.

Somalia

But even among Muslim populations, the *ṣūfī* brotherhoods' integrative role is definitely in evidence, as I.M. Lewis's 1984 account of the *Qādiriyya*, *Aḥmadiyya*, and *Ṣāliḥiyya* brotherhoods in Somalia reveals.[34] The first of these can be found among the nomadic northern Somali tribes, segments of which identify themselves with the holy clans of those who introduced *Qādiriyya* in the country. In this way these Somali tribes are able to claim Arab descent.

Operating among the sedentary populations of southern Somalia, the other two orders have laid emphasis on the establishment of agricultural communities (*jamāʿa*s) on lands allotted to them by the local tribes. This has turned the *jamāʿa*s into part of the local descent system. From this position, the *jamāʿa* members act as teachers or unofficial religious judges among the tribes.[35] At the same time, *jamāʿa* members, whose original *ṭarīqa* associations may have been lost, transforming them into descent groups clustered around the tombs/shrines of their founders, are subject to conflicting loyalties between their own *shaykh*s and the tribal leaders.[36] The whole picture is particularly complex, with the *jamāʿa*s functioning as intermediaries between tribal groups, but also as factors that accentuate the slow demise of the local lineage system through the transformation of the existing communities into independent settlements modeled on themeslves. So as Lewis argues, in the nomadic north sufism works harmoniously with the lineage structure whereas in the semi-nomadic and sedentary south it appears to work against it.[37] On the whole, Lewis maintains that, as in other Islamic societies, in Somalia the *ṣūfī* brotherhoods have traditionally functioned as channels of alliance between the tribes and that today they represent the roots of new urban political parties.[38]

Algeria

This relationship between sufism and politics is explored by F. Colonna in an article on the religious aspects of Algerian resistance against French colonialism. Colonna argues that in nineteenth-century Algeria the *ṣūfī* brotherhoods had enormous power, mainly because the majority, if not all, the Algerian *ʿulamāʾ*, perhaps the only literate social group,[39] belonged to their ranks.

From that position, the brotherhoods offered perhaps the only channel of resistance against the French occupation until the middle of the century. After that, their power started diminishing. Two reasons were behind this. First, until that time the occupation of their land was perceived by the Algerians in a fragmented way.[40] So each community reacted on an *ad hoc* basis, trying to oust the French from its own territory. Most uprisings were headed by *ṣūfī* brotherhoods – which often took the *jamāʿa* form described earlier by Lewis – considered by the French to be subversive by definition.[41] It was only after the al-Muqqrānī uprising of 1871, in which *shaykh* al-Ḥaddād of the *Raḥmaniyya* order played an important role, that the French coordinated their colonial project at the national level, thus wreaking havoc on Algeria's social structures. The 1873 and 1877 laws for the redistribution of land, the expansion of the secular French legal code to cover the entire country, the excessive taxation of the population, outright repression, and the appointment of official *ʿulamāʾ* were among the measures put into practice.

Clearly, the *ṣūfī* brotherhoods were unable to combat the enemy at this level. They may have had a lot of local centers in many towns and they could bring together distinct tribal populations, but they could not conceptualize the idea of a national level and consequently could not react appropriately. When the segmentary structure of the country was destroyed or at least seriously eroded, the power of the brotherhoods could only decline.[42]

The second reason why *ṣūfī* brotherhoods did not manage to continue wielding their traditional power in modern Algeria is related to the appearance of a new movement at the turn of the century, the Muslim reformers. Unlike the brotherhoods, which always retained some autonomy and drew their followers mainly from the rural areas, reformist Islam presented a united political front and, what was of utmost importance, appealed more to the urban bourgeois.[43]

These were now the heart of Algeria, whose tribal past had been destroyed and were on their way to becoming an urban class society. Reformist Islam was totally against sufism, which it presented as mere superstition, and accused many of the orders as well as members of the religious aristocracy of having reached an understanding with the colonial administration. Furthermore, the reformists presented a relatively cohesive nationalist program and stressed the importance of education, especially in Arabic language and culture as ways of combating French influence.

This being the case, in the post-1870s conditions the reformist movement was in a far better position to act against French colonialism. When Algeria got its independence, this situation continued as the state intervened in favor of Islamic reformism.[44] Islam was made into the official religion of the country, a corps of state *'ulamā'* was established, and the brotherhoods were legally banned. As Colonna writes, "a change in tribal/urban relations, the establishment of a strong central power, and finally the emergence of one or even of a number of bourgeoisies"[45] gave rise to the emergence of a unified religious sphere that fosters hierarchical oppositions (sufism vis-à-vis reformism) directly determined by what is going on in the social, political and economic spheres of society.[46]

Egypt

Regarding Egypt, a relatively different picture emerges from a 1960s historically informed ethnographic account of the *Ḥāmidiyya Shādhiliyya* order given by M. Gilsenan. The order was established in the 1920s, and by the 1960s it had between twelve and sixteen thousand members in Cairo and other urban centers of the Nile Delta. As Gilsenan argues, until the 1920s the Egyptian brotherhoods offered their members an "organised associational life" bringing together people of different socio-economic classes. The possibilities such an interaction afforded to those involved with the brotherhood were obviously great, but they were soon lost in the whirlwind of Egyptian modernization. Professional politicians, army officers, landlords, and journalists started gradually to take over much of the work done hitherto by the brotherhoods, offering new communication channels between the less privileged and the bureaucracy or, more generally, the state.

On top of this, the economic position of the brotherhoods declined through harsher taxation and the confiscation by the state of large tracts of their arable land, as well as through the promotion of new values and novel practices, e.g. modern education, which ran counter to what sufism stood for. That meant that the most prosperous and well-educated classes now shunned the brotherhoods, leaving them to those from the lower urban and rural classes. In itself this was deleterious for the future of the brotherhoods as it robbed them of their inter-class character.

Ḥāmidiyya Shādhiliyya, Gilsenan writes, managed to work its way through much of this, perhaps because its founder, Salāma b. Ḥasan Salāma (1867–1939), was himself a low-ranking bureaucrat with a first-hand knowledge of the system. Claiming Prophetic ancestry, Salāma was a pious, low-key man who steered the brotherhood away from all forms of ecstasy and the performance of miracles. Moreover, the brotherhood was provided with a strict code of behavior and a tight organization, something that enabled the hierarchy to trace its members all over Egypt and to offer immediate assistance to all those who were in need. In other words, the *Ḥāmidiyya Shādhiliyya* could boast of working along the same lines as the modernized state bureaucracy. Unfortunately, Gilsenan has not returned to the subject after the 1960s so as to see how the brotherhood coped with the rising tide of Islamism whose local associations today offer communal assistance similar to that offered by the *ṣūfī* brotherhoods, while also placing their members in a more politically informed transnational framework.

THE WORLD OF SPIRITS

Like all religious traditions, Islam is also characterized by a populous realm of spiritual entities, some better defined in nature and character than others. The generally accepted name for this class of entities is *jinn* although localized Islamic traditions use other names as well, such as *riḥ*, *shayāṭīn*, *ʿafārīt*, *khayṭ*, or *ghwāl*. For now, these names can be treated as synonyms. However, situating them in their respective ethnographic settings points towards diverse understandings of the generic *jinn* category. Nonetheless, they all refer to the commonly held view of the *jinn*, as this is given in the *Qur'ān*, especially in 6: 100.

As we learn from the relevant note found in most annotated editions of the *Qur'ān*, and from the dominant textual and popular traditions throughout the Middle East, the *jinn*s were created out of fire – unlike man, who was created out of clay. Like man, however, the *jinn*s may believe or disbelieve in God and will be called to account on the Day of Judgment. In certain ethnographic settings (Egypt, the Sudan, Tunisia, Morocco), King Solomon, or, alternatively, *shaykh* ʿAbd al-Qādir al-Jīlānī, is thought to control all types of *jinn*. A distinction, too, is made between *shayāṭīn* proper, pictured as the children of Satan, and the rest of the *jinn*s.[47] In that sense, *jinn*s are seen as malicious or mischievous, but not beyond redemption.

There are different kinds of *jinn* reflecting the variety of the human world. Thus, we have Muslim, Christian, Jewish, and pagan *jinn*s, male and female, Arab, Ethiopian, and black (African), high- or low-class ones. Sometimes, even a distinction by professional guilds is proposed, thus making the world of *jinn*s eerily similar to ours. This world is situated either underground or between the earth and the sky although simultaneously it is also held that *jinn*s inhabit, or perhaps infest, areas of the human world associated with water, humidity, blood, or dirtiness. These may include streams, springs, wells, caves, grottoes, hollows, marshes, baths, drains, toilets, sewers, and refuse dumps, but also slaughterhouses, graveyards, back-alleys, deserted houses and ruins, unusual trees and rocks.

People, especially women and children, should avoid such places lest they be attacked by the resident *jinn*s and suffer misfortune or a variety of ailments ranging from headaches and general malaise to paralysis and madness. If that is unavoidable, they must try to protect themselves by invoking God's name or by carrying special amulets. People are also prone to attacks when they are angry or frightened and when they go through liminal periods such as pregnancy or marriage. In the event of an attack, which takes the form of possession, the spirits are exorcised by specialists associated with *ṣūfī* brotherhoods or by independent religious healers. Treatment includes *Qur'ānic* readings over the patient, the use of amulets, incense, and spells, and the drinking by the patient of a solution of water and the ashes of burnt *Qur'ānic* texts. A huge variety of treatises and popular tracts related to *jinn*-induced illness can be found throughout the Muslim world. In that respect, knowledge and practices pertaining to *jinn*s can easily be associated with various forms of magic, spell-writing, divination, and the evil eye, as well as the world of the saints who provide spiritual defenses against, and cures from, *jinn* attacks.

In addition to all this, throughout the Middle East and North Africa we find beliefs in what Crapanzano calls "named-*jnun*."[48] These are endowed with a more fully developed character, appearance, and family relations than the rest of the *jinn*s, as well as with preferences and tastes whose satisfaction they seek by possessing their victims permanently. Not amenable to exorcism, named *jinn*s initiate a symbiotic relationship with their hosts in the context of which they voice their demands for "luxury" items (clothing and accessories, perfume, food items, cigarettes, and alcoholic beverages), animal sacrifices, and the regular celebration of ceremonies where their hosts dance ecstatically to the tunes of special music. Although in most other respects these entities resemble ordinary *jinn*s, the aforementioned traits result in their differentiation from the former, at least in the eyes of their followers, the majority of whom are women and men of lower social status. Amongst the best-known cases in the anthropological literature on spirit possession which deals with these practices are the *zār* cult, which is very popular throughout the Nile valley and parts of the Arabian Peninsula, and the Moroccan cult of *Aïsha Qandisha*.[49] It is to some of these works that I shall turn to flesh out the rather sketchy account of the spirit world offered above and to move from a folkloric presentation of exotic practices to a more anthropological discussion of the relevant issues.

Indeed, the use of anthropological analysis that goes beyond folklore and a paratactic presentation of beliefs in *jinn*s and other cognate spirits is imperative if we wish to place our present discussion within the context of the "orthodoxy" production process which governs much of our analysis of Islamic discourse. As it were, belief in, and practices related to, spirits comprise a locus superbly situated in the field of contestation on Islamic authenticity and in all politically animated discussions among Muslims and others on the importance of the local. As such, its anthropological analysis should be seen as an integral part of all studies of living Islamic traditions.

Syncretism/Anti-Syncretism

Reading accounts on spirit possession in a Muslim context, we are presented with the view that most of these spirits, earlier called "named-*jnun*," can be seen in syncretic terms. Now syncretism is a contested concept that has been used in various ways by both social scientists and members of the public. In their well-received 1994 Introduction on the subject, Shaw and Stewart pointed out that "'[s]yncretism' . . . is not a determinate term with a fixed meaning, but one which has been historically constituted and reconstituted."[50] It would thus be more profitable "to focus upon processes of religious synthesis and upon discourses of syncretism. This necessarily involves attending to the workings of power and agency."[51]

In doing so, Shaw and Stewart pair syncretism with its opposite term, anti-syncretism, which is often related to originality and authenticity, and promoted among others by "religious movements which are characterized as 'fundamentalist' or 'nativist'."[52] Several other issues are also critically discussed, the most relevant to our discussion being the following two.

First, the view that syncretism should refer to religion, describing situations where two different traditions interact. Shaw and Stewart disagree with this, reminding us that religion is a culturally constructed Western category whose content and boundaries are historically contingent. Thus problematizing the boundaries between religion and culture, they bring forward the potentially brutal politics of identity that inform areas of religious discourse such as religious dissemination, missiology, conversion, indigenization, and religious reformation in the name of an imputed authenticity. From such a perspective, to use the example of spirit possession, practices associated with spirits not specified in a locally dominant Islamic textual tradition can be analyzed as either "illegitimate" syncretism or as cultural expressions of faith, pointing to an indigenization or inculturation of the locally dominant religious tradition.

The former view, rare in modern anthropology, is held by neo-orientalists as well as by those actors in the field who identify themselves with hegemonic versions of religious "orthodoxy." These include militant Islamists and conservatives, as well as elite and middle-class members who are closer to a *sharīʿa*-minded Islam. For them, possession and other ecstatic practices are aberrations of the uneducated masses. The latter view is held by those anthropologists who are critical of their own "classical" traditions and gravitate toward theoretical positions such as historical anthropology, post-structuralism, or theory of practice. It is held too by representatives of religions with strong missionary traditions such as the Roman Catholic Church, which has reasons to legitimate an African or a Melanesian Christianity. Lastly, it is also held by those religious innovators who see in syncretism a strategy promoting their communities' interests. As Shaw and Stewart write, "we cannot assume 'popular' syncretism to be discursively unavailable."[53] Still, one should not stretch the point too far. As will be seen in the ethnographic examples below, as a rule possession cults' clientele tend to perceive their practices in a way mirroring that of their detractors: as exemplary proofs of their Islamic "orthodoxy," whose condemnation only demonstrates the ignorance of those higher in the social – and often ethnic – hierarchy. Obviously, issues of class and ethnicity are not far from the surface in the context of such debates.

Second, the view that

> [S]yncretism may be (or perhaps only looks like) a form of resistance, because hegemonic practices are never simply absorbed wholesale through passive "acculturation"; at the very least, their incorporation involves some kind of transformation, some kind of deconstruction and reconstruction which converts them to people's own meanings and projects.[54]

However correct this might be, Shaw and Stewart emphasize, a careful analysis of the ethnographic data suggests that syncretic practices both subvert *and* promote cultural or religious hegemonic traditions. As they write,

> [t]he appropriation of dominance and the subversion of dominance may be enacted at the same time, in the same syncretic act. Subversion may even be an unintended consequence of a syncretic process in which actors intend to appropriate rather than subvert cultural dominance. These conundrums of agency and intentionality make syncretism very slippery, but it is precisely its capacity to contain paradox, contradiction and polyphony which makes syncretism such a powerful symbolic process . . . Nor are anti-syncretic forms exempt from such contradiction.[55]

This formulation captures perfectly the complexity one encounters in the study of possession cults in the Middle East and North Africa, especially in the latter, as the predominantly Arab North African Muslim societies were, until the nineteenth century recipients, of huge numbers of African slaves, while the adjacent regions of sub-Saharan Africa further south were slave-hunting grounds and frontiers of the Muslim world, despite the existence of African sultanates that spread from the present-day southwestern Sudan to the Atlantic.

In a world of stupendous cultural and ethnic variation, where "true" Arabs and black Africans were almost ideal types in a hierarchical continuum of descending social status, with the latter considered subhuman slaves, Islam – and to a degree Arabism – provided a common idiom that explained both differences and similarities. Fluid enough, it was formulated and reformulated in a context of shifting political alliances and betrayals, wars and revolutions, economic booms and busts. In a world that Gellner's "pendulum theory" cannot envisage due to its complexity and constant movement, it would not be inappropriate to talk about Islamic subcultures nested within each other, feeding from each other, while being in continual competition over meaning and political and economic ascent.

These harsh realities are still part of today's world in the wider area, further complicated by the legacy of colonialism and the dashed hopes of the post-colonial state. Spirit-possession practices, traditionally central in this game of animating ethnic, cultural, and religious identities, are still important and flourishing. Obviously, their present form and sociological significance within the wider field of local Islamic ritual practices differ from those of previous historical moments. However, interpreting their contemporary situation and tracing their changes through time is a worthwhile task that sheds light on an aspect of Islamic discourse rarely addressed by anthropologists, other than specialists on possession cults or on religion or ritual studies.

Indeed, most books on Islam or Islamic societies, those written by anthropologists included, do not discuss beliefs and practices related to spirits, besides the token reference to the *jinn*s. So despite expressions of disdain toward the distinction between "orthodox" and "popular" Islam as orientalistic constructions, anthropologists discuss spirit possession as part of a people's or group's experience only in a piecemeal manner and under the rubric of culture rather than Islam or religion. The present account, situated next to discussions of the *Qur'ān*, the pilgrimage, Islamic modernism and Islamism, seeks to overturn this division of labor. At a different level, taking into account the popularity of such practices among women, it also demonstrates the importance of female practices as complementary to and interdependent with those of men – without suggesting that they end at spirit possession.

The *Ḥamadsha* and Other Examples from North Africa

Crapanzano's 1981 study of the Moroccan *Ḥamadsha* brotherhood is still widely read by anthropologists studying spirit possession and healing cults. For our present purposes, the study's significance lies not so much in its heavily psychoanalytic approach to possession and possession trance, which one may feel overshadows some more solid sociocultural considerations, but in the fact that phenomenologically the *Ḥamadsha* straddle the distance between *ṣūfī* orders and possession cults *proper*. Crapanzano's rich descriptions concerning the structure of the *Ḥamadsha* brotherhood and its ceremonial life provide us with a rare insight on the ways in which *ṣūfī baraka* and the power of spirits work together within a single experiential universe guided by Islamic precepts and Moroccan cultural categories, even while we treat his explanatory model with caution.

The *Ḥamadsha* clientele are followers of the eighteenth-century *ṣūfī* saints Sidi 'Ali ben Ḥamdush and Sidi Ahmed Dghughi.[56] After discussing the legends concerning the saints' acquisition of *baraka*, Crapanzano focuses on the villages where they are buried, describing their mausoleums and the adjacent shrines of *'Aïsha Qandisha*, a female *jinn* closely related to them. Almost half of the villages' inhabitants are descendants of the saints. Both descent groups are organized according to the Bedouin segmentary model and headed by two administrators (*mizwar*) who control their financial affairs and whose authority is extended over each village respectively. Among their principal sources of income are the proceeds from the pilgrimage to the tombs and the shrines, the ceremonies celebrated by the brotherhoods, and the earnings of the saints' properties.[57]

Besides financial wealth, the saints' descendants are also endowed with *baraka*. Though all of them possess *baraka* due to agnatic descent, some are considered to possess more *baraka* than others. This is due to personal characteristics, but can take an institutional twist as well, as in the cases of the *mizwar* and of highly respected elders. As for the *Ḥamadsha*, none of the saints' descendants belongs to the brotherhood, whose activities they treat "with a mixture of scorn and respect."[58] In other words, the *Ḥamadsha* do not possess *baraka* naturally, they are recipients of it.

To find the *Ḥamadsha* we must move from the saints' villages to their lodges (*zāwiyya*s) in the city of Meknes and the nearby shanty-towns. The city *zāwiyya*s are dedicated to either one of the two saints, but all pay tribute to *'Aïsha Qandisha*. Their enclosed courtyards function as stages for the celebration of ceremonies and as burial grounds for those who, for a fee, want to be near the saints' *baraka*, thus hoping to gain access to paradise. Also in the *zāwiyya* courtyards there are fig trees dedicated to *'Aïsha Qandisha*, where the faithful tie bits of cloth "as signs of various promises to the she-demon . . . if a child is born."[59]

The city *Ḥamadsha* include the adepts, the devotees, and the musicians. Members of the lower classes, the adepts are illiterate men who attend most *zāwiyya* meetings and act as ritual assistants. They are often stereotyped as "black" (Africans of slave descent). The adepts are not hierarchically organized, though one of them acts as *zāwiyya* leader (*muqaddim*). All *muqaddim*s are chosen unanimously by the adepts and approved by the *mizwar*s, under whose authority lie all *Ḥamadsha zāwiyya*s. Brotherhood membership is not hereditary.

The devotees are those male and female followers of the two saints who participate in the *Ḥamadsha* rituals. Most of them are devoted to the brotherhood because they have been cured from illnesses caused by *'Aïsha Qandisha*. The cure may have been effected by the adepts or by a pilgrimage to the saints' tombs. During the ceremonies, devotees dance ecstatically, while some slash their heads with knives, a practice characteristic of the *Ḥamadsha*. The musicians (oboe-, guitar-, and recorder-players) are professionals attached to the order long term. Each *zāwiyya* has its own musicians, although there are overlaps. The musicians are of great importance as they perform the tunes which animate the *jinn*s that possess the devotees during the ceremonies, thus leading their hosts to trance.

Each *Ḥamadsha zāwiyya* celebrates three types of performance; the one-day curing ceremonies of *lila* (night), the Friday afternoon *ḥaḍra*, and the name-day ceremonies celebrated seven days after a child's birth. In all three types, participants are thought to receive the saints' *baraka* and, where this applies, to be cured by spirit-induced illness – which again is seen as a manifestation of *baraka*. As a rule, the participants offer the *zāwiyya* gifts (candles, bread, sugar, or couscous) and small amounts of money or, when this is required by the saints or by *ʿAïsha Qandisha*, make sacrifices.[60] Theoretically, the money and gifts collected at the ceremonies are presented to the saints' descendants through their respective *mizwar*s. In reality, though, a percentage is disbursed among the *zāwiyya* adepts.[61]

In the shanty-town *zāwiyya*s Crapanzano distinguishes between the members and the devotees, but here the former are more pro-active than their corresponding city adepts in that they stage performances for a fee. This is because the whole spirit of the shanty-town *Ḥamadsha* is geared towards the *jinn*s; the saints are still present, but in a rather mechanistic way.[62] More precisely, the saints' *baraka* is seen as the channel through which the harmful effects of possession by the *jinn* are set right, leading to the recovery of the victims for whom the ceremonies are celebrated.

No fully formed theological explication seems to be available to the devotees and brotherhood members, but this does not mean that they lack something. Discursive analysis is only part of the *Ḥamadsha* experience of the "supernatural" and, perhaps, not an important one at that. Transmitted through the entranced participants in the *Ḥamadsha* ceremonies, the *baraka* effects a state of health for patients, actualized and perpetuated through following a regime commanded by the *jinn*. In its essential requirements, this regime consists of actively participating in the saints' cult and in the *Ḥamadsha* ritual practices, activities which Crapanzano describes in two chapters focusing on the pilgrimage to the saints' tombs and *ʿAïsha Qandisha*'s shrines, and on the *Ḥamadsha ḥaḍra* or ecstatic dances in the context of the one-day ceremonies (*lila*).

Finally, in a chapter that owes much to psychoanalysis and, rather unfortunately, little to sociological considerations, Crapanzano offers a more detailed picture of the relationship between the two *ṣūfī* saints and *ʿAïsha Qandisha*. As he argues, the *jinn*-induced illness afflicting the *Ḥamadsha*, at least the men, "is conceived at some level of consciousness as an inability to live up to the ideal standards of male conduct."[63] This Crapanzano relates to "the often arbitrary, harsh, and inconsistent behavior of the Moroccan father towards his son,"[64] which provides the latter with an ideal of male behavior, but demands that he accept it unquestioningly and meekly – that is, in a feminine manner.

When this contradiction is experienced in the form of a spirit-induced illness, the resolution comes from the transformation of the female *jinn* "from a force disruptive to the social and moral order into a force to preserve that order."[65] This is achieved with the assistance of the saints' *baraka*, "the symbolic equivalent of semen, virility, and the principle of patrilineality."[66] More specifically, possession by *'Aïsha Qandisha* represents the feminization of the patient who ritually enacts his own castration by slashing his head. Acquiring the saints' *baraka* and following the demands of the female *jinn*, the patient is rehabilitated in society. The symptoms disappear and once again he can act out his male role successfully. However, this does not imply a positive identification with the male ideal model. The patient is enabled to function along the lines suggested by the model because he receives the *baraka* of the saints, themselves exemplary models of social order, and because he obeys the demands of the (female) *jinn*, abandoning himself periodically in renewed acts of self-mutilation when participating in *Ḥamadsha ḥadra*s. So the resolution implied in *Ḥamadsha* therapy between *'Aïsha Qandisha* and the two *Ḥamadsha* saints, Crapanzano claims, involves a reconfiguration of their symbolic attachments that allows patients to overcome their illness/feminization, but only temporarily, as new episodes of illness can always afflict the *Ḥamadsha* clientele.

Besides the Moroccan *Ḥamadsha*, I would like to mention briefly a couple of other examples from nearby Tunisia, which exhibit in different ways this close interconnection between spirit-possession practices and sufism. The first one concerns the congregation of Sīdī Bel Hassen Essadli, a middle-class brotherhood operating in Tunis. As Ferchiou describes it, the official session of communal *dhikr* (*ḥaḍra*) of Sīdī Bel Hassen displays a marked gender dichotomy. On the one hand, we observe the male devotees chanting an introductory litany (*ḥizb*) comprising of *Qur'ānic* verses and invocations to God and then entering the *dhikr* with mounting enthusiasm, which may lead to a "state of collective trance."[67] On the other hand, we see the female devotees who initially stand silently in a contiguous room observing the men. As the latter start performing the *dhikr*, the women become progressively animated by their possessing *jinn*s under the watchful eyes of the female guardian of the sanctuary (*wakīla*). When the men enter into a state of collective trance, many women follow them in a parallel manner, only they are possessed by the *jinn*s. It is then, Ferchiou concludes, that we may encounter "speaking in tongues," when some of the spirits "talk" through their female hosts.

The second example comes from the brotherhoods of Sīdī Saad in Tunis and Sīdī Mansour in Sfax. Both instances Ferchiou describes as belonging to the *stambali* possession cult, a practice dominated by the black African community of Tunisia. As she writes, the celebrations start in their respective *zāwiyya* on a Thursday with the sacrifice of a black he-goat. In charge of the ritual is a group of five or six musicians and a female assistant (*'arīfa*), who has the power of divining. The ritual includes invocations of Prophet Muḥammad, of Bilāl, the first *mu'adhdhin* of Islam, and of *shaykh* 'Abd al-Qādir al-Jilānī of the *Qādiriyya* brotherhood.

> The possessed, all women, dance to the low-pitched sound of the *goumbri* [a type of guitar], and, as their possessing spirits are invoked, one by one they enter a trance. Sometimes, the *'arifa* attempts to exorcise spirits with massage and symbolic gestures. However, exorcism is not the ritual's essential goal. Rather, the cult has a therapeutic function and as such, aims at placating the spirits by pleasing them . . . The ceremony ends with the invocation of Nana 'Aisha, a member of the black series of spirits, who is associated with night and with blood.[68]

After the brief presentation of one more ethnographic case, where several congregations celebrate their possession cults in the suburban Tunis *zāwiya* of Saida al-Manoubiya through invoking their respective patron saints with the accompaniment of drums, Ferchiou concludes her account with a short discussion of the cult devotees' social profile. As she writes, the possessed women tend to come from the poorest sectors of the population. They often come from migrant rural families or from impoverished families of urban artisans. In most cases, their initial possession episode, perceived as illness, can be related to a critical moment: "loss of virginity, in a context of traditional control of sexuality; a sentimental deception or forced marriage; a natural abortion; a still-born child or the death of an infant."[69] But equally important for Ferchiou seems to be the fact that many of these women are obliged to enter the labor market and, certainly, this creates tensions with the traditional female model. "Today, to be employed outside means for women to fail in their roles as wives and mothers and to desert their home."[70] Spirit possession, especially in its incorporation within the widely accepted "traditional" *ṣūfī* religious system that prevails throughout North Africa, offers such women a means to articulate the tensions they experience in a socially approved or at least socially understood way.

The *Ṭumbura* Cult

The *ṭumbura* spirit-possession cult in the Sudan is another example of the blending of sufism and spirit possession.[71] The difference, so to speak, between this and the *Ḥamadsha* and other possession cults discussed above is that *ṭumbura* devotees are not *formally* associated with any particular *ṣūfī* order. Still, cult officiants claim that *ṭumbura* is part of the *Qādiriyya*, the biggest *ṣūfī* order in the country, a claim which *Qādiriyya* officials expressly deny. In all cases, what cannot be denied is the centrality of the *Qādiriyya* founder, *shaykh* 'Abd al-Qādir al-Jilānī, in *ṭumbura*'s symbolic universe.

Ṭumbura is practiced in the shanty-towns and low-class neighborhoods of the urban centers of the predominantly Arab Northern Sudan. However, there are very few, if any, devotees of Arab descent among the cult's clientele; the people of *ṭumbura* – *nās ṭumbura*, as they call themselves – come from the Western Sudan (Dār Fūr), the South and the Nuba Hills. A fair percentage of them are slave descendants, while the rest are migrants from the above-mentioned areas and, in the eyes of the Northerners, members of enslaveable peoples. This is perhaps among the reasons why the Arab Northerners have always considered *ṭumbura* an un-Islamic and barbarous practice, indeed a proof of its devotees' assumed baseness and ignorance, if a proof beyond their slave descent was ever needed.

Ṭumbura belongs to what I have called elsewhere the "*zār* cult complex."[72] This includes a number of distinct cultic practices that surround the *zār* spirit and are loosely associated with different ethnic groups, social categories, and regions of the Sudan. The best-known cult of the "*zār* cult complex" is *zār boré* – our next example – which is mainly associated with lower- and middle-class women of Arab descent. Other *zār* cults, now almost defunct, are *zār Nyamānyam* (the *zār* of the Azande) and *zār Sawākniyya* (the *zār* from Sawākin on the Red Sea).

Distinguished from the malevolent *jinn*, *zār* is an amoral and capricious spirit whose cult, similar to the *Ḥamadsha* as far as it concerns spirit-induced illness, is spread throughout Islamic Africa and the Middle East. The spirit appears in many guises, usually taken from the historical experience of its devotees. Thus, among the *ṭumbura* people the spirit modalities include the *Nuba*, the *Banda*, and the *Gumuz*, representing pagan African tribes to which many devotees originally belonged before their ancestors' enslavement by Arab Northerners; the *Sawākniyya* and the *Lambūnāt*, associated with the old Red Sea port of Sawākin, from which thousands of slaves were exported to Arabia and Egypt; the *Bābūrāt*, associated with the ships that transported the Anglo-Egyptian army to the Sudan in the 1890s, a development that led to the colonization of the country and the abolition of slavery; and the *Bāshawāt* and the *Khawājāt*, also related to the Anglo-Egyptian slave liberators and colonial administrators of the Anglo-Egyptian Sudan.

In the *ṭumbura* universe, then, through its modalities the invading spirit represents aspects of the *ṭumbura* people's collective historical self. This self they sometimes label *Sūdānī*, an adjective that until the 1920s did not refer to all Sudanese, its formal contemporary translation, but to those of African descent who had been subjected to enslavement.[73] However, the cult devotees turn this on its head, declaring the *Sūdānī nās āṣlī*, the "original people" and lawful owners of the land. In this manner, possession by *zār ṭumbura* implies the gathering of the devotees' fragmented subaltern self and the construction of a positive self-identity: rather than brutish slaves, the *ṭumbura* devotees present themselves as the original people of the land whose ancestors had been unlawfully enslaved by the Arabs and who are still regarded by the latter as inferior.

Besides the identity, behavioral traits and characteristic attire of the *zār ṭumbura* spirit modalities, this rearticulation of the self through possession and membership of the *ṭumbura* cult is also demonstrated in the songs of the cult which are separated into categories tied to each individual modality of the spirit. The songs are themselves often conflated with their corresponding spirit modalities thus creating further divisions and bringing into sharp relief additional characters or scenes associated with the modalities: the *Banda* spirit modality refers to the *Banda* tribe of southwestern Dār Fūr, who are often identified with the Azande; some of the *Banda* songs mention Babīnga, N'gurma, and Zingiabah, who can be identified with members of the Azande royal genealogies.[74] In a similar manner most *ṭumbura* songs describe scenes from the historical experience of the *Sūdānī* people. Tales of enslavement are intertwined with accounts of military exploits and political plots, creating a picture – obviously fragmented and mythologized – of the *Sūdānī* people not as subhuman slaves, but as a wrongly subjugated social category with a tragic history.

In all that, we can see that possession by the *zār ṭumbura* spirit articulates the differences between the dominant Arabs and the subaltern *Sūdānī*, turning upside down their historically informed relationship of subjugation. It does, though, something else, too.

Arab hegemony over the *Sūdānī* has always been political and economic as well as cultural. When the slaves were transported to the North, they were Islamized and, in due time, Arabized in terms of manners and cultural characteristics (rites of passage, kinship organization, attire, language). Such a religious and cultural conversion was also desired by the slaves themselves, as it created a space wherein a common idiom could be used in the never-ending negotiations between masters and slaves. In that respect, it was common, too, for freed slaves and their descendants to appropriate their erstwhile masters' tribal identity.[75] Nonetheless, the Islamized and Arabized slaves and their descendants, as well as all those destitute twentieth-century migrants from the same regions, have remained second-class Muslims and half-caste Arabs in a society proud of its (self-proclaimed) Arab ancestry and Islamic heritage.

Here, too, *ṭumbura* membership reformulates this relationship of power. Having symbolically inverted the Arab–*Sūdānī* relationship in the aforementioned manner, *ṭumbura* membership also allows the devotees to present themselves as descendants of Adam and Eve, i.e. as true human beings rather than as "speaking animals" and as true Muslims, as good as any other Arab or non-Arab. This is done by presenting *ṭumbura* as a veritable Islamic practice and its members as devout Muslims. We can approach this at two levels.

First, all *ṭumbura* ceremonies start with and contain throughout invocations to God, Prophet Muḥammad, Adam and Eve as progenitors of the human race, and a host of important *ṣūfī* saints of the Sudanese tradition. Second, the spirit itself is associated with *shaykh* ʿAbd al-Qādir al-Jilānī of the *Qādiriyya*, a *ṣūfī* order that has been traditionally more open than others to non-Arab subalterns. Not only is the *shaykh*'s green banner one of the four *ṭumbura* flags and his Y-shaped staff is held by all officiants when reciting invocations, but initiation into the cult, as well as the celebration of the closing of the Ramaḍān fast and of the Prophet's birthday, involve sacrifices in the name of the *shaykh*. Additionally and contrary to other possession cults, given the fact that *ṭumbura* devotees are irrevocably cured of the spirit-induced illness on condition of their full initiation into the cult, *shaykh* ʿAbd al-Qādir al-Jilānī appears as a source of *baraka* that transforms their reality and gives meaning to their everyday life. In other words, if possession by the *zār* guides people into the hands of *ṭumbura*, when cured by the officiants, they become lifelong devotees under the protection of *shaykh* ʿAbd al-Qādir al-Jilānī.

Lately, *ṭumbura* has been getting closer to the feminine cult of *zār boré*. For this, its relationship with *shaykh* ʿAbd al-Qādir al-Jilānī is becoming more tenuous, while the possessing spirit acquires centrality in a context of recurrent illness episodes. It seems, then, that from providing a *ṣūfī*-like organizational framework for subalterns, *ṭumbura* is now becoming a cult attracting female subalterns who would only be admitted with difficulty into the *zār boré* of the Northern Arab lower- and middle-class female devotees.

Such a transformation is logical. The *Sūdānī* self-identity "traditionally" articulated by *ṭumbura* is not relevant to current political and cultural developments. Islamism, new configurations of ethnic relations, and new forms of identity politics among more recent migrants to the Arab North are defining contemporary realities. If the slave descendants are not so keen any more (after three to four generations) to keep alive a *Sūdānī* identity that ties them to a stigmatized past, the younger migrants who enter *ṭumbura* have every reason to "remember" their Nuba or Fūr ethnic identity – the Gumuz are almost extinct, the Banda have lost much of their power and are now living mainly in the Central African Republic, and the port of Sawākin has been virtually abandoned for almost one hundred years – and to situate the cult and its symbolic universe in their ethnic Islamic tradition. New types of negotiations are needed that *ṭumbura*'s blend of possession and sufism cannot adequately serve without undergoing transformation.

The *Zār Boré* Cult of the Sudan

The Sudanese cult of *zār boré*, also known as the *red wind (rīh al-aḥmar)*, is our last example from the spirit world, which I have sought to situate within the premises of Islamic mysticism and to discuss in relation to sufism. The difference between *boré* and the possession cults discussed above is that *boré* appears to be further removed from the cult of the saints, although this does not diminish its

Islamic character in any way as the practice is very firmly situated within the Sudanese Islamic tradition representing an important dimension of the people's everyday experience with the sacred.

Practiced mainly by married lower- and middle-class women of Arab descent, *boré* is the best known of all practices of the "*zār* cult complex," both in urban and rural settings. In that sense, *boré* is a women's cult and more generally part of a female Sudanese religious economy, interdependent with, and complementary to, male religiosity and devotional practices. As in all previous examples, the spirit never leaves its host and, like the *Ḥamadsha*, *stanbali*, et al. but unlike *ṭumbura*, has to be kept satisfied with periodic celebrations and the offering of special items. In terms of its ontology and in relation to their host, *zār* manifestations are not seen as modalities of a single spirit, but as distinct entities representing the Other, the world *outside* the sociocultural environment of the cult devotees.

From this point of view, participation in *zār boré* can be linked to the tensions experienced by its mainly female devotees in their everyday effort to live up to the ideals posed by their specific cultural milieu in the face of a constantly encroaching outside world, an open field of opportunities and dangers at all levels. In a more technical language, cult participation has to do with the management of the self in conditions of sociocultural change. As Janice Boddy (1989) argues, it allows its female devotees to "de-naturalise," but not to negate, their own world and deal with their "cultural overdetermination" as women in a patriarchal Muslim society.

Having studied *zār* in the Northern Sudanese village of Hofriyat, Boddy argues that through allegory and the experience of possession-trance episodes the cult opens up the experiential universe of its devotees and offers another, off-centered, understanding of their everyday reality. She writes that in Hofriyat, just as in many other cultural settings in the Muslim Sudan and in the Middle East in general, "women are the inner core of village life: fertile, enclosed, domesticated; bound by custom, husbands, and kin; threatened by violations of interiority and its attendant values."[76] Having undergone pharaonic circumcision and infibulation, women become "a metonym for the resilience of village society in the face of external threat . . . [and] 'symbols of the homeland.' "[77] Their literally "enclosed, domesticated and bound" circumcised bodies stand for the "essence of femininity: uncontaminated, morally appropriate fertility, the right and the physical potential to reproduce the lineage or found a lineage section."[78] In other words, Boddy argues, marriage is revealed as "an *unsteady* means to use her fertility gift, to produce spouses both for her husband's kin, as required, and for her siblings' children and other personally relevant kin so as to consolidate her own support."[79]

"Unsteady" is the key word here. Clearly, this cultural ideal cannot be always realized as the gift of fertility may elude some women, albeit temporarily. This being the case, women are engaged in a continuous negotiation with men – husbands, brothers, fathers, and indeed with the patriarchal social order of the village as a whole – in order to live up to this culturally cherished ideal. As we read,

> the Hofriyati woman walks a tightrope in gale force winds: she must have children – not too few or too rarely lest her husband and others doubt her fertility, but not so many that she expends the source of her attractiveness and her husband loses interest.[80]

Enter here the *red wind zār* spirits which, as has been suggested, attack mostly *married* women. As in all cases described in Sudanese ethnography, but also in Egypt and in other Middle Eastern societies where the cult thrives and women find themselves in similar social positions, possession by the *zār* is directly connected with fertility, sometimes explicitly so. Complaining of illness and exhibiting symptoms such as boredom, apathy, depression, bad dreams, chills, chest pain, hemorrhage, etc. which are then divined to be the results of possession by the *zār*, that is to a *natural agent*, a woman avails herself of "a culturally sanctioned medium for articulating her dysphoria."[81] In this context, and through associations with the *red* female blood of the menstrual flow, "the *zār* provides a suitable idiom for articulating and meaningfully constructing women's anxieties having to do with their fertility."[82] Or, in the words of Constantinides who studied the same phenomenon on the outskirts of the Sudanese capital, "through spirit possession cults women who, for internal or external, physical or emotional reasons, are not adequately approximating to their culturally defined potential, express the nature of their problems through the symbolic behaviour of the cult's activities."[83] However, and here is the crucial point for both Boddy and Constantinides, in the ceremonies cult devotees not only symbolically register what is wrong with their social reality, but also somehow imply that things may improve and that the current problems may be overcome.

To understand this, we have to consider the identity of the spirits. As has been suggested earlier, *zār boré* spirits represent the Other, the world outside the sociocultural environment of the cult devotees. In the case described by Boddy, these take the stereotyped forms of *Darāwīsh* holy men, *Ḥabashī* male and female personas from Ethiopia, *ʿArab* spirits from the Red Sea hills and the desert *Hadendawa*, *ʿAbabda* and *Beni ʿAmer* tribes, the *Khawājāt* Europeans or Westerners, as rule symbolized by the British ex-colonial masters, the *Bāshawāt*, representing the even earlier Turco-Egyptian conquerors of the country, the Gypsy *Ḥalibs*, the West African *Fallata*, who have made their way into the Sudan as pilgrims to Mecca and as economic migrants, and the *ʿAbīd*, the African slaves from the South, whose descendants are still numerous everywhere in the Northern Sudan.[84] Similar pantheons are given in all ethnographies of *zār boré* in the Sudan, as well as in other Middle Eastern societies.

Possessed by what Lewis has called "a fluid historical mirror of the world of male Sudanese experience"[85] and Constantinides "a panorama of the recent historical past,"[86] the female *boré* devotees participate in well-orchestrated possession rituals which owe much of their evocative symbolism to traditional Northern Sudanese wedding ceremonies. Indeed, the person for whom the ceremony is celebrated is called "bride (*ʿarūsa*) of the spirit." But besides formal correspondences and structural parallels between possession and marriage, Boddy takes one more step arguing that, being "a muted expression of adult women's consciousness,"[87] *zār boré* uses the wedding imagery "as its foil, its allegorical 'pretext' "[88] in order to focus attention upon the values and significances of the hegemonic discourse that this imagery encodes. This, however, is done without forcing either favorable or negative conclusions. In that sense, *boré* is "counterhegemonic: it places an alternative construction on lived experience without denying the validity of culturally salient categories."[89]

Perhaps, Boddy continues, this may bring a change of outlook among the participants.[90] In other words, *zār boré*'s therapeutic efficacy lies in the possibility of effecting an experiential rift in the cultural as well as physical *enclosure* that overdetermines women's everyday life.[91]

Having said all this, one would think that, being an integral part of Northern Sudanese culture, *boré* can be situated without much discussion in the local *Islamic* universe. However, on closer inspection, we discover that things are more complicated than that, as we are confronted with a situation similar to what we saw with *ṭumbura*, albeit expressed in more hushed tones. While *ṭumbura* is roundly dismissed by the dominant Arab Northerners on account of its alleged un-Islamic character and its association with the low status of its subaltern non-Arab devotees, with *boré* things are different. On the one hand, the fact that *zār* is a type of *jinn*, that rituals start with the recitation of the *fātiḥa* and the invocation of Prophet Muḥammad and Bilāl, and that there are special rituals celebrated on the occasion of annual Islamic festivals has prompted many anthropologists to argue that *zār* participation "in many ways parallels men's participation in the religious brotherhoods."[92] And, of course, if that is not enough – in a sense it shouldn't be – we should listen to the devotees themselves, ordinary Arab Muslim women who proclaim their cult purely and utterly Islamic.

On the other hand, in a not unanticipated manner, *zār boré* is disapproved by most Northern Sudanese men on two grounds. First, they dismiss the very existence of the *zār* spirit, which is not mentioned in the *Qur'ān*, and when not reviled the cult is usually ignored by most *ʿulamā'* and *ṣūfī* masters. However, they do so half-heartedly and without much conviction as many amongst them have witnessed its potency and its miraculous cures, sometimes within their own families. Second, irrespective of its ontological existence, most men disapprove of the cult's social functions and see it as an opportunity for women to come together, dance, smoke, drink, and behave in a totally "un-Islamic" manner beyond appropriate social (read "male") surveillance.

Still, perhaps because of its immense popularity, the cult has always been tolerated except during the early 1990s, when Islamist fervor and state religious puritanism were exceedingly high. Since then, the situation has returned to normal with *boré* celebrations organized regularly and in a relatively open manner, the only impediment being the high cost.

Interestingly, too, with the afore-mentioned exception, since the 1980s *boré* has been recognized as an expression of Sudanese tradition: i.e. the dominant tradition of the Northern riverain Arab tribes, "traditionally" presented as the country's defining tradition. Academics and television presenters describe *boré*'s folkloric value and allude to its transformation from a cult into a club. In this manner, at least for an intellectual minority, it seems that *boré* has left the lower world of popular religious practices for the heights of disembodied national culture.[93] For the majority – detractors, skeptics, and the cult's clientele – all this may sound quite right, though quaint, but the issue remains. The cult's Islamic credentials are still a bone of contention. In that sense, *boré* should be seen as yet another instant in the never-ceasing process of defining Islamic "orthodoxy." This is so not only in the Sudan, but in all Muslim societies where the "*zār* cult complex" can be found. As for the relationship with the *ṣūfī* brotherhoods, I do not think that this can be founded on evidence from the cult's inner logic and ceremonial life. For this reason, I read Constantinides' statement on the parallels between *zār* and *ṣūfī* order participation at the level of social functions and of course as a proof of what Lewis has called "dual spiritual economy" in Islam, with the two branches, male and female, being "interdependent and complementary."[94]

6

Islamic Reformism

The term *iṣlāḥ*, which today is translated as reform, is repeatedly found in the *Qur'ān* covering a wide range of cognate meanings stressing what could be rendered as "making an effort to produce something good."[1] When we move to the *sunna* of the Prophet, the term acquires additional meanings, referring to the faithful following of the *Qur'ān* and the example of the Prophet and to the defense against unacceptable religious innovation (*bid'a*). Paired with *iṣlāḥ*, we often find the term *tajdīd* which can be translated as renewal. Though both terms denote a return to the normative texts of Islamic tradition as the way to improve society, the former indicates adherence to the views of the forefathers, while the latter allows for new interpretations through the exercise of *ijtihād*.

In the course of centuries what Voll has termed the *iṣlāḥ-tajdīd* tendency has always been present in Islamic history as a continuous process aiming at the perfection of human understanding of the religion and at the promulgation of binding rules in accordance with it. Thus *iṣlāḥ-tajdīd* has taken many forms in the effort of Muslim thinkers and activists to meet in Muslim terms the challenges of their generation. For this, *iṣlāḥ-tajdīd* tendencies should not be restricted to the efforts of the religious visionaries, social reformers, and leaders of Islamic political movements. Among these are numbered: Ibn 'Abd al-Wahhāb (1703–87), who spearheaded the violent purging of Islam in eighteenth-century Arabia and became the ideological founder of the contemporary conservative Saudi Arabian regime; Muḥammad Aḥmad (+1885), the Sudanese protonationalist revolutionary who assumed the title "*al-Mahdī*," suggesting that after him will come the Day of Judgment; and Ḥasan al-Bannā (1906–49), who was allegedly assassinated by the Egyptian authorities for his political activities as leader of the Muslim Brotherhood. The term should also cover the efforts of many among the great *'ulamā'* religious scholars and jurists of Islamic tradition: Muḥammad Ibn Idrīs al-Shāfi'ī (+820), who was the first jurist to formulate the rules governing the use of *ijmā'* and *ijtihād*; Aḥmad b. Ḥanbal (+855), who founded a particularly conservative legal school; Abū

Ḥāmid Muḥammad al-Ghazzālī (1058–1111), who combined the strict legalistic positions of the *ʿulamāʾ* with sufism; Aḥmad b. Taymiyya (+1328), who stressed the comprehensiveness of Islamic law and bitterly attacked both *ṣūfī* extravagance and the intellectual inertia of the *ʿulamāʾ*; and Sayyid Jamāl al-Dīn al-Afghānī (1838–97), who asked for the reopening of "the gate of *ijtihād*." As Eickelman has perceptively pointed out: "*[t]he distinction between reformist and 'radical' Muslim thought and movements is more a fine gradation than a sharp boundary and centers upon the disposition towards political action.*"[2]

Especially during the period of colonialism, the calls for the reformation and the renewal of Islam were part of the wider Arab Renaissance movement (*al-Nahḍa al-ʿArabiyya*), that emerged at the turn of the twentieth century when the Ottoman Empire was relatively liberalized under the increasing influence/ pressure of Europe. Many Muslim thinkers of the era thought that something quite radical had to be done if their societies were to liberate themselves from the shackles of foreign domination and to shake off the general lethargy that had characterized all sectors of public life for a very long time.

For those who later became known as Muslim reformers the solution to this problem was a return to the "roots" of Islamic tradition as well as a judicious adoption of all those elements of European culture which could prove useful to the general reformation and revival of society. Practically, the latter meant the adoption of technological innovations and of organizational modes pertaining to the army, the bureaucracy, and the economy. In that sense, as a movement of "return to the tradition" while keeping its eyes turned to the future, Islamic reformism fashioned Islam into a modernizing force in society: the quest for an authenticity (*aṣāla*) based on the tradition of a normative Islam judiciously interpreted through the practice of *ijtihād* would allow Muslim societies to move forward on the path of a modernity close to that of European societies.

As will be seen in the following pages, in spite of its significance, Islamic reformism has never managed to turn itself into a popular movement. It has always remained an intellectual trend, although one that has substantially colored government politics towards religion throughout the Middle East and North Africa and has opened up Islamic discourse to a dialogue with non-Islamic philosophical and political traditions. For this reason, the present chapter is the least ethnographic in the book and should be read as a brief intellectual biography of reformism through the consideration of some of its proponents. Nonetheless, it is certainly important in the context of the overall analysis, as it reveals that the process of "orthodoxy" production – the red line that goes through all my analysis of Islamic tradition – is here too conspicuously present in the effort of the reformist intellectuals to formulate the most apposite Islamic answer to the great issues of their times. Here, then, is perhaps the most fitting place to quote G.K. Chesterton's basic matrix concerning "orthodoxy," as this is quoted in turn by Žižek, namely that "the search for true orthodoxy, far from being boring, humdrum, and safe, is the most daring and perilous adventure."[3]

THE *TANẒĪMĀT*

To put all this in perspective and to appreciate the political implications of Islamic reformism, we should start with the state of affairs in the late Ottoman Empire. Perhaps for the first time in the modern history of Muslim societies, the trend of an eclectic adoption of European models with the expressed purpose of modernizing the state took a definite form during the reigns of the Ottoman sultans ʿAbd al-Mejīd (1839–61) and ʿAbd al-ʿAzīz (1861–76). Triggered by the mounting bureaucratic and economic problems of the Ottoman Empire in a period of increasing European pressure, their reforms concerned the political and economic reorganization of the empire, and are today known as *Tanẓīmāt* (literally, orders or regulations) from the name of the official edicts which announced them. As Yapp argues, the *Tanẓīmāt*, especially those of 1839 and 1856, are perfect examples of reforms which initially were restricted to the reorganization of the army, but were subsequently extended to other sectors of social life, albeit not always successfully.[4] A full application of the reforms that the *Tanẓīmāt* envisaged would have transformed the Ottoman Empire into a more or less secular polity of Ottoman citizens irrespective of religion or ethnic affiliation.[5] The Islamic law would still be upheld, but only in those areas of social life pertaining to personal status such as family and inheritance law.

As it was, the *Tanẓīmāt* effected a measure of modernization according to Western standards, but at best the results were mixed. That was partly because the *Tanẓīmāt* were rooted in a European tradition of state organization that was based on a particular type of relationship between state and society that was absent from, and to a large degree misunderstood by, the Ottomans.[6] It was also partly because the *Tanẓīmāt* were not liberal reforms, but a forced bureaucratic experiment which, it was hoped, would allow the empire to continue functioning in all possible ways to the advantage, of course, of the bureaucracy which had promulgated them. And all this was in a period of an advancing, triumphant European imperialism. With the accession of Sultan ʿAbd al-Ḥamīd II in 1876, things took a decisive turn toward authoritarian governance for the next three decades until the Young Turks' 1908 revolution and the outbreak of World War I in 1914. Soon after that, in 1923, the Ottoman Empire was dissolved and what was left of it became the secular nation-state of Turkey.

It is in the problematic and authoritarian character of the *Tanẓīmāt*, which promoted the secularization and modernization along Western lines of an empire in decline, that we discern some of the first signs of modern Islamic reformist thought.[7] Its first organized appearance was in the 1860s and 1870s with the Young Ottomans movement.[8] One of its leaders, Nāmīq Kemāl, accused the government of having lost control of the state to the encroaching European powers which were aided by rapacious and corrupt Ottoman ministers. What was needed was a new system of government control based on a new system of parliamentary representation. For the Young Ottomans and Muslim reformists such as Nāmīq Kemāl, this new system was not to be imported from Europe as it already existed as part of Islamic tradition right from the beginning: it was the model Muslim polity of Madīna that was governed by the Prophet after the *hijra*.[9] Based on this model, the reformers of the era argued, the true reforms that the government should promulgate could be easily accepted as part of the people's Islamic tradition, not as a sign of forced Westernization. In this way, the empire would benefit from all the technological and other innovations that could be imported from Europe without losing its Islamic character. As Perry writes, the Young Ottomans were the first movement in history that envisaged an articulation of Western models with a "correct" interpretation of Islam, that is the reformist interpretation.[10]

SAYYID JAMĀL AL-DĪN AL-AFGHĀNĪ (1838–97)

This line of thought was not an isolated example. On the contrary, it was part of a wider current that had started to affect most Muslim societies in the Middle East and North Africa. Outside the restricted boundaries of Ottoman Turkey, the towering intellectual personality of Islamic reformism was Sayyid Jamāl al-Dīn al-Afghānī. A contemporary of the Young Ottomans, al-Afghānī was a thinker with particularly strong political views, which often landed him in prison or sent him into exile. His message was simple: Muslims should unite in order to defend themselves against European imperialism, but they should do so not under the iron fist of dynastic rulers. In the reign of Sultan ʿAbd al-Ḥamīd II, who presented himself as the caliph of all Muslims, that was a dangerous message.

But al-Afghānī was equally critical of the *ʿulamāʾ*, accusing them of following the dogma of *taqlīd*, thus precluding the rise of any new and exciting thought. In their hands and in the hands of repressive rulers, "Muslim society" – al-Afghānī thought in terms of the one and indivisible Community of Believers – had entered a prolonged period of deep decline.[11] The only way out, al-Afghānī preached, was a return to its original Islamic traditions, while keeping its eyes open to catch anything useful that the present situation could offer, such as European political ideas, technology, and bureaucratic organization.

As far as the return to a pristine Islam was concerned, al-Afghānī preached a return to the original texts of the tradition, but in a critical manner. For this, he fervently supported the opening of "the gate of *ijtihād*" as the means for a radical reinterpretation of the tradition and a much-needed modernization of Islamic law.

Turning to the benefits that Europe could supply, besides the obvious technological innovations and models for bureaucratic organization, al-Afghānī was also ready to adopt some political ideas. Thus, despite its European origins, al-Afghānī did not consider nationalism to be anti-Islamic. On the contrary, he believed that both pan-Arabism and the various versions of local nationalisms were equally useful in the struggle against colonialism, on condition that they did not interfere with the people's Islamic principles.[12]

Al-Afghānī was a great thinker. Perhaps he was rather unsystematic in his treatment of the various issues he was concerned with and a bit too enthusiastic in adopting ideas that could promote all sorts of political causes as they developed. But his lasting influence in Islamic reformist thought cannot be overestimated. Of particular significance was his exile from Egypt to France in 1879, because during that period he had the opportunity to work with a number of Egyptian intellectuals and political activists who would later play a central role in Islamic reformism and the nationalist movement. Among them were Muḥammad ʿAbduh, Saʿd Zaghlūl, ʿAdīb Isḥāq, Ibrāhīm al-Laqqānī, and ʿAbd Allāh al-Nadīm.

MUḤAMMAD ʿABDUH (1849–1905)

ʿAbduh had studied theology and Islamic sciences at al-Azhar University in Cairo. He was initially drawn to mysticism, but following his acquaintance with al-Afghānī he showed a marked interest in Islamic reformist thought. The two met in Paris where ʿAbduh was exiled because of his participation in the 1882 revolution of ʿUrābī *Pasha* – which led to the occupation of Egypt by the British.[13] In 1889 ʿAbduh returned to Egypt and was somehow reconciled with the government despite the latter's subservience to the British whose consul-general was the real power behind the throne. ʿAbduh's "modern" and moderate views on Islam carried him to the office of the Grand *Muftī*, the highest Egyptian judge, and to membership of the legislative council of the country.

From these positions, ʿAbduh proposed a number of reforms in the system of higher education, especially in relation to al-Azhar Islamic university. His recommendations included the reinterpretation of the *Qur'ān* and the Prophetic *ḥadīth* in the light of contemporary Egyptian realities, and the protection of Islam from Christian and generally Western influences. In his vision, Islam – and in particular the Islam of the Prophet and his Companions, unadulterated by Western influences and mystical accretions of the sufist type – was the real "sociology," "the science of happiness in this world as well as the next."[14] So for ʿAbduh and the Muslim reformers the return to the roots of the tradition and the reformation of Islamic discourse were conflated.

The contemporary political developments in Egypt left their mark on ʿAbduh's thought. Although he considered the prevailing socio-political conditions in Egypt satisfactory, he was in fear of Egypt's becoming secularized. For him, this meant the rupture of Egypt's social structure at all levels. Already, he could detect signs of this in the parallel functioning of two educational and legal systems, a traditional Islamic and a modern one, which produced two types of educated Egyptian. Hence his insistence on a return to a modernized Islam as the only solution to this problem.

On this point, ʿAbduh was particularly clear. Like his teacher al-Afghānī he regarded logic and revelation as the two principles guiding human experience. As he argued, rationality proved that humanity was in need of prophets in order to understand things which were obscure. At the same time, it showed that prophethood had to stop somewhere, more precisely at Muḥammad, the last of the prophets. From there on humanity should abandon itself to God. In that sense, ʿAbduh claimed that both Islam and science are children of logic, itself a gift given to humans by God in order that they should follow His will.[15] He also claimed that Islam constituted the middle way between complete secularization and anti-science Christianity. Lastly, ʿAbduh was ambivalent toward the idea of nationalism. As a Muslim, he believed in the paramount importance of the one and undivided Community of Believers. As an Egyptian he loved his country and its history, something that attracted him to nationalism. So for him Egypt was a microcosm of the Community of Believers and his ideas for its government were rooted in the thought of the medieval Muslim thinkers. What was needed was an enlightened ruler who would govern in accordance with Islamic law and after consultation with the leaders of the people. This model was close to constitutional monarchy, but ʿAbduh believed that Egypt was not yet ready for it. For this reason, he appeared to be prepared to work with the British overlords for a period of time during which they would educate the Egyptians on how to govern themselves.

MUḤAMMAD RASHĪD RIḌĀ

ʿAbduh's views were further developed by his disciple Muḥammad Rashīd Riḍā (1865–1935). Riḍā's overriding concern was the safeguarding of Muslim unity. He was critical of mysticism, accusing its adherents of neglecting their religious duties in favor of venerating individual *shaykh*s – a weighty charge in view of the strong collective character of the five pillars (examined in chapter 4) – and of seeing Islam as a passive religion where everything depends on God.[16] At the same time, Riḍā criticized the *ʿulamāʾ* for obscurantism, urging them to unite and reinterpret the *Qurʾān* and the Prophetic traditions following the principle of *ijtihād*. In this light, he also believed that the Community of Believers could only benefit if Muslims exploited the intellectual wealth of the West, for the simple reason that it really belonged to them. By this, Riḍā meant that the roots of Western progress were in the knowledge that the Europeans had taken from the Arabs of the Holy Land and of Spain.[17]

So for Riḍā, Islam represented at the same time the solid and unchangeable foundation of everything there was, but also a malleable and dynamic tradition which could absorb social changes and rethink some of its own principles and practices in a manner that would not hurt its eternal and immutable nature. But how was that possible?

Riḍā distinguished between two kinds of beliefs and practices; those governing the relations between God and humanity and those governing the relations between human beings. Whatever belonged to the first category was unalterable and had been revealed once and for all in the *Qur'ān* and the *ḥadīth*; hence his dislike of sufism whose practices he viewed as unlawful accretions to the revealed truth of God. However, whatever belonged to the second category should not be governed by a formalism of the *taqlīd* type, but should be approached with an open mind and always in accordance with the prevailing historical conditions. In this, Muslims were enjoined to do nothing more but to imitate the companions of the Prophet who were admonished by Muḥammad to practice their religion not for the sake of sterile dogmatic adherence, but out of inner conviction.

But here Riḍā set two important preconditions. First, when a specific clause of Islamic law goes against a more general clause based on a widely held moral value, then Muslims should follow the general clause and disregard the particular ruling. Second, in all the cases where the *Qur'ān* and the prophetic traditions do not give clear guidance, the faithful should proceed according to their reasoning and the general principles of Islam.[18]

These views led Riḍā to offer some policy suggestions of a very controversial character on issues which, even today, are part of the debate about human rights and the nature of Islamic tradition in the modern world. The first one concerns apostasy from Islam, an issue that was at the forefront of the Western media in the 1980s after Ayatollah Khomeini's ruling against Salman Rushdie for his book *Satanic Verses*. The then spiritual and political leader of Iran sentenced Rushdie to death, accusing him of apostasy from Islam whose Prophet his book had profaned, denigrated, and vilified.[19]

Riḍā did not follow the traditional view on the matter of apostasy, as presumably Khomeini did for theological as well as for political reasons. In Riḍā's view, a distinction should be made between those whose apostasy endangers the unity and well-being of the Community of Believers and those whose apostasy is a personal matter with no social consequences. In the first case the apostate should be punished by death. In the second he should be left alone. Since, as a rule, such a distinction is not made and the Community of Believers, through the *ʿulamāʾ* who reach a consensus (*ijmāʿ*), declares all apostates guilty, the Community is committing a grave mistake because its decisions contradict a more general Islamic principle according to which there is no compulsion in religion. This is an example of Riḍā's first precondition mentioned earlier on the relationship between a specific legal ruling and a general doctrinal principle.

The second case concerns the so-called holy war (*jihād*). According to Riḍā, *jihād* can have only a defensive character and should be waged only in those cases in which the Community of Believers is under attack. The propagation of Islam should take place only peacefully, through persuasion, except in those cases where Muslims living among unbelievers are obstructed from practicing their religious duties.

The third case concerns the prohibition of charging interest in all economic transactions between Muslims. Riḍā believed that indeed this is the best system there is, but reminded his audience that his contemporary early twentieth-century Islamic societies were under constant siege from imperialist Europe, something that was not true in the times of the Prophet. For this reason, Riḍā invoked the general principle of necessity according to which an illegal act becomes legal under certain conditions. He thought that the prevailing conditions made it imperative for Muslims to organize their economic system along the lines of capitalism and to accept the importance of charging interest.

Lastly, the fourth case is related to Riḍā's views on women's rights. Here Riḍā exhibits a particularly conservative attitude toward the issue. He believed that women should participate in a dynamic and creative manner in the life of the community, just as during the early days of Islam. Their faith and their religious and social duties are exactly the same as those of men. However, Riḍā continued, reality itself showed that men were superior to women in strength, intellectual power, and will for knowledge. For this reason men should control women, but in a flexible manner which takes into consideration female needs.

CONTEMPORARY MUSLIM REFORMIST THINKERS

Islamic reformism did not disappear with the deaths of al-Afghānī, ʿAbduh, and Riḍā, the three intellectuals who in a way could be seen as its founding fathers.[20] Although it did not manage to inspire large numbers of people, a point I discuss later in this chapter, Islamic reformism is still a vital trend in Islamic thought, whose adherents contribute a great deal to contemporary debates concerning the nature of Islamic discourse and its relation with Western religious and philosophical traditions. Just to give an indication of the current state of affairs I shall present the work of three reformist Muslim intellectuals, two *sunnī* and a *shīʿa*.

Shaykh Muḥammad Saʿīd Ramaḍān al-Būṭī (1929–) is dean of the School for Islamic Law at the University of Damascus, Syria, and a preacher in two of the central mosques of the city, Mawlānā al-Rifāʿī and Tinjīz. He has also written a great number of books on Islam and is considered the most popular preacher on Syrian radio and television.

Al-Būṭī believes that the present conditions make the use of *ijtihād* of paramount importance for all Muslims and argues for the establishment of an institutional body comprised of the most important *'ulamā'* which will respond in a collective way to the problems that contemporary Muslims are faced with.[21] But unlike the Islamists and many of the forefathers of Islamic reformism discussed earlier, who extend the right of *ijtihād* to all Muslims without qualification, al-Būṭī maintains that only those who have a deep knowledge of Islamic law should be allowed to express binding opinions on legal and other matters without clashing with Islamic orthodoxy. His reasoning here appears to be based on common sense. What will happen, al-Būṭī asks rhetorically, if a person with no knowledge of civil engineering tries to build a house? What will happen if a person with no knowledge of medicine offers pharmaceutical advice to a patient? The same is true with the Islamists, al-Būṭī maintains. They shout about the correct application of Islamic law, while most of them know very little about it.[22] Their *ijtihād* is totally cut off from the history and the wider context of the Islamic tradition.

The same seems to hold true, according to al-Būṭī, for many Islamic reformers. Citing as an example 'Abduh's and Riḍā's wholesale dismissal of whole sections of Islamic tradition, such as sufism, the Syrian intellectual argues that the forefathers of Islamic reformism were not in a position to understand and to appreciate the fine distinctions between Islamic legal concepts, nor did they have an adequate intellectual grasp of Islamic theology to allow them to judge the orthodox character of any given argument. For example, al-Būṭī continues, not all legal clauses (*aḥkām*) are of the same significance or are endowed with the same degree of permanence. Some *aḥkām* are absolute and categorical, so they cannot be reinterpreted through the exercise of *ijtihād*, whereas others can.[23] A deficient understanding of this has led people like 'Abduh and Riḍā to dismiss not only those elements of mystical Islam which are indeed problematic from a legal point of view, such as "emotional" sufism (*al-taṣawwuf al-wijdānī*), but also elements which are perfectly orthodox in character, such as "ethically oriented" sufism (*al-taṣawwuf al-akhlāqī*).[24]

If that is not enough, a deficient understanding of Islamic law led some of the Muslim reformists of the past to eschew the traditional distinction between the four major schools of law, which all Muslims treat as part, indeed a cornerstone, of their legal tradition, and to elevate reformism as a trend which goes beyond, i.e. it abolishes, all four.[25] For al-Būṭī this is a serious offense against the very basis of Islam's universality.

As a scholar of religion, al-Būṭī is mainly interested in the progress and well-being of the entire Community of Believers through the development of what he calls "modern Islamic civilization" (*al-ḥaḍāra al-islāmiyya al-mu'āṣira*).[26] For al-Būṭī, the contemporary world is guided by a secularized and materialistic ideology which is actively promoted by Western neo-colonial forces whose aim is to distance people from God, just as has happened in the West. For this reason, he believes that Islamic societies should return to a model of life that is based on the *'ibādāt*, that is the liturgical duties of Muslims according to the Islamic law.[27] This will lead to the establishment of Islamic states, in the context of which the faithful will understand that as far as their liturgical duties are concerned the boundaries between the social and the private spheres of action are obliterated. In this vein, laying emphasis on the collective character of prayer (which I have discussed in chapter 4), al-Būtī describes the mosque as the cornerstone of Islamic state (*al-ḥajar al-asāsī al-awwal fī binā' al-dawla al-islāmiyya*) and as the highest symbol of unity, equality, and harmony between the individual and the Community of Believers, as well as between the latter and the ruler of every Islamic society. Still, al-Būtī does not discuss the necessary steps that would lead to the establishment of Islamic states, but he is categorical that the whole process should be a gradual and peaceful one.

Lastly, al-Būtī emphasizes the importance of the nation-state, suggesting that this is the only guarantee for the eventual emergence of Islamic states. In this context, he considers religion (*dīn*), culture (*thaqāfa*), patriotism (*waṭaniyya*), and nationalism (*qawmiyya*) as the four most important characteristics of the ideal nation-state.[28] It is perhaps because of such positions that al-Būtī has been characterized as an apologist of the Syrian government, which is not known for its particularly warm feelings toward Islam or for its respect for human rights. He himself denies the charges, arguing that there is a fine, but nonetheless very real, line that separates rebellion against government from insubordination.[29]

Holding such positions, al-Būtī does not belong to any political party or movement. Although he believes that many of the ills that have befallen the Muslim world are the result of Muslims' desire to adopt Western mores and tropes, he is still convinced that the way forward lies with the dialogue between the Muslim world and the West and in the mutual exchange and accommodation of ideas and practices.[30]

The example of al-Būtī is interesting on two counts. First, although he is critical of many tenets propagated by earlier Islamic reformers, he should still be seen as part of this trend because of his adherence to the exercise of *ijtihād* and because of his belief that a dialogue between the West and the Muslim world is both possible and useful. This reveals the gamut of different positions which may be included under the label "Islamic reformism." It also reveals, more than other cases perhaps, that the process of "orthodoxy" production should not be seen in relation to more or less distinct dividing lines, but between currents of thought that dwell along reformists, Islamists, and conservatives. This will be seen again in the following two chapters in reference to Islamist activists. Second, al-Būtī's timidity in relation to direct forms of political action should be seen in the light of the harsh and often violent political reality of contemporary Syria under the *Ba'th* party for the last sixty years or so. It should be remembered here that mere membership of the Muslim Brotherhood, the most prominent organization among the outlawed opposition, "is still punished by death under Law 49 of 1980."[31] This shows that raising a critical voice is much more dangerous that some Western liberal activists and academics may be ready to concede and that intellectual trends should always be positioned within their own specific socio-political frameworks, lest the sense of proportion be lost.

The second contemporary Muslim reformer I would like to introduce is Ḥusayn Aḥmad Āmīn, a retired diplomat who read law and English literature in Cairo and London respectively. Although not so well known by the Egyptian public as al-Būṭī is in Syria, Āmīn has certainly left his imprint on Islamic reformist thought in Egypt through three studies on the position of Islam in the contemporary world that he published in the 1980s.

Āmīn's main point is that all arguments about Islamic discourse should be based on a firm and systematic knowledge of Islamic history. Armed with this knowledge, one could immediately see that while in the beginning the Islamic discourse was moving along with the wider socio-political developments of society, there came a time when specific political decisions led to its gradual debilitation, especially in what concerns Islamic law. What he sees as even more pathetic is that today this depressing situation is considered by many as something perfectly natural, simply because it is mistaken for the "genuine Islamic tradition."[32] In other words, all those who are today demanding the full implementation of Islamic law, think of it as an eternal, unchanging, and unalterable aggregate of legal rules which can be applied everywhere, at any time, and in the same manner. Such people, Āmīn argues, confuse the ossification that the law has suffered at a particular point in time for an alleged traditional nature.

Alternatively, a historically informed approach to Islamic tradition should start with the Prophet himself. In his works Āmīn stresses three points. First, the Prophet was an ordinary man, a person who committed errors just like everybody else.[33] Second, the very revelation of the *Qur'ān* was a long process characterized by fragmentation and discontinuities as each revelation was inextricably tied to particular events and often functioned as a commentary on them or as a way of presenting some wider idea. Indeed, many *Qur'ānic* verses were themselves abrogated when fresh developments changed the situation which had led to their revelation. Third, the initial reaction of the Meccan trading aristocracy against Muḥammad's prophetic message was of an economic and political nature, as the new monotheism was detrimental to the interests of its members. This, Āmīn writes, is not even mentioned in the biographies of the Prophet, which as a rule constitute hagiographies rather than historical studies. But this is not all. This ahistorical picture of the Prophet was further magnified by the alleged "discovery" of *ḥadīth* which were clearly non-authentic. For Āmīn, this invention took place because it suited those who wanted to cloak their activities or ideas with an aura of Islamic legitimacy. That was, after all, what made many of the early religious scholars and jurists formulate criteria for securing the authenticity of each and every *ḥadīth*.

Among the examples from the *Qur'ān* that Āmīn cites as a clear proof of the processual and deeply historical character of Islamic tradition and, consequently, as a justification for the reformulation of the Islamic law, are the veiling of women and the punishment for theft. Starting with the former issue, Āmīn argues that if one were to situate the *Qur'ānic* verses 33: 59 and 24: 31 in the historical context that had led to their revelation, the emerging picture would be significantly different from what most Muslims might think today.[34]

The first verse, Āmīn writes, concerns the need to differentiate in a categorical manner between free Muslim women – who were admonished to be covered – and female slaves – who were usually uncovered. As it was, before the revelation of that particular verse, many of these female slaves used to dress in the same way as the free Muslim women in order to be able to walk around freely and to visit secretly and with impunity their free-born lovers. As all misunderstandings concerning the identity of a woman discovered at night outside her house should be avoided, Muslim women were advised to follow a particular dress code. And even then, Āmīn claims, this code most probably concerned exclusively the Prophet's wives, not every single Muslim woman. The second verse, the Egyptian reformer continues, refers specifically to a tradition that was widespread during the era of the Prophet, according to which many women went about with their breasts uncovered. According to this version, the sentence is related to this particular tradition. In both cases, Āmīn concludes, since in contemporary Muslim societies there are no female slaves nor any women going about with uncovered breasts, both verses should be declared null and void and should not constitute the basis for regulating the dress code of contemporary Muslim women.

In a similar manner Āmīn argues that verse 5: 38, stipulating the severence of a hand as the appropriate punishment for theft of property, should not be applied today because the character of the act itself has been radically transformed. Thus, while in seventh-century Arabia the theft of property was considered to be a particularly heinous act, as it could cause someone's death if, for example, his camels – the only means of transportation at the time – or his water supplies were illegally appropriated by another party, today there are other much more serious crimes than those, such as corruption and embezzlement. But in all these cases Islamic law has not been changed accordingly.

The third reformist intellectual is the Iranian ʿAbd al-Karīm Sorūsh, who has emerged as one of the most important *shīʿa* theologians of recent times. His prolific and wide-ranging oeuvre covers most of the areas of contemporary reformist Islamic thought, with special emphasis on questions concerning the nature of Islamic government, the importance of democracy and tolerance, and respect for human rights. Significantly, all these issues are not discussed at the level of political proclamation or planning, but in terms of a philosophical exposition concerning the place of religion in general and Islamic revelation in particular in today's secularized world.

Investigating the nature of morality in an ever-changing world of fallible people, Sorūsh puts at the center of his conceptual universe the concepts of justice, courage, and moderation.[35] These are the three cardinal virtues that true religion propagates and can be said to rise above the relativity that characterizes social life. Freedom is important too, but it is understood more as a reality emanating from the above three. This being the case, a religious government cannot be anything but tolerant and observant of human rights, in other words "democratic," combining reason and revelation in order to provide the people with a government that satisfies their needs while following the will of God.[36]

But for Sorūsh, "democracy" is not a concept necessarily connected with liberalism, which he accuses of excess relativism that may lead to secularism and atheism, or a political reality where anything and everything is "subject to referendum and debate and . . . nothing has a solid and an a priori 'foundation.' "[37] Rather it "is a method of harnessing the power of the rulers, rationalizing their policies, protecting the rights of the subjects, and attaining the public good."[38] In other words, democracy rests on and promotes the same moral values as religion, namely justice, courage. And moderation; this, significantly, makes respecting human rights a necessary condition of a government's religious character and not a sign of surrender to relativistic liberalism, as some religious thinkers appear to suggest. Democracy then provides the checks and balances agreed upon rationally, and religion, as the bulwark of morality, guarantees the smooth functioning of democracy.[39]

In itself, such a model of a democratic religious government rests on a particular conceptualization of religion that is fully historicized by self-reflective subjects. For Sorūsh this is an absolute precondition if religion is to survive in the present-day secularized world. But how is religion's absolute and transcendental character to be reconciled with historical change? How can eternity be reconciled with temporality?

Sorūsh's answer is given at two levels. Firstly, he distinguishes between religion (*dīn*), which remains constant, and religious knowledge (*maʿrefat-e dīnī*), which undergoes change.[40] This allows Sorūsh to accept the Prophetic revelation of Islam as true and flawless, while conceding all jurisprudent interpretations of it as essentially incomplete and subject to error. As he states, "[t]he last religion is already here, but the last understanding of religion has not arrived yet."[41] Secondly, and following from this, Sorūsh refuses to distinguish between doctrine and its history when it comes to justifiability. In other words, a set of ideas, say communism, cannot be approached critically *in abstracto*, that is independent of the specific way in which it entered historical reality, in our case the pre-1989 socialist world. For Sorūsh "doctrines are entirely testable and . . . history is the arena of their trial and error,"[42] which means that errors, false interpretations, and even harsh and violent practices perpetrated in the name of doctrinal truth and purity are part and parcel of the doctrine itself.

Arguing that religion is sent by God to humanity with all its faults, Sorūsh naturalizes religion and situates it in "an immutable natural process of evolution,"[43] where revelation and human reason cannot but work together. This makes Sorūsh a true follower of Islamic reformist ideas, but with a critical difference. Contrary to most of the other Muslim reformers we have discussed in the previous pages, his distinction between religion and religious knowledge prevents him from attributing normative status to any single particular interpretation of Islam, such as the Islam of Prophet Muḥammad and his Companions which even today is still presented as the "Golden Era" of Islam by reformers and Islamists alike. Still, Sorūsh commits the same sin as all Muslim reformers and Islamists in essentializing Islam, advocating the separation of "the fundamental from the tangential and accidental."[44]

At a more practical level, all this makes Sorūsh a critical thinker whose moderate ideas are in sharp contrast with the more radical views that dominate contemporary Iran. In particular, his critical stance toward "West Toxication" (*gharb zadegī*), which either rejects the West wholesale or tries to imitate it blindly,[45] and the importance he attaches to cultural allegiances[46] with the aim of claiming for Iranians an identity anchored in tradition (nationalism Islam), although dynamic and supple enough to be engaged in a fruitful dialogue with the world in general, do not endear him to the Iranian clerical establishment. Indeed, Sorūsh does not flinch from describing it as "a government without theory and doctrine."[47] How much these ideas can influence some of its more flexible and adaptable members or can become the basis of an alternative political platform is difficult to say.

ISLAMIC REFORMISM AS A POLITICAL MOVEMENT

How successful Islamic reformism has been in helping Muslim societies to manage Western influence in ways harmonious with Islamic tradition is a rather misleading question, for two reasons. First, it presupposes an isomorphic presence of Islamic reformism in different societies and an uncritical approach to Islamic tradition that completely disregards local conditions and the particularities of distinct national political histories. Second, it presupposes a well-organized reformist popular movement with well-articulated theoretical positions delineating a well-defined terrain of differences which could be dealt with by the promulgation of specific policies.

Most of these factors are not, and cannot be, accounted for. What could be discussed instead, but again only superficially, is the impact of Islamic reformist central ideas and concepts on the political discourse of Muslim societies. Properly speaking, this project belongs to the field of political science rather than to the field of social anthropology (although political anthropology would have much to offer had the ground been prepared through detailed ethnographic studies in different Middle Eastern societies, an element that today is altogether absent). This being the case, in the present context only some tentative generalizations can be offered.

To start with, it should be observed that Islamic reformism did not dominate, either ideologically or politically, the fight against colonialism. That fight was successfully conducted in conditions arising from the political realities produced by the collapse of the Ottoman Empire and the two world wars and by forces which approached Islam as part of an Arabist nationalist history, i.e. as a dimension of the Arab sociocultural heritage and as "the most eloquent expression of its genius."[48] With the gaining of independence in the 1950s and 1960s, Islamic reformism and Islamic discourse in general receded further into the background, leaving the nationalists to dominate the political field until the 1970s. After that, encouraged by government failures and crumbling living standards in a perceived environment of increasingly assertive Western predominance, Islam was reintroduced in the 1980s mainly in the guise of Islamism, the cousin so to speak of reformist Islam.

From another perspective, Muslim reformists, especially of the earlier period, were among the first to try to make Muslim populations – mainly the middle classes and members of the bureaucracy – more aware of their own history and tradition in Islamic terms, thus putting a face, one out of many, to their differences from the West. At the same time, Muslim reformers have never stopped arguing that taking refuge in past glories is not an answer to contemporary problems and that the discursive character of the Islamic tradition has to be openly acknowledged so as to include whatever the West may have to offer. In this way, Muslim reformers have been and continue to be, the main representatives of the Islamic discursive tradition which sees the West as an opportunity, not as a threat. Lastly, it must not be forgotten that the early Muslim reformers were among the first to introduce into the political discourse of the Middle Eastern and North African Islamic societies concepts such as democracy, citizenship, and human rights articulated in what they saw as "traditional" Islamic discourse. In that sense, Islamic reform was instrumental in the exploration of the new space that modernization opened up in the colonized Middle East and North Africa, and in the reordering of social life, what Asad calls "a new moral landscape."[49]

At the same time, it is evident that Islamic reformism has always been more of an intellectual trend with important political ramifications, rather than a fully fledged political movement addressing its message to the upper and middle classes who could envisage themselves as self-governing citizens and autonomous subjects. As such, reformism has not managed to come to grips with everyday practical difficulties, except in a fragmented manner, for example in education and the judiciary, and even there it has produced recommendations that have been assimilated by the secularizing modernity of the state. Most of its otherwise brilliant thinkers have been unable to produce either a new comprehensive theology in the context of modernity or a new and dynamic legal framework for Islamic law. Correspondingly, at the level of political practice we cannot talk about a reformist movement with an organized leadership and popular base; we cannot even talk about reformist mosques, that is mosques where the Friday noon *khuṭba* can be seen as part of a wider program of political agitation comparable to that of Islamist groups.

As it is, Islamic reformism has been flourishing among intellectuals, academics, political analysts, writers, and bureaucrats. The cases of the three contemporary reformers mentioned earlier show this very clearly, as well as the views of other Middle Eastern intellectuals who have offered comments on the subject. For example, in a discussion on human rights in the Middle East between Dwyer, a professor of law at Cairo University, and ex-minister Gamāl Abū al-Magd it is maintained that contemporary Egyptian reformers do not belong to any specific organization, but constitute an *ad hoc* group of people with similar ideas who work on the same issues and consult each other's publications.[50] Indeed, as the editor-in-chief of *al-Shaʿb* newspaper, ʿAdil Ḥusayn, said to Dwyer in another interview, the problem is not so much that Muslim reformers are not in a position to give the right answers, *but that they are unable to form the right questions.*[51]

Consequently, it should perhaps also be mentioned that Islamic reformism has often become a weapon in the hands of politicians, some of whom may initially have had an organic relationship with it before political realities guided them elsewhere. Thus, besides those who followed a university career, many "successors" of the leaders of early twentieth-century Islamic reformism, such as Saʿd Zaghlūl, Ṭāha Ḥusayn, and Muḥammad ʿAlī Jinnāḥ, became secular nationalists, but obviously showed some sympathy for Islamic reformism ideological positions. Known as "the father of all Egyptians", Saʿd Zaghlūl was the embodiment of Egyptian national emancipation until his death in 1927.[52] Ṭāha Ḥusayn was accused of apostasy by Rashīd Riḍā and the conservative *ʿulamā'* of al-Azhar for his 1926 book *On Pre-Islamic Poetry.*[53] His efforts to secularize Egyptian history has been continued by a younger generation of intellectuals, such as ʿAbd al-Raḥmān al-Sharqāwī.[54] Lastly, Muḥammad ʿAlī Jinnāḥ became effectively the founder of the state of Pakistan.

ISLAMIC REFORMISM AS AN INTELLECTUAL/PHILOSOPHICAL TREND

Most critical reviews of Islamic reformism discuss whether the ideas of the first reformists, such as Jamāl al-Dīn al-Afghānī and Muḥammad ʿAbduh, were based on firm philosophical foundations or on an array of concepts from Islamic discourse as well as from Western philosophical traditions that had been utilized in an expedient and politically opportunistic manner. To my knowledge, one of the most concise and well-argued critiques of Islamic reformism has been put forward by the Syrian-born philosopher and sociologist Aziz al-Azmeh.

As al-Azmeh argues, when Islamic reformism emerged in the lands of the Ottoman Empire its aim was to salvage "the intellectual credibility of the Koran and other foundational texts" *and* to adopt "the inevitable tropes and values of modernity."[55] Accepting the principles of Western evolutionism, Muslim reformers suggested that religion follows the laws of human evolution because man is "by nature a rational and a religious animal."[56] This allowed them to make a direct connection between religion and utility that had clear political implications. For example, al-Afghānī argued that religious solidarity provides society with "unanimity, unity of direction and demand of victory over those who contest it."[57] This led him to assert that on the basis of their shared Islamic tradition Muslims comprise a "Muslim nation" which can successfully withstand European cultural, economic, and political assaults.[58]

So religion is not only important in a transcendental manner; it is also useful as a weapon in the field of politics. But of all religions, al-Afghānī continued, the most effective one in pushing the faithful down the road of moderation, trust, and truthfulness – the three basic truths that all true religions teach or, in other words, the best suited to provide a true and hence useful experiential framework for moral agents – is Islam because it is the only religion that fully accepts God's absolutely transcendental nature *and* human rationality.

However, for al-Afghānī and for the rest of Muslim reformers up to the present day, the faithful have distorted the "real" meaning of Islam through the adoption of *taqlīd*, i.e. the blind imitation and unquestioning acceptance of the existing doctrines, and through the incorporation of non-Islamic practices and beliefs, such as the cult of the saints. The only way to correct this would be the reopening of the "gate of *ijtihād*."[59] Only this could guarantee a "true return" to the fundamental principles of religion (*uṣūl al-dīn*) in a spirit of renewal (*tajdīd*) and reformation (*iṣlāḥ*) that would allow Muslims to hope for a better future.

According to al-Azmeh, this line of reasoning is unsound. He argues that Islamic reformism conceptualizes its own version of Islam as normative Islam which then opens to interpretations according to the principle of general utility;[60] this is how we should understand the reformers' call for reopening the "gate of *ijtihād*." This call for textual reinterpretation is problematic because it disregards the historical context in which the original texts and the traditions of the first Muslims that have been accorded normative status were formulated; or, to be more accurate, it disregards *all* historical context, thus making Islam amenable to *every* context. So in the reformist discourse the normative and the pragmatic are conjoined in a manner that enables actors to move to and fro according to their own political purposes. As a result, the logic of worldly rationality and the rationality of Islamic law – to which a purported universality has been attributed – are amalgamated, transforming the Islamic law into a "metaphor for legality."[61] But who is to guarantee the validity of this translation and interpretation except the very people who advocate it? As al-Azmeh writes,

> There is therefore no justification in reason or in history for this translation, nor any credibility for it, except its being based on an exclusive normative status given to a name – Islam – which is represented by an absolutely normative source, that is, the Koran and the early period of Islam and on the desire to impose meanings on it that indicate modernity . . . With this, history is ensnared: it is supposed to contain modernity. Modernity is also ensnared, by assuming its correspondence with that supposed past.[62]

So for al-Azmeh the basic problem of Islamic reformism lies in its ahistorical and philosophically untenable nomination of a particular interpretation of Islamic tradition as normative and its investment with characteristics of modernity.

This is not the view taken by historian Omnia Shakry in her study on early twentieth-century Egyptian women set on the path to modernity, especially in relation to the upbringing of children. Shakry's work is of particular importance because it focuses on Egypt of the 1900s, that is on a country and a period when Islamic reformism was particularly strong, and on a subject which was at the heart of the modernizing project. Here I shall not refer to the rich material on the ways in which Egyptian reformers debated the character of mothering and child-rearing, trying to infuse it with a modernist ethos, but on the theoretical underpinnings of their debate. Based on Asad's understanding of Islam as a discursive tradition, Shakry argues that, instead of seeing Islamic reformism as an effort to bring together Islamic tradition and a particular type of Western modernism, we could see it "as part of an Islamic discursive tradition . . . [and as an] attempt to formulate an Islamic modern."[63] This view, Shakry maintains, is in accord with a mode of historical consciousness which has always been present in Islamic tradition and which works around the concepts of decline (*inḥiṭāṭ*) and reform (*iṣlāḥ*), renewal (*tajdīd*) and revivification (*iḥyā'*).[64] Being formulated and enacted within historical time, this tradition of *tajdīd-iṣlāḥ* does not seek to re-create a glorious past as imagined by the reformers, but to introduce definitive policies that "reflect historical specificities of time and place."[65] So what Shakry is actually suggesting about Islamic reformism is what I meant when I argued that at a more general level the *umma* itself can be seen as that transhistorical subject toward which God's transcendental Truth is addressed, creating it out of nothing, a subject historically obliged to transform this Truth in lived experience, in every case according to the exigencies of the particular historical conditions. For Muslims in general, and for Muslim reformers in particular, this is their duty in this world.

Shakry's view of Islamic reformism is of particular importance because it shows that a felt need for change in early twentieth-century Egypt did not derive from the West, nor did it take its particular form through imitation.

Rather, it came from within society itself and was expressed in terms of Islamic tradition as a historically specific effort to create an Islamic modernity. Shakry's analysis demonstrates two points: first, that despite its elitist intellectualism, the reformers' reading of the situation was more or less correct and addressed real social problems, needs, and dilemmas. Second, that the Egyptian reformers did adopt concepts such as "progress" and "social backwardness" from the early twentieth-century Western vocabulary of modernity, as that had entered the space of anti-colonial struggle, but they invested these concepts with a moral dimension which sprang from within their reading of Islamic tradition, which was different from the discourse of Western modernity, based as the latter was on "the affirmation of the world's autonomy, of its self-sufficiency in terms of reason, knowledge, and action."[66]

7

Islamism: A General Overview

During the last two decades or so Islamism, preliminarily defined as a particular form of Islamic assertiveness with clearly visible political traits and sometimes explosive methods, has become one of the most easily recognizable terms in the Western world. It has also become equally infamous through its direct association with violence and its alleged relation to cultural backwardness. Significantly, in the post-9/11 era of the so-called "War against Terror," Islamism has been often presented as the most dominant intellectual and political trend within Islamic tradition in terms of a pathogeny, as if it were a sociocultural malaise that has afflicted Islamic societies and now threatens the whole world. Indeed, medical language has been liberally applied by those who agonize about whether Islamism will "spread" throughout the Muslim world, "contaminating" even those Islamic societies such as Jordan or Tunisia which many commentators call "modern," or whether it will "affect" the Muslim immigrant communities of Europe. Especially in the West, then, but increasingly among the elites of most Muslim societies too, Islamism is seen as a cancer that should be treated urgently and drastically.

In this chapter I present the conceptual framework within which Islamist groups articulate their discourse. In the following chapter I shall concentrate on a small number of topics which differentiate between the groups. This formulation enables me to consider together a variety of groups, organizations, and individuals without obliterating the differences between them.

TERMINOLOGY

Among Western commentators and scholars, Islamism came into prominence after the 1979 Iranian revolution. Since then it has been described by a variety of terms such as Islamic extremism or militancy, Islamic resurgence or revival, political Islam or Islamic fundamentalism. All these terms are more or less unsuitable for describing the phenomenon, as they are either emotionally loaded oversimplifications or are based on questionable socio-political assumptions.

Extremists and Militants

Thus, "Islamic extremism" or "militancy" point almost exclusively to violence, fanaticism, and terrorist acts as the sociological traits of Islamism *par excellence*, obfuscating everything else. Certainly, violence – spectacular violence, to be more precise – is often used by members of certain Islamist organizations, but as a rule the majority are engaged in peaceful activities, such as humanitarian aid (*zakāt* in practice), education, and health services, as well as the Muslim equivalent of "pastoral care." But even when violence is used extensively, this must be analyzed in political terms rather than demonized as mindless bloodlust. History demonstrates that yesterday's "terrorists" or "rebels" can be tomorrow's political interlocutors.[1]

Resurgence and Revival

Terms implying "resurgence" or "revival" are also inappropriate if they allude to an alleged state of collective passivity which has been now disturbed somehow by the concerted act of Muslim activists.[2] At the same time, though, we have seen that throughout Islamic history the concept of renewal (*tajdīd*) has been used by the actors themselves in their discourse on socio-political movements and intellectual trends. Revival, then, or neo-revival, can be a useful term if it refers to a demand with a long history springing from within the Islamic discourse, a demand which seeks to act as a bridge between the past and the present and to reconcile current realities with the stipulations of the Islamic vision.[3] In that sense, contemporary Islamism is but a phase of an old historical movement, not a new phenomenon.

Political Islam

As for "political Islam," this term too is problematic if it implies that in the Islamic tradition religion and politics constitute *in principle* two distinct realities and spheres of social practice in the same manner as in modern established Christianity and, by extension, in today's secularized world. Given the history of this distinction in the West, it is evident that political Islam represents an aberration, an undesirable contamination of politics with religion – rather than vice versa – which can only foster fanaticism and violence. Moreover, the term has an evolutionist ring in it, as it describes an allegedly unhealthy situation over which Western societies prevailed long ago on their way towards "progress."

All these things do not mean that in Islamic tradition there is no distinction between religion and politics as such. Islamic law does distinguish between *ʿibādāt*, referring to the eternal and immutable obligations of humans towards God, and *muʾāmalāt*, referring to relations between humans and more specifically to what could be called civil transactions. As part of human history, the latter can be modified in accordance with the prevailing social conditions, but in ways that obey the principles of Islamic law which reflect the eternal will of God, even if this is only at the level of ideology. In other words, any distinction between religious and non-religious affairs that one could envisage in the context of social life and political practice of Islamic societies does not presuppose "the negation of man as worshiping being, as *homo adorans*: the one for whom worship is the essential act which both 'posits' his humanity and fulfills it"[4] that constitutes the essence of secularism. It can be argued, then, that the integrative character of Islamic tradition is based upon the rejection of a distinction between religion and state[5] or upon the *programmatic* rejection of secularization.[6]

Fundamentalism

Equally problematic is the term "Islamic fundamentalism," which routinely has negative connotations.[7] The term itself is a loan from the American Protestant Evangelical movement, which I find utterly different from Islamism.[8] To restore a degree of clarity, then, to a point of great political import that is generally accepted out of habit rather than thoughtful consideration, I shall dwell on the matter in some detail.

As a matter of fact, Protestant fundamentalism – especially in the USA, which provides us with the prototype version of the phenomenon – works as a double act. At one level, it could be argued that it focuses on the strengthening of personal faith (something that leads to the rebirth, in the sense of restoration, of the person through the radical reformulation of individual consciousness) and neglects the restructuring of the social order.[9] At another level, though, a closer look would reveal that Christian fundamentalism does encourage the restructuring of social order as it promotes specific policies and fosters a wider social ethos characteristic of the vision it serves. Especially in the USA, this is done through the implicit equation of the individual values of the born-again believer with "American values," which are then presented as universal.[10]

However, such a restructuring of the social order does not constitute the ultimate aim of Christian fundamentalism. The latter can be identified at the apocalyptic level as the participation of all "true" believers in the final victory of God and the establishment of a new cosmic order. We are thus faced with a contradiction situated at the epistemological foundations of Christian fundamentalism.

On the one hand, we have the notions of *individualism* – "true" believers are saved as individuals, not as church members, so hence the stress on a private rather than personal relation with Christ despite the considerable pastoral work that Evangelical Christians are proud of – and a *free (i.e. market) economy*, the privileged topos for the structuring of autonomous individuals responding to the operations of the spirit. On the other hand, we have an instrumentalist approach towards the state stemming from a particular reading of the American Founding Fathers and from an implicit identification of America with the "City on the Hill" or with "New Jerusalem."

This contradiction can be resolved only at the apocalyptical level with the millenarian destruction of the current order and the establishment of a paradise of autonomous individuals. Significantly, and this is a further issue, this affinity between fundamentalism and neo-conservatism affords fundamentalism a vantage point within the secular framework of the globalization process. This is sociologically curious but theologically explicable. Nonetheless, given the enormous economic interests and missionary zeal of many fundamentalist organizations, it makes the whole affair even more volatile politically. The gradual elevation of "terror" "into the hidden universal equivalent of all social evils"[11] and of Ussāma bin Lāden into the looked-for "new militant figure"[12] is its latest and more extreme manifestation.

All this is in contradistinction to Islamism.[13] First, individual aspirations and personal behavior are subordinated to the strictures of a (supposedly) well-defined legal and political framework within which the *umma* ought to function. Second, despite the belief in an apocalyptic *telos*, the main concern is with the here and now, with history. Divine will and human condition both call for the establishment of functioning Islamic states, thus banishing apocalypse almost entirely from view. All that matters is the present, which should be molded according to a vision of what there was, the seventh-century Madīnan state of Prophet Muḥammad. At that time, the Muslim kingdom of God was established; contemporary believers are enjoined to reconstitute it, not by returning to it, but by applying its principles in the modern world.[14]

This being the case, I cannot agree with Roy's otherwise very interesting analysis on Islamism and neo-fundamentalism, as he calls it, which is basically concerned with understandings of Islamism in the West and through the Internet. When he claims "What is Islam? The answer has to be individual, not so much in terms of elaborating new theoretical answers . . . but in terms of self-appropriation of the answer" and "[t]he self is the truth; faith, not religion, is the truth"[15], he is being inaccurate. There are, of course, such instances within the wide Islamic world, but theologically and sociologically they do not reflect Islamism. As he himself writes, Roy rests his case on phenomenological similarities between revivalist movements, such as anti-intellectualism, and "a religious consumerism applied to the supermarkets of Faith."[16] But while this is so for Protestant charismatic movements and for certain representations of Roman Catholicism, they mean different things in the case of Islamism, whose followers, even when they reside in the Afghan wilderness or the dark recesses of the World Wide Web, see themselves as members of the *umma*, the Community of Believers, which they wish to defend against infidels and apostates. Not to put too fine a point on it, Islamist movements of all kinds represent in that sense a protest rather than a Protestant-type movement.

It is not with born-again Protestant fundamentalists that Islamists should be compared. Rather, they should be likened to the fourth-century monastic movement, whose adherents sought refuge in the Desert (literally and metaphorically) in order to save the (Christian Byzantine) Empire. Although the monks and nuns "left society" and its temptations, they took "society" with them in order to change it. To a certain degree, this holds true for contemporary monastics as well. For such people, individualism is a heresy and history is where the Kingdom of God makes its presence felt until it impregnates it with grace, thus restoring its true nature. Although Muslim eschatological icons do not feature widely in Islamist discourse, they are present in the hope of establishing a true Islamic state in the here and now. For Islamists, the eminently social vision of an all-embracing *umma* is an acutely historical strategic target.

For the same reason, one should distinguish between Islamism and millenarianism,[17] a not so distant cousin of fundamentalism, although the two share some characteristics such as equality, homogeneity, the maximization of religious, as opposed to secular, attitudes and behavior, and acceptance of pain and suffering even to the point of undergoing martyrdom. Strictly speaking, the archetypal trait of all millenarian movements is not simply the negation of the *present* order of things in favor of another one that is mandated by God(s) or the ancestors, but the repudiation of *all order that proceeds from within the realm of human praxis*. This, as we saw, is not the case with Islamism whose political vision is very much this-worldly.

ISLAMIST DISCOURSE: AN OVERVIEW

It would now be pertinent to present a general outline of Islamist discourse and of the way this has been received by some Western commentators, especially in relation to Western modernity, before moving to a more detailed discussion in the following sections.

Principles

Inspired by the seventh-century Madīnan polity headed by the Prophet himself, Islamists argue that every single believer and the society as a whole should follow *exclusively* and with no deviation God's will as expressed once and for all in the *Qur'ān*. This means three things: first, Islam cannot and should not accommodate historical changes, like those discussed by the Muslim reformers we encountered in the previous chapter. It must remain in its pristine and allegedly "authentic" form of its first days, when the Prophet and his immediate companions were still alive. Second, Islamic injunctions, such as those connected with the five pillars or those associated with the punishments for crime stipulated by Islamic law, should be actively enforced at the social level. And third, each Muslim society should be headed by a government which derives its legitimacy *solely* from the fact that it applies Islamic law to all facets of social and individual life.

In this vision the state is the ultimate expression of the collective will of the *umma*, the imagined Community of Believers, as this is realized at every historical moment through discursive practices sanctioned by Islamic tradition. An Islamic society, then, should be nothing less than an Islamic state exclusively governed by Islamic law, which Islamists understand as a closed and well-articulated system of unalterable legal rules.[18] Members of this state are not autonomous individuals and free citizens in the European Enlightenment tradition, but subjects of God under the sovereign power of His law and members of the Community of Believers which they should never endanger by their own individual acts. That is why leaving the fold of Islam through conversion to another religion or through unbelief (a woolly term open to abuse) is considered a crime (apostasy) in theory punishable by death.[19]

Thus defined, the members of this ideal Islamic society have nevertheless an important prerogative-cum-obligation: they are expected to rise against their government if the latter does not uphold Islamic law and acts in ways openly inimical to the principles of Islam. How this is agreed upon on a particular occasion is part of the ongoing struggle for the production of "orthodoxy" that affects the whole realm of Islamic discourse. Taking into account that, except in Iran, Afghanistan under the *Ṭālibān*, the Sudan and Turkey, Islamists have never come to power, this prerogative takes the form of minority political struggle, sometimes violent but more often communitarian and ideological.

Proposed Policies

Concerning the importance of the *Qur'ān* and its binding character in relation to social reality, such views do not differ substantially from those held by the majority of Muslims. Where Islamists differ is in the practical application of all this, especially in taking seriously their vision as a practical guide for everyday behavior and in holding the rulers and their allies personally liable for any presumed misapplication of the holy writ on penalty of deposition or, for the most extreme, death.

Indeed, in varying degrees many Middle Easterners do consider their governments to be inefficient, corrupt, and insincere in their Islamic beliefs, and do regard the West as an opponent of Islam in a generalized and ill-defined manner that is focused on specific US and European views on Palestine, Iraq, and elsewhere. Islamists, though, remaining rigidly steadfast in the purity of their vision, actively accuse their governments of being apostates and unbelievers who have sold out to the Americans and the West in general and are acting in unison with the Israeli state.[20] For them, to remove such governments and to combat their perceived patrons and allies is not only an appropriate political option; it is a religious duty. Hence the violence perpetrated by the most extreme Islamist elements against government targets and all the perceived enemies of Islam. Two classic examples, an internal and an external one, are the 1981 assassination of Egyptian President Anwar Sadat, who had made peace with Israel,[21] and the 9/11 terrorist attacks in the US for its role in the Middle East.

But violence reflects only a tiny minority of Islamist activities. The main policy option of Islamism in all its organized forms, whether political parties, professional associations, or cultural organizations, is to promote a vision of an Islamic modernity through a "call to Islam" (*daʿwa al-Islāmiyya*). As will be seen in detail later, this process endeavors to make Islam, as understood by the Islamists, more visible in everyday life mainly through preaching, advancing an Islamic public awareness, assisting the poor, promoting an Islamic code of dress (especially for women), and organizing seminars, talks, and discussions on spiritual subjects and current affairs. The end result of *daʿwa* and the strategic aim of the movement is what has been called "Islamization from below."

At this point, it is important to remember that "Islamization from below" may very well be actively promoted by Islamist organizations, but it operates within the parameters of a more diffused, almost vague but certainly strongly felt, sociocultural current that has been sweeping the middle and lower classes. Yearning for a "return" to an "authentic" Arab Islamic culture in the face of growing political and economic uncertainties, this inchoate sensation that drives people to pay closer attention to their religion and/or tradition, acquires increasingly more ideological coherence through the more concrete politics of the "Islamization from below" process. In this manner, this diffused popular current becomes progressively part of a specifically Islamist imaginary regime and the fantasies by which it is accompanied. In other words, the Islamist movement provides in a concrete and easily digestible form a political platform and a venue for concerted action on what many people do feel anyhow, but in a less distinct manner.[22] This point is significant for three reasons. First, it explains how culturally conservative segments of the population can often become fellow travelers of the Islamists without necessarily adopting their specific political strategies. Second, it demonstrates that the Islamist message is vague enough to include the variety of positions that occupy the conservative end of the spectrum. Third, it shows how the Islamist discourse on Islam constructs versions of Islam which are equally essentialized and "orientalistic" as those of their political adversaries and which owe much of their programmatic coherence to an unacknowledged adoption of Western modernistic elements. I shall return to this later in the chapter in relation to women's issues.

Struggling with Western Modernity

The roots of the Islamists' *current* ideological positions can be found in the recent history of their societies. According to them, Muslim societies fell victims to colonialism not because they were abandoned by God, but because they had distanced themselves from Him in an ungodly effort to imitate the West. After the end of colonialism, the various national governments which have taken over have followed more or less the same path. Not only have they not "returned" to God, but they have tried to enforce systems based on alien, i.e. Western, ideas such as democracy, socialism, the secularization of society, a market economy, and consumerism. The "proof" that all this has not worked is the fact that poverty has soared, social inequalities have become even more pronounced, corruption and moral degradation are the order of the day, Muslim solidarity has been severely eroded, and the Muslim world has been repeatedly attacked by the infidels in Iraq, Afghanistan, Palestine, Kashmir, Chechnya, Bosnia – and all this despite the "blessing" of the black gold which flows abundantly in many Middle Eastern and North African countries.

This picture has made many scholars in the West approach Islamism as a reaction of sections of the Islamic Community of Believers to what can be called "the failure of the modernization process," which has allegedly led Islamic societies to the protracted socio-economic and political stagnation they are currently experiencing. This position appears to be further supported by the fact that Islamism has many adherents among the lower middle classes who often hold university or college degrees, but cannot translate their qualifications into economic advancement and upward social mobility.[23]

"The failure of the modernization process" argument may explain part of Islamism's appeal among certain segments of the lower middle classes in the big urban centers. It does not, however, allow us to see the more general picture as it severs Islamist discourse from its theological foundations and historical antecedents – what I called in the previous chapter "the ever-present *iṣlāḥ-tajdīd* tendency" – advancing a rather shallow ideological and economistic/utilitarian position based on problematic assumptions.[24]

What we are told in effect is: "Had the Islamic Middle East been modernized, the 'problem' of Islamism would not have been encountered." According to this view, "the failure of the modernization process" is related to the absence from the Muslim world of an equivalent of the Enlightenment, which would have relegated religion to its "natural" place, the private domain, just as has supposedly happened in the West. But for unclear reasons, the argument continues, this did not happen. Islam has clung to the center of people's experiential horizons, thus making it impossible to expect the emergence in the Middle East of the notion of post-Enlightenment citizenship and all that comes with it.[25] In this bleak picture, an allegedly "reactionary" ideology fostering irrational religious violence complicates an already "intractable problem."

Though such views are not always openly articulated by the proponents of "the failure of the modernization process" argument, they are nonetheless its logical outcome as well as a proof of its untenability. Simply put, the whole argument is unashamedly evolutionist and ethnocentric, taking Western modernity as the opposite of tradition, as a synonym of secularization, and as the only system that can ensure economic prosperity, political stability, and social peace in the world.[26]

But tradition is neither static nor opposed to modernity. As has been consistently maintained throughout the present work, Islam *is* a discursive tradition precisely because Islamic discourse is dynamic, fluid, and ever-transforming within the parameters of a highly political ongoing project of producing "orthodoxy" through the interminable reinterpretation and re-evaluation of texts and practices. To view tradition otherwise would simply be to associate it with stagnation. Especially in the context of the present discussion, the emerging picture would be that of an irrational non-Western world of religious fanaticism, fettered by the weight of tradition, while social change-cum-progress can come only from the West.

Such views are not only sociologically mistaken; they are also politically questionable, especially in the current political climate. The present economic recession and political corruption in the Middle East should not be seen as symptoms of "the failure of the modernization process." Rather, they should be seen as effects of the long-term and systematic dislocation by colonialism and neo-colonialism of relatively well-integrated systems of values that gave meaning to locally held world conceptions, the profound disturbance of everyday life, the crumbling of all political structures, the near total destruction of the checks and balances of local systems of government, as well as of the superficial and mechanistic application of certain Western models by successive post-colonial regimes which, with precious few exceptions, appear to have been promoting their own interests. In reality, even when the rule of law, citizenship, and secular nationalism, democracy itself, socialism and/or the market economy are (rhetorically) espoused, this is not necessarily because they are recognized as genuine popular demands, but because they can serve otherwise authoritarian regimes and corrupt oligarchies as badges of an ill-conceived and window-dressing progressivism. This is what causes popular discontent that may lead to terrorist activities when other legitimate means of mainstream political expression are prohibited.

This brings us to the importance of local conditions. Having the elegance of most generalizations, presuming to offer neat answers to difficult questions, "the failure of the modernization process" argument disregards the complexity of local conditions which often run counter to its premises. For example, it would be inaccurate to suggest that the hugely popular and well-organized Lebanese and Palestinian Islamist organizations Ḥizb Allāh, HAMAS, and Islamic Jihad antagonize the people's nationalist feelings and desire for meaningful sovereignty or that they can be seen as a direct result of an encroaching secularization of society. Rather, the emergence and increasing popularity of Islamists in the area are directly associated with factors such as the Israeli occupation, the inability of the nationalist movement at particular historical moments to articulate credible alternatives, the divide-and-rule practices of Israeli policy, the inherently fractious nature of the Islamist movement itself, the involvement of foreign powers such as Iran, Syria, Saudi Arabia, and Jordan, as well as the local repercussions of important regional developments such the 1979 Iranian revolution and Afghan resistance to the Soviets in the 1980s, the 1982 Israeli invasion of Lebanon and the ensuing Palestinian massacres and the 1987 Palestinian uprising. All this has offered Islamists an opportunity to spread their influence to the wider population despite their violently "Stalinist" methods.[27] The same kind of analysis would allow us to study the popularity of Islamism in Egypt, the Sudan, Algeria, and other Arab Muslim countries of the area.

Following this logic, we can still maintain that economic stagnation and political corruption *are* contributing to the popularity of Islamism in its current form, but only in so far as the movement in all its local forms portrays foreign occupation, corruption, cronyism, absolutism, and state-sponsored terrorism *as non-Islamic vices*, which, in a sense, they are in the same way as they are un-Christian and non-democratic. As for the complicity of the West in all this, at the level of politics it is an observation repeatedly made by numerous Western and non-Western commentators and current affairs analysts, while at the level of principles – i.e. how far can capitalism at its current stage be reconciled with Islamic, or indeed with Christian, values – it is an issue debated by equally numerous social scientists, philosophers, and theologians.

Having said that, one is tempted to suggest that, in the end, the role of the West in the current emergence of Islamism in general and of terrorist activities in the name of Islam in particular lies not so much in its direct political subjugation and economic exploitation of the Middle East, the Muslim world, the Arabs, the Third World, the Other, or whichever historical subject we choose to elect. Rather, it lies in a Western philosophical certainty in positing quite effectively as universal its *own* Truth and – *pace* Evangelical Protestantism, which has been woven into the very fabric of Western modernity, perhaps at the cost of its own otherwise transcendental nature – its belief in infinite material progress in a secular world.[28] At this point, Ziauddin Sardar is close to the mark when he writes that "[t]he key difference between the west and the rest is that non-western cultures comprehend humanity primarily in terms of its limitations, its finiteness."[29] Such attitudes on the part of the West are found arrogant by many Muslims in the Middle East and elsewhere.

To conclude then this section, *in its present form* Islamism has been empowered by adverse international, regional, and local socio-political developments experienced within a context of prolonged economic stagnation and endemic political corruption that afflicts Middle Eastern societies. On top of this, it has also been empowered by what is seen as Western arrogance in forcing its own conception of the world to be recognized as the only valid one. All other alternatives, especially those claiming religious status, can exist but only as such: as alternatives of equal significance from which autonomous individuals can freely choose. But in this way, all such alternatives, be they Christian, Muslim, or something else, lose their claim to eschatological finality, to expressing in full and exclusively the total meaning of the world.

At the same time, as an enterprise for constantly redefining "orthodoxy," i.e. as an intellectual and activist current within the wider parameters of the "orthodoxy" production project, Islamism has been running throughout Islamic history. As a guardian of society's Islamic morals against those perceived to be internal and external foes, and as a struggle for the continual renewal of the Islamic vision in the time-honored tradition of *iṣlāḥ-tajdīd*, what we today call Islamism has always been present. With different names and in different socio-political environments it has always functioned as a more or less comprehensive critique of existing "orthodoxy." Thence its present discourse on "returning" to a "real" Islam and reclaiming a pristine "authenticity." But all these terms, despite the views of contemporary Islamist activists who give them a literal gloss, have a peculiarly modern ring. Islamists may talk about an "authentic" past, but they do so from the vantage point of a present from which there is no escape. I shall return to this theme in the following pages.

ONE OR MANY ISLAMIST MOVEMENTS

The previous section gave us an overview of some of the core Islamist tenets, especially in their complex relation to Western modernity. In this section, I shall follow up that discussion, considering in detail the Islamist positions on a number of central political issues that concern all Middle Eastern societies. To cover more ground and highlight what I regard as the most interesting areas for discussion, I have organized the material around the question of the ideological and organizational singleness and multiplicity of the Islamist movement. The discussion is completed in the next chapter.

Simply put, my point of departure is Roff's thesis that we have one and at the same time many Islamist movements.[30] Exploring first the catholic[31] and supranational character of Islamism, I shall identify five ideological positions which most Islamist groups share. These positions emanate from specific and equally shared interpretations of the *Qur'ān* and other theological treatises of the Islamist textual archive, although they may lead to a variation of tactics and strategies. Different considerations, such as the wider political climate or local action constraints, do play a considerable role in what is actually done in the end. This, however, does not annul the basic ideological kinship upon which the catholic character of the Islamist vision and its political agenda are based.

At the same time, there are a number of outstanding differences between Islamist groups that go beyond the level of tactics and the adoption of specific strategies and which reflect a substantial diversity of views at the level of ideology. No doubt, their existence is related to local socio-economic and political conditions in each case. But I take them to be of another kind altogether from the differences in political praxis mentioned in the previous paragraph. Such differences will be explored in chapter 8.

The Catholic and Supranational Character of Islamism

We can identify five issues or discursive areas which can be found in all instances of Islamism.

The establishment of Islamic states

Islamism is catholic in its appeal and the nature of its vision because its central tenet everywhere it operates is the establishment of Islamic *states* in all Muslim societies, i.e. states governed exclusively by Islamic law. However, neither the exact nature of such a state nor that of Islamic law itself finds all Islamists in agreement. Both issues are debated among organized groups and wide circles of sympathizers and interested members of the public from different socio-cultural environments and with varied historical experiences.

Certainly, such debates are also common among the *'ulamā'* religious scholars, but there is an all-important difference: the Islamists, especially those occupying prominent positions within their organizations, are not always graduates of Islamic schools or universities so they do not possess the extensive theological and philosophical knowledge that the legally inclined *'ulamā'* of institutional Islam would deem appropriate. As a result, the positions they outline tend to be criticized for their alleged mechanistic character and lack of firm theological and philosophical foundations.[32] On the positive side, as a rule Islamist positions are formulated in an everyday language unencumbered by theological and philosophical terms, thus being easily accessible to most people. Their seeming deficiency in sophistication, with all the practical shortcomings that implies, is compensated by their popular – some say populist – accessibility. One is tempted to note that one of the most intractable issues of Islamic tradition, the character of an Islamic state, is transformed by Islamists into an everyday discussion topic among the faithful, not only among the *'ulamā'* or other doyens of the Muslim intelligentsia, but also those whom Asad calls "unlettered Muslims."[33] Here we see the production of "orthodoxy" process in its most "democratic" garb.

The approach to the West

The second reason why Islamism is catholic in its appeal and the nature of its vision has to do with the way it relates itself to Western discourse. In line with the already mentioned "authenticity" thesis, Islamists claim that philosophically Islam is totally independent from Western discourse, which they understand as more or less uniform and homogeneous in the manner discussed in the Introduction. This claim is also advanced by other non-Islamist Muslims, though not with the same eloquence and fervor, as it has not been expressly elevated into an emblematic statement carrying direct political load. And what is more, those whom we have called in the previous chapter Muslim reformers argue that the dialogue with the West at the level of ideas and practices is, if not outright beneficial, at least impossible to avoid.

On closer inspection, although clamoring about Islam's discursive independence, Islamists do not equate Western discourse with modernity itself. On the contrary, they distinguish between modernity as a discursively independent framework of action that is highly conducive to the development of technological innovation and "progress" and modernity as a discursive topos specific to Western societies, whose philosophical and moral implications are by and large inimical to religion.

This distinction allows Islamists to argue that technological innovation and "progress," though intimately associated with the modern condition, can nonetheless be detached from their wider Western ideological context and be employed by Muslims for the improvement of their own societies as if they were mere tools. Indeed, there are some amongst them who maintain that many technological innovations and scientific discoveries were initially made by the Arabs during the first centuries of Islam or that they were mentioned in the *Qur'ān* prior to their actual (i.e. technical) realization. In the first case, the West is presented as receiver of a pre-existing Arab Muslim knowledge, while in the second one it merely confirms pre-existing *Qur'ānic* wisdom. It is not by chance, then, that many of the most respected Islamist ideologues noted how important technology and science are to Muslims, so far as they do not divert their attention from God:[34] typical of these are Ḥasan al-Bannā (1906–49) and Sayyid Quṭb (1906–66) of the Muslim Brotherhood, the most important and populous Islamist organization with centers in Egypt, the Sudan, Syria, and Jordan, as well as Mawlānā Abū 'l-Aʿlā Mawdūdī (1903–79) of the Jamāʿat-i Islāmī of Pakistan.

In the same context, it should be noted that, in addition to applied technological knowledge, contemporary Islamists find another part of Western science particularly useful for the Muslim community: modern economic theory, and especially international finance, whose methods and tools are extensively employed by Islamic banks and international financial networks all over the world.[35] This is revealing because, although in theory Islamism criticizes Western capitalism (and socialism) for being a crude form of materialism, in practice it promotes a type of Islamic economy which can be described as "an 'enlightened' form of capitalism" or "Islamisation of capitalism."[36]

Islamist claims to philosophical and moral independence for Islam have been strongly criticized by several researchers. As it is pointed out, technological innovations and scientific concepts cannot be separated from their wider discursive context nor can they be used as free-floating "objective" tools as their existence is intimately connected with the particular production logic and organizational structures that made their appearance possible in the first place. Furthermore, besides technological innovations and scientific concepts, Islamists also employ many abstract concepts which do not originate with Islam, such as "state," "democracy," "human rights," and "the people." According to Zubaida, this allows one to discern commonalities between Islamism and populist nationalism, which parallel those between Islamism and enlightened capitalism that we noted earlier.[37]

Lastly, there is a third point of criticism which will be fully discussed in chapter 8, but will be briefly mentioned here in order to complete the picture. Alongside whichever concepts it may appropriate from Western discourse, Islamism approaches certain issues which are at the center of its discourse, such as the idea of family, in a manner that implicitly owes much to Western philosophical ideas, especially those of the first decades of the twentieth century. As will be argued later, this is of significance not only because it demolishes Islamism's claims to philosophical and moral independence from Western discourse, but because it demonstrates that the conditions within which the movement itself acquired its present form have left their mark on the way it approaches social reality.

This brief consideration of the relationship between modernity and Islamism suggests that to describe the latter as a retrogressive form of Islam that proclaims a "return" to an Islamic golden past – a position advanced by many detractors of Islamism in the West and elsewhere, but also by many Islamist intellectuals too – is simply not correct. We have seen that the situation is much more complex. On the one hand, just like many conservative Islamic regimes (such as those in Saudi Arabia and the Gulf shaykhdoms), Islamism appears on the surface to be a fairly conservative movement in its choice both of texts (which, apart from the *Qur'ān* and the Prophetic traditions, includes an array of medieval theological treatises) and of ideological positions (such as gender relations and female dress code). On the other hand, compared with the same conservative regimes, Islamism comes across as a particularly progressive and modernizing force, not only in its incorporation of technology and science as a means to further its political ends – after all, most Gulf countries are at the cutting edge of technological innovation, including information technology – but in the actual manner in which this is realized and in the way it shapes social relationships; for example, gender relationships within the organizational frameworks of the Islamist movement are anything but "traditional" when compared with those in Saudi Arabia and the Gulf.[38] The apparently confusing spectacle of an ultra-modern services sector coexisting with the ultra-"traditional" kinship arrangements that characterize Saudi Arabia is far from the vision of most Islamist organizations, which in any case see the Saudi regime as hypocritical and non-Islamic.[39] How far this suggests that the Islamist vision constitutes an Islamic modernity is difficult to say, because Islamists themselves do not provide any definition of such a concept. Most relevant discussions remain at a descriptive level and possess a rather programmatic character which is captured in the often-used motto of "Islamizing modernity." One thing is certain: just like all "returns," Islamists' quest for an "authenticity" cannot escape the coordinates of the present.

Defining the enemy

The third reason why Islamism is catholic in its appeal and the nature of its vision has to do with the fact that in all its versions it does battle against the same enemies: the West and its local allies in the Muslim world. This is different from the previous point, concerning independence from Western discourse, but it is of equal importance. As has been mentioned above in the Introduction, although the West is a historical cultural construction, a dynamic project rather than a fixed reality, it is often seen by millions of people in the Middle East in an essentialist and negative manner. In that respect, the process of globalization is understood as a concerted effort on the part of this monolithic and objectified West to corrupt, take over, and finally destroy the moral principles and organizational structures of the Islamic world. The standard anthropological view of globalization, that "[t]he world system, rather than creating massive cultural homogeneity on a global scale, is replacing one diversity with another,"[40] is replaced by more trenchant views of an essentialist nature.

These views are clearly reflected in the statements of many Muslim leaders and intellectuals and are not confined to Islamist circles. Thus, the Sudanese ex-prime minister Sādiq al-Mahdī rejects "the West's version of modernization" which he equates with "Westernization," arguing that modernization "can and must be divorced" from the "cultural and historical expressions" of the West.[41] Likewise, Ḥasan al-Turābī, the National Islamic Front leader and until recently strong man of the Sudan, maintains that in itself the West does not constitute an enemy of Islam, except in relation to specific policies that are designed against the Islamic world.[42] In a similar manner, Rashīd al-Ghannūshī, the exiled leader of the Tunisian *al-Daʿwa* political party, denounces the respect the West has shown toward the writer Salman Rushdie for the injurious manner in which he has attacked Islamic religion and traditions in his work *Satanic Verses*.[43] Lastly, the Pakistani anthropologist Akbar Ahmed sees in the establishment of a "global civilisation" the "triumph of the West," which he credits not only with expansion, bubbling with scientific ideas, economic plans, political ambitions, and cultural expression, but also with the death and destruction of everything non-Western, ethnocentricity, arrogance, and racism. As the opposite of this dark picture, Ahmed proclaims Islam a positive force with huge universal potential.[44]

Such pronouncements on the West by well-known Muslim activists and intellectuals, which could be easily multiplied, are part of an extensive bibliography on the subject. The roots of this literary output go back to the ways in which Muslims have depicted Europe since relatively early and is certainly not confined to Islamist tracts and outright denunciations of the West and everything that this may stand for.[45] But of immediate interest are various studies and other literature on the relationship between Islam and the West authored by Islamist activists during recent decades, especially after the 1979 Iranian revolution; this includes republications of much earlier works which are now finding an expanding readership.

The texts I am referring to can be divided into three basic categories. The first concerns new editions of classical (i.e. late medieval) studies on Islamic law and politics, such as those of Aḥmad Ibn Ḥanbal (d. 855) and Ibn Taymiyya (1263–1328).[46] Some of these works have come to acquire cult status among members of Islamist organizations comparable to that of Marx or Mao among leftist intellectuals and students of the 1960s. What is interesting about such works, which are invariably difficult to approach if only for their highly formulaic language and complex structure, is their contemporary introductions and textual notes. There the present-day editors try to demonstrate the relevance of the masters' analyses to contemporary problems experienced by Muslims worldwide.[47]

The second category of Islamist publications include the studies of well-known and highly respected Islamist intellectuals and activists, as well as those of less-known writers whose work has all the credentials of an intellectual endeavor with political implications.[48] Among the former we have Ḥasan al-Bannā, Sayyid Quṭb, and Mawlānā Abū 'l-A'lā Mawdūdī, the three grand masters mentioned earlier in the chapter, whose works are constantly republished. They all refer to the West and the various ideologies associated with it in a highly disparaging way. For example, Mawdūdī was a determined opponent of secular nationalism and an advocate of Islamic universalism. In his view, "Western civilization strikes at the very roots of that concept of ethics and culture which is the base of Islamic civilization . . . Islam and western civilization are like two boats sailing in totally opposite directions."[49]

Among the lesser-known, but not necessarily less important, contemporary Islamist activists and thinkers we come across similar conceptualizations of the West and its relation to Islam. Here the list of authors and the ways in which they discuss the issue could be endless.

Thus, Khursid Ahmad (1995) and Jabal Muhammad Buaben (1996) discuss how Western intellectuals, such as A.J. Arberry, H.A.R. Gibb, P.K. Hitti, W. Muir, D.S. Margoliouth, and W.M. Watt, allegedly misrepresent Islam and Prophet Muḥammad; while the Palestinian Ismail Bagi al-Faruqi accuses the West of spiritual bankruptcy and of contaminating the Muslim world with the "despicable Western virus" of nationalism. For him the only way forward is that of revival and reform.[50] On his part, Maulana Wahiddudin Khan (1997) goes one step further, attempting to demonstrate *Qur'ānic* superiority in comparison to Western scientific and philosophical tradition. In the same vein, Israr Ahmad asks for the launching of a high-powered academic movement to effect a change in "the educated intelligentsia of the society"[51] and Hasan Hanafi promotes a new social science, occidentalism, as a response of the colonized to Western domination.[52]

Of specific interest are also the views of Islamist women activists. Thus, Maryam Jameelah, an American Jew converted to Islam, equates modernization with Westernization, which brings in its train evolution, relativism, and secularism,[53] and argues that the "real" purpose of Western academic study of Islam is the subversion of "the Islamic cause" and the frustration "of any attempts for a genuine Islamic renaissance."[54] Agreeing with Jameelah, the Egyptian Islamist Ṣafīnaz Qāzim, maintains that we are now living in a "euro-ameri-zionist age," which nonetheless will "fall" just like the Roman and Persian empires and will be succeeded by the age of Islam.[55] Lastly, Ḥība Ra'ūf, who belongs to a younger generation of Islamist activists, accuses the West of wantonness and of promoting individualism in a manner that, to a certain extent, goes back to the style and content of Sayyid Quṭb's ideas.

The third category of Islamist publications that should be considered concerns texts presenting the views of more radical groups and organizations. These works use the *Qur'ān*, the Prophetic *ḥadīth*, and classical treatises on Islamic law and theology as foundation stones for their analyses, but on the whole their character is much more overtly political than intellectual, propagandistic rather than exploratory of ideas. They are calls for political agitation, but not necessarily for violence. Peaceful admonition blended with criticism of governments and elites is also propagated.

Such publications, already mentioned in the context of our discussion of religious merchandise in chapter 3, can take the form of longer or shorter books, brochures, leaflets, or pamphlets. Some of them discuss current issues and concerns of the Muslim community, such as Palestine, Iraq, and Afghanistan, while others are republications of older material and deal with more general, but, in the eyes of many, equally pressing issues, such as the establishment of Islamic states.

This type of material is usually sold or distributed in bookshops, kiosks, markets, study-centers, party offices, universities, *Qur'ānic* schools, and mosques, as well as on the Internet. At the same time, their availability seems to be directly related to the general political climate and freedom of the press, as their content is invariably critical of the powers that be and revolutionary in its intentions. Often, it is easier to find such material, written in English, in London than in Cairo or Khartoum, although in the current political climate such material may be in short supply almost everywhere. As before, the examples that follow are indicative.

Arguably, one of the best-known and infamous publications of this type is *The Neglected Duty* by the Egyptian ʿAbd al-Salām Faraj. There the author presents his own interpretation of Ibn Taymiyya's theories, according to which those Muslim leaders who do not promote the establishment of Islamic states should be assassinated. The book has become widely known through its association with the 1981 murder of Egyptian President Anwar Sadat.[56] As far as I know, this is the only Islamist propaganda text that has been fully studied and presented in an English-language publication (Jansen 1986), together with responses from representatives of Egyptian institutional Islam.

The following three examples concern publications of Ḥizb al-Taḥrīr, a political party with branches in many Middle Eastern and North African countries, as well as in several Western capitals. The Ḥizb al-Taḥrīr was founded in 1952 by *shaykh* Taqī al-Dīn al-Nabahānī, a West Bank Palestinian. As Milton-Edwards notes, "its philosophy was decidedly pan-Islamic and anti-colonialist."[57] Fiercely against nationalism, whether Arab or Palestinian, the party called for "the immediate destruction of current state systems in the Middle East through jihad . . . [and] the resurrection of an Islamic state."[58] Ḥizb al-Taḥrīr never became a mass movement in Palestine itself and played only a minor role in Jordanian political life. Nonetheless, it is still present in the area, in other Arab states in the Gulf and North Africa, as well as in the West.[59]

In a large number of pamphlets and books that are distributed throughout the Arab world and the West, Ḥizb al-Taḥrīr propagates its main ideas which are still uncompromising and revolutionary. As we read in some of its recent publications, Islam is a complete way of life whose implementation should be enforced by the state.[60] For this reason, the establishment of an Islamic state, or more specifically, the re-establishment of the caliphate is not only a practical necessity, but also a religious obligation. What exactly this entails is described in a number of publications, some of which are the work of al-Nabaḥānī himself.[61] Interestingly, in an earlier publication, *Khilafah is the Answer* (1989), the tone is much more messianic than in Nabaḥānī's measured analysis. For example, after the quotation of some Prophetic *ḥadīth* showing that the re-establishment of the caliphate is near, we read that

> the Muslims will open Rome, the capital of Italy, the home of the Pope and the stronghold of Christianity, and . . . will remove the state of Israel and eliminate the Jews living in it. The opening of Rome and the destruction of Israel will be achieved by the Khilafah state, an indication that the state will be a major superpower as it was before.[62]

Lastly, in a 1996 publication in which the party presents its ideology and practices in more detail, we read that the establishment of the caliphate would involve a "struggle against the *Kufr* colonialist states which have domination and influence on the Islamic countries," as well as a "struggle against the rulers in the Arab and Muslim countries" which do not follow "the rules of Islam."[63] Despite the romantic and utopian character of the whole project, the re-establishment of the caliphate as the only solution to Western hegemony (which is discussed in terms of neo-colonialism in a manner that reminds us the discourse of leftist organizations) has given Ḥizb al-Taḥrīr prestige among younger activists who see in the West an insidious enemy of the Muslim world.

At the same time, if we place in a broader spectrum of political options the solutions that Islamists propose in order to thwart Western hegemony of the Middle Eastern societies, we could call them "a 'Third Way' that accepts capitalism but seeks to contain the inequality it engenders by an all-encompassing moral law and the moral activism of the faithful."[64] In addition, the Islamist "Third Way" is characterized by easily discernible traits of *petit-bourgeois* nationalist populism, which have been present in previous ideologies that have flourished in the Middle East, such as Arab nationalism and Arab socialism.[65]

The condemnation of mysticism

The fourth reason why Islamism is catholic in its appeal and the nature of its vision is that it always opposes all types of mystical tendencies which can be found in every Muslim society. There are two main reasons behind this enmity. The first one is doctrinal. Islamists preach a pristine puritanical form of Islam at the center of which is God and the *Qur'ān*. For them, the fact that *ṣūfī* masters and other saintly personalities are considered to be intermediaries between God and believers and are often venerated by the latter is simply unacceptable. Additionally, the various practices which are part of mystical Islam, be they witchcraft rituals, ecstatic spirit-possession cults or astrological and other divinatory techniques, are considered to be mere superstitions which have nothing to do with Islam *per se* as Islamists understand it. So Islamic education in the form of seminars or study groups that Islamists invariably provide to the community has a dual purpose: on the one hand, to "free" believers from superstition and on the other to teach them the "real" Islamic values and practices. It is this uncompromising spirit and will to cleanse religion from "ungodly accretions" that led followers of the Islamist Wahhabī movement to attack Mecca and Madīna, as well as other holy cities of Islam, at the beginning of the nineteenth century, demolishing tombs, mausoleums, and shrines of Muslim personalities, including that of the Prophet himself.

The second reason, which often goes unacknowledged, is that for Islamists the existence of *ṣūfī* brotherhoods and the veneration of saintly lineages provide alternative, that is, antagonistic, foci of religious and political allegiance which divide the Community of Believers along sectarian or even tribal lines.

In societies where sufism is especially strong for historical reasons, this network of sacred obligations cannot be easily distinguished from political relations at the local level and from their economic implications. This situation can turn Islamists and the *ṣūfī* establishment into political opponents in a very direct and uncompromising manner. This has been the case in the Sudan where until the 1989 Islamist-backed military coup the two major political parties were closely associated with sufism.

This inflexible and unyielding position of Islamists toward mysticism raises a number of interesting issues. As has been illustrated in chapter 5, mysticism is an integral part of Islamic tradition as this is realized in each individual Muslim society. To show enmity toward it demonstrates that the Islamists approach Islamic tradition in a singularly circumscribed manner. After all, some of the most important historical personalities among those well versed in scriptural Islam, like al-Ghazzālī, were actively involved with mysticism. Such enmity is not strange. As with every political or religious ideology, the invocation of tradition is always a very selective and entirely political process. Assuming the form of "truly" interpreting the tradition or of "cleansing and purifying it from all those ideas and practices which have contaminated it in the course of time," tasks that many sincerely see as their political or religious duty, it also amounts to a manipulation of the past in the light of present demands.

In the case under discussion here, this puritanical ethos has always been present in Islamic history under many guises. Thus, the seeming antithesis between the traditionalist *ʿulamāʾ* and the *ṣūfī* mystics that was discussed and deconstructed in chapter 5 is part of that broad trend. The same is true for the Islamic reformers whose enmity towards mystical Islam was noted in chapter 6. Even the late eighteenth- and early nineteenth-century movement of neo-sufism opposed the ecstatic character and metaphysical tendencies of the *ṣūfī* orders.[66]

But although this widespread condemnation of mysticism correctly demonstrates that there are very important points of contact between the various visions of Islamic tradition, we should equally remember that it is the Islamists in particular who, more than anyone else, reject all forms of mystical Islam in the name of renewal of the faith and in favor of a particularly legalistic version of tradition, which centers around the establishment of Islamic states and the full application of Islamic law, seen as a closed system of rules. In that sense, it is as if Islamists roundly reject the idea of local(-ized) Islam, that is, the idea that in every society Islam takes on a particular color according to the local cultural milieu, promoting instead a one-size-fits-all Islam which would be the same everywhere in the world.

Individualism and the position of women

The fifth reason why Islamism is catholic in its appeal and the nature of its vision has to do with the position it accords to the individual in relation to society, as well as with its broader ideological stance concerning "women's issues," that is, the issues related to the rights, role, and status of women in society.

Starting with the individual, this is conceptualized first and foremost as a member of the Community of Believers, always under the absolute will of God and the power of His law. This does not mean that the individual as such ceases to exist, but that the concept is understood in a fundamentally different way from that in Western secular societies. As we saw in chapter 4, each and every human being is individually responsible for him- or herself in the eyes of God. However, each individual fulfills his or her divinely prescribed role, that is, is impregnated with meaning at a deep existential level, only as a member of the Community of Believers. In that sense, the individual Muslim is at the very center of Islamist discourse.[67]

At the level of political structures, the practical implications of this position are enormous. As Stork notes, "[t]he individual citizen, as an autonomous, contract-making self, is a peculiarly modern and Western discourse"[68] and should not apply to Islamic societies. That means that while in the West the ultimate source of law, philosophically as well as legally, is the people, in an Islamic society as imagined by the Islamists the highest authority is God. Consequently, personal and human rights are of a different order from those in the West.[69] Significantly, this view is not an Islamist peculiarity, but applies to Islamic discourse in its entirety, although it seldom affects the politics of Muslim societies at the level of government politics.[70] As Asad notes, "[t]he Islamic *umma* presupposes individuals who are self-governing but not autonomous. The *sharīʿa*, a system of pracical reason morally binding on each faithful individual, exists independently of him or her."[71]

Concerning women's issues, Islamists' invariably restrictive views on polygyny, female attire, social mobility, and occupation have been heavily criticized in the West. Most people in Europe and America believe that in Islamic countries women are oppressed, in some places more than in others. They also believe that the Islamist vision of society is more repressive than, say, that of Muslim reformists. Veiling, female circumcision, and women's position in Afghanistan, Iran, and Saudi Arabia constitute everyday markers indicating violations of women's rights. In all cases, Islam is seen as a common denominator and the ultimate source of the problem.[72]

Anthropologists and other observers of Islamic societies know that things are much more complex. As Eickelman writes, it would be highly inappropriate to identify a normative Islamic tradition (here in relation to the position of women) when Muslims themselves vigorously debate the issue.[73] Indeed, what exactly is considered to be normative at each historical juncture and in each community is intimately related to what has been called time and again in the preceding chapters "production of orthodoxy." In that sense, we cannot talk about the "position of women in Islam" or "sexuality in Islam," without running the risk of reproducing orientalistic modes of thought.[74] Moreover, issues related to the position of women in specific societies should be explored from various points of view, religion being only one of them. As Hale rightly points out, "[t]he aim . . . is to avoid automatically conflating patriarchal gender relations and religiously sanctioned patriarchal codes."[75]

Certainly, this does not stop Muslim conservative thinkers and Islamists, even Muslim reformers, from seeing their respective versions of Islam as supplying the total and all-encompassing blueprint for gender relations. Still, an analysis of their positions should strive to uncover the internal dynamics of their discourse and to elucidate its relation to the material conditions that sustain it. What follows, then, is not a discussion of "women's position in Islam," which if made would exhibit untenable essentialist presuppositions, but an introductory presentation of the ways in which personalities and organizations of the Islamist movement approach the role of women in Islamic societies and the movement itself.

Islamist discourse on women's issues contains a number of principal elements, which function as points of departure for the various more specialized arguments on polygyny, veiling, female occupation, etc.

First, when confronted with unsavory facts, such as degrading veiling, female circumcision, or absence of political rights, Islamists acknowledge that in the Muslim world the position of women – vis-à-vis that of men, where men and women are seen as categorical objects – is not ideal. However, they attribute this to a poor understanding of Islam, the harmful influence of local customs and superstitions, and the general social malaise they associate with corrupt governments. This proposition enables them to defend Islam's "real" views on women and to appropriate them for themselves, arguing that these will be implemented when they come to power. Second, Islamists maintain that Islam's "real" views on women, just like Islam as a whole, have been either innocently misunderstood in the West or (the most prevalent view) have been intentionally misrepresented as part of a wider "Western conspiracy."[76] In reality, they argue, Islam is a particularly progressive tradition in the way it approaches women and their position in society. Third, to prove this, Islamists approach all discussion on women's issues in a comparative and highly polemic manner vis-à-vis the perceived "position of women in the West," which they stereotypically describe in distinctly dark colors, emphasizing a woman's unenviable position as a sexual object. Fourth, this strategy allows Islamists to couch their arguments in a framework of an Islamic "authenticity," which they present in terms of (re)instating an alternative – and hence "true" – Islamic identity in the face of morally and politically pernicious Western influences facilitated by conniving local elites. Lastly, Islamists' positions on women's issues are close to those of institutional or establishment Islam, that is, the versions of Islam promoted by governments and the *'ulamā'* hierarchies.[77]

This last point is particularly significant for the following reason. It has been often argued that, despite all publicity, as a political movement Islamism has failed in its effort to effect regime changes and to establish Islamic states in the wider region of the Middle East, except in a very few cases which can all be explained away as special: Iran, after a popular revolution; Afghanistan, after foreign occupation, civil war, and total collapse of the state and society; the Sudan, after a brutal army coup; Turkey, after the discrediting of all alternatives and in a much diluted form.[78] From this point of view, terrorism is actually seen as a veritable proof of this failure in the sense that spectacular sporadic violence is the only strategy left to an otherwise marginal(-ized) form of religious fanaticism.

The problem with this view is its narrow definition of politics as something that can be clearly observed at the level of electoral results and public administration. As an anthropologist I would open up the political to the vista of cultural practices and the field of identity politics, and would approach Islamist discourse as an instance of what I have earlier called "Islamization from below." This is the discursively articulated dimension of a much wider popular trend towards cultural "authenticity" that is supported by all sorts of conservative voices whose position in society has never been questioned. In terms of this current, the politics of culture and the culture of politics cannot and should not be formally distinguished. It should be remembered, then, that when I discuss Islamist views on women's issues in the pages that follow, I do so having as a background this wider and pervasive social consensus.[79]

Polygyny and Female Occupation

I would first consider the issues of polygyny and female occupation.[80] True to their "misunderstanding/misrepresentation of the Islam" thesis, Islamists, together with other conservative Muslim thinkers, assert that *in reality* polygyny is practiced only under very specific conditions and is legally sanctioned according to very strict rules.[81] Even then, it has nothing to do with the male sexual appetite and everything to do with alliance building between different descent groups and with more generalized concerns of economic and political nature. In other words, polygyny is presented as a strategy integral to traditional (Muslim) social structures and as a practice regulated by Islamic law with wisdom and prudence.[82] Nonetheless, Islamists appear to discourage polygyny in the present conditions, without condemning it in principle.

But there is another, evil, kind of polygyny, the argument continues, that is prevalent in the West in three different forms: first, through successive marriages and divorces, what they call serial polygyny; second, through the keeping of mistresses alongside lawful wives, which is presented as a particularly widespread practice; and third, through habitual sex between unmarried partners.[83] In all this, women are conceptualized as sexual trophies and objects of desire used by men for their own pleasure. Lastly, the argument emphasizes the sorry fate of single mothers, the vast number of children born outside wedlock, the hell of prostitution and the illegal sexual trade, domestic violence, VD and AIDS, all of which, it is claimed, are either absent from Islamic societies or at least much less in evidence. In this context, it is the value of family itself that becomes the focus of Islamist discourse as the nurturing and secure nest/cell at the foundations of all real Islamic societies.

Concerning women's professional occupation and, implicitly, their right to move freely outside their homes and their role in politics, once more Islamists find themselves in broad agreement with most conservative Muslims, though in the end some do envision women outside the traditionally understood household. They all agree that men and women are equal in the eyes of God, but different in their natural tendencies and disposition. This takes men outside the house, charging them with the making of material provision for the family, and keeps women within the house, entrusting to them the noble job of raising children and looking after all domestic affairs.[84] Islamists also emphasize that, according to Islamic law, women are *entitled* not to work outside the house whereas men are *obliged* to provide their families with all that is necessary for their material well-being and happiness.[85] Still, there is a considerable gray area in the thoughts of many Islamists concerning women's implication in Islamist political struggle.

One of the best-known Islamist groups, the Palestinian HAMAS, itself a wing of the Muslim Brotherhood, devotes two articles of its *Charter* to the "role of Muslim women." Impressive as this might be, a close reading of the text shows that the group does not really depart at all from the general view on the subject that was outlined in the previous paragraph. For instance,

> The women in the house and the family of Jihad fighters, whether they are mothers or sisters, carry out the most important duty of caring for the home and raising the children upon the moral concepts and values which derive from Islam; and of educating their sons to observe the religious injunctions in preparation for the duty of Jihad awaiting them.[86]

Turning to individual preachers and activists who influence public opinion, *shaykh* Muḥammad Mitwāllī al-Shaʿrāwī, a popular Egyptian radio and television preacher, argues that man can work outside the house because God has endowed him with logic, while woman should be responsible for her household because God has given her emotions.[87] However, *shaykh* Muḥammad al-Ghazālī, another well-known Egyptian Islamist, is equivocal on the matter. He maintains that according to God's economy women should lovingly serve their husbands and their home rather than practicing jobs incommensurable with their nature, while he agrees that there are jobs suitable for women outside their household. Even in a state of war against Islam, al-Ghazālī suggests, women could assist men in "the treatment of the sick, preparation of medicines, transport of the injured . . . and carrying out some managerial duties."[88]

A similar equivocation can be found in the work of Yūsuf al-Qaradāwī, another prominent Egyptian Islamist-cum-conservative intellectual, who is head of the *Sharīʿa* Faculty at the University of Qatar and whose work has been translated into English.[89] As Karam writes, al-Qaradāwī's preferences are for women "servicing" their husbands and that even in a state of war their role could be seen as an extension of their domestic tasks.[90] However, in a 1992 book on the priorities of the Islamic movement, al-Qaradāwī appears adamant that women should be engaged in Islamic work in a forceful manner and independently of men. Urging women to stand up for their rights, as these are described in the *Qur'ān* and the Prophetic *ḥadīth*, al-Qaradāwī acknowledges that "men have never allowed women a real chance to express themselves and show special leadership talents and abilities that demonstrate their capability of taking command of their work without men's dominance."[91] Indeed, these are weighty claims which can be reconciled with other statements of al-Qaradāwī only with difficulty. But in all cases, they do not annul his insistence that when talking about gender relations, *equality* is not an issue; what is at the center of his thought, just as with any Islamist, really, as well as with the majority of conservative Muslims, is God-ordained *complementarity* between the sexes. In al-Qaradāwī we have a fine example of how Islamist thought can move from the chartered areas of more traditional conservative thinkers.

The views expressed by female Islamist activists, such as the Egyptian Zaynab al-Ghazālī, Ṣafīnaz Qāzim, and Ḥība Ra'ūf, are not altogether different. The first, a veteran Islamist campaigner who was imprisoned and tortured in the 1950s, even denies the existence of separate "women's issues" arguing that both men and women, in their own distinctive and complementary ways, have to do their natural God-given duty. And "[w]oman's role in society is to be a mother, to be a wife . . . To build men . . . to build great women who build men to become a great *umma* [nation]."[92] We see here how prominent the link between family and the Muslim nation is. On her part, Ṣafīnaz Qāzim maintains that "Allah gave certain different blessings to men and women, but these are partial differences that do not mean inequalities – there is a unity of kind."[93] Accordingly, Qāzim is strongly critical of feminism, which she depicts "as a sister to Zionist ideology, and part of [the] grander 'euro-ameri-zionist' scheme"[94] mentioned earlier.[95] Besides this, Qāzim accepts that women participate effectively "in building their emerging societies,"[96] but we are not told exactly how this can take place.

Lastly, Ḥība Ra'ūf, who belongs to a younger generation of Egyptian Islamists, clearly states that women should be "allowed to occupy the highest public functions *as long as they [are] qualified*."[97] In this, Ra'ūf includes even military service, as for her the Islamic nation (*umma*) is in a state of war. But as Karam rightly points out, this is done mostly through the politicization of the family and a blurring of the public/private distinction. This does not really negate the patriarchal bias of the male Islamist ideology: once in power,

Islamists can send their women home to carry on their good work from within the family.[98]

Such underlying tensions between male and female Islamist sub-discourses have been successfully examined by, among others, Hale (1996, 1997), an anthropologist working in the Sudan. Hale's argument is based on Mernissi's position, that "much of the Muslim world experiences a competition between newly urbanized middle- and lower-middle-class men and semiemancipated women from predominantly middle-class urban backgrounds,"[99] whose social position improved especially during the reign of secular nationalist regimes.

Following this logic, the Sudanese National Islamic Front (NIF) promotes ideological positions which allow women to work, but only if their occupation does not question male hegemonic ideological claims and do not adversely affect the material interests of middle-class Sudanese men. This implies that Sudanese Islamists envision female professional occupation only in terms of meeting otherwise insurmountable financial difficulties. In all other cases, it is decreed that women should stay at home and raise their children, thus living up to the most cherished Islamic ideals of family and motherhood. In other words, the Sudanese Islamists, just like their counterparts elsewhere, approach women's issues with a romanticized vision of woman as "traditionally" Muslim.

But even if that were so, then the Sudanese Islamists should be positively inclined towards the professional activities of the great mass of usually illiterate lower-class women, as it is self-evident that these are directly associated with the latter's terrible state of impoverishment. But no, this does not happen, because in the eyes of the NIF followers such activities do not promote Islamic ideals. On the contrary, they run counter to their romanticized view of Muslim woman as a good wife and mother, who, enjoying the blessed safety and comfort of her household, is not obliged to sell tea or vegetables in the market, make and sell alcoholic beverages, or prostitute herself in order to feed her family.[100] The romanticized NIF vision of Muslim woman has little or no relation to the harsh realities of the great mass of unemployed impoverished women of the shanty-towns and the third-class residential areas who, in a sense, are the unrecognized heroes of Hale's sensitive ethnography.

The Veil

Islamists consider female veiling to be obligatory for *all* Muslim women, a view they share with many conservative Muslims. This is explained in a number of ways, most of which display a clear patriarchal bias. For al-Shaʿrāwī veiling affords women a measure of security, while it also functions as a source of respect. When all women are veiled, he proclaims, men's natural instincts cannot be inflamed so a number of otherwise regrettable incidences such as rapes and indecent behavior can be avoided. Not only can individual women feel secure, but aging wives can be comforted that their husbands will not compare them to younger and more presentable ladies. In all cases, then, for al-Shaʿrāwī veiling appears to work towards protecting marriage and family from non-conjugal strains.[101]

Al-Ghazālī, also, advocates the extensive use of veiling, but differs from al-Shaʿrāwī and most conservatives in that he accepts women's right to be active in the public sphere. In the same vein, he argues that "'women have a right to make themselves beautiful . . . but not to display their charms.'"[102] Similar views are held by al-Qaradāwī, who asks,

> Is it fair to disparage and sneer at a young woman who veils her face because she is convinced that her action is in tune with Islamic teachings and through which she seeks Allah's acceptance, and yet keep silent about another who walks about in the streets or seashores or appears on television or movies almost naked, deliberately seeking to provoke the instincts, claiming that she is simply excercising "personal freedom" which is sanctioned by the constitution?[103]

Lastly, Ṣafīnaz Qāzim, one of the female Islamists mentioned earlier, offers the additional explanation about veiling that "it forces men to deal with a veiled woman on an equal footing, because they will be attracted by her mental rather than her physical attributes."[104] This is a view shared by many young women members of Islamist organizations and by others whose ideological views place them at the conservative end of the spectrum.

So for Islamist activists and sympathizers veiling is intimately related to the position women should have in a fast-changing social milieu – allegedly threatened by Western secularism – and to the role they should play within the Islamist movement, the only bulwark against this menace. In other words, veiling has the status of an unambiguous ideological position and a clearly discernible political dimension. This, Hodgkin writes, is what differentiates the contemporary veil-as-political statement from the veil of the previous generations, which had a "traditional" character as the only appropriate female apparel, and as such its use rarely, if ever, became part of a rhetoric.[105]

Still, it would be misleading to accept a dichotomous discourse that differentiates between a "traditional" non-political veil and one expressive of an Islamist political affiliation. As it happens, the so-called "traditional" veil of the previous generations (which I take it to refer to the veil worn by women of "traditional" urban or rural Muslim societies, a rather imprecise description at best) has invariably been intimately connected with issues of social status and stratification, class and group identity. Islamic morals, cultural propriety, and power relations have always jointly informed an individual's total social being, as Abu-Lughod's 1988 classic anthropological study on veiling among Egyptian Bedouin has shown.

Similarly, current uses of the veil are equally rich in meaning and should not be necessarily associated with *active* participation in the Islamist movement.

Rather, they should be seen within a wider context of responses to questions related to identity and "tradition" in fast-changing socio-political environments. For example, in its contemporary form, veiling appeared in 1970s Egypt among female university students, that is among the first women who took advantage of the educational opportunities offered by the relatively new post-colonial nationalist state. For them it was a symbol of empowerment that also signified respect for Islamic traditions. It enabled them to "declare their difference from their uneducated relatives without jeopardizing their respectability."[106] Progressively, the practice was appropriated by middle- and lower-middle-class working women as well as by educated young women from rural areas, where female education often appeared as an un-Islamic innovation that questioned women's assumed natural domesticity. For such women, veiling signifies a "return to roots" closely associated "with a sense of crisis in both political and economic realms."[107] It allows them to move symbolically and practically in the public sphere, but also signals that they do not see this "relative freedom" as their natural right. It "helps clarify to themselves, to husbands, and to coworkers, that they work in the face of economic uncertainty to aid their family and not because it is their personal desire."[108] In more political terms, "[f]or the economically exploited and socially disadvantaged the return to *hijab* [veil] is both a protest against the consumerism of the élite classes and against westernization."[109]

Be that as it may, when we move into areas where politics routinely assume direct confrontational forms, veiling is often employed as a weapon in the context of political struggle. Such an area is the Gaza Strip. The campaign for veiling started in the late 1970s when the predecessor of HAMAS, *al-Mujamaʿ al-Islāmī*, "sought to impose or, as they saw it, 'restore' the *hijab* [veil] for women in Gaza."[110] In doing so, the organization endowed the veil, which already existed among the older generations, with new meanings which suited its intention of portraying the struggle against Israeli occupation as a religious and not a nationalist one. In that climate, where the nationalists rather than the Israelis figured as the immediate enemies of the Palestinian Islamists, many women who elected to move around uncovered were harassed by *al-Mujamaʿ* supporters. Not wearing the veil was considered by the latter to be a trait of the internal enemy or "collaborator," together with the use of drugs, pornography, alcohol, "engaging in illicit sexual relations or even social gender mixing."[111]

The arrival of the Palestinian National Authority in Gaza in July 1994 improved the situation only superficially. As Hammami writes, "[u]ltimately, this suggests that while the Authority adopts the classic Arab nationalist modernist approach to social and gender relations, on the ground it is still competing with Hamas, using a discourse of social morality."[112] Plainly, both the typical Arab secular nationalist view of woman as a pillar of society, which may often take the form of token emancipatory policies – a phenomenon that can be observed in many Middle Eastern societies – and the Islamist discourse on women as guardians of the Islamic traditions and mothers and wives of the faithful, are based on romanticized portraits of women and both espouse a puritanical ethos.[113]

Authenticity, Tradition, and Modernity

Islamists' discourse on "authenticity," especially their romantic view of woman as personification of an "authentic [Islamic] culture,"[114] suggests that their way of understanding Islamic tradition suffers from the same type of essentialism as that of classical Western orientalists and contemporary neo-orientalists. In all cases Islam is perceived as something ideal that exists outside history and human praxis; therein lies its assumed "authenticity" that, in Islamists' eyes, society should make every effort to reclaim, even if this is not always welcomed by the actors, as the Gaza example has shown, and even when it leads to terrorism. So the spectacle of veiled women who would preferably stay at home does not simply signify a religious awakening in the face of everyday difficulties attributed to inept governments and an encroaching West. Rather, it testifies to the workings of an Islamist discursive regime that articulates through specific strategies real popular socio-economic problems and experiential anxieties in a vision of a reclaimed "authenticity." This vision is put to the service of an allegedly better future, far removed from the present state of social, political, and moral corruption.

But there is something more in all this which concerns the way this image of "authentic" Islam is constructed. Commenting earlier in the chapter on the Islamist claims to Islam's philosophical and moral independence from Western discourse (pp. 205–6), I maintained that in reality propositions on issues central to Islamist discourse *do* owe much to Western philosophical ideas. The example of women and family discussed above is particularly instructive.

As Abu-Lughod writes concerning Egypt, in the modernist Islamist family model the two spouses are conceptualized as marriage companions enjoying a sincere and fulfilling relationship with each other in an environment *where all other kin and social relationships are either absent or unimportant.* In other words, the model that the Islamist discourse presents us with as "authentically" Islamic is that of a nuclear family where women are fully dependent on their husbands and disconnected from their own descent groups, other women, and the wider community. But this model has nothing "traditional" in it, as it is in total contrast not only with what was the norm in the pre-colonial days, but also with the lived experience of women in contemporary rural and semi-urban Egypt.[115]

Based on the historical analyses of Mitchell (1991) and Shakry (1998), Abu-Lughod argues that the model's sources should be sought among the elite feminist agenda advanced at the turn of the previous century by reformers who had adopted ideas and practices from contemporary Western Europe, based on the perceived socially inferior position of women in Egypt.[116] These ideas were later adopted by the early nationalists, who appealed to both the bourgeois reformist dreams and to the conservative middle classes' assumptions about marriage,[117] and subsequently by the Nasser regime, whose "support for women's work and education" progressively spread to "the upwardly mobile lower middle classes from whom the Islamists draw much of their support."[118] In the process, all connection with Western notions was conveniently, and perhaps sincerely too, forgotten not only by the Islamists, but also by those nationalist circles who first explored these ideas about women's status in a modern state.[119]

Unfortunately, we have no comparable material from other Middle Eastern societies. My own observations from the Sudan, which were peripheral to my main ethnographic concerns, confirm that middle- and upper-middle-class urban families as a rule do follow the nuclear model, in that they live separately from the extended family and their wider descent group. How many of them are favorably disposed toward the Islamist message that is articulated by the government, it is difficult to say; veiling amongst the women and the award of public works contracts to influential *abū digin* (as men with beards, sign of Islamist persuasion, are locally known) could be indicative of political affiliations, but no more than that. One thing is certain, though, as I had the opportunity to observe myself and to discuss with many friends and relatives: generally, it is highly unusual for middle- and upper-class Sudanese women to make their appearance at any type of social gathering. Or to put it differently, among the lower classes women are far more visible and mobile.

But can this be attributed to Islamism as such? The previously mentioned "Islamization from below" process can perhaps be more plausibly associated with what I observed in the field. But even then, one should be careful. A historical study could reveal that in urban Sudan, just as in Egypt, this situation has been a long-time characteristic of urban social life, but not necessarily for the same reasons as in Egypt. For example, from a purely ethnographic point of view studies on spirit-possession cults throughout the Middle East indicate that these have always attracted lower- to lower-middle-class women, as those from the higher classes lead more restricted social lives because they have to conform with the locally espoused Muslim ideals. And certainly this is true for most women in particular societies in the Arabian Peninsula and Central Asia; let us remember post-*Ṭālibān* Afghanistan.

Finally, one should be careful not to generalize about the decline in the importance of kinship ties among Islamists. Judging from the Sudan, once more, it would not be inaccurate to suggest that kinship ties have always been very important in the construction of political power networks among the governing elites. There have been very specific tribal groups among the riverain northern Arabs who historically have found themselves in positions of power, as well as very specific families who have managed to participate in government. This did not stop after the 1989 Islamist military coup. Of course, such arrangements have always been characterized by a male or, should we say, patriarchal bias. Ethnographically speaking, little is known about the female members of such families. Nonetheless, the whole picture brings forward a different side of Islamist discourse from that of the Egyptian material.

Local traditions, often religiously inflected, urbanization, "Islamization from below," active support of the Islamist message, and intricate articulations of a purist Islamist message with time-honored political strategies and local alliance practices could all be equally implicated in the social mapping of kinship relations and family structures. This does not invalidate the previous consideration of the Egyptian Islamist model which, after all, discusses the position of women rather than kinship itself. However, it implies a multi-factoral approach and suggests that more studies of localized Islamist discourses should be conducted, which should always be situated within the wider social and economic context.[120]

8

Islamism at the Local Level

Having discussed in the previous chapter the catholic and supranational character of Islamism, I shall now examine the differences between Islamist organizations at the local level, concentrating on five points concerning ideology and political practice.

SUNNĪ AND *SHĪʿA* ISLAMISM

The first point refers to the differences between *sunnī* and *shīʿa* forms of Islamism. Now, this does not mean that the point at issue is the degree in which *sunnī* and *shīʿa* Islam are receptive to radicalism; such an approach would betray an essentialism of the worst kind.[1] Rather, it has to do with how certain traits characteristic of the two traditions, such as the standing of their religious scholars and jurists (*ʿulamāʾ*) in their respective visions, are reflected in the politics of *shīʿa* and *sunnī* Islamist organizations.

Simplifying a complex situation, one could argue that at the level of political praxis and political cooperation the main difference between *sunnī* and *shīʿa* Islam concerns the positioning of the *ʿulamāʾ* within the Islamist movement. As we saw in earlier chapters, despite the wide range of ideological positions advanced by the *ʿulamāʾ* of the *sunnī* tradition, the *sunnī* religious jurisconsults are a rather conservative presence which guards society against the inroads of modernity and all types of innovation (*bidʿa*) through closely adhering to the principle of *taqlīd* (blind imitation) rather than to the practice of *ijtihād*.

For this reason, and aside from any tactical alliance with members of their guild sympathetic to the Islamist cause, the majority of *sunnī* Islamist activists roundly denounce the *ʿulamāʾ* as a class of religion specialists who have created an ossified and inflexible form of Islam which legitimates corrupt regimes only to feather their own nest as paid lackeys of the political establishment. And if that were not enough, Islamists also claim that it is this very complacency of the *ʿulamāʾ* that has made the Muslim world fall prey to secularism and

Western domination. The very "essence" of *sunnī* Islamism's "democratic" approach to doctrinal interpretation where the subject is vested with a singularly authoritative voice[2] and to forms of mass organization and practice, such as the self-regulating piety assemblies and *da'wa* groups, seems to antagonize many elements of today's institutional Islam.

Among the *shī'a* Muslims the situation is different. Just like the *sunnī* religious scholars and jurists, the *shī'a 'ulamā'* are also regarded as the sole institutionally authentic guardians and interpreters of Islamic vision, but with an added caveat related to the historical enactment of the *sunnī–shī'a* theological differences. As we saw in chapter 1, due to the historical circumstances of its emergence and later development, *shī'a* Islam is considered by its adherents to be the religion of the oppressed and the disadvantaged who fight against the forces of evil until the end of time. Then the Hidden *Imām* will emerge from his occultation and, together with other eschatological figures, will lead the community to the final victory. Until that time, though, society is to be guided by its *'ulamā'* who are engaged in the reinterpretation of Islamic law through the vigorous practice of *ijtihād*. This is an essential part of the delegating of the Hidden *Imām*'s political authority during the period of his occultation to the religious scholars of the era, with the leading *'ulamā'* being closer to the masses than their *sunnī* mainstream counterparts, whose discourse is often heavy in political neutrality and legal formalism. This closeness does indeed take theologically specific forms with the elevation of the most prominent amongst the leading *shī'a 'ulamā'* to the status of "models of imitation" and "the virtuous *faqīh*."[3]

Within this context, a direct politicization of the *shī'a 'ulamā'* does acquire practical meaning. This is what happened in post-revolutionary *shī'a*-majority Iran with the establishment of *vilayeti-i-faqi*, a "clerical theocracy" under Ayatollah Khomeini, who extended the *Imam*'s *executive* functions to the religious scholars and jurists to a degree hitherto unknown.[4] As Sivan writes,

> With the victory of the Usuli school in the mid-19th century, the Iranian Shi'a developed a hierarchy of ulama, something rare in the world of Islam: above the rank and file mullahs stand the mujtahidun (authorities on matters of jurisprudence), and above these the mataji al-taqlid ("models of imitation," prominent figures of authority . . . members of the last group were supposed to recognize one of their rank in each generation as the supreme marja' . . . This is the same "Virtuous Jurist" (Faqih) that Khomeini speaks of in his revolutionary teaching, and in whose hand he sought to vest not only religious authority, as was accepted until then, but also political rule (wilaya or wilaya 'amma, a concept that orginally referred to the authority of the Hidden Imam).[5]

In these circumstances, an Islamist discourse of the kind routinely encountered in the *sunnī* world could not appear in contemporary Iran. Far from being denigrated, as in *sunnī* radical Islam, in *shī'a* Islamism the religious scholars are by definition leaders of the movement and the community.

Another prominent example of *shīʿa* Islamism operating outside Iran comes from the *shīʿa* minority of Lebanon, first with the mid-1970s *Imām* Mūsa al-Ṣadr's Movement of the Dispossessed and the subsequent radicalization of the local *shīʿa* community during the protracted civil war and then with the 1980s emergence of the Ḥizb Allāh movement that has managed to be transformed into a major force in current Lebanese politics, especially after its proclaimed victory over Israel, whose troops withdrew from southern Lebanon in 2000.[6]

In Ḥizb Allāh, the most popular *shīʿa* Islamist organization in the Middle East, we have a community-oriented movement waging a defensive *jihād* against Israel that is based on a strong *shīʿa* theological foundation as developed by Khomeini and on the "traditional" *shīʿa* view of martyrdom.[7] At the same time, and in seeming contradiction with its ardent radicalism, the movement has managed to strike a balance between its avowed aim of establishing an Islamic state in Lebanon and its participation in constitutional Lebanese politics.[8] The two strands of the party's political thought are brought together in a successful blending of Islamic rhetoric and nationalist liberation. Recently, taking into account Iraqi resistance against US occupation, this has taken the form of a more expansive Islamic nationalist discourse explicated by none other than Ḥizb Allāh's spiritual father and most prominent *shīʿa ʿālim* in the region, al-Sayyid Muḥammad Ḥusayn Faḍl Allāh.[9]

At the level of political theory, this phenomenon has been analyzed in terms of Ḥizb Allāh's discourse on oppression and non-compulsion to Islam, arguing that, contrary to *sunnī* Islamism, the *shīʿa* Islamism of Ḥizb Allāh does not possess a " 'taqfīr' – declaring the infidelity of adversaries – discourse. Above all, it is the oppressors who are anathematized, regardless of their religious identities, political leanings or religiosity. Furthermore, the party does not equate secularism with oppression or sin."[10] This enables Ḥizb Allāh to distinguish between the occupying Israeli forces, which together with the USA represent "the greatest abominations in our era,"[11] and the sectarian system of Lebanese institutional politics or secularist Syria, both of which they can assail ideologically while working with them in terms of practical politics.[12]

The above analysis works well within its own reference framework, which is the movement's own ideological agenda. However, one would feel that Ḥizb Allāh's political accommodation with the Lebanese political establishment could also be fruitfully examined through careful consideration of the movement's economic base in the rural communities of southern Lebanon and especially of the position of its *imāms* and other leading personalities in the local structures of power. How has the Lebanese civil war and the Israeli invasion, which saw high numbers of fatalities among the *shīʿa* population, mass evictions, and resettlements, as well as "the mass exodus from the South instigated by the destruction of southern produce, Israel's economic blockade of the region, and the flooding of Israeli goods into the Lebanese market,"[13] affected the economic basis of local *shīʿa* religious families? And how has the emergence and strengthening of a Syrian-sponsored political elite affected their local political standing in the south? Could the current situation be seen as one more step in the downward spiral of the 1950s and 1960s described by Gilsenan when he wrote that

> the Learned Families . . . were being forced more and more into a rather limited religious role . . . Indeed, Shiʿite culture in its local forms, with its ideology of learning and descent, had become for them more a restriction for their own comprehension of, and action within, the new order. To remain economically and politically important one had to leave the village, develop other relationships and bases of influence and social authority.[14]

If that is the case, could one conceive of Ḥizb Allāh's emergence and its gravitation towards a nationalist accommodation – without losing sight of its ultimate goal, the establishment of an Islamic state in Lebanon – as a reaction to such kinds of socio-economic enfeeblement at the local level? And if yes, what is the role of descent in the mapping out of the political and religious power matrix in the *shīʿa* Lebanese south? Being an anthropologist, Gilsenan duly emphasizes the "double ideological role" of descent

> as a principle of religious and moral authority and a link with the figures by reference to whom the community is defined (the Imam and the heroes of Kerbela); and as a mode of definition and a drawing of boundaries around an elite that predominated in production and the village economy and that had a monopoly over vital cultural resources.[15]

ELEVATION TO POWER AND PRAGMATISM

A second important difference between Islamist organizations at the local level has to do with the policies pursued in the event of their accession to power and with the relations they cultivate from this position with other Islamist groups within and without. Besides its practical significance, the issue exhibits some theoretical interest as well, because of the widely held view of Islamism as a political theory that borders on the utopian or the unworkably fanatical. The devious question, then, is whether Islamism can retain unsullied its assumed ideological purity and political intransigence when it becomes the state ideology or adopts a more pragmatic profile. For Western political analysts and strategists as well as for incumbent Middle Eastern governments and ruling elites, the first is a much-dreaded possibility; the second an indication of political hypocrisy. In both cases Islamist groups can be equally discredited and, if necessary, prevented from participating in elections.

The material we have at our disposal consists of four cases only, and particularly divergent from each other at that. These are Iran, Turkey, the Sudan, and Afghanistan. In all other places, no Islamist group has managed or been allowed to form a national government. Still, if one could venture a suggestion, with the exception of Afghanistan (which in any case was forced to change rather dramatically) the other three examples indicate a progression toward less radical political options. As Roy argues,

> [b]y entering the political game, Islamist movements also brought in social groups that felt excluded from politics . . . have helped to give root to nation-states and to create a domestic political scene . . . the only real basis for future democratisation, even if these movements were not promoting democracy.[16]

In general, I would be reluctant to accept Roy's formulation, which sees this process as a move from "utopia to conservatism" mainly because, in terms of the previously mentioned *iṣlāḥ-tajdīd* tendency for renewal in Islam, as well as in relation to their championing of the free and vigorous exercise of *ijtihād*, the Islamists remain ideologically distinct from all shades of Muslim conservatives, for example the Saudis and the other Gulf monarchies. In that sense, Roy's claim that "[t]oday there are no Islamists in Iran. The former revolutionaries have turned into either liberals or conservatives,"[17] is rather stretching it. Just as in Turkey, the Sudan, and indeed everywhere in the Muslim world, in Iran too (co)exist more or less revolutionary, pragmatic or conservative Islamists, all of them involved in the process of "orthodoxy" production.

The Case of Iran

Being the seat of the first Islamic revolution that has dislodged a powerful oligarchy long supported by the West, Iran has been considered already at some length. What can be added with respect to the present discussion is that in a period of explosive regional political developments the Iranian leadership is marred by serious internal discord over ideological disputes. These concern mainly the source of legitimate power and affect the very substance and nature of the political process. On the one hand, hardline regime ideologues argue that clerical prerogatives, emanating from the *vilayeti-i-faqi*, the spiritual authority, and juristic autocracy of the supreme *faqīh* and reflected in the crucial role of the all-powerful Council Guardians appointed by him, take precedence over democratic parliamentary procedures, as they are understood in the West. The crisis over the summary disqualification of several hundreds of reformist candidates from running in the 2004 elections is among the highlights of this struggle.[18] On the other hand, the moderates among the Iranian *'ulamā'* ask for a greater degree of openness, but do not offer a well-thought-out alternative vision that goes beyond the necessities of ideological pragmatism and the strictures of populistic economics. True, the moderates' job is significantly hampered by what amounts to outright state repression, but that aside, their own efforts at pursuing their aims are not characterized by any sort of reformist zeal nor do they point toward any form of liberal socio-political vision. After all, they all come from the same ideological womb of Iranian revolutionary shīʿism as developed by Ayatollah Khomeini.[19]

Leaving the stage of internal politics, it is on the foreign-relations front that things have moved on from where they were ten or more years ago, when the West was roundly vilified and the revolution appeared to spare no effort to export itself to the rest of the Muslim world. The Afghan war came and went leaving behind a sizeable American force dangerously close to Iran's eastern borders with no overt reaction on the part of Tehran. Then, a few years later, the same scenario was repeated on Iran's western borders with Iraq. No love was ever lost between the Iranians and either the Afghan *Ṭālibān* or the Iraqi *Baʿth* party, but still the pincer movement must have been strongly felt by an unusually subdued Iran. What is more, a number of American and European officials have been visiting Tehran on a variety of issues. Thus far, the most serious development concerns Iranian intransigence to Western pressure concerning its nuclear program. Further afield, in Lebanon things look just the same as before, as Iranian support of Ḥizb Allāh continues almost undiminished, though these days Ḥizb Allāh is more of a paragon of peace due to what they consider to be a decisive victory over Israel in southern Lebanon. Also, as has already been discussed, Iranian and more generally *shīʿa* forms of Islamism are not all that friendly toward *sunnī* Islamist organizations from the Muslim Brotherhood to *al-Qāʿida*.

This being the case, and given the international political atmosphere, a career diplomat, a well-informed journalist, a political scientist, even an anthropologist, would agree that in Iran it is as if the hardliners have been given a carte blanche (or a new lease of life) in what concerns the internal political scene in exchange for Iranian deference in matters concerning Western and other interests in the wider region. This may not say much about the ways in which political realities are experienced on the microlevel, but it speaks volumes about the spectrum of alternative policies on the macrolevel. The world's most important Islamic revolution, the proof in the eyes of many in the Muslim world that the impossible may well be within grasp, is facing the consequences of its own significance.

The Case of Afghanistan

The second example of an Islamist-run society comes from a neighbor of Iran. Afghanistan under the *Ṭālibān* proved to be the only Islamist regime that adamantly refused to acknowledge the West as "a point of reference."[20] To a certain extent, one could not help but imagine that besides all other strategic aims that the Afghan war may have served, there was a punitive element involved in it as well. But all this does not concern us in the present context.[21] There are three points which I would like to consider here.

The first one concerns the worldview of the *Ṭālibān* regime itself. On the surface, one could presume that it was the assumed sheer impossibility of the terrain and the history of previous Afghan wars which emboldened the *Ṭālibān* leaders to offer safe haven to all sorts of fugitive Islamist activists, completely disregarding world opinion. At a deeper level, though, it was their messianic fervor to create a confederation of Islamic states from Samarkand to Karachi that guided their strategic imagination and gave them perspective. In this project, which went further than state-building in its theological aspirations, every helping hand and every dollar, either from abroad or, for some, from local poppy-fields and drug-trafficking, were welcomed not only for practical reasons, but as palpable signs of Muslim unity and portents of God's providence.

With the benefit of hindsight, what is astonishing in all this is the *Ṭālibān* regime's lack of knowledge and understanding of the outside world. They did not, could not, fathom that their chances of succeeding in their sacred mission were really non-existent, as the bigger players in the area, Pakistan included – despite the sympathy felt towards them by segments of the intelligence services – would cut them down to size if they actively strove to export their Islamic revolutionary vision. Prior to 9/11, the *Ṭālibān* had already been accused of having broken every rule in the book with respect to democracy and human rights, but had been left more or less to their own devices for a relatively long period of time. They might have been seen as religious fanatics, but they checked the Russians and hated the Iranians. What really tipped the balance was their audacity, their foreign ambitions, and, in the end, their disastrously mistaken political assessment of the situation: that the USA, as the hegemonic Western power, would not dare to react to provocation. That alone would prove that an Islamic revolution was indeed possible. Lastly, if all that was not enough, Afghanistan's strategic location in an abundantly rich but politically volatile region of South Asia also played a role in the final decision taken by G.W. Bush's Republican administration.

Another element that is worth mentioning concerns the already hinted-at negative comments that the *Ṭālibān* regime had been receiving from the West long before the "War on Terror" rhetoric assumed its privileged position in the discursive arsenal of the latter. Central to this criticism were the plight of Afghan women and the absence of Western-type democratic procedures in public administration. On their part, the *Ṭālibān* argued that the essence of their system was to restore Afghanistan's "real" Islamic traditions which years of foreign occupation and political mismanagement had all but destroyed. In this perspective, their views on women and their disrespect toward Western democracy were part of such a restoration of "true" Afghan Islam – a view expressed in the now-defunct *Ṭālibān* website, www.taleban.com. Still, the situation could be read from a different perspective.

As it happened, the majority of the *Ṭālibān* were ethnic Pasthun. Their women have always been heavily covered in full-body veils, similar to those of many Arabian Peninsula societies, and severely restricted in terms of movement and education. In no way were such practices *Ṭālibān* innovations. Equally, the Pasthun have never practiced parliamentary democracy at the level of the tribe, ordering their affairs in a traditional fashion that vests the elders' assembly with executive authority; parliamentary democracy such as existed at the national level only reached the Pasthun in very practical terms that had to do with their relations to central government.[22]

Until the emergence of the *Ṭālibān* administration such practices were scarcely mentioned in the press and were generally thought of as tribal custom. True, they did not sit well with Western sensibilities concerning gender and human rights, but such was the remoteness of Afghanistan that the subject was never accorded the same status as mass media stories about women's rights in Saudi Arabia or female circumcision in southern Egypt and the Sudan. As for their Islamic character, Pasthun practices were duly recognized by specialists as part of "tribal Islam"[23] without ever losing their ethnic luster. It was only after the *Ṭālibān* established their harsh "theocracy" and equated Pasthun culture with authentic Afghan Islamic tradition that Western analysts and the media reacted in a negative manner; even this, however, did not challenge the assumed identification of Islamic/Pasthun tradition, and more importantly did not associate the current situation in Afghanistan with the international political factors which had assisted the *Ṭālibān* to power.[24]

Lastly, the third point of the *Ṭālibān* case that should be mentioned is the bewilderment or even contempt that the *Ṭālibān* version of Islam has encountered from other, more urbane Islamists. A characteristic example is that of Rashīd al-Ghannūshī, the exiled leader of the Tunisian Islamist party *al-Daʿwa*, who maintained that he was ashamed of the situation in Afghanistan, which in his view had nothing to do with Islam. In al-Ghannūshī's eyes, the Ṭālibān promoted a decadent form of Islam.[25] Similar views were also expressed by members of the Muslim Brotherhood all over the Middle East. It remains a matter of political judgment to assess the degree to which the Afghan war itself played a role in the airing of such views at that particular period.

Inescapably, the admittedly harsh *Ṭālibān* regime will be forever connected with the 9/11 terrorist attacks against the USA and with the name of Ussāma bin Lāden. Besides the ruptures that a brutal war and an equally brutal "peace" brought to an already ravished land, conditions that cannot yet be properly studied by anthropologists due to security constraints, just as in the Sudanese case (see below pp. 232–5), the Afghan case has demonstrated the deep relationship between Islam and ethnic politics in Central Asia, in other words the ways in which Islam is dialectically related to local conditions.[26] Such a connection is not always present. Indeed in many other examples from the Middle East and elsewhere it was class that allowed for an interpretation of local forms of Islamism. However, in those cases where the idioms of religious extremism and ethnicity feed off each other, the result can be highly explosive, especially when ethnic groups spill over international borders or when they collectively comprise post-colonial nation-states. It goes without saying that only good ethnographic studies could provide the necessary information in all such cases. However, it should be remembered that, quite understandably, the current political climate does not encourage anthropologists to enter the fray.

The Case of the Sudan

In the Sudan things have evolved considerably during the last two decades. As a long-term trend poised to acquire an air of permanency, the overt politicization of Islamic discourse in the Sudan became clearly noticeable during the last years of Ja'far Numayrī's military government (1969–85). Numayrī's crowning achievement was the 1972 Addis Ababa agreement that ended the civil war between the Northern Arab Muslim-dominated government and the African Southern Sudan Liberation Movement. However, in the following years the regime pursued increasingly authoritarian and contradictory policies. With little to show at the economic front and with the Addis Ababa agreement in tatters, Numayrī tried to save his government by moving closer to the Islamists of Ḥasan al-Turābī, leader of the Muslim Brotherhood (ICF) and its post-Numayrī-era successor, the National Islamic Front (NIF).[27] The culmination of this rapprochement was the 1983 implementation of the so-called September Laws, an inclement and politically expedient version of the *sharī'a* that would apply to all Sudanese irrespective of religion.[28] The transformation of the Sudan from a (supposedly) socialist federal republic into an Islamic state and Numayrī's opportunistic Southern policy led to the resumption of the civil war and the end of his government.

The 1985–9 civilian administrations that followed did not repeal the September Laws or address Southern grievances over Northern socio-political and economic dominance because they themselves traditionally imagined the Sudan to be an Arab Muslim country. In all this, the NIF's role was paramount as it "represented the self-consciously maximalist position in favor of assimilation on the basis of a cohesive Arab-Islamic national identity";[29] all the other Northern popular forces agreed with this, but did not dare to express it forthrightly. It is indicative that in 1987 Turābī was boldly pontificating on the relationship between the Islamist movement and the state: "what matters in fact is who controls the state, and for which purpose, rather than by what means."[30]

In June 1989 Lieutenant General 'Umar Ḥasan Aḥmad al-Bashīr established yet another military dictatorship. Turābī's NIF furnished the new regime with its abrasive version of Islamism, championing the enactment of Islamic legal penalties, founding the Popular Defence Forces (PDF), and declaring the war against the Southern forces (SPLA) a *jihād*.[31] In the same period, the Sudan aspired to become a global center of Islamism, organizing international conferences on militant Islam and offering a safe haven and training camps to numerous Islamist activists, including Ussāma bin Lāden.

But more than that, at a cultural level, the NIF's cadres started promoting their own version of Islam with the financial assistance of groups from Saudi Arabia and the Gulf States. Thus, the ban on alcohol production and consumption was zealously upheld,[32] a form of monochrome veiling started to replace the much looser and more richly colored local female *thawb* on penalty of flogging, large numbers of women civil servants were pensioned off, and gender segregation was imposed on public transportation. As ʿUmar Bashīr stated, "the ideal Sudanese woman 'should take care of herself, her children, her home, her reputation, and her husband.' "[33]

For the middle classes, who had enjoyed the relatively prosperous and politically vibrant 1960s and 1970s and who had hailed the end of Numayrī's regime in 1985 as the beginning of a new era of peace and economic growth, the new situation was intolerable. No wonder so many of them left the country to work abroad. As for the lower classes, who populated the impoverished neighborhoods and the ever-expanding shanty-towns around the urban centers of the North, Islamization did not mean much in itself. It was one more name for government corruption, inefficiency, and brutality. In any case, those of non-Arab descent, who had lived all their lives through the ebbs and flows of a continuous Arabization and Islamization process, had been long accustomed to the arrogance of the Northern Arabs, although public floggings of women for selling tea or food in the market was a worrying development. But perhaps besides the cynicism that my non-Arab friends and informants[34] from the shanty-towns displayed towards the government, there was a deeper fear and uncertainty this time: the habitually considered "second-class Muslim" non-Arab Sudanese now had to conform with the new model Arab Muslim, much less amenable to the openness and malleability of Sudanese traditions.

The educational system, too, was fully Islamized, with ideological orientation classes introduced in a segregated secondary education, access to higher education conditional on enrollment in the PDF, and the English language completely banned from university classes, even with regard to reading lists. But worst of all was the development of "a sophisticated patronage system that attracted support for careerist reasons [by both students and university teachers] by providing scholarships to study abroad, financial credit to establish businesses, and employment for university graduates in Islamic banks and firms."[35]

In business, too, there was a sustained attempt to promote a new Islamic ethos with the aggressive expansion of Islamic banking even in sectors of the economy that were far from ready for it. In that respect, it was pronounced that the country would aim at economic autarky rather than succumb to outside pressures, with President ʿUmar Bashīr defiantly declaring "we will eat our own maize and we will spin our own cotton" in a period of repeated crop failures, impending famine, and mounting debt to the IMF. At a less heroic level, Islamic financial assistance to the populace often took the form of personal loans which differed little from party hand-outs aiming at winning political support. It is rather questionable if such tactics could kickstart a moribund economy, especially as they included thousands of ill-conceived projects as well as the fattening of obscure bank accounts in respectable European and Middle Eastern financial institutions. Lastly, in the sphere of public religious ceremonies the activities of the *ṣūfī* orders were seriously hampered, while other more Islamically "suspect" practices, such as all sorts of ecstatic spirit-possession cults, were banned altogether.

At the same time, outside the capital, in the war-ravaged provinces of the South and the Nuba Hills, new forms of bondage (or slavery) emerged. Whole African populations were genocidally dispersed, and forced settlements euphemistically called "peace camps" were established, where wholesale rape programs were instituted for the production of a new Arab Muslim Sudanese generation. In the meantime, the death of the *jihādis* from the North was duly celebrated according to new and compelling forms of popular imagination: no funerary rites for the Muslim heroes of the *jihād* against the animists and the Christians of the South, but joyful weddings with the heavenly *banāt al-ḥūr* celebrated atop the martyrs' graves. In the grim atmosphere of the 1990s, the NIF version of Islam painted over generations-old ethnic and racial differences and disguised, however thinly, all structural inequalities of the post-colonial era.

That things started to change was not so much due to outside pressure in an era of dawning American unilateralism – when, for example, the USA bombed a factory in the capital or when it demanded Ussāma's expulsion (he was duly sent to Afghanistan) – but mainly to two internal developments: the prospect of exploiting oil reserves to a degree hitherto unknown and the realization that the civil war was unwinnable.

Indeed, the exploitation of oilfields in the North–South border areas upped the stakes tremendously and complicated the war effort on both sides. The possibility of financing the war with oil money was definitely considered, but as the investment and expertise had to come from abroad there were obvious limitations to such a scheme. And then, some time later, the "War on Terror" was declared by G.W. Bush.

It was during that period that the government realized that it had to change course. Turābī and the NIF were summarily dismissed and some sort of parliamentary elections were staged. Islamism remained at the center of the regime's ideological agenda, but without its previous internationalist fervor and its violent excesses.[36] Then, with US encouragement, the government and the SPLA came to an agreement on power- and wealth-sharing. This is a welcome development, but does not mean that the country will automatically put the past behind it. The recent humanitarian disaster in Dār Fūr, whose non-Arab peoples have been left outside the North–South framework for peace and development, suggests otherwise. In the meantime, the government plans to augment its oil production, while new roads are paved that will give landlocked Ethiopia access to a newly refurbished Port Sudan on the Red Sea. Still on the US list of the states that sponsor terrorism, the Sudan is looking for an exit and a future in the shape of an oil-rich autocracy.

The Case of Turkey

The last example of a society governed by an Islamist administration is Turkey, a country that for many, Turks and non-Turks alike, balances precariously between the Middle East and Europe. It is in this context that the recent entrenchment of Turkish Islamism should be considered.

With a thinly veiled authoritarianism of the Kemalist military-dominated National Security Council (NSC) and the tacit support of the major political parties, the Islamists were kept outside parliament until the end of the 1980s.[37] In 1991, forming a coalition with two right-wing parties, Necmettin Erbakan's Islamist Welfare Party (Refah) gained 40 seats in the Assembly; this almost quadrupled in 1994 and Refah "emerged as the largest political party of all with 158 deputies, and 22 per cent of the vote overall."[38] Two years later, when all attempts by the secular establishment to form a workable government without the Islamists failed, Erbakan became head of the government. However, the Islamist victory was short-lived as in June 1997 Erbakan was forced to resign because of "explicitly pro-secular moves" by the armed forces, the NSC, and the state prosecutor.

A new political organization, the Virtue Party, was established by the Refah hierarchy, but this time the agenda was different. Having learned from the past, Islamists removed completely from their discourse all ultra-nationalistic and chauvinistic references, declared support for Turkish membership of the EU, and embraced democracy and gender equality. Significantly, the headscarf issue was treated in terms of personal freedom and human rights rather than religion, thus transforming it into an issue of "cultural" rather than "political" Islam.[39] Still the NSC was not impressed, and in 2001 the Virtue Party was duly outlawed.

In 1999 Bülent Ecevit, a left-wing veteran politician and old-style nationalist, became prime minister, but his rule was beset by political intrigues, accusations of corruption, a currency collapse, and a 9.4 percent economic contraction. In the midst of all this, on November 3, 2002, the Justice and Development Party (AKP), which had succeded the banned Virtue Party, won 34.3 percent of the popular vote, becoming the first party in 15 years to win a total majority of seats in the Turkish National Assembly. After some legalistic hurdles that included trial for sedition, the leader of the party and ex-mayor of Istanbul, Tayyib Erdoğan, became prime minister in March 2003.

As Jenkins argues, right from the beginning the AKP has presented itself as "a conservative rather than a religious party"[40] although its leadership and the core membership identify themselves with the Islamist movement. The impression one gets is that the government is in no hurry to force through measures which could incur the wrath of the NSC, while the latter understands that, ultimately, it should respect the will of the people; a party with 34 percent support cannot be banned with impunity. Be that as it may, until now the government has achieved rather mixed results, with its economic program amounting to the announcement of isolated populistic measures and its foreign policy being somewhat contradictory and indecisive. Still, the AKP, and Erdoğan personally, managed to wrest from the EU a definite date (October 2005) for the commencement of entry negotiations.

The future will show how the AKP will combine an Islamist agenda with a secular type of parliamentary democracy. If they succeed, Turkish Islamists will be hailed as the first such modern example. However, analysts should not rush to reach general conclusions. Just as Kemalism is a *sui generis* Turkish ideology, so Turkey's version of Islamism is another, despite its familial resemblances to other similar ideologies and organizations. To see Turkey as the battleground where Islamism will eventually show its "true colors" in relation to democracy is simply mistaken, as the socio-economic conditions prevailing at each historical moment and the political developments with which they are dialectically articulated are constantly in motion and refuse to bow to essentialist readings of social reality and the concepts with which we attempt to describe it.

Indeed, Turkish Islamism is a case for an in-depth study of the ideological permutations that in the long run shape an Islamist political program and of the intertwining of an Islamist movement with the self-proclaimed secular state and its inner logic. Briefly put, Islamist success in Turkey during the 1990s was due to the melding together of a number of different constituencies, which included parts of the disaffected lower and middle classes – peasants, workers, small and medium-sector businessmen, some bureaucrats, and Muslim intellectuals – in an effort "to contest the hegemony of the ruling elites in the *cultural* and political field"[41] during a period in which the main political parties were locked in an acrimonious circle of corruption and economic scandals.

At a deeper level, though, Islamists never really veered from the *logic* of the secular Turkish state, which, lest we forget, defined the "conditions of possibility"[42] within which they worked. They may have promulgated several laws that did bring into question some time-honored policies of the Kemalist establishment, but in the end they did not question the state itself; rather they worked as another face of the state, less tainted with past failures, but locked with the secularists into a strenuous confrontation in which each side defined the other as the complete opposite of itself.[43]

Wearing the mantle of a Turkish/Islamic "authenticity" the 1990s Islamists advanced as bearers of a new and more inclusive vision. When Erdoğan and the AKP came to power in March 2003 the new administration showed itself to be a much more acquiescent follower of the traditional road of Turkish nationalism within the context of Turkey's European orientation than its predecessor Welfare Party. Whereas Refah attacked the "conditions of possibility" within which it worked and lost at the hands of the Turkish "deep state," AKP has been attempting to transcend them through the enunciation of a clear pro-European Westernizing rhetoric which in certain areas has been concretized into specific policies, such as the abolition of the death penalty and the denunciation of torture. Thus, instead of frontally attacking the Kemalist status quo, the (New) Islamists are besieging the "deep state" of Turkey on its own ideological ground: Westernization and Turkish nationalism.

In this process, the AKP Islamic rhetoric has also been affected. One could argue that the AKP is not offering a well-designed *Islamic* political program, not even to the (not inconsiderable) extent of its predecessor Welfare Party. Or is it? To take as an example the infamous headscarf affair, which has served as *cause célèbre* for both secularists and Islamists, the government's insistence that covering the head is not *really* religious but cultural, and as such can be condoned, can be construed as a clear policy statement: by defining Islamic practices as cultural rather than political it provides a space for their enactment and for the emergence of a more nuanced Islamic discourse. It is this transformation of Islam into a cultural idiom of a Europe-oriented modern society which has allowed the AKP to accept with some impunity from the "deep state" the authority of the European Court of Human Rights in Strasbourg over the issue, brought to it by Layla Sahin, a medical student who was refused her degree because she appeared at the graduation ceremony wearing a headscarf. In comparison with all previous religious parties in Turkey, this type of "relativizing" the content of Islamic tradition, however defined, is indeed new.[44]

But this redefinition of Islam as a cultural idiom within a vision of a democratic European Turkey may have a drawback, at least in terms of electoral power. The core of AKP's constituents, who see "themselves as Muslims [sic] first and Turks second,"[45] are not directly interested in Turkey's relationship with the EU, nor in the successful organization of a NATO summit in Istanbul, nor, even, in the relationship between their country and the USA. The (qualified) acknowledgment of the government's achievements over these issues, which makes up the bulk of worldwide reporting and analysis of current conditions in Turkey, comes from those who did not vote for it and remain sceptical of its "true" intentions. On the contrary, for those who actually voted for it, the promulgation of Islamic policies, not only in connection with the headscarf, but also in relation to education and public morality, may appear higher in their agenda.[46]

DEMOCRACY AND PLURALISM

A third difference between Islamist organizations at the local level concerns their views on representative democracy and pluralism; this is a political issue unrelated to the essentialist, ahistorical, and, ultimately, wrong question on the "relationship between Islam and democracy."[47] Allied with the free market economy in its various forms and the political values of European Enlightenment, Western-type democracy has today acquired the status of the "natural" situation for humankind.[48] In this capacity it has also been associated with Western expansionism and has been used as ideological cover during the Cold War for the establishment of various forms of dictatorship in countries supposedly under the threat of communism or anarchy and more recently in the so-called "War against Terror." Moreover, authoritarian regimes in the Middle East and elsewhere are paying lip-service to the democratic principle, while rigging elections to achieve ridiculously high majorities. It is in this general context that the positions of Islamist intellectuals and movements on democracy should be considered.

Discussing the "commitment to the electoral principle" in the Middle East, analysts, most often political scientists, have not reached a final conclusion. In a recent work reflecting this state of affairs, Piscatori (2000) echoes Waterbury's earlier thesis on democracy without democrats[49] and distinguishes between three schools of thought.

The first one is linked to the wider intellectual environment of Islamic reformism and sees no contradiction between elections and Islamic principles.[50] The second school of thought dismisses the very notion of democracy as non-Islamic because it is based on contractarian and voluntaristic assumptions. This is the view of Sayyid Quṭb and Ḥasan al-Bannā of the Muslim Brotherhood, the leader of the Algerian Front Islamic du Salut (FIS), ʿAlī Belhaj (b. 1954), and *shaykh* Muḥammad Mitwāllī al-Shaʿrāwī, the popular Egyptian preacher mentioned earlier.[51]

The last school of thought is a compromise between the previous two and is linked with Mawlānā Abū 'l-Aʿlā Mawdūdī of the Jamāʿat-i-Islāmī. Mawdūdī's "theo-democracy" accepts that the majority of Muslims should somehow elect an advisory body (*majlīs shūra*) which will have legislative authority. *Shūra* refers to an advisory process that goes back to the days when Prophet Muḥammad governed Madīna. Together with the concepts of *ijtihād* and *ijmāʿ*, which should be obviously exercised by the members of this body, *shūra* lies at the basis of those approaches which present Islam as coexisting with the "principle" of democracy.[52]

Be that as it may, the socio-political reality within which the various Islamist groups operate is much more complex and dynamic than any schools of thought may suggest. Piscatori himself makes this perfectly clear in his study where he discusses the actual policy positions of several Islamist groups throughout the Middle East. What can be seen from this exposition and from the rest of the literature on the subject (which, unfortunately, includes very few anthropological works) is that, actually, most Islamist organizations do participate in elections when they are allowed to do so despite the fact that ideologically they may oppose majoritarianism and the model of parliamentary democracy. As Esposito and Piscatori have argued, to all intents and purposes, some sort of democracy has come to be considered a *sine qua non* condition of contemporary politics.[53] Even organizations portrayed as hardline, which may also use violence or have a history of violent confrontation with the state, such as HAMAS, Ḥizb Allāh, the Algerian FIS, and the various Muslim Brothers' branches in Egypt, the Sudan, or Jordan are engaged in some kind of pluralistic politics. Maybe their charters do decry the role of democracy and the importance of elections and maybe their vision does center upon the establishment of Islamic states governed exclusively by *sharīʿa*, but their positioning within their respective political fields shows them as active players in the give and take of the electioneering process at various levels, as hesitant actors operating within existing political structures. In that sense Roy's suggestion that "the Islamists did contribute to laying the basis of greater democracy"[54] is correct, although the follow-up, that "Islamist parties thus contribute . . . to the 'secularisation' of politicals,"[55] I find difficult to accept. His distinction between "the emergence of a secular society as such," which does not happen, and "the reaffirmation of the autonomy of the political,"[56] which allegedly does, is foreign to my understanding of secularization as discussed in the Introduction. The following case studies may illustrate some of these points.

The Jordanian Muslim Brotherhood

Since the opening-up of the Hashemite regime in the late 1980s, the Jordanian Muslim Brothers have come up with a strong parliamentary presence, although the crown has retained its hegemonic position.[57] As Wiktorowicz (2000, 2001) argues, this might be related to the Brothers' effort to protect their extensive network of social services from the state's repressive policies, though, simultaneously he acknowledges that it makes them more vulnerable to state regulation through bureaucratic control. His other example, the smaller Salafi movement, which never made a pact with the Jordanian state, has opted out altogether from the latter's regulatory system in order to retain its independence.

A reliable analysis of the Brotherhood's position in contemporary Jordan is difficult to make in the absence of in-depth local studies and of rich ethnographic descriptions that capture its day-to-day activities and the ways in which it has ingrained itself in the structure of the local communities. Moreover, developments are fast and often take nasty turns as they move in parallel with political developments both in Jordan and in the wider region. For example, a

September 2004 crackdown by the state against senior Brotherhood members has been interpreted by analysts and the press as qualitatively different from previous brushes with the authorities; these include the clash in 1994, after the government had signed the peace agreement with Israel, and the 1997 confrontation, when the Brotherhood boycotted the elections protesting allegedly unfavorable election provisions that promoted tribal and pro-establishment candidates.

The accession to the throne of ʿAbdullāh II and the 2003 electoral success of the Brotherhood (it won 16 seats in the 110-member legislature) in a period of tremendous political upheaval and military adventures have made things even more complicated. The crackdown in the fall of 2004 was ordered because the government felt that the Brotherhood had overstepped the invisible line between agreeable political criticism and inflammatory rhetoric. The nine senior Brothers amongst those arrested were accused of preaching in mosques without obtaining official licenses and of inciting the public to violence against the West and the USA in particular. In the event, last-minute talks between the Brothers and Prime Minister Faysāl al-Fayez led to the release of the Brotherhood *ʿulamāʾ* and the retraction of all arrest warrants. It seems though that the system allowing peaceful cohabitation between the Islamists and the government is reaching its limits.[58]

HAMAS

On the western bank of the river Jordan, HAMAS has adopted "a strategy of political adjustment" which, for Mishal and Sela, must be "explained in terms of its ability to bridge the gap between opposing considerations of practical needs and normative requirements, representing its dual commitment to both sociocommunal values and religious-nationalistic beliefs."[59] While rejecting the Oslo Accords, HAMAS did not launch a frontal attack on the new order. It remained a "highly doctrinaire, activist movement" committed to armed struggle against Israel, but grudgingly recognized the Palestinian Authority (PA) as a *fait accompli*. It has never accorded it legitimacy, but nonetheless encouraged its own members to join "the civil service and the PA's operational apparatus."[60] At the same time, it has stepped up its violent campaign against Israel, often in collaboration with the much smaller but more intransigent Islamic Jihad. Lastly, as Mishal and Sela emphasize, just like the PLO, HAMAS also

> has two sets of leaders, those "outside" and "inside" the [occupied] territories, with the former in control of the latter. The outside group is more closely identified with Hamas's ultimate goals and grand vision, and the inside group focuses on local grievances and close-to-home issues . . . Whereas the "outside" was more reluctant, the "inside" leadership took a more positive approach to the idea of establishing a political party and running in the elections.[61]

In that sense, even at the level of the movement itself the pursuing of participatory politics and armed struggle can be linked with a parallel, and certainly intertwined, line of authority. Which type of action will eventually dominate has to do with the relative positioning of its adherents in the wider political structure, especially now that HAMAS has become government.[62]

The Egyptian Muslim Brotherhood

Like their Jordanian counterparts, in Egypt, too, the Muslim Brothers have followed a similar trajectory of rapprochement with the state, though the latter has proved itself much less hospitable than the Jordanian one toward those who 50 years earlier had vowed to seize it violently. Thousands of executions and decades in Egyptian prisons have left the Egyptian Muslim Brothers numb. Their prolonged confrontation with the state, alternated with periods of relative relaxation of security measures (which, significantly, have never reached normalization), have made it obvious that turning Egypt into a fully fledged Islamic state is perhaps impossible, except at an extremely high price which neither they as an organization nor Egyptian society as a whole were ready to pay. The conciliatory gestures towards Islam made by the Sadat government provided the opportunity for the initial partial rehabilitation of the organization. And partial it remained, because the Brothers were not legalized as a political party.[63] The same policy has been followed by Sadat's successor, Hosni Mubarak, who has unleashed a real war against the more radical Islamists since the early 1990s, while he periodically rounds up members of the Brotherhood and bars access to its Internet sites.[64]

Nonetheless, in the context of an authoritarian state which seeks to define and monopolize the content of Islamic tradition,[65] the necessary political space has been constructed for the Egyptian Muslim Brothers to work from, either with or through other parties or as independent candidates. In this way, the Brothers have not only managed to send representatives to parliament in 1984, 1987, 1995, and 2000, but also to a number of professional associations, such as the lawyers' and journalists' syndicates. The Brotherhood's current supreme guide is Muḥammad Mahdī Akīf, whose 1954 death sentence was commuted to 20 years' imprisonment. In a recent interview he emphasized that his

> number one mission . . . is to struggle for legality as a politcal group . . . "Confrontation with the state is a futile task, particularly now . . . the only mechanism now is to educate the people, orient them with the true precepts of Islam, and promote a sense of justice in society."[66]

On the other hand, much smaller Islamist organizations, such as the (Egyptian) Islamic Jihad and the Gamāʿa al-Islāmiyya, which traditionally resort to outright terrorist actions and do not possess the extensive social network of the

Muslim Brothers, have either been crushed by the Egyptian state or forced to renounce violence.

How far this accommodation has served the Egyptian Muslim Brothers' long-term purposes and effectiveness remains to be seen. In a sense, to a far greater extent than their Jordanian chapter, the Egyptian Muslim Brothers appear to have been constantly worried about a government backlash if they overstep their tacitly approved, but nonetheless nebulous, margins of freedom. A good example is the analysis by Gehad Auda (1991) of the uncertainty that characterized the Brotherhood's response to the first Gulf War. On the one hand, more than a decade later, and with the emergence of much more extreme forms of Islamist action, it could be argued that at the level of national politics, including the shaping of Egyptian foreign policy, the Egyptian Muslim Brothers are becoming less influential.[67] On the other hand, other analysts are emphasizing the quiet revolution that I have referred to earlier on, which is the comprehensive and multi-layered "Islamization from below," a process which, in the name of "authenticity," brings together the various sorts of Islamists with the numerous strands of conservative but politically less agile Muslim lower and middle classes. Thus, in an 1995 article entitled "Islamists Set the Social and Political Agenda in Egypt," Metzger quoted Aḥmad ʿAbd Allāh, a former student activist, who nervously argued that "[a]l-Azhar has become more and more conservative" and informed his readers that "recent fatwas from al-Azhar reflect more the views of the Muslim Brotherhood than of the government."[68] And this was only a few months after a government raid against the Brotherhood.

Islamism in Yemen

Our next example comes from Yemen, where the government has been fighting against Islamist groups since its rapprochement with the USA in 2002. Hundreds of militants have been rounded up, including a number of alleged *al-Qāʿida* officials. The situation in Yemen is particularly complicated by the fact that tribal leaders, rather than the government, control a large and relatively inaccessible portion of the country. In this conservative and impoverished corner of the Arab world,[69] which is reputedly awash with weapons, stringent anti-Americanism is blended with local discourses on Islam and the ideals of personal autonomy and tribal pride. Among the personalities whom the government would like to do away with is Ḥusayn al-Hūthị̄, a *shīʿa* Zaydī leader, whose militia is based in the mountainous area of Marān. Al-Hūthị̄ is accused of promoting violent anti-US and anti-Israel protests. Especially since 2000, the government has been repeatedly accused of detaining suspects without charging them. The government has denied this and counters that "up to 250 terrorist suspects have been released after going through an 'education' process run by the Dialogue Committee which focuses on peace and tolerance in

Islam."[70] Since 2000 Yemen has been the theater of several murders of Christian foreigners and prominent secular Yemenis,[71] as well as of two major bombing incidents against US and French vessels. Some of the suspects are in the USA while the rest are being tried in Yemen.

Islamism in Tunisia and Morocco

Moving to the western part of North Africa, we are confronted with three distinct cases. In Tunisia the government has followed an invariably repressive policy against the Islamists, especially since their "powerful showing in the April 1989 elections, in which they won 12 percent of the national vote."[72] Rashīd al-Ghannūshī, the president of *al-Daʿwa* party, has been living in exile in Europe where he has published extensively on issues related to Islamic politics and has become a respected figure among Islamist intellectuals. Be that as it may, what is peculiar about Tunisia is that the country has not suffered major terrorist attacks nor has it been associated with international terrorism networks or with international Muslim fighters, such as those who participated in the Afghan war in the 1980s.[73] In this context, Tunisian Islamism is deemed to be a parameter of local politics with few international ramifications.

To an extent, the same was true of Morocco until the government of King Muḥammad VI toughened its position vis-à-vis Islamism after the 9/11 attacks and turned the screw further after the May 2003 Casablanca and March 2004 Madrid bombings, which killed 39 and 190 people respectively. These events have upset the balance that characterized the relationship between the King and the Islamist movement throughout the 1990s.

The crucial year was 2002 when, on the one hand, the moderate Islamist Justice and Development Party (PJD) came third in the September national elections and, on the other, Morocco joined the US-led "War on Terror." The wrath of the state fell on the salafist Islamic fringe, although the dividing line with the PJD moderates was significantly blurred. Throughout that year an increasing number of people associated with a group based in the shanty-towns north of Casablanca, al-Ṣirāṭ al-Mustaqīm – the *Straight Path*, an evocative name claiming all the "orthodoxy" credentials it could – were arrested on account of various offenses, ranging from murder to religious and anti-state propaganda.[74] The same group was later identified as the culprits behind the Casablanca bombings, though the sweeping security operations also extended to other groups with similar ideology, such as al-Takfīr wal-Ḥijra. Since then, and especially since the Madrid bombings, in which many Moroccans were implicated, the perennial question concerning links with *al-Qāʿida* has been high on the agenda.[75]

The trials for the Casablanca attacks took place in the summer of 2003. Of the 87 defendants, who included four *imāms*, four were given the death penalty, while the others received sentences from 10 months to life imprisonment. But that was only the tip of the iceberg as "[a]t least 700 [were] brought to court through the summer charged either with direct involvement in the Casablanca attacks, or – in most cases – with other offences arising from alleged sympathy with what the authorities call the 'Jihad Salafist current,' or alleged plans for attacks in other cities."[76]

What is interesting with Morocco is how PJD Islamists reacted to this overwhelming state authoritarianism. Right after the Casablanca blasts, the government-aligned press stepped up its already-running anti-PJD campaign. Ignoring the differences between distinct types of Islamist discourse, they blamed the PJD "for preparing the ground for extremism and for being fellow travellers of Bin Laden sympathizers."[77] Denying the charges, the party roundly denounced terrorism and supported the introduction of a draconian anti-terrorism law, which the government passed only days after the bombings in the face of considerable opposition from several human rights organizations.[78]

But the most stunning concession on PJD's part was its decision to scale down the number of candidates it fielded in the 2004 municipal elections, thus robbing itself of an almost certain electoral victory. They did this, the Islamists declared, so as not to complicate further the situation in Morocco and thus frighten away tourists and foreign investors.[79] Many have suspected a backroom deal between the Islamists and the king. Whatever the case, it appears that the PJD Islamists have decided that in the current historical conjunction it is safer to concentrate on the improvement of their already existing social network and to further nurture their roots within the local communities. On his part, the king has been equally careful to maintain the balance between his title as *amīr al-mū'minīn*, the "Commander of the Faithful," and his image as the architect of modern Morocco. In a royal decree concerning women's status one can spot some progressive measures concerning marriage and divorce, but the already existing *sharīʿa*-minded core of the relevant legislation has not been questioned.[80] Perhaps, both the Palace and the PJD are mindful of the Algerian quagmire next door, if not for any other reason, because neither side feels particularly strong.

Islamism in Algeria

The Algerian case is paradigmatic of how devastatingly wrong undemocratic politics can go when the winners of national elections, here the Islamic Salvation Front (FIS), are prevented from assuming power. The 1990s Algerian civil war shocked the world with its ferocity as well as with its opaqueness and the conspiracy theorizing that engulfed it.

Since independence from France in 1962, after a guerrilla war still admired by many liberal intellectuals and politicians in Europe, Algeria had constructed an image of a modernizing socialist society blessed with considerable oil reserves. However, in the 1970s the country entered a protracted recession, which was further aggravated by the post-1973 international fall in oil prices.

Politically, too, the one-party regime of the National Liberation Front (FLN) became increasingly authoritarian, especially after 1979 when Chadli Benjedid replaced the independence hero Boumedienne.

Popular anger exploded in October 1988 with extensive urban riots over unemployment and poverty and against the economic policy of the government, but most seriously over its failure to honor its social contract with the people. The FLN was delegitimized in the eyes of the people, 50 percent of whom were under 25 years old and had not experienced the country's anti-colonial struggle against the French. For them, the FLN was the party that had condemned their age group to 85 percent unemployment and had sold the country's independence to the IMF and the World Bank.

Accepting the inevitable, the regime embarked on a project of political liberalization. It was then that the Islamist FIS emerged as the main beneficiary of popular discontent.[81] The roots of Algerian Islamism can be found in the mid-1970s when a large number of private and publicly sponsored mosques and Islamic educational establishments were built, initially "as a social and political counterweight to . . . leftist opposition groups."[82] That gave Islamists a sizeable and influential constituency in the 1980s, which they later augmented by attracting large segments of the disaffected lower and middle classes, especially the youth. With the FLN unable to inspire the national imagination and identified with the sectarian interests of the bureaucracy and the army in a stalled economy, the FIS stepped into its place ready to take over. Blending populism with Islamic rhetoric, the party of the sober middle-aged professor ʿAbāssī Madanī and the younger firebrand *shaykh* ʿAlī Benḥaj won the first round of national elections in December 1991, a period complicated by the first Gulf War.[83] That was too much for the real wielder of power in Algeria, the armed forces, who canceled the elections. A few months later, they deposed the president and took direct control of the country themselves.

The outcome of all this was a civil war which cost Algeria tens of thousands of lives. Often, the massacres of villagers were so gruesome and stage-orchestrated that they gave birth to all sorts of conspiracy theories, linking together the Islamists, the secret services, the army, the oil industry, and, naturally, the French ex-colonial masters and the American CIA.[84]

More recently, the situation has been kept somewhat under control. After the administration of General Liamine Zeroual (1994–9) a nominal return to democracy has been improvised through the organization of elections in which the army – often called the *décideurs* – has imposed its own candidates, like Abdelaziz Bouteflika in 1999 and again in April 2004. In a climate of "national reconciliation" an amnesty was declared and the FIS armed wing disbanded, without this resulting in the legalization of the party, though smaller organizations, such as the Armed Islamic Groups (GIA) have continued their violent campaign. But the real issue, *the nature of the state and the identity of those who represent it*, has not been seriously addressed.[85]

This goes beyond economics and religion, secularism and Islamism. It is related to legitimacy and to the existence of a national vision which can incorporate all Algerians – something like the original vision of the FLN before the independent Algeria was turned into a fully-fledged rentier state.[86] But no one can be certain whether the FIS, had it been allowed to contest the April 2004 elections, would have been able to position itself as a credible alternative. Though its leaders Madanī and Benḥaj were released from prison in July 2003, it would be difficult to envisage the party as part of the future Algerian political landscape. It is indicative, I think, that the moderate Islamist party of ʿAbd Allāh Jabāllāh took only 5.02 percent of the votes in the recent presidential elections with a 58 percent voter turnout; by comparison, the 1991 FIS victory was the product of a 40 percent voter turnout.[87]

The above discussion has shown that whatever theoretical positions on democracy the various Islamist movements may hold, it is national governments which often scorn pluralism.[88] Perceiving the virtual exclusion of Islamists from parliamentary politics as a policy of containment and as insurance against a more or less assumed future danger – that elected Islamists will never resign – many Muslim governments in the Middle East (and beyond) are thus commited to three policy positions which may prove deleterious to regional stability.[89] First, they deny their people as a whole the fruits of an open and free society and of a just and representative political system; systems that deny legitimacy to any single popular mass movement cannot by definition be open and democratic. Second, they allow themselves to be uncritically portrayed as bedfellows of the West, whose strategic vision they seem to have adopted as a prop against internal liberalization. Third, they refuse to distinguish between mass-organization Islamist movements with diversified policies, which mainly include social work and in very specific cases armed struggle usually related to national liberation targets, and small radical groups whose main, if not only, strategy is terrorism.

The last point is of some importance because it exposes the two-level hegemonic discourse of most Middle East governments and elites, a discourse that is partly reproduced by their Islamist adversaries. At one level, the exclusion of all kinds of Islamists is legitimated in terms of an allegedly clear-cut distinction between politics and religion. At this level, governments present themselves as agents of a modernizing project that operates on the basis of non-culturally specific principles of a purportedly quasi-technical universal probity, such as nationalism and social cohesion, economic/market and political constraints and opportunities. Avoiding identification with secularism and all discourses derived therefrom, most Middle East governments and elites struggle within the parameters of a particular Western-type modernity, a discursive topos where religion-inflected politics has no place, except at the mildest of forms that can be harmlessly depicted in terms of cultural heritage.

At a second level, as has been shown in chapter 3, the very same governments present themselves as guardians and exclusive interpreters of Islamic "orthodoxy." Loudly declaring the *sharīʿa* as the basis of legislation, they lambast Islamists, from the Muslim Brothers to Ussāma bin Lāden, for corrupting the meaning of God's law and misusing Islamic tradition to further their own political purposes. In this operation of "orthodoxy" production, governments or governing political parties may even ask the religious scholars of the state, usually the *ʿulamāʾ* of the most prestigious theological college, to issue a *fatwā* concerning the matter in hand. It is this part of hegemonic discourse that is partly reproduced by Islamists in the sense that they, too, are engaged in the same "orthodoxy" production project, although with very different results.

THE PLACE OF NATIONALISM IN ISLAMIST DISCOURSE

A fourth difference between Islamist organizations at the local level relates to the position of nationalism in their respective discourses. The two most important figures who have influenced the way modern Islamists approach nationalism are the Indian Mawlānā Abū ʾl-Aʿlā Mawdūdī and the Egyptian Sayyid Quṭb. Before 1947 Mawdūdī fought against the "secularist 'Muslim nationalism' of Jinnah,"[90] but when Pakistan was finally established, he embraced it and fought to turn it into an Islamic state.[91] Still, his ideal remained the establishment of a world state governed by *sharīʿa*. On his part, Sayyid Quṭb came in contact with Mawdūdī's ideas as early as the 1950s, but it took him a decade to reach a more theoretically astute and politically intransigent thesis against nationalism. Like other Islamists of that period, the Muslim Brotherhood ideologue was initially friendly towards pan-Arabism, at the time the dominant ideology of Nasserist Egypt and of much of the Middle East outside the Arabian Peninsula. This attitude was not born out of any deep philosophical conviction. Rather, it was related to the fact that Arabism and Islam had always been closely intertwined throughout Muslim history, so Islamists like Quṭb could approach Arabism as a stage in the process of establishing a transnational Islamic state.[92]

Nasser's clash with the Brothers and the harsh experience of imprisonment and torture undergone by thousands of them, Sayyid Quṭb included, changed all this. Pan-Arabism and nationalism became associated with a trenchantly secular state inimical to Islam. In Quṭb's theoretical schema, nationalism was simply a constitutive element of *jāhiliyya*, the new barbarity, which was compared to the pre-Islamic state of pagan Arabia.[93] The enemy, then, was the state itself, an effective beast cloaked in the garb of popular revolution and democracy.[94]

Similar conclusions were reached by Syrian and Lebanese followers of Mawdūdī and Quṭb in the 1970s and 1980s, such as Saʿīd Hawwa, Marwān Ḥadīd, Fatḥī Yakān, and Saʿīd Shaʿbān. Again, the road to such radical positions was directly associated with regime brutality and the advent of military elites,

Hawwa's "most depraved social group."[95] In such a political climate and in terms of the radicalism it introduced into Islamist discourse, it is no surprise that radical groups would put into practice the message "the fight against the enemy nearest to you has precedence over the fight against the enemy farther away."[96]

Still, if this is how the battle lines were drawn on the front line of ideological purity, on the front of mass-organization politics things were remarkably, though not unusually, more opaque. The selfsame organization that Sayyid Quṭb had founded eventually came in from the cold in order to participate in the electoral process at all levels. As discussed earlier, state repression continued under both Sadat and Mubarak, but the Muslim Brotherhood managed to become a mainstream Egyptian political power, though still illegal. The same is true with every mass Islamist organization. In this way, a distinction has been created between these organizations and those smaller and more radical groups which still follow the path of violent confrontation with the state.

On the part of the bigger mass organizations, this does not signify a theoretical reappraisal of their understanding of nationalism. It is rather a tactical (or perhaps strategic) movement of *real politik*. Nothing misleading in this: it is a political decision dictated by the conditions that Islamist mass movements found themselves in in the 1980s and 1990s and which brought home a number of points concerning policy orientation.

First, the state proved much more difficult to overthrow than had been predicted or hoped. Moreover, its repressive power managed to deliver a relatively efficient structural blow to the middle echelons of Islamist bureaucracies, partly neutralizing their decision-taking mechanisms and frustrating their organizational capabilities for overt political action.

Second, at the same time, the state proved incapable of delivering economic dividends to the middle classes, who saw their living standards plummeting. That offered the Islamists the opportunity of moving into the only area that had been left open to them: the provision of municipal services. These activities were orchestrated within the wider, open-ended project of what I have called the "Islamization from below process" which, in the case of the Brotherhood for instance, became the cornerstone of the movement's political and ideological discourse.

Third, society at large did not embrace the idea of the state's violent destruction and a "return" to a poorly thought-out form of post-national Islamic state/khalifate. Outside the most militant circles, the idea looked utopian, and was finally quietly put aside. From Turkey, Jordan, and Egypt to Tunisia, Algeria, and Morocco, Islamists have been voted in not to bring about Muslim unity, but mainly because they are seen as less corrupt and more straightforward than the incumbent governments with their faded visions and repressive policies. I am not arguing here for the primacy of material needs over abstract ideals (see the bread and sugar riots of the late 1980s in various Middle Eastern capitals), but for a dialectic relation within an Islamist discourse that was popularly imagined within the existing coordinates of political practice.

Lastly, the first Palestinian *intifāḍa* (starting in 1987) and the 1982 Israeli invasion of Lebanon created a new dynamic. Through HAMAS and Ḥizb Allāh, Islamic opposition to the occupation has given credence to a new type of "Muslim nationalism" that shares elements with the territorially based "secular nationalism."

For HAMAS, nationalism is "a religious precept" and a "nationalist is a Muslim who seeks to eject trespassers or enemies from Muslim land."[97] This religious quality of Palestinian nationalism that HAMAS has been promoting results in a radically different political program from that of the PLO, whose nationalism is secular and in response to the violation of Gellner's "nationalist sentiment."[98] Whereas the PLO accepts a two-state solution of sorts for the Palestinian question, HAMAS views the whole of Palestine, from the Mediterranean coast to the river Jordan, as a Muslim *waqf* partly occupied by the Jews, a foreign *religious community* and Muslim foe *par excellence* since the days of the Prophet. It is in this sense that the Palestinian liberation struggle is conceptualized as a *jihād* and HAMAS presents itself as a credible alternative to the PLO. Still, this uneasy combination of Islam and territorial nationalism aiming at the production of a localized Palestinian Muslim identity is very impoverished when it comes to details. All we are told is of the eventual establishment of an Islamic state, but what form such an entity may assume is not clearly spelled out. And as Milton-Edwards notes, there is no mention at all of this as "the first step towards the creation of a dar al-Islam irrespective of borders and boundaries."[99]

Coming to the Lebanese Ḥizb Allāh, we see the party proclaiming itself "a nation tied to the Muslims in every part of the world," although gradations of Islamic solidarity and ideological kinships are accepted as existing within this *umma*.[100] This acknowledgment allows the party to accommodate its belief in Ayatollah Khomeini's *vilayeti-i-faqi* system of government without submitting itself to Iranian suzerainty. In all this, Ḥizb Allāh seems to have gone a step further than HAMAS in that it has articulated theoretically that Islam can "both 'recognise and embrace' different cultures and nationalities," as long as nationalism does not become "an intellectual identity" that opposes "affiliation to Islam."[101] Such a marriage between Islam and nationalism has allowed Ḥizb Allāh to expand its appeal in two ways. First, the party has coopted Arab nationalism in order to defeat Israel, and, second, it has successfully managed to integrate itself into Lebanese national politics.

ISLAMISM AND VIOLENCE

We thus come to the last difference between Islamist organizations at the local level, which refers to the position of violence in their respective discourses. As the role and type of violence perpetrated by Islamists have been widely transformed over the decades, I concentrate here on the period after the 1979 Iranian revolution, thus covering what is often called "new radicalism." Be that as it may, in terms of what has been said in the previous paragraphs, we can distinguish between mass Islamist organizations that promote a variety of peaceful social and cultural activities within the community and those, usually smaller, organizations that mainly pursue a violent confrontation with the state.

At a descriptive level this distinction is generally correct. There are, however, two important points which should be considered. First, among the mass Islamist organizations there are some which, beside their mainly peaceful activities ranging from kindergartens and *zakāt* committees to free literacy classes and dental clinics in low-income areas, often have an armed wing. These include HAMAS, Ḥizb Allāh, and the FIS. This dual strategy is politically and morally legitimized in the eyes of their supporters by the assertion that they are struggling against either an invading foreign power, like Israel, or an internal foe who has acted unlawfully, like the Algerian army which annulled the 1991 elections. Thus, despite the ferocity of their struggle, it would be wrong to see such organizations simply as resistance movements that would cease operations after they have succeeded in their bellicose efforts. Rather, as in the case of Ḥizb Allāh, they will continue functioning as political parties involved in the management of peace as well as of charities supplying services to the community.

On the other hand, the smaller more radical Islamist groups, like the Palestinian Islamic Jihad, the Egyptian Jihād al-Islāmī and Jamāʿa al-Islāmiyya, and the Algerian GIA, as well as *al-Qāʿidā* and the Saudi Arabian Islamist cells allegedly associated with it, use violence as their main weapon against a foe that is politically defined as such in purely ideological terms, and they accord a secondary position to forms of community service that may have been attempted within the limits of state legality. Such peaceful endeavors are subordinated in their almost 1970s Leninist notion of the necessity of the utter destruction of the state and its supportive ideological apparatus. In that respect, such "armed-struggle-first" groups put little faith in the "Islamization from below" line that the Muslim Brothers and other mass movements pursue.[102]

Second, size cannot be directly linked to a group's proclivity to violence. In other words, smaller outfits are neither by definition nor by necessity more prone to violence. It is rather that groups which have elected the path of confrontation with what they consider to be an ungodly opponent tend to be small and tightly knit. This is mainly for reasons of operational security, except when they function in conditions of generalized warfare, like resistance movements (e.g. the Palestinian Islamic Jihad) which are nonetheless organized in small cells, or when they take advantage of the interstices of a leaking international system at all levels, geographical, political, and virtual, like the elusive *al-Qāʿida*.

Having distinguished between mass Islamist organizations pursuing a dual peaceful/violent strategy and smaller, more militant groups which on all counts operate outside legality – and leaving aside nationwide organizations, such as the various chapters of the Muslim Brothers and the Tunisian and Moroccan Islamist parties, which all implement Islamization-from-below policies – we can now distinguish between two types of political vision and, as a consequence, reveal a qualitative differentiation between two kinds of violence which is of great political significance.

On the one hand, the mass Islamist organizations that follow a dual operational strategy do so along the lines of a long-term political plan which, ideally, will enable them to come to power either in a newly constituted, and preferably Islamic, state (Palestine) or in a pre-existing nation-state (Lebanon). In their case, violence is practiced within the structured framework of strategic possibilities open to a mass resistance movement on its way to political domination.

On the other hand, the militant Islamist groups that follow a strategy of confrontation with the state do not see themselves as political entities governing a future polity whose bureaucratic and administrative mechanisms, its precise social and economic policy characteristics, and its security arrangements they have accurately theorized. All we have is a romantic/utopian pronouncement on the future state's Islamic nature. In this context, the violent campaign against the state and its internal and external sojourners does not follow the logic of the seizure of the state and accession to power. The state for them is not a castle that should be taken by force, so consequently their practice constitutes moments of personal/collective resistance to state authority and the logic of its mechanisms.

This stance, as can be glimpsed in Sayyid Quṭb's writings, has important moral and existential elements that cannot be properly understood outside the ethical horizon of Islamic eschatology and what this entails for the world. It is exactly this separation at all levels – ideological, political, operational – that gives their (violent) practice its phantasmagoric, spectacular, and in the end terrorizing character. Even then, of course, there are differences of degree which may underlie qualitative variations, but on the whole the scheme I propose works for all such militant groups, from the splinter group that assassinated the Egyptian president in 1981 or those who attacked Copts and foreign tourists in Egypt in the early 1990s to the Algerian village massacres of the mid-1990s, the attacks against foreigners in Saudi Arabia, and the internationalized violence associated with *al-Qāʿidā*.

As Sivan argues, this kind of organization characteristic of the militant groups discussed here is close to the idea of party vanguardism,[103] as well as, I would add, to the approaches developed through a peculiarly Islamically inflected Guevarism. From this perspective, as a revolutionary practice that has been repeatedly followed in the West and elsewhere, the waging of a violent campaign against the state should be seen historically and should always be critically approached from within the specificities of the local context. It is only in this way that Islamic violence, just like all types of political violence, will not be judged and summarily dismissed according to a generalized and ahistorical morality of a dubious universal character, which in turn would be based on the invocation of Man as generalized subject outside historical, class, or gender determinations.[104]

This is exactly what the "War on Terror" campaign is not doing. As Aretxaga has written, the "War on Terror" has taken what I have called earlier the phantasmagoric, spectacular, and terrorizing traits of this type of Islamist violence to their extreme, producing "a fictionalized and absolutized enemy."[105] In this manner it has set the stage for a titanic conflict between the "powers of Good" and of civilization, on the one hand, and the "powers of Evil" and barbarity, on the other.[106] This war, the US neo-conservative and evangelically informed ideologues and their allies around the globe warn us, will be long and arduous, but not because the enemy is difficult to triumph over, but because the struggle itself is placed outside history. To quote Aretxaga:

> [t]he current "War against Terrorism" is unfolding . . . around a double temporal structure, as an arresting time in which historical time itself . . . is arrested. In contrast to historical time, the structure of this timeless war is characterized by the temporality of waiting, waiting for the next attack, waiting for the spread of a virus, waiting for the killing of terrorists, waiting . . . as a prolonged moment of suspension and anxiety, of terror transformed into spectacle, of terror that is also a thrill, of terror that focuses and binds into a new sense of patriotic affect.[107]

For Aretxaga, this strategy is disastrous as it strikes directly at the very core of the Western system of liberal values that (supposedly) underlies parliamentary democracy. As she writes,

> the war on Terrorism might indeed create the very enemy it is seeking to eradicate . . . setting the stage of war not as a state of exception, but rather as a permanent state of affairs in which the state of exception has become the juridical norm and the legitimating right of police and military intervention.[108]

But it could be also argued that the "War on Terror" unleashed by the West does something more than that: it also structures the murderous qualities of certain types of Islamist violence, indirectly giving credence to the message of its leaders. This is an important point, because it reveals the interdependence of modes of violence, Islamist and state terrorist in our case, and the creation of "a closed dynamic of mimetic violence that can reproduce organized terror ad infinitum, narrowing if not closing the space for political engagements of other kinds."[109] It is not then that terrorizing violence does not exist and that it is not perpetrated by Islamist militants indiscriminately against people.

It certainly does, and one cannot but feel that its reprehensible, indiscriminate, and murderous aspects should be morally condemned by all political ideologies and all religious traditions. But Terrorism as a categorical concept that allows for the declaration of an unending war in a timeless frame against a demonized Other and for a consequent limitation of civil freedoms – Aretxaga's "permanent state of exception" – is an entirely different issue, a structural effect influencing terrorists and anti-terrorists alike.

And with this, I come to the last point of my discussion of Islamist violence, namely its relationship with violence in general. What I suggest is that Islamist violence – both when practiced within the structured framework of strategic possibilities open to a mass resistance movement *and* when it acquires an autonomous character that places it outside the premises of mass political action and into the hands of a self-defined and self appointed ideological/operational elite – should not be seen in isolation from the wider use of political violence in each and every society under consideration. In other words, Islamist violence should be always analyzed in conjunction with state violence. This is not because Islamist violence is somehow causally related to state violence,[110] but because the state is by definition the entity that organizes *structurally* social coercion in the name of legitimate governance. This holds true for both Western bourgeois class societies and for the post-colonial Islamic societies of the Middle East and North Africa, and should not be neglected by researchers, even when Islamic violence takes the form of indiscriminate murder or when it is associated with other causes, such as those of the criminal and abhorrent hostage-taking in a North Ossetian school in September 2004. Taking into consideration Russian expansionism can help us contextualize massacres like this, without in any way condoning them.

Lastly, viewing violence perpetrated by Islamists as a specific spectrum of modes of violence within a wider framework hegemonically organized by the state, may allow us to see it not as a unified and monolithic structure, but as "a dimension of people's existence, not something external to society and culture that 'happens' to people" but as "socially and culturally constructed."[111] From this point of view, we are enjoined to remember that Islamists, too, are victims of violence, either at the grand level of the "War on Terror," ranging from wholesale armed invasion to incarceration in legal and extra-legal prisons, or at the equally lethal level of continuous manhunts, beatings, and targeted assassinations.[112] Indeed, it would not be far-fetched to situate Islamist violence within the wider structures of what could be called "(sub)cultures of violence," thus indicating the systemic value that violence has taken in specific socio-cultural contexts, say the Arab Palestine, Iraq, or even Syria, Saudi Arabia, Egypt, and other Middle Eastern states exhibiting a high degree of authoritarianism. From this point of view, Peteet's analysis mentioned in the preceding note could be fruitfully employed in contexts other than that of occupied Arab Palestine.

The same is true of Jean-Klein's more recent (2001) article on Palestinian nationalism and resistance. There the author discusses "self-nationalization," "a process wherein ordinary persons fashion themselves into nationalized subjects, using distinctive narrative actions and embodied practices that are woven into the practice of everyday life."[113] I find a most expressive point in Jean-Klein's analysis in her reference to a mother's report of the arrest of one of her youngsters as a heroic act of resistance: "What do you mean 'They took him!'? He *went*!"[114] Like Peteet, Jean-Klein does not focus on Islamists. However, as the aforementioned statement suggests, her analysis may shed light on Islamist activism, especially on the ever-growing tide of suicide bombings. Perhaps for obvious reasons, this practice has not become a subject of anthropological inquiry. Its tremendous political gravity and the acute moral problems it poses make analysts timid and hesitant to approach it. Clearly, the historically hallowed discourse of martyrdom as an act of heroism and negation of the self in favor of something superior and community-oriented does not seem to capture the reality of suicide bombers.

Notes

INTRODUCTION

1 See Lewis 2003a, b and Pipes 2002, 2003. For less polemical studies which look for either ideological confrontation, see Berman 2003 (esp. chs 3 and 4) or political incorporation, see Huntington 1993 and Zakaria 2004, most articles in *Foreign Affairs* on the Middle East and studies of the *Center for Strategic and International Studies*, Washington DC, such as *The Future of Islam-West Relations* and *The Future of Islam and the West: Clash of Civilizations or Peaceful Coexistence* (http://www.csis.org/islam). For the pre-9/11 era, see Modood 1997: 4 on "Islamophobia" as a form of cultural racism and Bjorgo 1997 on anti-Muslim feelings amongst members of the European middle classes. On stereotyping at the level of popular representations, especially in the post-9/11 era, see Goody 2004 (esp. ch. 4 on the Islamic Other); Gumbel 2001; Abdel-Latif 2001b on media representations of history in the US; and Thomson 2001 on the Hollywood unidimensional and shallow representations of "Evil" and terrorism. See also Holland 2001: 5 on the similarities in the representations of Ussāma bin Lāden and Lex Luthor, Superman's evil adversary.

2 Geertz, 1971: v.

3 Eickelman 1987: 18. See also Eickelman 1982a: 1–2.

4 Asad 1986: 14. More recently, another author who has employed the concept of "discursive tradition" is Muhammad Qasim Zaman in his study of the position of religious scholars in contemporary Islam (2002).

5 As Gefou-Madianou 1999: 26–7 has noted: "as a discipline anthropology should always be in a state of crisis," thus echoing in the post-anthropology-as-cultural-critique era (Marcus and Fischer 1986) Raymond Firth's view (1981: 200) of anthropology as an indiscreet, provocative, and uneasy science. This apart, the literature on the subject is vast; maybe it really says something about the state of affairs in the field.

6 Gilsenan, 1990: 15.

7 In the words of Faure, "we cannot simply dismiss the traditional view [of tradition] as purely ideological" (1996: 10). Rather, we should bring forward the "heterogeneity or multivocality of the tradition" which has been silenced as "[t]he historical narrative tends to reproduce the homogenizing effects of the

traditional account by reinforcing its linearity even when it would seem to question its content." Faure refers here mainly to texts internal to the (Buddhist Chan/Zen) tradition, as well as to scholarly writings about the tradition.

8 All *Qur'ānic* quotations come from the English translation of the *Qur'ān*, revised and edited by the *Presidency of Islamic Researches, IFTA, Call and Guidance*, and offered free of charge by the Saudi Arabian Embassy in Athens, Greece, as "a gift from the Custodian of the Two Holy Mosques King Fahd Ibn Abdul-Aziz for the spreading of Allah's Word." This is almost identical to the annotated translation (1975) of Abdullah Yusuf Ali of the Islamic Foundation, Leicester.

9 Eickelman 1989: 258–62.

10 Asad 1986: 17. I am not sure if anyone ever tried to produce something along these lines for Islam or for any other religion. Even David Gellner's *Anthropology of Buddhism and Hinduism* (2003), a well-researched study raising important theoretical issues, is more circumscribed in the subjects it considers. See for example Gellner's second chapter, esp. pp. 58–9, where he raises the question "What should the anthropology of Buddhism be about?"

11 Cf. Lindholm 2002 for an analysis of these trends.

12 As Starrett (1997: 282–3) observes, "there is relatively little comparative ethnographic work on different Muslim societies."

13 To these one should add the numerous newspaper articles which approach critically the policy options followed by many Western governments toward Islamic societies in the context of the "War on Terror." Especially for the immediate period after the 9/11 terrorist attacks, for the British press see among others Fisk 2001a, b, 2002, and Freedland 2001.

14 I.M. Lewis 1999: 116.

15 Quoted in Ahmed and Shore 1995: 29.

16 Eco 2001: 2.

17 Gramsci 1973: 212.

18 To put it in Marilyn Ivy's words, it "is as much a discursive construct as an objective referent" (1995: 1).

19 Halliday 1996: 3. Appropriately, Halliday's book is called *Islam and the Myth of Confrontation*.

20 Having explained my understanding of the term, I shall not use quotation marks around it in the rest of this book.

21 Eickelman 1989: 3. See also Hourani 1993: 2. As Hodgson (1977i: 60–2) writes, the term has disadvantages. First, "[i]t cuts the Iranian highlands in half – the western half ('Persia') having been assigned to the Mediterranean [British Imperial] command, the eastern half ('Afghanistan') to the Indian command." Second, the term implies it is part of some "East" – that is, all civilized lands but the occidental, taken as somehow forming a civilization or a region to which something distinctive may be ascribed, set off as one entity against the "West" as another. Hodgson's historically correct but rather idiosyncratic term was the "region from Nile to Oxus."

22 Originally the region was called "Near East" – a term that is still employed in Germany; "Middle East" referred to "the territories which extended from Iran to Tibet. These two terms were used in those senses down to the end of the First World War" (Yapp 1987: 1).

23 In the present volume I do not deal with Muslim–Christian relations. Those interested can consult O'Mahony 1993, 1996, 1999, 2001; Fitzgerald 1999; Ayoub 1999; Abu-Rabi 1999; and Nielsen 1995b. The two basic premises underlying this bibliography are that both Muslims and Christians believe in the same God and that they can learn from each other. For more critical approaches which refer to the restrictions imposed on Christian minorities, see Goddard 2000 and Michel 1985, 1992. From a Muslim point of view, see Nasseef 1986; Rahman 1986; and Hamidullah 1986. In all cases, the relations between Muslims and Christians in the Middle East cannot be discussed only in theological terms. As the cases of Lebanon, Egypt, and the Sudan suggest, each one is directly related to local sociocultural dynamics and political considerations. Taking into account the different social positioning of Lebanese Christians, Egyptian Copts, and southern Sudanese Christians in their respective societies, it would be a folly to attempt any generalization.

24 In general parlance political developments have led to a near identification of the Arab world with the Middle East – though not necessarily vice versa. This tendency results in (i) excluding Turkey from the Middle East altogether, thus favoring its European Union candidacy; (ii) putting aside the differences between Arabs and Iranians in favor of a differently positioned *sunnī* and *shiʿa* distinction; and (iii) in making the position of Israel in the area even more exceptional.

25 Halliday 1996: 27–30.

26 Cf. Lindholm 2002: 13.

27 Abu-Lughod 1989: 280.

28 Said 1991: 105, 299. See also Hodgson 1977i: 315–18. More recently, Roy (2004: 12–13) has made a similar point in his effort to correct a tendency among several analysts who pass value judgments on an "essentialized" Islam on the basis of the political realities in the Middle East.

29 For those interested in the subject, Nielsen's *Muslims in Western Europe* (1995a) offers a good general introduction, although political developments and migration trends may soon render it dated.

30 Robertson 1992. As he writes, "our main task now is to consider the ways in which the world 'moved' from being merely 'in itself' to the problem or the possibility of its being 'for itself'" (p. 55).

31 Giddens 1990: 175. See also Giddens 1991. For a concise discussion of sociological theories of globalization, see Waters 1995.

32 Friedman 1996: 311.

33 Appadurai 1996: 307.

34 Hannerz 1987: 555.

35 Ibid.: 557. Cf. Smith 1996 for a resurrection of the nearly abandoned concept of "culture area."

36 Hannerz 1992: 222.

37 The wording here is indebted to Asad 1996 and 2003: 70–2. In both publications Asad argued against the notion of "resistance," which one could see implied in Hannerz's 1987 article, because it presupposed "a particular kind of deep motivation . . . attributed to an essentialized subject-agent" (2003: 72). Asad 1996 disputes this, arguing that

> we should not assume that every act is the act of a competent agent with a clear intention . . . there are certain circumstances and conditions which may or may not be immediately available to the consciousness of the person engaged in those activities but which constrain and structure the possibilities of his/her own actions. Whether such actions are undertaken reluctantly or gladly is another matter. But what is crucial here is: what it is that one is, in a sense, obliged to do by the structuration of conditions and possibilities, not the consciousness with which one does them, and the gladness, anger, or resentment with which one does them. This doesn't mean, of course, that people have no consciousness. It means that we are looking at the wrong thing if we look to consciousness to understand the changing patterns of our lives. For that, we ought to be looking at the circumstances by which possibilities are patterned and reshaped.

38 Featherstone 1996: 11, 12.
39 See among others Casanova 1994; Chadwick 1995; MacIntyre 1967; Taylor 1998; and Asad 2003.
40 Schmemann 1995: 118, 129.
41 Eschatology is a complex term. Here it refers to the central hope of the Church, i.e. the establishment of the Kingdom of God at the end of time. As meta-history, though, this hope has been already introduced in history through the resurrection of Christ. All monotheistic religions are eschatological, albeit in different ways.
42 Asad 2003: 25.
43 Ibid.: 193.
44 Indeed, these are characteristics of all "traditional" forms of religiosity, though they may be absent from certain modern forms of it usually associated with New Age.
45 Ibid.: 205. Strictly speaking, Egypt was not a British colony. To simplify things, I have refrained throughout the present book from distinguishing between the various forms of colonial subjugation, such as mandates, protectorates, trust territories, and condominiums. Like the generic notion of "colonialism," they are all specific forms of imperialism.
46 Ibid.: 235.
47 An exception is Roy, who quite rightly points out that "in the Middle East . . . [secularization] is mostly associated with dictatorship, from the former Shah of Iran to President Ben Ali of Tunisia" (2004: 3).
48 Zakaria 2004: 150–1.

CHAPTER 1 THE ISLAMIC COMMUNITY THROUGH HISTORY

1 Florofsky 1972: 19.
2 Even the idea of "Christiandom" lacked the legal presumptions of what Hodgson (1977i: 57–60) calls "Islamdom."
3 As MacIntyre 1981 [2003], Asad 1986, and Zamam 2002 have shown, the existence of disagreements and contradictions, as well as the development of sustained internal criticism and lines of argumentation are constituent parts of all traditions. In a similar manner, one could suggest that in a monotheistic tradition that will

find its completion eschatologically, the doctrine itself, as well as the practices with which it is dialectically related, remains always an approximation; it is an ongoing process in tension with the world rather than a finished product. From another point of view, of course, one could argue that this is an accurate description of all historical processes.

4 Those non-Muslim monotheists who dwelt among the Muslims were distinguished in terms of their religious creed (for example, Christians or Jews) and constituted self-governing communities (*dhimmis*) under Muslim protection. Needless to say that this sanitized legalistic picture was often violently upset as the various *dhimmis* were part and parcel of political processes. Still, it should be stressed that compared with Europe and the Americas only very rarely did religious differences lead to forced mass conversions, wholesale massacres, and genocidal purges. See Courbage and Fargues 1996.

5 Hodgson 1977i: 298.

6 Hitti 1991: 103.

7 For the study of Muḥammad's life, see Watt 1953, 1956, 1961, and Rodinson 1976. See also Hodgson 1977i: 146–86; B.S. Turner 1978: 31–8; Hitti 1991: 111–22; Esposito 1992: 7–19. Of all these, the study that discusses the role of Muḥammad in the establishment of Islam and analyses his mission in sociological and anthropological terms is that carried out by Turner. There the author considers Weber's view on early Islam in relation to the latter's theory on charisma. Cf. Weber 1964a: 358–73; 1964b: 46–59, 262–6.

8 The principal language of Pakistan and the surrounding areas.

9 Recently, this view has come under critical revision.

10 For a detailed discussion of the term *umma*, see pp. 44–8.

11 Paraphrasing Mauss, Messick (1993: 3) describes the *sharīʿa* as a type of "total discourse," where all institutions are simultaneously religious, legal, moral, and financial. Similarly, in Calder's analysis of the term in the *EI* (pp. 321–6), the *sharīʿa* is placed in the broader historical context of the Arab-speaking populations of the monotheistic Middle East of the first centuries of Islamic history and it is suggested that the term refers to the entirety of a prophetic religion, both for Arab-speaking Jews and Arab Christians of the same period.

12 Voll 1982b: 4.

13 One of the many examples of the symbolic meaning of the battle of Badr which could be cited is the large number of modern military exercises which carry that name. A relatively recent example is the Egyptian army exercise in 1996, Badr 96. Thirty-five thousand soldiers took part and it included taking over a canal and then liberating a town under siege. It is obvious that this canal was the Suez and that the enemy was the Israelis. Once again, within the framework of the exercise of course, the Muslims were shown to be victorious over the unbelievers.

14 Very early in Islamic history we come across genealogies which connect Muḥammad to Abraham through Ishmael in a line parallel to those connecting Jesus through King David and Isaac – Ishmael's younger brother – to the patriarch of Semitic monotheism. In that respect, "the genealogy of Muhammad is a sacred charter that links a seventh-century Arab from the small Meccan tribal group of

Quraysh with the God of Abraham revered by Jews and Christians in their respective revelations" (Varisco 1995: 147). This fictitious account was employed by medieval Arab genealogists as a template for Arab tribal structure.

15 Except for Persia.

16 North Africa was conquered by AD 715, but did not achieve political unity under caliphal rule. For the Arabization and Islamization of the local Berber populations, see Brett and Fentress, 2002: esp. ch. 4.

17 See ch. 5.

18 See ch. 3.

19 See *sharī'a*, *EI*: 323.

20 See Watt 1991: 85–8; 1994: 82; Said 1991: 59.

21 See Hourani 1991; Watt 1991; Cardini 2001. For early Arab Christianity and apologetics, see Griffith 1992.

22 That is, the fifth century after the emigration (*hijra*) to Madīna and the eleventh century of the Christian era. Mentioning the AH calendar when referring to certain events allows us to appreciate their importance in the temporal context of Islamic history.

23 For the changing perceptions of the crusades see Watt 1991: 77–82, Ahmed 1992: 172, and Esposito 1992: 163. In all cases, the Muslims of the time of the crusades did not consider these Christian campaigns in Palestine to be anything more than the usual attacks of barbarians, considering the Franks the same as the Asian tribal attackers (for the early Arabic ethnography of barbarism, see al-Azmeh 1992). In fact, in the relatively long period of the crusades, the politically divided Islamic entities of the area often formed opportunistic alliances with some of the local Christian populations. It must be remembered here that in several patches of the wider historical Middle East and Africa, Christians were reduced to a minority possibly as late as the thirteenth century. See Courbage and Fargues 1996.

24 See Hodgson 1977ii: 437–500.

25 See Braudel (2001: 157). As the French historian wrote: "in 1526, when the Turks gave the coup de grace to Christian Hungary (Battle of Mohacs) it is clear that a resurrection of the whole of Islam, under a Turkish and Sunni guise, signaled everywhere and without contradiction the victory of the traditional religion and the Orthodox faith."

26 Hodgson 1977iii: 101–2.

27 Ibid.: 109.

28 As Inalcik (1995: 125) argues, "these laws . . . were based on rational and not religious principles and mainly concerned the areas of public and administrative law."

29 Hodgson 1977iii: 133.

30 Yapp 1987: 59. In this context, we should also consider the issue of the Ottoman capitulations. The term refers to a long-standing "policy of arranging with the foreign Christian communities (and hence with their governments) that they should govern their own internal affairs through consuls . . . and that they had accorded favourable terms of trade" (Hodgson 1977iii: 141). In time, this policy proved injurious to the Ottoman state as it strangled its trading possibilities and assisted in the creation and strengthening of a semi-"foreign" Christian and

Jewish merchant class (*Levantines*) who were neither Ottoman nor occidentals, but looked to Europe for protection.

31 For the *Tanẓīmāt*, see pp. 176–7. The bibliography I have consulted includes Hodgson 1977iii: 230–3; Yapp 1987: 108–14; Hourani 1989: 45–9; Mardin 1989; Inalcik and Quataert 1996: 762–6; Zürcher 1997: 52–74; and Quataert 2001: passim.

32 For a discussion of the wider intellectual and socio-political framework, see Mardin 1989: 124–46 and Karpat 2001.

33 Toprak 1993: 630–1; Zürcher 1997: 173–202.

34 Samatar 1992: 5. This is not a Muslim peculiarity. Old Testament prophets followed a similar logic (von Rad 1965).

35 Eickelman 1989: 3.

36 For the notion of post-colonialism, see Childs and Williams 1997; Loomba 1998; and Ashcroft 2001. See also the reader of Williams and Chrisman (1994) for an impressive selection of classical articles on the subject.

37 There are many references stating that *shīʿa* Muslims are an Islamic sect (Klein 1985: 230). In this way, the *sunnī* are indirectly considered as "orthodox" believers without however condemning the *shīʿa* as heretics. This is not correct. Despite the diverging theological and political views of *sunnī* and *shīʿa* Muslims, their difference has not taken the form of a distinction between "orthodoxy" and "heterodoxy."

38 Modern-day Iraq is a perfect example of this.

39 In the present context, the terms *imām* and caliph are used as if they were synonymous. For a more detailed discussion of the term *imām*, see p. 99.

40 The term "Ayatollah" refers to a high-ranking official in the Iranian clerical leadership of religious scholars-jurisconsults. In the literature it is written with a capital A, unlike similar titles we have come across, such as sultan or caliph.

41 Esposito 1992: 47.

42 Ibid.: 48–50.

43 As Eickelman 1989 suggests, any discussion of the Alevi identity and practices reveals that religious identity is always inextricably bound to relations of dominance and authority; that Muslims themselves can "maintain distorted perceptions of significant 'others' within the community" (p. 287), and that traditions like that of the Alevi with no "high scholarship and carriers of 'high' formal learning" (p. 288) can survive in the face of modernization and the danger of sweeping away particularism.

44 The concept of the *Mahdī* appears in *sunnī* theological treatises as well. The majority of messianic figures who declared themselves to be *Mahdī* were *sunnī* mystics and warriors. The best known is Muḥammed Aḥmad (+1885) of the Sudan. See among other sources, Holt 1977; Voll 1979; Trimingham 1983: 93–6; and Kapteijns 1985. For a critique on the meaning of *Mahdī* and a comparison with the alternative Islamic vision of the Wahhābī movement of the Arabian Peninsula, which to this day provides ideological support for the Saudi Arabian government, see Voll 1982a.

45 According to Turabi (1993: 11), this is the characteristic which brings *shīʿa* Islam close to the definition of an infallible Christian Church, whose path is guided by the Holy Spirit.

46 Ahmed 1993: 51.
47 He did not disallow it either.
48 Gellner 1987: 138.
49 Ibid.: 142. See also Sivan 1989.
50 Eickelman 1989: 279–80.
51 Fischer and Abedi 1990: 13.
52 Ibid.: 15. At the same time, though, Fischer and Abedi (1990: 14) remind us of a commonplace truth for all rituals, namely the coexistence of drama and deep religiosity with profanization and an obscene sense of humor, as life outside the ceremonial context continues. For example, the man playing Zaynab, Ḥusayn's sister, always had a big mustache. When someone from the audience made a rude comment "he would show his mustache from under his chādor . . . and would respond to propositioning with such retorts as, 'Yes, I'll sleep with you; bring your mother too.'"
53 Gilsenan 1990: 61–71.
54 Sivan 1989. As Sivan has clearly showed, in Iran the meaning of the stage performances of the Ḥusayn drama has been progressively moved in the 1980s towards more openly political renditions and interpretations that went along with the revolutionary ideology of the Khomeini regime and with the developments in the Iran–Iraq war.

CHAPTER 2 THE FOUNDATIONS OF ISLAMIC DOCTRINE AND THE COMMUNITY OF BELIEVERS

1 Cf. Fischer and Abedi 1990: 148–9.
2 See Asad 1986: 15; Eickelman 1989: 262ff.
3 For many Muslims, the archetypal *Qur'ān* existed with God before the creation, hence the concept of *al-nūr al-Muḥammadī*, the cosmogonic light of Muḥammad as source of life. This view is particularly widespread in mystical Islamic texts, especially those of the neo-*ṣūfī* Aḥmad b. Idris (+1837). See O'Fahey 1990: 175; Thomassen and Radtke 1993: 19.
4 This is disputed by Watt and Bell 1990: 41. See also *al-Kur'ān*: *EI*: 405.
5 Hallaq 1997: 8.
6 Watt and Bell 1990: 83, 84.
7 Bloch 1974; 1975; 1986: 182, 184; 1989: 44–5.
8 Hodgson 1977i: 471–2; ii: 510; Ahmed 1993: 95–6, 110.
9 Eickelman 1989: 306.
10 Ibid.: 307.
11 This is also in accordance with the *Qur'ān*, 33: 21.
12 See Klein 1985: 27–9.
13 See *ḥadīth*: *EI*; Burton 2001: ch. 6; Hallaq 1997.
14 Hallaq 1997: 13, 17–8.
15 Fischer and Abedi 1990: 105–8.
16 Hallaq 1997: 125.
17 Ibid.: 1. "*Mujtāhid*" is a technical term representing a status conferred to someone by others. One cannot declare oneself *mujtāhid*.

18 Hodgson 1977i: 315–18.
19 I disagree with Hodgson. At least from the point of view of the Eastern Orthodox theological tradition, the grace of God through Jesus covers the whole world, making it anew.
20 The rabbis interpreting Talmudic law did not differ from the rest of the faithful in their relationship to God.
21 Hodgson 1977i: 329. A similar argument has been advanced by the Eastern Orthodox and Roman Catholic churches concerning the infallibility of the Church (*ecclesia*). This is presumed to be guided by the Holy Spirit and as such to be the only possible historical subject to interpret the sacred texts authoritatively and to form a Holy Tradition. This is questioned by the Protestants.
22 Hallaq 1997: 1.
23 Ibid.: 117.
24 Ibid.: 19.
25 Hodgson 1977i: 330.
26 Though until the period of European colonialism it remained a jurist law. See Brown 1997: 365.
27 Hallaq 1984: 21. As the exercise of *ijtihād* was of paramount importance to the functioning of law the religious scholars and jurists of the day were naturally interested in dealing with the problem.
28 Ibid.: 13.
29 Just like *mujtāhid*, "*mujāddid*" is a technical term conferring status.
30 See *idjtihād*: *EI*; Gibb 1947: 13; Schacht 1982: 70–1.
31 Hallaq 1984: 19.
32 Ibid.: 32.
33 Hallaq 1997: 213–14.
34 Asad 1993: 222–3.
35 Asad 2003: 197.
36 Asad 1986: 14.
37 Cf. 1 Peter 2: 10 where we read "for you once were not a people, but now you are the people of God."
38 Barth 1992: esp. 23–4.
39 Combs-Schilling 1989: 223.
40 Ibid.: 105. See also Geertz 1971 where the author discusses Moroccan kingship in terms of intrinsic and contractual legitimation. The former is related to the royal descent line that goes back to Prophet Muḥammad and ʿAlī and the latter to the *sunnī* institution of the *baʿy* (oath of allegiance). Geertz argues that this double legitimation allows the king to present himself simultaneously as leader of the entire *umma* and as representative of a particular type of a local mystical tradition of Islam.
41 Combs-Schilling 1989: 228.
42 Makris 2000.
43 Holt 1977: 45ff.
44 The riverain Sudanese Arabs include those populous tribes who live in the Nile basin. These had been the tribes wielding political power in the region corresponding to the contemporary state of the Sudan.

45 For the Sudanese civil war and the contest of identities, see among others, Beshir 1968, 1975; Deng 1973, 1995; Lesch 1998; Jok 2001; Johnson 2003. Though non-anthropological, all these studies capture the minutiae that really lend the events their dramatic character and bring to the surface the long historical structures that shape contemporary cultural visions and political realities.
46 Smith 1991 [2000]: 96.
47 Vatikiotis 1980 [2000]: 41.
48 Ibid.: 52.
49 Ibid.: 44.
50 Ibid.: 105ff.
51 Dwyer 1991: 75–6.
52 Gellner 1985: 35ff.
53 Gellner 1993b: 76.
54 Ibid.: 80.
55 I.M. Lewis 1986: 95.
56 Gaffney 1994: 29.
57 Asad 1986: 10–13.
58 See also Eickelman 2002.
59 The term *salafiyya*, which has been widely used to describe Islamic modernism, implies an effort to return to the premise of *al-salaf al-salih*, the "venerable ancestors" of the *umma* who lived in the era of the Prophet and the four rightly guided caliphs. As a movement, *salafiyya* attached little importance to the state as a unit for the implementation of Islamic law and promoted the resurgence of the caliphate.
60 Hobsbawm 1995: 70.
61 Cole and Kandiyoti 2002: 189.
62 Zubaida 2002: 211. Cf. Chatterjee 1989, 1993.
63 Zubaida 2002: 211.
64 Cole and Kandiyoti 2002: 194.
65 Zubaida 2002: 214.
66 Zubaida 1993: 148–9.
67 Ibid.: 170.
68 Nothing strange in all this. As Eickelman (1989: 270) has shown, just like everybody else Muslims have multiple identities which coexist and function in particular ways according to the prevailing historical conditions.
69 Zubaida 1993: 172.
70 Ibid.: 177.
71 Ibid.
72 On the contrary, as Hefner (1997: 8) argues with reference to the Muslim societies of Southeast Asia, the state appears as that particular type of organization which, theoretically at least, allows Muslims to work for the total religious and political transformation of society. It is also interesting to see the history of terms such as "nation," "people," or "state." See Eickelman 1989 for a revealing summary of the history of the term "*millat*," at times translated as "the people" in nineteenth- and twentieth-century Iran, as well as valuable notes on terms such as "*al-sha'b*" and "*al-jamāhīr*," which have been used by communist and socialist Middle Eastern regimes.

73 Gupta and Ferguson 1992: 7.
74 Appadurai 1997: 21, 33.
75 Eickelman and Piscatori 1996: 137–8.
76 As well as, I would add, net-spaces, a cross between Appadurai's techno- and mediascapes (1997: 33).
77 Eickelman and Piscatori 1996: 139–41. Together with the British Commonwealth and the newly founded International Criminal Court, the OIC is one of the very few significant international bodies the USA does not belong to.
78 A friendly publication once called it a "lethargic and ineffectual grouping" (Jansen 1995: 10).
79 Eickelman and Piscatori 1996: 142.
80 Eickelman and Piscatori 1996: 145.
81 The other side of satellite TV is that it provides viewers in Muslim countries with images of the West much more benign than those reported by the national press, radio, and TV, thus complicating even further the images of the West. For example, how could the American soldiers in Iraq be the same as the smiling or heroic characters in Hollywood movies and TV sitcoms?
82 Anderson 2002: 302.
83 Eickelman 2002.
84 This, I think, can be also detected in the process of "objectification of Islam" discussed by both Eickelman and Piscatori 1996, and Starrett 1998, as will be seen in detail in the following chapter.
85 An interesting article on Islam on the net that was posted very soon after the 9/11 attacks was Gary Bunt's (2002). It contains a wealth of information concerning sites of Islamic character.

CHAPTER 3 AUTHORITY AND KNOWLEDGE

1 For a discussion of the term *ʿilm*, see Hallaq 1997: 15, 19 and the entry *ʿilm al-kalām* in *EI*. See also Hodgson 1977i: 255. For the concept of *ʿilm* in Islamic mysticism, see Schimmel 1975: 17ff.
2 As Quataert (2001: 167) argues, only 2–3 per cent of the early nineteenth-century Ottoman subjects were literate.
3 This is true for Christian monasteries as well. See *masdjid*: *EI*.
4 Hourani (1991: 163) puts the first appearance of *madrasas* in eleventh-century Baghdad.
5 In modern Arabic, the term "*madrasa*" means "school." A *Qur'ānic* "school" is called "*kuttāb*." Before the emergence of the Western-style educational system in the Middle East and North Africa, the two terms were synonymous, though the latter referred almost exclusively to primary education. For the early history of the institution, see Hodgson 1977ii: 46–9; Hitt 1991: 410–11, 660–1; Inalcik 1995: 285.
6 Eickelman 1989: 312; Mitchell 1991: 83–4. See also Eickelman 1982b.
7 See *masdjid*: *EI*; Hourani 1991: 164–5.
8 Mitchell 1991: 84.
9 For example, the standards of instruction and the content of knowledge imparted in several *madrasas* of the mid-eighteenth-century eastern Sudan were very

different from those of, say, thirty to fifty years later when the area had become the target of some very important missionaries from the Ḥijāz, who belonged to the Idrīsī neo-*ṣūfī* tradition (Trimingham 1983; O'Fahey 1990), and from the period 1821–98 when the country was under the Turco-Egyptians, who had introduced Egyptian *ʿulamāʾ* friendly to the government in an effort to co-opt the local population (Hill 1959), and later under the Mahdist regime that practiced a strict form of early Islamism (Holt 1977; Voll 1979).

10 As the *waqf* system is primarily governed by "traditional" legal rules and edicts, it is often based on oral agreements rather than on written legal contracts, a fact that compounds difficulties from the point of view of a modern bureaucracy. See Benthall (2002: 153) for the case of Oman. For a brief presentation of land reform in Egypt since the era of Muḥammad ʿAlī, see Anderson 1968. In all events, the absence of documented land-titles does not concern *waqf* lands only. As Taher Helmy, president of the American Chamber of Commerce in Egypt and a member of the ruling party's Policies Committee, argues, "[n]inety-two per cent of Egypt's property owners hold their real estate assets as extralegal – that is, unregistered and without a title" (2004: 5). For *waqf* history, see the relevant entry in *EI*.

11 The post of religious endowments minister is not without its dangers. See, for example, the assassination of the Egyptian *waqf* minister Muḥammad Ḥusayn al-Dhāhabī in 1977 by the militant Islamists of al-Takfīr wal-Ḥijra, an offshoot of Jihād. al-Dhāhabī was among the most renowned *ʿulamāʾ* of al-Azhar. Takfīr wal-Ḥijra is still operating in Egypt, but has received serious blows from the security forces. In July 2004 another seven members of the banned group were arrested north of Cairo (Halawi 2004b: 2).

12 Eickelman 1989: 307–8.

13 Mitchell 1991: 101.

14 Messick 1993: 3.

15 See *masdjid*: *EI*; Hourani 1991: 167–71: Rahman 1984: 33–5.

16 el-Shayyal 1968: 118–19.

17 And even then a semblance of independence was retained.

18 Mitchell 1991: 87.

19 See also pp. 224–5.

20 In the West this is typical of many self-confessing Christians, who may accuse their established Church and its clergy of all the sins in the book, while continuing to participate in the rituals at which the same "unworthy" Church ministers officiate.

21 Gilsenan 1990: 31.

22 Ibid.: 32. Again, this is not a Muslim peculiarity. To take just one example, in his preface to Moltman's highly acclaimed, almost popular, classic *Theology of Hope* (2002), Buckman advises readers to skip chs 1 and 4, where the author places his work within the wider German theological tradition and the philosophy of history. Admittedly, these are very difficult texts to follow.

23 At the level of discourse, this can be partly attributed to an innate conservatism in the classical Islamic political theory and to its aversion to anarchy and populist insubordination even when the political authorities act unjustly.

24 As an anthropologist, I am rather ill disposed toward distinctions of the "central" versus "peripheral" type. However, in the context that Zeghal is using the terms it is clear that it is a matter of distance from political authority in a well-defined institutional environment. Naturally, as in all cases where similar distinctions are employed, what is labeled as "peripheral" yields to comprehensive sociological description only with difficulty. But at least Zeghal recognizes that and directly relates it to punitive measures on the part of the government (1999: 386). More refined in this respect is Zaman's extended study of the *'ulamā'* in Pakistan and in selected Middle Eastern societies. Though he adopts Zeghal's distinction, he writes that "[t]he activities and attitudes of the contemporary 'ulama are more accurately ranged along a broad spectrum of options and possibilities, however, than they are fixed in mutually exclusive or dichotomous groupings" (2002: 134). I shall return to this point later in the chapter.

25 Zeghal 1999: 388; Moustafa 2000: 14; Zaman 2002: 147–8.

26 Mentioned in Zeghal 1999: 380.

27 Roy 1994: 96–7.

28 Zeghal 1999: 377.

29 Ibid.: 380.

30 Ibid.: 387.

31 Ibid. Strictly speaking, no market can be totally "deregulated," as some of those involved, in our case the *'ulamā'*, retain many of their institutional prerogatives vis-à-vis the new "entrants," in our case the Islamists.

32 Zaman 2002: 148.

33 Ibid.: 149. Cf. Ismail on conservative Islamism in Egypt: "conservative Islamist discourse is articulated by the right-wing party al-Ahrar and elements of the Muslim Brothers, as well as by segments of the state apparatus, the official newspapers, and the state-run mass media. It is produced in relation to a particular set of material conditions and finds support among various class fractions tied to the rentier economy" (1998: 219).

34 For al-Qaradāwī's latest visit to the UK in the summer of 2004, see the various articles in the British press. They were overwhelmingly negative in tone, calling the *shaykh* a "race-hate cleric" (Waugh 2004: 5) who spreads his "gospel of hate" in London (Lebrecht 2004: 13).

35 Zaman (2002: 141) offers a characteristic example concerning the highly respected Jām'iyyat al-'Ulamā'-i-Islām, a Deobandi organization formed in 1945 that "has played a considerable role in Pakistani electoral as well as agitational politics" (p. 119). When the Jām'iyyat organized a large international conference in Peshawar, Pakistan, in April 2001 to celebrate the achievements of the Deoband movement, among the messages read to the half-million audience gathered for the occasion were those of Ussāma and the *Ṭālibān* leader *mullah* Muḥammad 'Umar.

36 See el-Shayyal 1968: 122–4.

37 To the question of the Mamlūk governor, "Why did the *'ulamā'* disobey the government?" *'ālim* Sayyid 'Umar Makram responded that the legitimate rulers of the country were the *'ulamā'* themselves, those who follow the *sharī'a*, and the Ottoman sultan, who in practical terms could do very little from far-away Istanbul (el-Sayed 1968: 273).

38 Baer 1968: 147. Vatikiotis calls this process bureaucratization of the *'ulamā'* (1980: 300), arguing that the government tried to turn the *'ulamā'* from a social category whose political antennae were often attuned to the popular feeling into a part of the state bureaucracy.

39 Starrett 1998: 104.

40 Ibid.: 116.

41 Ibid.

42 Ibid.: 8.

43 Eickelman 1992.

44 Ibid.: 650.

45 See Messick 1993 for a discussion of the manner in which Ottoman and Yemeni reformers of the nineteenth and twentieth centuries transformed Islamic law into a modern legal system, destroying in the process the discursive flexibility and interpretative polyphony that traditionally characterized it. Referring to Messick and to his own work in Egypt, Starrett (1998) maintains that the condensed manner in which Islam is taught in Egyptian schools really represents a new Islamic tradition that has its roots in the historical one, but should not be mistaken for this.

46 For example, Starrett (1998: 113–14) shows how Islamic statements and imagery are incorporated in the science textbooks, where God is presented as the power that makes the world meaningful. Equally interesting is the manner in which scientific research is presented as part of a divine plan to boost the progress of the Egyptian nation financially and politically and to increase the status of Arab scientists.

47 Ibid.: 9.

48 It should not be supposed that religious instruction is necessarily at the center of the government's education policy. As in other countries, this is based on other deliberations associated with the economy and the job market. See Khalil (2004: 2) concerning a recent conference in Egypt entitled "Towards a Knowledge Society: the Future of Education in Egypt." From the public's side, see Houtsenen 1994 on traditional *Qur'ānic* education in a southern Moroccan village. As the author argues, villagers prefer *Qur'ānic* to modern schools for a number of reasons. First, they find them less expensive. Second, they do not require regular attendance, so children are periodically available for agricultural work. Third, they see them as repositories of local traditions. Fourth, they more easily accept traditional teachers than their modern counterparts, whom they classify as alien. Fifth, they argue that in any case the knowledge imparted in modern schools is too theoretical to be applied in everyday life and concentrates on areas already saturated by jobless graduates.

49 el-Menshawy 2004: 3. For many, this decision is associated with the general political atmosphere. For example, 'Alī Abū Laban, an MP associated with the outlawed Muslim Brotherhood, argues that after a *fatwā* (religious decree) asking for a *jihād* against aggressors in Iraq was issued by the Grand *Imām* of al-Azhar, *shaykh* Muḥammad Sayyid al-Tantāwī, the US administration was pressing the Egyptian government to rein in al-Azhar. Although Tantāwī later retracted the *fatwā* amd repeatedly met with the American ambassador in Egypt, the pressure

continued, "with an [American] congressman even asking for Al-Azhar to be added to the US's list of terrorist groups" (ibid.).

50 Hirschkind 2001b: 16.

51 This does not mean that the model of Islam imparted in Saudi religious education does not exhibit the characteristics identified above by Starrett. Doumato (2003), in a post-9/11 article on Saudi school texts on Islam, discusses some additional characteristics which Starrett did not consider in his 1998 study, viz. the manner in which relations between Muslims and non-Muslims are depicted and the idea of martyrdom. As Doumato suggests, the overall picture emerging from the school texts is not so much one of hatred toward the West as the promotion of the idea that Muslims are somehow under siege and have to stick together, both at the level of the kingdom and at that of the *umma* as a whole.

52 Parsons 1966: 4.

53 For a concrete case, see Bledsoe and Robey's 1986 article on the social uses of Arabic literacy among the Mende of Sierra Leone for concealing and manipulating knowledge. Though they do not dismiss Goody's position on the importance of literacy for communication, they criticize him for neglecting "the equal potentials of writing for obfuscation, concealment of meaning and lying" (p. 203). As they write,

> [w]e believe that writing, because it is tangibly visible but potentially semantically opaque, is just as well suited for facilitating secrecy as for facilitating communication of a literal message. Moreover, writing does not replace the oral idiom but comprises one component of the total pool of potential knowledge that the Mende strive to attain and manipulate in competition with others. In fact, the Mende seem to value literacy not *in spite of* the difficulty of attaining it, but *because* of it. (p. 222)

This is similar to what happens in Arabic-speaking Muslim societies, the only difference being that there Arabic is also used for everyday verbal and written communication besides its employment in the context of Islamic discourse.

54 Ong (1997: 127) points out that the Semitic alphabet, of which Arabic is an example, is deeply related to the non-textual human world.

55 Parry 1985: 204–5.

56 Ibid.: 207, 210. In this spirit, one could offer a similar interpretation of the importance attached to *Qur'ānic* calligraphy, to the one offered by Goody (1995: 157–8), thus weakening further his argument on the importance of writing.

57 Fischer and Abedi 1990: 106.

58 *Qur'ān*, 6: 7.

59 Watt and Bell 1990: 40–4.

60 The version that most of us are likely to encounter is the Ḥafṣ form of 'Āṣim from Kūfa.

61 Fischer and Abedi 1990: 106.

62 Ibid.

63 Ibid.

64 This emphasis on correct and precise reproduction is not an Islamic peculiarity. According to Parry, it can be found in many traditional societies:

> [I]t has been motivated more by a concern with the precise reproduction of the sound than by a concern with the retention of the meaning it conveys. The words in themselves have power once they are vocalized. For this power to become manifest they must be pronounced with precision and exactly the right intonation. Wrongly accentuated they may have an effect opposite to the one intended. (1985: 209)

65 See also Messick 1986, 1993. Discussing the interpretation of the *sharīʿa* in Yemen, both publications emphasize the importance of orality in Islamic tradition and the significance of interpersonal relations between teachers and students.

66 See p. 225.

67 Comparing the Christian, Jewish, and Islamic traditions, Fischer and Abedi (1990: 147–8) argue that the Christian one sees the world as realization of the Logos and language as a representation permitting the decoding of the Logos. The Jewish tradition stresses the effort to conceptualize the meaning of everything through a mode of argumentation that accepts both oral and textual forms as equally in need of hermeneutic exploration. The Islamic tradition sees the text as an inferior form of recording the Word, insisting for example that both the Jewish Torah and the Christian Gospels are erroneous representations of God's will. This being the case, Islamic tradition seeks the true meaning of the world behind the veil of illusory appearances, behind the reality of texts.

68 Especially in the case of inventories of Islamic phrases in Arabic (*adʿiyya*, sing. *duʿāʾ*) which the faithful can use in all sorts of everyday occasions – before going to sleep or when waking up, before and after meals, when purchasing a new garment, as well as in case of illness, accidents, visiting people, or expressing certain feelings – we can see elements of local traditions and language idioms becoming globalized as proper forms of Islamic etiquette. See Alvi 1997.

69 T.M. Lewis 1986: 107.

70 The anthropological view of "authenticity" as a quality always conferred in the present according to the logic of the "orthodoxy" production process does not contradict this.

71 This is not an Islamic peculiarity. It is a central position of the Roman Catholic Church (http://www.newadvent.org/cathen/15006b.htm) and of Eastern Orthodox Christianity (Florofsky 1972), though not of Protestantism.

72 Cf. Zaman 2002: 28.

73 Weber 1964b.

74 From this perspective, one should contrast this type of Islamic devotional literature, even in its coarser form of popular pamphlets and tracts, to the self-help "How to . . ." manuals we come across in the West. Interestingly, the orientalistic belief widely held in the West concerning "Eastern wisdom" does acknowledge a distinction between "Zen Meditation . . ." or "Karate Shotokan in Thirty Simple Lessons" from "real" work with a teacher/master/sensei who, preferably, has had some firsthand instruction out there. Thus, for those who consider themselves to be "seriously" into such practices, using manuals can be excused

only as a first introduction to the Way or as mnemonic devices which can be consulted whenever one's memory has failed to register or to assimilate what the teacher demonstrated in practice.

75 Even the now extensive use of audiovisual techniques and the Internet has added a new dimension in this process that goes beyond Parry's distinction between "scribal" societies and those with more advanced printing techniques.

76 Hirschkind 2001b: 6.

77 Ibid.: 7.

78 Ibid.: 19.

79 Ibid.: 21.

80 Ibid.: 23.

81 Hirschkind 2001a: 624.

82 As the one studied by Mahmood (2001) in relation to prayer. See below pp. 100ff.

83 Hirschkind 2001a: 627.

84 Ibid.: 632.

85 Ibid.

86 Hirschkind 2001b: 16.

87 Ibid.

88 Ibid.: 17.

89 Ibid.: 25.

90 Hirschkind 2001a: 641.

91 Eickelman 1982a.

92 Hirschkind 2001b: 25–26.

93 Ong 1982: 135.

94 Starrett 1998: 94.

95 Cf. Nasr 1992.

96 Georges 1976: 161, quoted in Finnegan 1992: 113. Finnegan's questions concerning "local conceptions about change, stability and transmission in verbal expression" (ibid.), as well as those concerning the socio-economic position of performers and other participants in the production and consumption of oral arts, form today the backbone of anthropological approaches to the study of oral traditions that consciously avoid the pitfalls of a narrowly positivistic historicism.

97 Such accomplishment is first and foremost a central concept of revelation and an epistemological foundation of an eschatology already inaugurated with, or in, the revelation of the *Qur'ān* to Prophet Muḥammad and the foundation of the Muslim *umma*, the people of God. Seen in this light, Islamic discursive tradition can rest on the certainty that the *Qur'ān is* complete, but Islamic sacred history *is not*, in the sense that it has not yet found its intended full meaning since it is still unfolding and will unfold until the Day of Judgment (*al-Yaum al-Dīn*) or Last Day (*al-Yaum al-Ākhir*) (cf. Klein 1985: 84ff). As the past is subsumed in the present, not passively but in order to sacralize it, that is to reveal its sacred nature, the future is called upon as the *telos* (from the Greek *teleiosis*: accomplishment, perfection) and the end of history and the fulfillment of God's promise to His Community. This, I think, is a way of reading Asad's previously mentioned notion

that "[a]n Islamic discursive tradition is simply a tradition of Muslim discourse that addresses itself to conceptions of the Islamic past and future, with reference to a particular Islamic practice in the present" (1986: 14).

98 Tonkin 1992: 2.

99 Ibid.: 5.

100 Caton 1990: 155.

101 Ibid.: 177. In his discussion of the Malay Chewong's myths, songs, and spells Howell moves a step further arguing that "instead of treating each category of formal speech acts as a separate enterprise in any one culture, making whatever social, symbolic or structural connexions as may be appropriate, all genres of formal speech acts within a society should be looked at together as one discourse" (1986: 82). Howell's point is certainly valid, but might be difficult to work in the context of a complex society. The Chewong number around 260 individuals. Howell did his fieldwork among the eastern part of the tribe.

102 Tonkin 1992: 8.

103 Cf. Vansina 1985.

104 Barber 1989: 14.

105 Bloch 1989: 27. See also Bloch 1975. For a clear exposition of Bloch's theory concerning the political dimensions of rituals, see his historical ethnography of Merina circumcision (1986) and his more theoretical study on violence and ritual (1992), where he marshals ethnographic material from different societies.

106 Bloch 1989: 37.

107 That is why eloquence is of cardinal importance for the *'ulamā'*. The lack of it indicates imperfect knowledge of the subject and inability to demonstrate its innate truth. Interestingly, Muktadar al-Ṣadr, the *shī'a 'alim* of Najāf, Iraq, who raised the Mahdī Army against US and government forces in the summer of 2004, was dismissed by other *shī'a 'ulamā'* as an upstart with no real knowledge because, among other things, he lacked eloquence.

108 Ibid.: 44.

109 Ibid.: 38.

110 Connerton 1995: 58.

111 Ibid.

112 Ibid.

CHAPTER 4 THE FIVE PILLARS

1 Al-Bukhārī, al-Fatḥ, 1/49, quoted by *shaykh* Muḥammad Ṣāliḥ al-Munājjib n.d.: 3.

2 Hitti 1991: 100–1.

3 See *Qur'ān*, 6: 137, 109; 10: 23; 31: 24, 31.

4 Ibid.: 112.

5 Asad 1993: 221–2. Asad argues that Islam differs from the other two Abrahamic monotheisms as it rejects both the notions of "covenant with God" (Judaism) and of "kinship with God" (Christianity). Be that as it may, as far as Christianity is concerned things are more complicated since the image of men as "sons of God" coexists with that of men working for God in the same manner that

slaves work for their masters. See for example 1 Cor. 7: 21. For the position of slaves in early Christianity and the cognate image of believers as slaves of God, see Kyrtatas 1987.

At the same time, we must emphasize a point common to all three traditions, that the relationship between God and man cannot take place in the abstract, but only within the framework of a community of believers. From this point of view, the members of the *umma* do not constitute autonomous subjects. Just as in Christianity and Judaism, the relation between the creature and the Creator informs the notion of individual freedom.

6 Watt and Bell 1990: 28.

7 *Qur'ān*, 33: 40.

8 Cf. Gellner 1993a: 72–5.

9 Every prayer is a "ritual prayer" in a particular way. Here the term is used to emphasize its institutionalized status and its specific legal characteristics. That means that there are other prayers which are not "ritual," such as personal prayers uttered by the believer, mystical ones, prayers for the dead, etc. See Eickelman 1989: 287. In a recently published extended essay on prayer Marcel Mauss (2003) stresses the ritual character of the prayer, defining it as "a religious rite which is oral and bears directly on the sacred" (p. 57). Though Mauss's study is cast in a quasi-evolutionist form that has been long abandoned by anthropologists, it still contains important insights into the nature of the phenomenon, especially in relation to its social rather than individual character.

10 For other prayers, see Issa 1996a.

11 *Qur'ān*, 2: 142–50; 4: 43; 5: 6, 58.

12 http://www.islamknowledge.com/unity_amongst_muslims.htm.

13 *Ṣalāt: EI.* As for women, they can pray in the mosque, but are not encouraged.

14 See Old Testament 1 Kings, 1: 8; Daniel, 6: 2.

15 *Qur'ān*, 2: 137ff.

16 See among others, Ahmed 1990: 27; B. Lewis 1990: 25; Makris 2000: 98, 99, 101, 220. As will be seen later in this chapter and in chapter 5, this equality among believers is theoretical rather than actual.

17 Delaney 1990: 516.

18 Ibid.: 293. Delaney does not specify if this is her interpretation or if it was suggested to her by her informants.

19 Mahmood 2001: 829.

20 Ibid.: 833.

21 Ibid.: 844.

22 Ibid. Cf. Mauss (2003), where prayer is classified as an "oral rite" as distinct from the "manual" ones which "consist in movements of the body and of objects" (p. 56). Though Mauss is perfectly correct in stressing the importance of *formal ritual speech as action* in the context of prayer, he is unable to see the latter as an activity involving the human totality – praying body and mind – as Mahmood does. Cf. Anthony of Sourozh (1999a, b), as two ordinary (standard, I would say) examples from within the Eastern Christian Orthodox tradition which show that Mahmood's innovative anthropological approach on prayer has always been part of the Church's experience.

23 Tapper and Tapper 1987: 72.
24 Ibid.: 84.
25 Gilsenan 1990: 167.
26 See for example Brenner 1993.
27 Makris 2000: 29–30.
28 Lewis 1986: 97.
29 Another anthropological study of the *ṣalāt* whose conclusions about the collective character of the ritual prayer are close to mine is by Bowen (1989) and concerns four Indonesian societies. Very briefly, as the ethnographic area is far removed from the Middle East and North Africa, Bowen makes three points of interest. First, "[t]he individual structuring of worship in turn shapes and is shaped by public discourse about its proper form" (p. 611). Second, prayer can be taken to provide a model of and a model for society which then shape the manner in which distinctions are made between Muslims and non-Muslims, as well as between Muslims from different societies (pp. 612–13). In the first case, Bowen mentions examples from West Africa, where the crucial question is not "Are you a Muslim?" but "Do you pray?" In the second case, the ethnographic examples come from Indonesia, Iran, and Afghanistan. In the latter, the Pashtu-speaking *sunnī* Durrani distinguish themselves from the Uzbeks, i.e. non-Pashtu-speaking *sunnī* Muslims, with reference to their view of *ṣalāt*. See also Tapper 1984. Lastly, Bowen maintains that anthropologists have not shown great interest in analyzing the Muslim prayer because "[t]he ṣalāt is not structured around an intrinsic oppositional or semantic core. It cannot be 'decoded' semantically because it is not designed according to a single symbolic or iconic code" (p. 615).
30 *Qur'ān*, 62: 9.
31 Klein 1985: 142.
32 For the *ḥadīth* which concern the *ṣalāt al-jumʿa*, see http://www.islamknowledge.com/Jumah.htm.
33 See *khuṭba: EI*.
34 Gaffney 1994: 120.
35 Ibid.: 123.
36 Asad 1993.
37 For details, see Issa 1996b.
38 Cf. Reinhart 1996: 124.
39 For a detailed discussion of these issues, see *zakāt: EI*.
40 Weiss 2002: 9.
41 Pfeifer 1997: 155, 157.
42 Ibid.
43 Cf. *Qur'ān*, 2: 275; Abu-Saud 1993: 8; Brahimi 1996: 8; Rahman 1964. See also Iqbal and Mirakhor 1987 and Stiansen 1999, 2003 on Islamic banking.
44 See for example Zubaida 1997: 60–1 for Egypt.
45 Weiss 2002: 16–17.
46 Ibid.: 16.
47 Ibid.: 17.
48 This is an entirely different matter from the rather dated discussion concerning the presence or absence of classes in non-Western societies. For an anthropological view, see Bloch (1985: esp. 152ff), where he discusses the introduction

to anthropology of Althusserian concepts concerning the articulation of multiple modes of production in traditional societies. This led to the discussion of the class issue in such societies, especially by French anthropologists working in Africa. See Bloch 1984: esp. ch. 4 by Emmanuel Terray. There, discussing the Abron Kingdom of Gyaman, West Africa, Terray suggests that in non-Western societies we come across classes-in-themselves rather than classes-for-themselves. That means that "[t]he exploited class does not succeed in constituting itself as a political force capable of unified action at the level of the total society, and confrontations remain enclosed within the boundaries of local communities" (p. 111). Unfortunately, no author from Bloch's 1984 edited volume makes any reference to Islam, except in passing.

To find such references we must go to Rodinson's classic *Islam and Capitalism* (1966 [1980]). There Islam is understood within the parameters of an enlightened orientalistic discourse as a tradition friendly to free trade and capitalism, but powerless in the face of strong dynastic states (p. 89). Rodinson's Islam seems to converse with history, but it remains strangely unaffected by it. This becomes clear when the French orientalist calls upon the Muslim masses to embrace socialism, as there is no other "third way," "using" [*sic*] Islam in the context of class struggle (p. 288). But in order to have any chance of succeeding in this effort, Islam should "pass through a deep transformation, through an *aggiornamento*" (p. 293). This will allow the Muslim masses and their leaders to understand that, despite its distortions, Marxism is the only way forward (p. 294). For a critical discussion of Rodinson and other intellectuals such as Samir Amin and Peter Gran, who theorized on the relationship between Islam, capitalism, and Marxism, see Binder 1988: ch. 6.

49 Weiss 2002: 18.

50 Throughout my discussion of *zakāt* I refrain from introducing local trade unions into the picture. That would require an altogether different context of analysis which is remote from the subject of this book.

51 Weiss 2002: 22.

52 Ibid.: 24–5.

53 See Norton 1995, 1996.

54 Hann 1996: 21, 22.

55 Ibid.: 16.

56 Antoun 2000: 445.

57 Ibid.: 456.

58 Ibid.: 459.

59 Ibid.: 460. For an urban setting, this time in Cairo, Egypt, see Singerman 1995, especially her discussion of private voluntary organizations as a mediated distribution point (pp. 246ff). Singerman's *sha'bī* informal networks should be seen in connection with the equally difficult to define and certainly more restrictive "Islamic parallel sector," mentioned on p. 74.

60 Although I have refrained from introducing the trade unions into the present discussion, I should point out that I do not regard them as a secular counterweight to Islamic organizations. As will be seen in chapters 7 and 8, in many Middle Eastern countries, such as Egypt, the Sudan, or Jordan, many trade unions have served as bastions of Islamist action.

61 These are characteristics of what anthropologists have called "audit cultures." See Strathern 2000; although that edited volume concentrates more on the academy, it provides interesting general insights on the new forms of accountability that have become prevalent in Western societies.

62 Benthall 2002: 156–7.

63 Ibid.: 157.

64 Ibid.

65 Benthall 1999: 36.

66 See also Benthall 2002: 159. I am not sure if Mauss (1979: 10) understands this difference betweeen *zakāt* and alms-giving when he refers to *Qur'ān*, 64: 15–18, encouraging his readers to substitute for the word "*Allāh*" the word "society." On his part, Sayyid Quṭb knew quite well all the implications of his argument. As we read in a short ethnographic vignette from Morocco, where *zakāt* is not a legal obligation, the recipients of it do not resent it in any way. "'This isn't charity,' [the donor] retorted. 'This is zakat. Our honor is to proffer zakat, her [the woman who received it] honor is to use the zakat. All is provided by God, not by us . . .'" (Bowen 2002: 265).

67 Benthall 2002: 161.

68 Benthall 1999: 32–4.

69 Seesemann 2002: 106–8.

70 Ibid.: 107.

71 Ibid.: 111.

72 Ibid.

73 Ibid.: 114.

74 Fischer and Abedi write that "the primal Qur'ān, called the *Umm al-Kitāb* ("mother book"), which resides in the seventh heaven, descended to the heavenly sphere on the twenty-seventh, nineteenth, twenty-first, or twenty-third day of Ramaḍān, and thence via the angel Gabriel into the heart of Muhammad" (1990: 103). The two anthropologists argue that this indeterminacy concerning the exact date is not to be clarified because it encourages prayer. It is believed that "prayers on the night of revelation are worth a thousand prayers any other time" (p. 463).

75 Muḥammad Ṣāliḥ al-Munājjib n.d.: 4. In http://www.ummah.org.uk/ramadhan/.

76 Buitelaar 1993: 17. Focusing on Morocco, this is the only long anthropological study of Ramaḍān.

77 See, for example, Buitelaar 1993: 78.

78 *Qur'ān*, 2: 183.

79 Alī 1975: 72.

80 See Douglas 1985: esp. ch. 3.

81 Besides the specialized bibliography on the subject, which mainly concerns historians of religion and Arab Studies scholars, the best introduction to *Qur'ānic* and *ḥadīth* injunctions on the Ramaḍān fast can be found in Buitelaar 1993: ch. 1.

82 Ibid.: ch. 2.

83 See for example http://www.ummah.org.uk/ramadhan/ and submission.org/ramadan.html.

84 Fischer and Abedi 1990: 18.
85 For example, what is the status of a girl menstruating for the first time but saying nothing to her parents?
86 Muḥammad Ṣāliḥ al-Munājjib n.d.: 3–6.
87 In all commentaries on the subject women are not presented in an active role.
88 This rule applies to married couples as well as to a man and his concubine.
89 In *Qur'ān* 2: 183 the verb usually translated as "that you may (learn) self-restrain" is *waqā*.
90 See, for example, http://www.isd.usc.edu/~~jnawaj/ISLAM/PILLARS/FastFiqh.html; http://www.holidays.net/ramadan/story.htm;qss.org/articles/ramadan/toc.html; http://www.ummah.org.uk/ramadhan/.
91 Muḥammad Ṣāliḥ al-Munājjib n.d.: 4.
92 Such views are close to the understanding of fasting advanced by the tradition of the Eastern Orthodox Church. See Hopko 1984iv: 146–50; Ware 1964: 306–7.
93 Cf. Bakhtiar's suggestive title *Ramadan: Motivating Believers to Action* (1995). This edited volume discusses the manner in which believers are motivated to action through participating in and understanding the Ramaḍān fast. Interestingly, the language and the terms that it uses are close to what could be called New Age terminology.
94 Buitelaar 1993: 3.
95 Ibid.: 3.
96 Ibid.: 58–9.
97 Ibid.
98 Ibid.: 60.
99 Ibid.
100 Ibid.: 61.
101 Ibid.: 161ff.
102 Ibid.: 181.
103 Ibid.: 54.
104 Ibid.: 94.
105 Ibid.: 96.
106 Ibid.: 131.
107 Ibid.: 133. Buitelaar refers to Eickelman 1976: 137.
108 Kenyon 1991a: 33.
109 See ch. 5.
110 Buitelaar 1993: 68ff. Significantly, Buitelaar associates them with the Gnawa teams, which are related to African slave descendants.
111 Bellér-Hann and Hann 2001: 160.
112 Ibid.
113 Starrett 1995b: 54.
114 Ibid.: 65–6. In his article on cassette-*da'wa* Hirschkind (2001b: 10) cautions agaisnst placing too much emphasis on "the commercial aspect of the cassette-sermon" for two reasons. First, the preachers themselves very rarely have "formal contractural relations with the tape companies and receive no remuneration from the sales of their tapes." Second, "the majority of tapes listened to in Egypt . . . circulate through the practices of borrowing and exchange."

115 Amin 2004.
116 Ibid.
117 Armbrust 2002: 341.
118 Ibid.: 346.
119 Cf. Hobsbawm and Ranger 1993. In all cases, as Bhabha (2000: 2) has argued, the encounter with the "other" has made impossible "any immediate access to an originary identity or a 'received' tradition."
120 Armbrust 2002: 347.
121 *Economist*, Dec. 16. 2000: 48.
122 Another version called the early morning *suḥūr* lunch *intifāḍa*, thus drawing a parallel between the struggle of the Palestinian youth against the Israelis with the struggle of the believers to overcome thirst and hunger during the fasting hours.
123 *Al-Ahram Weekly*, 2003: 1.
124 The pilgrimage to Madīna is considered to be a pious act (*fiʿl al-khayr*) and not a religious duty (*farḍ al-wājib*); hence its non-obligatory legal status (Metcalf 1996: 184).
125 For examples see ch. 5.
126 See Levtzion 2000.
127 Cf. Fischer and Abedi 1990: 159.
128 For the pilgrimage tradition in West Africa with special reference to the nineteenth century, see al-Naqar 1972.
129 Yamba 1995: 131.
130 Ibid.: 153.
131 All the items considered to be necessary for the *ḥajj*, such as *iḥrām*, a special belt for banknotes and passport, a small plastic pillow to be used during nights out in the open, a prayer-mat that can double as a mattress, an umbrella for the sun, and a plastic container for water, are sold separately or in the form of a special pilgrimage kit in all Muslim countries.
132 In her previously mentioned ethnography of a Turkish village in Anatolia, Delaney (1990: 518–19) describes the departure of the pilgrims from the village and the guides' role during their long journey to Mecca. The figures concerning costs mentioned by the author in her 1991 account (p. 304) are old, but nonetheless give an indication of the financial difficulties involved in the project. It should be added here, that, perhaps "naturally," the pilgrimage to Mecca has become a multi-million dollar business for both governments and the private sector. For example, the Egyptian company *Deyar* has recently initiated the "*ʿUmra* via Egypt" program by signing agreements with numerous tourist operators in Morocco, Tunisia, Libya, Turkey and *Egypt Air*, Egypt's national carrier. According to the agreements, pilgrims to Mecca would spend a number of nights in Egypt, thus increasing the country's tourism-generated income. The company is now set to expand its program to the Muslim communities in Europe (El-Din, 2004b).
133 The description that follows comes from Wolfe 1994.
134 By and large, these photographs, which can be seen in books, posters, or the Internet, are among the scant photographic material from the *ḥajj* that reaches the outside world.

135 Cf. Fischer and Abedi 1990: 160.
136 Ibid.: 163.
137 The respective biblical verse is Genesis, 16: 7.
138 For practical reasons, the *ḥajj* authorities have designated a particular area near the central mosque of Mecca where pilgrims can fill their receptacles with Zamzam water to carry to their home communities.
139 According to Combs-Schilling (1989: 74), who did her fieldwork in Morocco, during the whole day the pilgrims refrain from food and water and do not make any effort to keep away from the fierce sun. For all these privations, it is believed, God will forgive their sins as well as those of every single Muslim in the world.
140 For the symbolism of the pillars, see Fischer and Abedi 1990: 164.
141 Although the sacrifice of the ram is widely considered to be part of the *ḥajj* ritual, it is not a legal obligation for Muslims.
142 For the hygiene situation and the various measures taken, see Delaney 1991: 308–9.
143 This may have been adopted from a similar practice among Christian pilgrims to the Holy Land in Palestine.
144 Bellér-Hann and Hann 2001: 167.
145 Fischer and Abedi 1990: 165.
146 Bellér-Hann and Hann, 2001: 167.
147 See for example, *Ḥadjdj*: *EI*.
148 Eade and Sallnow 1991. For another typology of the pilgrimage, see also Morini 1984. Cf. Bowman 1991; readers can compare the *ḥajj* with his understandings of Roman Catholic and Eastern Orthodox Christian pilgrimages to Jerusalem.
149 Dubish 1995: 38.
150 Ibid.: 39.
151 Eade and Sallnow 1991: 3.
152 See for example Pearson (2000: 44) who describes the *ḥajj* as a remarkably efficient method for the integration of the worldwide community of Muslims.
153 Turner and Turner 1978: 250. See also Turner 1974: 274; 1989: 94–130.
154 Indeed, the figures given by Fischer and Abedi for 1987 are staggering: 21 million free one-litre bottles of drinking water; 3,420 Turkish butchers recruited to slaughter hundreds of thousands of animals whose meat is then distributed to the two and a half million pilgrims or put in deep freezes; 1,700 coaches operating round the clock in Mecca; etc. (1990: 169).
155 See Piscatori 1991: 8.
156 Fischer and Abedi 1990: 156.
157 Ibid.
158 Quoted in Whitaker 2005: 10.
159 http://www.muslimedia.com/archives/special-edition/ḥajj/hajj1.htm, http://www.muslimedia.com/archives/special98/ḥajj2.htm, and http://www.muslimedia.com/archives/special-edition/ḥajj/hajj2.htm respectively. The term "Haramain" (*al-ḥaramān*) refers to the two holy cities of Islam, Mecca and Madīna.
160 Delaney 1990: 515.

161 Ibid.: 1991: 117. According to Young (1993: 298), the idea of exile from paradise, which is at the basis of Delaney's analysis, cannot be found among Arabic-speaking Muslims.
162 Roff 1985: 85.
163 Delaney 1990: 520.
164 Ibid.: 521. This description goes against Turner's view of the pilgrimage as communitas, discussed in pp. 136–7 above.
165 See pp. 47–8 and pp. 103–5 (chs 2 and 4).
166 See p. 98 above.
167 Makris 2000: 98–9.
168 Male and female cult group leaders respectively.
169 For the association between slavery and the Sudanese Battalions, see Hargey 1981; Hill and Hogg 1995; and Makris 2000.
170 Zaman 2002: 4.

CHAPTER 5 ISLAMIC MYSTICISM

1 It should be noted, though, in many cases leaders of mystical brotherhoods are also esteemed religious scholars and theologians.
2 For another version, see Eickelman 1989: 288–9.
3 See Hodgson 1977i: 363–4.
4 See Schimmel 1975: 91–7; Hodgson 1977ii: 180–92.
5 See Schimmel 1975: 247–8; Hodgson 1977ii: 207–9, 216–17.
6 According to B.S. Turner (1978: 66), this "essential looseness" is a characteristic of all religious organization in Islam.
7 Sufism is almost exclusively male, hence the gendered character of the sentence.
8 For the various stages of preparation disciples have to pass from, see I.M. Lewis 1984: 137–8.
9 Geertz 1971: 45.
10 For more information about the ways *baraka* is transmitted, see Crapanzano 1981: 170, 174.
11 Geertz 1971: 44.
12 The term *karāma* (pl. *karāmāt*) also refers to those ceremonial dishes which are offered to God or the saints in order to secure good health (Abdullahi 1980: 17). They belong to the precautions people usually take to ensure their health and to avert disease which would otherwise befall them. Such offerings, which often have miraculous results, are called *karāmāt ʿāfia* and are divided into public and individual ones, depending on who is organizing them. For the Sudanese ethnographic context, see Holy 1991; Kenyon 1991a; Makris 2000; Nordenstan 1968.
13 In what follows I am heavily indebted to Gilsenan 1990: 75–115.
14 See ibid.: 82–3.
15 Weber 1964a: 324ff.
16 *Khāniqā* or *khānqā* in Persian.
17 For Morocco, see Crapanzano 1981: 169.
18 See for example, Warburg 1971 for a formative period in the history of the modern Sudan.

19 Strictly speaking, the mosque is not inherently sacred. As Hodgson (1977ii: 218) argues, the mosque is closer to the ancient Greek *agora* than to the Christian church.
20 Eickelman 1989: 300.
21 Ibid.: 301.
22 See also Crapanzano 1981: 170.
23 I have not actually studied the *zāwiyya*. The following description should be seen as the result of repeated visits and knowledge acquired during the last 15 years of my association with the country.
24 As Ibn Khaldūn (1986i: 222) writes, "the Sufis feed on *dhikr* exercises." For a broader presentation of *ṣūfī* liturgical life, see Schimmel 1975, as well as more localized studies which also cover saint worship, such as Trimingham 1983 and Karrar 1992 on the Sudan; Gilsenan 1973 on Egypt; Lewis 1998 on Somalia; Crapanzano 1981 on Morocco.
25 *Qur'ān*, 17: 110, 63: 9.
26 The well-known dance of the "whirling dervishes," performed in many European cultural venues by Turkish performers, is a *dhikr* technique of the Mevlevi brotherhood, which was established by Persian mystic and poet Jalāl-ud-dīn Rūmī (+1273). Obviously, the performance we see has been stripped of most of its mystical connotations to suit European artistic taste.
27 Eickelman 1989: 289.
28 Brett and Fentress, 2002: 148. Brett and Fentress's account (pp. 142–9) clearly show the positioning of the *zāwiyya*s in North Africa between the thirteenth and sixteenth centuries.
29 See McHugh 1994. See also Karrar 1992; al-Karsani 1985a, 1985b; O'Fahey 1973; Trimingham 1983: ch. 6. Of interest is also O'Fahey's 1990 biography of Aḥmad Ibn Idrīs, the nineteenth-century Moroccan mystic and teacher who played a central role in the formation of specific *ṣūfī* brotherhoods throughout North Africa. As O'Fahey characteristically writes (p. ix): "[t]wo states of the region, Libya and Somalia, are at least in part creations of the tradition associated with him."
30 See Ḍayf Allāh's *Kitāb al-Ṭabaqāt* (1985), a late eighteenth-century document, for accounts of the miraculous exploits of such holy men and their mediatory roles in the societies of the Nilotic Sudan.
31 See Makris 2000.
32 Trimingham, 1983: 217–22. Trimingham can be easily accused of "orientalizing" his material. However, his work contains a wealth of valuable primary information.
33 See Makris 2000.
34 See also Lewis 1998.
35 Lewis 1984: 140.
36 Ibid.: 145.
37 Ibid.: 147.
38 Ibid.: 142.
39 Colonna 1984: 109–10.
40 Ibid.: 113.
41 As Triaud (2000: 170) argues, French opposition to Islam was a direct heritage of the French Revolution and the separation between Church and State.

42 Colonna 1984: 114.
43 Ibid.: 109–10.
44 Ibid.: 117.
45 Ibid.: 118.
46 Hence Colonna (ibid.: 119ff) does not see the ultimate victory of reformist Islam in the emergence of an autonomous but not independent religious sphere in post-colonial Algeria.
47 In the *Qur'ān* Satan is presented as both a *jinn* (18: 48) and an angel (2: 32).
48 Arabic plural of *jinn* (Crapanzano 1981: 140).
49 See among others, I.M. Lewis 1986, 1989; I.M. Lewis et al. 1991; Crapanzano 1981 on Morocco; Kennedy 1967, Morsy 1991, and Natvig 1988, 1991 on Egypt; Constantinides 1972, 1977, 1979, 1991, Boddy 1989, Kenyon 1991a, 1991b, and Makris 2000 on the Sudan; Ferchiou 1991 on Tunisia; Ashkanani 1991 on Kuwait.
50 Shaw and Stewart 1994: 6.
51 Ibid.: 7.
52 Ibid.: 8.
53 Ibid.: 18.
54 Ibid.: 20.
55 Ibid.: 21.
56 Throughout this account I keep Crapanzano's transliterations.
57 Crapanzano 1981: 67.
58 Ibid.: 74.
59 Ibid.: 80. *'Aïsha Qandisha* is often called by Crapanzano a "she-demon."
60 *'Aïsha Qandisha*'s special love for blood is also attested by the fact that she induces many of her devotees to slash their head during performances. *Jinns*' predilection for blood is known throughout Morocco (Hammoudi 1993: 118, 131, 189).
61 Ibid.: 99.
62 Ibid.: 107.
63 Ibid.: 224.
64 Ibid.
65 Ibid.: 228.
66 Ibid.: 226.
67 Ferchiou 1991: 210.
68 Ibid.: 212. Observe the similarity between Nana 'Aisha and *Ḥamadsha*'s *'Aïsha Qandisha*.
69 Ibid.: 216. We will come across this relationship between possession and sexuality/fertility in our last example in this chapter, the Sudanese *zār boré* cult.
70 Ibid.: 217.
71 See Makris 2000. See also Kenyon's accounts on *ṭumbura* in the city of Sinnār (1991a, 1991b) in central Sudan for a wider perspective on the cult.
72 Makris 2000: 61ff.
73 Though, as mentioned in ch. 2, the legacy of slavery did not disappear.
74 See Makris (2000: 254–5) in connection to Evans-Pritchard (1971: 92–3).
75 See Glassman 1991 for an analysis of this among the slave populations of the Swahili coast. Glassman's thesis, in conjunction with my 2000 analysis of Sudanese

material, should be seen in the light of Wendy James's "subjugated knowledge" (1988: 139), concerning slaving systems and James Scott's concepts of the "weapons of the weak" and "hidden transcripts" (1985, 1990). As Scott argues, the hidden transcript "represents a critique of power spoken behind the back of the dominant" (p. xii). It is a counter-discourse that embraces gestures, speech, non-verbal insinuations, and practices, including spirit possession (pp. 141–2).

76 Boddy 1989: 114.
77 Ibid.: 74.
78 Ibid.
79 Ibid.: 183. Emphasis added.
80 Ibid.: 183.
81 Ibid.: 186.
82 Ibid.: 188.
83 Constantinides 1977: 83.
84 In relation to this, Boddy has been criticized for not offering an equally dynamic picture of the villager's world. See Abu-Lughod, 1993: 426; Makris 2000: 6.
85 Lewis 1986: 103.
86 Constantinides 1977: 72.
87 Boddy 1989: 340.
88 Ibid.: 339.
89 Ibid.: 340.
90 Ibid.
91 On this point Boddy has been criticized by Lewis (1990: 590) for not providing enough evidence to support her thesis on the liberating potential of *boré*.
92 Constantinides 1977: 64.
93 Hurreiz 1991.
94 Lewis 1986: 106.

CHAPTER 6 ISLAMIC REFORMISM

1 *Qur'ān*, 2: 220, 228; 4: 35, 114, 128; 7: 56, 85, 142; 11: 46, 90; 49: 9, 10; 28: 19. See also *iṣlāḥ*: *EI*.
2 Eickelman 1989: 316. Emphasis added.
3 Žižek 2003: 35. From G.K. Chesterton *Orthodoxy* (San Francisco: Ignatius Press, 1995).
4 Yapp 1987: 108–14.
5 See Mardin 1989: 109. According to Abu-Manneh, the 1839 Rescript was rooted in Islamic tradition, especially the *Naqshbāndī-Mujāddidī sūfī* principles, but by the 1850s its authors had disappeared from the scene and Western influences crept into the reformers' plans.
6 Cf. Asad 2003: 217. Asad's study mentions the *Tanẓīmāt* almost incidentally. However, it contains rare insights on Islamic reformism and the emergence of the secular in the Islamic Middle East.
7 A similar argument has been promoted by modern Turkish Islamists who cast the republican ideology of Mustafa Kemal (Atatürk) as another "imposition from above." See Navaro-Yashin 2002: 138.

8 See Perry 1992; Kassam 1993, 1994.
9 Mardin 1989: 122.
10 Perry 1992: 128.
11 Hourani 1989: 114.
12 In that sense, al-Afghānī did not participate in the debate about the nature of nationalism outside Europe, whether, that is, it was an imported ideology or not.
13 As Yapp (1987: 225–6) argues, the ʿUrābī revolution was brought about by the consequences of modernization.
14 Hourani 1989: 149.
15 As Geertz argues (1971: 105–6), Muslim activists like ʿAbduh followed two strategies simultaneously: on the one hand, they asserted that Islam and scientific reason cannot be in conflict with each other because they share no common ground, while on the other they claimed that Islam, and in particular the *Qurʾānic* text, encompasses all scientific thought. A true scientist, then, cannot be but a Muslim.
16 Hourani 1989: 232.
17 What he might be thinking of is that a number of ancient Greek philosophical texts had been introduced into the Latin West in their Arabic translation.
18 Hourani 1989: 233.
19 See Ahmed 1992: 169–77.
20 I say "in a way" because there were others before them who built the basis for the development of reformist ideas. Amongst them are Rifāʿ Badawī, Rafīʿ al-Taḥtāwī, Khayr al-Dīn, and Butrus al-Bustānī. See Hourani 1989.
21 Christmann 2000: 68.
22 Ibid.: 68–9.
23 Ibid.: 70.
24 Ibid.: 71. The term *al-taṣawwuf al-wijdānī* denotes all forms of ecstatic sufism.
25 Ibid.: 72.
26 Ibid.
27 Ibid.: 73.
28 Ibid.: 76.
29 Ibid.: 74.
30 Ibid.: 72.
31 George 2003: 92.
32 Abu-Zahra 2000: 84–5.
33 Ibid.: 88.
34 Ibid.: 96ff.
35 Soroush 2000: 113.
36 Ibid.: 128, 131ff.
37 Ibid.: 151.
38 Ibid.: 148.
39 Ibid.: 153.
40 Ibid.: 31.
41 Ibid.: 37.
42 Ibid.: 83.
43 Ibid.: 85, 150.
44 Ibid.: 22.

45 Ibid.: 159.
46 Ibid.: 163ff.
47 Ibid.: 23. For the ideas of Sorūsh, see also Cooper 2000.
48 Choueiri 2000: 78, 159. See also how Muslim nationalist intellectuals of the late nineteenth and early twentieth century rehabilitated the pre-Islamic *jāhiliyya* (pp. 37, 49, 75).
49 Asad 2003: 226.
50 Dwyer 1991: 75.
51 Ibid. This is too harsh. Such difficulties should be seen in the context of wider issues of political analysis. As another of Dwyer's Egyptian interlocutors suggests (p. 70), the task that the contemporary Egyptian Muslim reformers have to accomplish is much more difficult than that of the conservative Muslim thinkers. Whereas the latter consider more important the analysis of texts than the analysis of society (a project doomed to fail), the former have to come up with a much more general analysis of the social realities.
52 See Vatikiotis 1980.
53 Ibid.: 307.
54 Ibid.: 493. On Ṭāha Ḥusayn, see also Hourani 1989: 324–40.
55 Al-Azmeh 1996: 101.
56 Ibid.: 103.
57 Ibid.: 104.
58 Hourani 1989: 119.
59 See p. 43.
60 Al-Azmeh 1996: 106.
61 Ibid.: 108.
62 Ibid.: 109.
63 Shakry 1998: 151.
64 Cf. Voll (1983: 44), whom Shakry follows at this point.
65 Shakry 1998: 152. Still, Muslim reformers did accept the existence of an Islamic "Golden Era." In that sense, as al-Azmeh has suggested, they were as essentialist as their conservative detractors. Cf. Asad 2003: 220–1.
66 Schmemann 1995: 129.

CHAPTER 7 ISLAMISM: A GENERAL OVERVIEW

1 See Khalil (1998: 2) for the short memory and political opportunism that often characterize Western political practice in relation to these issues.
2 Cf. Vatin 1987: 161.
3 Cf. Esposito 1993: 119–20.
4 Schmemann 1995: 118.
5 Krämer 1997: 73. Though dominant, this is not the only view existing among Muslims. There are many who consider Islam part of their "cultural tradition" or an element of their identity and use the term "political Islam" in a rather derisory manner, perhaps because they are frightened of the political repercussions of an Islamist accession to power. For a more theoretically refined argument, see Flores (1997: 83) on the views of Muḥammad Saʿīd al-Ashmāwī, a

well-known Egyptian judge and reformist intellectual, who suggests that Islam has always been "an apolitical religion concerned solely with spiritual and ethical guidance." Even the early caliphate, al-Ashmāwī maintains, was really a "civil" government, not a religious one (Shepard 1996: 29). See also Fluehr-Lobban (2001) for a more general discussion of al-Ashmāwī's views.

6 It is in this respect that we must understand B. Lewis's assertion that "there is no equivalent to the term 'laity', a meaningless expression in the context of Islam (1991: 3)", rather than in the sense of a lived experience in the political field.

7 Ahmed 1992: 15.

8 Kepel 1995; Beinin and Stork 1997: 3.

9 Sennett 2002: 7.

10 Ibid.

11 Žižek 2002: 111.

12 Badiou 2003: 2.

13 Not to say to every non-Evangelical Christian Church as well, a point that is often overlooked.

14 Cf. Lind (2001: 21) for an analysis of a post-9/11 ideological convergence between circles of conservative Muslims, the American Evangelical Right, and the ecological movement. For an alternative view retaining the term fundamentalism, see Lawrence 1990 and Roy 2004. For Lawrence, all three fundamentalisms, Islamic, Christian, and Jewish, are "religious ideolog[ies] of protest . . . [against] the modernist hegemony in the High Tech Era" and nationalism (pp. 83, 87). Cf. Lechner (1990: 79). Typologically, this may be true, but in practice both Evangelical and Jewish fundamentalisms have been co-opted by the state, whereas Islamism has been routinely persecuted. From this point of view, Tariq Ali's *Clash of Fundamentalisms* (2002), where he argues for a deep ideological affinity between Islamism and the US-led "War on Terror," is certainly marketable but not accurate.

15 Roy 2004: 38.

16 Ibid.: 34.

17 A cognate term that is often used is "messianic movements." See Lewis 1989: 117–18, 156–7; Bloch 1992: ch. 6; Bowie 2003: 171–2; Morris 1998: 257; Turner 1989, 2002 [1969].

18 See Flores 1997: 86–8; al-Azmeh 1996: ch. 3; and for a detailed account of the party see Taji-Farouki 1996a and b.

19 See Hourani 1989: ch. 1.

20 Many of the positions that Esposito (1992: 163) finds characteristic of the Islamists are held by the general public and are routinely discussed in the cafés of Cairo and Amman.

21 The assassins of the Egyptian president considered him as the contemporary incarnation of the pharaoh, the symbol of absolute idolatry and irreparable estrangement from God. The term also refers to the absolute power of the state, a power that is antagonistic to that of God and His law. In the *Qur'ān* the pharaoh is presented as the godless and blasphemous opponent of Moses who had to be destroyed together with everything that he represented before a new socio-political and moral order could be created. See Golberg 1991: 17.

22 Cf. Ismail's "conservative Islamism" (1998) and Wickam's "parallel Islamic sector" mentioned in ch. 3 (p. 74), as well as Gad's article in *al-Ahram Weekly* with the title "Middle-Class Militancy" (2004).

23 See Hodgkin 1990: 93–4. Wheatcroft (2001: 8) notes that many of the 9/11 terrorists came from an affluent middle-class background.

24 This is often done by liberal intellectuals who decry the West's suspicious attitudes towards Islam. For example, Žižek (2002: 41) writes that while there is "no excuse for today's acts of horror . . . [the fact that Islam has been a tolerant religion for centuries] clearly demonstrate[s] that we are dealing not with a feature inscribed into Islam 'as such', but with the outcome of modern socio-political conditions." This is true. However, throughout the analysis one cannot be sure if Žižek is referring to Islamist terror or to Islamism.

25 This is how Salman Rushdie admonishes the Muslim world: "The restoration [!] of religion to the sphere of the personal, its depoliticization, is the nettle that all Muslim societies must grasp in order to become modern." Quoted in Hirschkind and Mahmood 2002: 351.

26 Indeed, there are some who talk about the existence of an Islamic culture of narcissism where the subjects see themselves as the eternal victims of history (Beaumont 2001).

27 See Milton-Edwards 1999 and Saad-Ghorayeb 2002.

28 See Asad 1996.

29 Sardar 1998: 267.

30 Roff 1987: 32. In my view, this formulation is more pertinent to Islamism today than Dekmejian's 1988 description of it as a polycentric movement (p. 18). See also Voll 1997 for an analysis reminiscent of that of Eickelman and Piscatori 1996 mentioned in ch. 2.

31 I use the term in its literal meaning "universal" and "of interest or use to all men" (*Concise Oxford Dictionary*).

32 This is the same kind of critique as that leveled by the establishment's political parties against the various organizations of the radical Left whose political program demands the destruction of capitalism, the demise of the state, and the emergence of new, mostly undefined, and usually unworkable, socialist relations of equality.

33 Asad 1986: 15.

34 See for example, Sivan 1990a: 25 and Esposito 1993: 125ff. The same is true for other more conservative Islamist personalities such as Fethullah Güllen from Turkey, who has written extensively on the relationship between Islam and science in an effort to reconcile Islam with the dominant laicist ideology of Mustafa Kemal (Atatürk) and his successors. See Shankland 1999: 81–2.

35 See Hale 1996: 192–3; Hodgkin 1990: 92; Medani 1997.

36 Choueiri (1996: 25) and Weiss (2002: 15) respectively. Cf. Žižek (2002: 133) on "capitalism without capitalism" – in place of Fukuyama's "Islamo-Fascism" – and an effort to resurrect Rodinson's idea of socialism as the only solution for Muslim societies, without the latter's orientalistic bias (1966 [Greek transln 1980]: 294).

37 Zubaida 1993: 33.

38 So, although one could agree with Roy (1994: 120) about the conjunction between "conservative fundamentalism" and Islamism, one should remain acutely aware of their differences at the levels of political organization and strategic objectives. The same holds for the relations between Islamists and Muslim reformers. Although both accept *ijtihād* and reject *taqlīd*, for the Islamists a great part of Islamic tradition, more precisely that which is related to personal status and family law, should not be reinterpreted. Generally for Islamists, the practice of *ijtihād* concerns only those areas which are not specifically covered by Islamic law in a definite manner (Esposito 1992: 194).

39 Perhaps this is also a trait of other "fundamentalist" religious ideologies, such as Evangelical Protestantism. With its antipathy towards ritualism and clericalism and with its straightforward language and "black and white" interpretation of reality, the Evangelical movement projects a more "modern" and user-friendly image than Roman Catholic and Eastern Orthodox Christianity, whose more nuanced discourses and rich liturgical universes appear too opaque and unacceptably "traditional."

40 Hannerz 1987: 555.

41 Al-Mahdi 1983: 239.

42 Al-Turabi 1995: 8.

43 Haeri 1998: 7. See, however, "Ghannūshī's appreciation for many of the accomplishments of Western civilization: empiricism and use of reason, modern science and technology, rejection of tyranny and championing of human freedom and responsibility, and the willingness to rebel against any oppressor" (Esposito and Voll, 2001: 113). This ties in well with our previous discussion on the Islamist view of modernity.

44 Ahmed 1992: 94ff. See also Ahmed 1993: 206, an interesting example of popularizing anthropology, and Ahmed and Donnan 1994.

45 See e.g. Lewis 1981; Blanks 1997; Cardini 2001.

46 For Ibn Taymiyya, see Hodgson 1977ii: 470–2; Hourani 1989: 18–22.

47 Sivan 1990a: ix.

48 Obviously, the examples that follow are only indicative, as the number of those involved is very high. Also, the specific works mentioned have been either translated into English or have been reviewed in English-language publications.

49 Maududi 1992: 13.

50 Esposito and Voll 2001: 28.

51 Ahmad 1986: 20.

52 Mentioned in Esposito and Voll 2001: 88–9.

53 Ibid.: 60.

54 Jameelah 1990: 16–17.

55 Karam 1998: 217.

56 Esposito 1993: 96.

57 Milton-Edwards 1999: 64.

58 Ibid.: 67.

59 For a detailed account of the party, see Taji-Farouki 1996.

60 Ḥizb al-Taḥrīr n.d.: 2–3.

61 See al-Nabaḥānī 1998.

62 *Khilafah is the Answer*, 1989: 44.
63 Hizb ut-Tahrir 1996: 25.
64 Hinnebusch 1996: 200.
65 See Vitalis 1997: 99.
66 The exact nature of neo-sufism and the content of its ideology are still debated. See O'Fahey 1990.
67 See for example the Muslim Brotherhood homepage (http://www.ummah.org.uk/ikhwan/index.html), where "building the Muslim individual" is described as the first of the movement's main objectives.
68 Stork 1997: 67.
69 Ibid.: 70.
70 When Ayubi writes that "If it can be argued that the concept of the State in Europe cannot be understood in isolation from the concepts of individualism, liberty and law . . . the Islamic concept of the body-politic cannot be understood in isolation from the concepts of the group (*jama'a* or *umma*), justice (*'adl* or *'adala*) and leadership (*qiyada* or *imama*)," (1998: 7) he does not take into due consideration lived realities.
71 Asad 2003: 197.
72 Cf. Enayat 1982: 92.
73 Eickelman 1989: 203.
74 Cf. Bouhdiba 1985 where the author discusses the issue in terms of "Islamic feminine," "Arab woman," "popular Tunisian opinion," and the like. Still, at the level of literary criticism, source commentary, and general sociological principles, the analysis has its merits as it allows for some plasticity.
75 Hale 1996: 187. See also Kandiyoti (1992) and Young (1993: esp. 285), who dismisses the notion of "Muslim patriarchy" as an orientalist construct. Similarly, in her widely acclaimed study of veiling and honor among Egyptian Bedouin groups Abu-Lughod (1988: 143ff) acknowledges the fact that the negative valuation of sexuality and the ritual pollution that is often associated with women *are* invariably expressed in religious, i.e. Islamic, terms. A closer look, however, reveals that such negative value is primarily associated with the social order, in the case of the Egyptian Bedouin with the importance attributed to patrilineal parallel-cousin marriage as a safeguard of the solidarity of agnatic kin groups.
76 Karam 1998: 210 (inverted commas in the original). See also pp. 186, 192, 216–17.
77 Ibid.: 176.
78 See Roy 1994.
79 As an Egyptian acquaintance was telling me, veiled women can be identified and these days their numbers are growing at an impressive speed. I do not deny the value of this assertion; however, I find the following example more indicative of how pervasive this consensus may be. To assist young pupils learning the Arabic alphabet, the Egyptian primary education language books contain photographs that correspond to particular letters. For the letter *m*, the corresponding photograph depicts a *muḥāggiba*, i.e. veiled woman (Starrett 1996: 132).
80 As Karam (1998: 177) rightly observes, polygyny and male control are not often discussed *per se*.

81 See for example, Muhammad Mahmoud (1996: 260) for Rashīd al-Ghannūshī's views on the subject.

82 Indeed, there are authors who choose to approach marriage as a strictly legal contractual agreement between two individual sovereign parties declaring that it can include a stipulation against further parallel marital unions (Begam 1980: 15). On closer inspection, however, the situation is proved to be more complex. It is true that marriage (*niqāḥ*) is *par excellence* a contract (*'acd*) in accordance with the *Qur'ānic* use of the term (Rayner 1991: 88), thus allowing for specific conditions, but not terms, to be stipulated (ibid.: 357). It is also true that the wife occupies the position of "a contracting party" rather than "a sale-object" (Coulson 2001: 14). However, "the husband, as a quasi-purchaser, occupies the dominant position" (ibid.: 15). More specifically, the Ḥanafī, Mālikī, and Shāfi'ī legal schools recognize that "any condition which seeks to modify or contradict the established rights of the parties . . . [such as] the right of the husband to take three additional wives . . . is itself void and regarded as non-existent while the contract remains valid" (ibid.: 189–90). Only Ḥanbalī law, for reasons which cannot be discussed here, endorses "the principle of individual freedom to regulate contractual relations" (ibid.: 190), and since the primary purpose of Middle Eastern reformers has been the amelioration of the position of women under the law, this has been adopted to varying degrees by many Arab countries (Egypt in 1926, Jordan in 1951). Nonetheless, generally the fact has remained that "the husband's established powers could not be curtailed without his free consent" (ibid.: 208). Besides the broadening of the law in a Ḥanbalī direction, some attempts to overcome this by way of *ijtihād* (see ch. 2) have also been made: first in Syria (1953), then in Tunisia (1957), where polygyny was prohibited outright, Morocco (1958), Iraq (1959), and Pakistan (1961). All in all, though, as anthropologists know very well, local practice, precedent, and cultural logic often work irrespective of the content and stated purposes of the law, be it Islamic or otherwise.

83 Ali n.d.: 1.

84 Indeed, for Islamists it is the importance of motherhood that prompts men to keep women within bounds. See Saktanber (2002: 221) for Turkish Islamists. At the institutional level more than 20 Arab countries have ratified the Convention for the Elimination of All Forms of Discrimination Against Women, the 1994 action plan of the International Conference on Population and Development. However, as a recent report of the Egyptian National Council for Women indicates in the Middle East and North Africa "[l]ess than one-third of women participate in the labour force, the lowest among all regions" (Ezzat 2004, 20).

85 Lamya n.d.: 3.

86 *Charter of Hamas*, article 18.

87 Karam 1998: 180–1. Interestingly, the *shaykh* maintains that these natural differences in disposition, which make men and women complementary, are based on chemical differences in their respective cells.

88 Quoted ibid.: 190.

89 Recently, al-Qaradāwī was not allowed to enter the USA "because of his support for 'martyrdom operations' in Israel" (al-Yafai 2004: 8). On the other

hand, British authorities did not find sufficient evidence of any criminal offense and allowed the *shaykh* to enter the UK.

90 Karam 1998: 194.

91 al-Qaradāwī 1992: 87.

92 Karam 1998: 210, 212.

93 Ibid.: 219.

94 Ibid.: 231.

95 This view belongs to a more general understanding of feminism by Islamist women activists as a response to the serious exploitation Western women have been subjected to in their societies by male chauvinism and capitalism. But even then, feminism is presented as an extremist ideology that seeks to equate women with men, thus denying their complementarity and, indirectly, the importance of motherhood. See Saktanber (1994: 116–19) for Turkish Islamism.

96 Karam 1998: 221.

97 Ibid.: 223.

98 Ibid.: 230.

99 Hale 1997: 238. See Mernissi 1988: 9. In an earlier publication Mernissi had made a similar point. As she argued with special reference to Morocco, "the state constitutes a threat and a mighty rival to the male as both father and husband . . . By providing a nation-wide state school system and an individual salary for working wives, daughters, and sons, the state has destroyed two pillars of the father's authority" (1975 [1985]: 172).

Be that as it may, the rise of Islamism in the 1990s and since has changed again the balance reaffirming the traditional religion-couched male bias.

100 Hale 1996: 199–200. It is not necessary to see such women as victims. We can also see them as active agents who, in many instances, take their life in their own hands and do not depend on husbands or other male relatives. In many cases, as Jansen (1987) has shown for Algeria, such women occupy positions which transform their marginality into mediatory power. Among the cases she examines we encounter the mistress of the baths, washers of the dead, servants of the saints, sorcery specialists, fertility advisers, and prostitutes but also service workers and career women. Having said that, it should be remembered that Jansen conducted her fieldwork in 1981–2, that is before the consolidation of the Algerian Islamist movement.

101 Karam 1998: 183–4.

102 Quoted ibid.: 188.

103 al-Qaradāwī 1995: 105.

104 Karam 1998: 220.

105 Hodgkin 1990: 85–6.

106 Abu-Lughod 1998: 250.

107 MacLeod 1992: 111, 113.

108 Ibid.: 122. See also her 1996 article (esp. p. 47) in Singerman and Hoodfar's edited volume (1996) which explores the role of the household in the social and political life of contemporary Egypt. Appreciating the mounting socio-economic difficulties afflicting lower-income urban households, may allow readers to contextualize the indirect appeal that characterizes Islamist discourse.

109 Watson 1994: 152.
110 Hammami 1997: 196.
111 Ibid.: 204. *Al-Mujamaʿ*'s slogan "how can uncovered women and men with Beatle haircuts liberate our holy places?" captured this logic very well (Milton-Edwards 1999: 111).
112 Hammami 1997: 207.
113 Ibid.: 206. At the same time, all emancipatory legislation should be in principle welcomed. See Karam 1998 (esp. chs 5 and 6).
114 Hale 1997: 235. See also Hale 1996.
115 Abu-Lughod 1998: 260.
116 Interestingly, Muslim reformers such as Muḥammad ʿAbduh and Rashīd Riḍā used similar language to that of Lord Cromer (1980ii: 539), the powerful British consul-general, when he described the "position of women in Egypt, and in Mohammedan countries generally . . . [as] a fatal obstacle to the attainment of that elevation of thought and character which should accompany the introduction of European civilisation."
117 For a comprehensive history of Egyptian feminism and its relation to nationalism and political rights up to the 1940s, see Badran 1995.
118 Abu-Lughod 1998: 263. In the same article, Abu-Lughod also discusses the ways in which modernist visions concerning education, work, and marriage have informed the plots of popular television serials (*musalsala*) in Egypt. For a more extended discussion of such productions, see Armbrust 1996. These serials, especially the Egyptian and Syrian ones, are very important channels of dissemination of such ideals due to their popularity throughout the Middle East, as I had the chance to discover myself when watching television in the Sudan.
119 Here Abu-Lughod has been influenced by the work of Partha Chatterjee of the *Subaltern Studies* group (1989, 1993), who problematizes the meaning of "authenticity" in the context of Indian nationalism.
120 See Hoodfar 1997 for the case of Iran. It is important to note here that since the 1990s in many Middle Eastern countries a long discussion has started concerning the establishment of academic departments and institutes of Women's or Gender Studies. In Egypt, this project has been explored by the American University in Cairo (AUC) with the participation of several well-known anthropologists like Cynthia Nelson, Lila Abu-Lughod, Sondra Hale, Soheir Morsy, Sorayi Altorki, and others. In 1998 the AUC published the proceedings of the *Arab Regional Women's Studies Workshop*, which had taken place the previous year (Nelson and Altorki 1998). In my view, among the issues discussed in the edited volume, four are the most important: first, the possibility of developing non-Western types of feminism in the Middle East; second, the possibility of developing types of Islamist feminism; third, the need to develop locally those theoretical tools which would correspond to the political practices and potentialities of the local feminist movement; and fourth, the need to analyze the legacy of the region's colonial past and the capabilities of its post-colonial present. All four issues are intimately connected with what many workshop participants called "the West/Middle East dichotomy" (p. 113) and with what Abu-Lughod called "East/West politics" (p. 63).

CHAPTER 8 ISLAMISM AT THE LOCAL LEVEL

1 See Zubaida 1993: 26ff.
2 Which nonetheless does not amount to embracing individualism as in the case of Protestant Christian fundamentalism.
3 See ch. 2.
4 See Saad-Ghorayeb 2002: 60.
5 Sivan 1989: 9. See also Sivan 1990b. For the concept of *wilayya* in *sunnī* jurisprudence, see Schacht 1982: 188.
6 For other examples of *shī'a* minority communities in the Gulf area, especially in Kuwait, Bahrain, and eastern Saudi Arabia, see Esposito 1997: 55–6.
7 See also Milton-Edwards (1999: 200) for a brief discussion of *shī'a* influences on the ideology of the *sunnī* Palestinian Islamic Jihād organization.
8 See Abdel-Latif 2004b.
9 See Abdel-Latif 2004d: 27. For some, Ḥizb Allāh's liberation rhetoric has a *shī'a* edge which has been coming out more and more sharply of late. As Asir and Fakiq (2004: 7) write, "[w]ith Shias throughout the region growing increasingly agitated with colonial injustice . . . what seems to be building up (among Lebanese Shia) is a situation that the French-designed Lebanese system may not be able to contain for much longer."
10 Saad-Ghorayeb 2002: 20.
11 Ibid.: 19.
12 Indeed, the nine-member parliamentary bloc of Ḥizb Allāh at that time supported a bill extending President Emile Lahoud's mandate for another three years. The bill is widely seen by many Lebanese parties as one more attempt on the part of Syria, Lahoud's major political ally, to extend its hold on Lebanon. For this reason it has been denounced by the USA and France, which passed a resolution in the UN Security Council condemning it. Still, Ḥizb Allāh's general secretary Sayyid Ḥasan Naṣr Allāh maintained that Syrian troops, who entered Lebanon at the onset of the 1975–90 civil war, should have remained, suggesting that at that point one should have sided with Syria against the USA and Israel (Fakih 2004: 5).
13 Saad-Ghorayeb 2002: 11.
14 Gilsenan 1990: 74.
15 Ibid.: 64. See also Piscatori (2000: 27) who, discussing the logic of Ḥizb Allāh moderation, stresses the decrease in financial support that the party started to suffer from the post-Khomeini Iranian leadership, the factionalism which isolated those who espoused more radical solutions, and the feeling that participation in elections could open previously closed doors in terms of influence and bargaining. And that included not centrally located players, such as other Lebanese political organizations and Syria, the power behind the scenes, but also "the large, landed families whom it had severely criticised" (ibid.: 28).
16 Roy 2004: 76.
17 Ibid.
18 Still, it would not be inaccurate to suggest that Iran is a more open society than Saudi Arabia or Egypt.

19 Besides these two factions, there is a sizeable number of genuine reformists in Iran who press for more radical solutions away from the current Islamist model of government.

20 Featherstone 1996: 12.

21 The only book-length study of the *Ṭālibān* is Ahmad Rashid's 2001 journalistic account of the history and policies of the regime. The basic points of his arguments can be found in his previous (1999) article in *Foreign Affairs*, where Rashid pleaded for US intervention.

22 This distance from central goverment institutions has been portrayed in a disparagingly orientalist style. See Hensher (2001: 4), who ridiculed the idea of an Ussāma bin Lāden trial by the *Ṭālibān* themselves in an Islamic court because they are nothing more than village *mullah*s adjudicating differences concerning sheep and goats.

23 See for example Ahmed and Hart 1984.

24 In a powerful critique, anthropologists Charles Hirschkind and Saba Mahmood (2002) take to task over-zealous American intellectuals who expressed their concern and anger with the plight of Afghan women as victims of the (male) fundamentalists, without referring to the role of the US and Pakistani administrations in the emergence of the *Ṭālibān* movement and without taking into consideration the long-term consequences that the internationally approved Afghan war might have had on the local population as a whole. For the authors, this betrays an unsophisticated view of fundamentalism/Islamism and a misplaced fear of public religion. Finally, I should also note another emblematic moment in the love-to-hate relationship between the *Ṭālibān* regime and the West: the February 2001 destruction of the Bamiyan Buddhist statues. See Goody 2004: 146ff.

25 Haeri 1998: 7.

26 Once more let me emphasize how otherwise progressive intellectuals, who shun the stereotyping of Muslims and try to contextualize current events, do not always understand the importance of this point. Let me quote Žižek (2002: 55), who argues that "even if terrorism burns us all, the US 'war on terrorism' is not our struggle, but a struggle internal to the capitalist universe": "we should 'deconstruct' Afghanistan itself; it never existed 'in itself', it was the creation of outside forces from the very beginning." Reading this quote in context and considering the writer's style, it certainly makes sense, but at a rather populist level. Even his "our struggle" remains tantalizingly vague. This is not enough when dealing with such issues.

27 See Johnson 2003: 55–7; Lesch 1998: 54–5.

28 Warburg 1990.

29 Ibid.: 68.

30 Sidahmed 1996: 192. From this point of view, it seems incredible that the same Ḥasan al-Turābī had argued four years earlier (1983: 244) that an Islamic government is basically a form of parliamentary democracy, as the Islamic law represents the beliefs, and hence the will, of the people. For Turābī's positions on Islam and politics, see el-Affendi 1991.

31 This was part of a much wider process called comprehensive *daʿwa* that was organized by the Ministry of Social Planning under ʿAlī ʿUthmān Muḥammad Ṭāḥa. See de Waal and Abdel Salam 2004: 89ff.

32 Indeed, such was the zeal of the regime that in 1995 the Ministry of Health banned the import of all medicines containing alcohol, including the vital anti-malarial chloroquine (Lesch 1998: 132).

33 Ibid.: 133.

34 I was conducting fieldwork in the country in the period 1988–9.

35 Lesch 1998: 143.

36 In the meantime, Turābī founded the Popular Congress Party. Later, he was put under house arrest for several months before being transferred to al-Khober prison. His personal assistant said that Sudan's ex-strong man had access to television and cooked food brought to him by his family on a daily basis. In an ironic twist, Turābī's son, 'Issām, asked John Garang, the secularist leader of the SPLA and Turābī's lifelong adversary, to intervene with the government on behalf of his father (Nkrumah 2004: 8).

37 Shankland 1999: 90–1. Still, as Nilüfer Göle (n.d.) argues, "[i]t would be an error to situate Kemalism only at the state level and Islamism only at the societal level." For the period up until the 1980s, see Toprak 1993. For an anthropologically inspired collection of articles on Islam in modern Turkey that presents the view of many Turkish intellectuals, see Tapper 1991.

38 Shankland 1999: 92.

39 Saktanber 2002: xvi–xvii.

40 Jenkins 2003: 53. More recently, the AKP was pronounced a conservative Islamic-oriented party (Boland 2004: 3). In another report, this time from the BBC, we read that "Turkey has a mainly Muslim population but a secular government" (http://www.news.bbc.co.uk/go/pr/fr/-1/hi/world/europe/3840133.stm).

41 Boland 2004: 3 (my emphasis).

42 Navaro-Yashin 2002: 7. See also the articles in the previously mentioned Tapper 1991 edited volume.

43 As Navaro-Yashin argues, "[a] dominant secularist discourse about Islam managed not only to imagine but, at least to a certain extent, also to produce truth about Islam" (ibid.: 32). While this may be true, at least to a certain extent, when positing the Islamists and the secular establishment as two faces of the state, we must always acknowledge their different relative distance from what could be called the "deep state."

44 Incidentally, the Court ruled against Sahin, declaring the covering of the head a religious practice in contravention of the university's secular character. On her part, following the same logic of cultural self-actualization, Sahin has appealed against the decision arguing that rather than being an expression of religious belief, the covering of the head indicates a manner of emphasizing her individuality. However, this does not imply an embracing of Western individualism, as Roy (2004: 192ff) seems to imply.

45 Jenkins 2003: 55.

46 The pro-Welfare Party taxi driver who said to Jenkins (2003: 63) in 1995 that "[i]f they lie or steal they may not fear the law, but I am sure they fear God" could very well be a contemporary AKP supporter. In terms of a political science analysis, Kalyvas (2003) has linked the "willingness to moderate" expressed by the party nomenclature to "electoral" and "nonelectoral constraints," the latter referring to the intimate connection between local elites and military establishments.

47 See ch. 2 above.

48 For a more complex analysis, see Zakaria 2004.

49 See Waterbury 1994 and the volume in which this article is included.

50 Interestingly, alongside prominent Muslim reformists such as Muḥammad Rashīd Riḍā and ʿAlī ʿAbd al-Rāziq, Piscatori mentions Yūsuf al-Qaradāwī, the prominent Islamist intellectual mentioned earlier (p. 217).

51 Piscatori 2000: 18. Perhaps here we could mention Abū Musāb al-Zarqāwī, the *sunnī* militant allegedly behind most bomb attacks in Iraq. As the BBC reported, al-Zarqāwī issued a warning against Iraqi elections saying that "[w]e have declared a bitter war against the principle of democracy and all those who seek to enact it." Reputedly, al-Zarqāwī has "attacked democracy as a springboard for 'un-Islamic' practices, claiming that its emphasis on majority rule violated the principle that all laws must come from a divine source" (http://news.bbc.co.uk/go/pr/fr/-/1/hi/world/middle_east/4199363.stm). Still, other considerations, such as the strengthening through elections of the Iraqi *shīʿa* community, should also be taken into account. In all events, without proper fieldwork it is impossible to contextualize such statements. Reporting them is certainly useful, but does not necessarily lead one to a deeper understanding of the local scene.

52 See Krämer 1996: 208; Leca 1996: 60. *Shūra* is one of these woolly concepts which can be used in all sorts of ways by skillful theoreticians, whom al-Azmeh has criticized for complete disregard of the historical context and lack of philosophical precision, see p. 190. The concept of *majlīs shūra* has been widely utilized in the Arab world. Usually, it constitutes an advisory body with little executive power, such as the Egyptian *Shūra* Council, parliament's consultative upper house. Significantly, the last *Shūra* Council in Egypt was largely boycotted by the opposition, which called it a "setback for democracy in Egypt" (El-Din 2004a: 2).

53 Esposito and Piscatori 1991: 440. However, how is one to interpret the words of Iranian President Muhammad Khatami who, in one breath, argued that bowing to the people's will, to *religious* democracy, is the only way forward (Dinmore 2001: 2)?

54 Roy 2004: 80.

55 Ibid.: 81.

56 Ibid.: 4.

57 See Milton-Edwards 1991 for a detailed analysis of the alliance between the Jordanian crown and the Islamists during the 1990–1 Gulf crisis.

58 See Abdallah 2004. For a more macroscopic view of Jordanian political life from the point of view of the monarchy, see Greenwood 2003. Though informative, from an anthropological point of view the study is limited in perspective as the author identifies the key "Jordanian policy-makers" in what he calls the "new liberal bargain" (pp. 250ff) as mainly the government/Palace and the businessmen, and to a lesser extent the Transjordanians working in the public sector.

59 Mishal and Sela 2000: 151.

60 Ibid.: 148.

61 Ibid.: 163.

62 Israel should be factored in here, as its targeted assassination policy directly affects HAMAS's lines of command.

63 And this despite the fact the organization had abandoned violence.

64 See for example Nafie (2004: 3) on the censoring by the Egyptian authorities of the Brotherhood's official website in September 2004, following the example of Saudi Arabia that had banned the site two months earlier. In a more somber note, the death (June 2004) in custody of Ākram Zuhayrī, the 40-year-old engineer and member of the outlawed group who was arrested on May 16 together with another 53 Brothers, has brought up once more the problem of prison conditions in Egypt (Halawi 2004a: 2).

65 What Shadid (2002: 254) calls "Egypt's moribund political landscape."

66 Abdel Latif 2004a. See in http://weekly.ahram.org.eg/ for a number of articles with up-to-date information and analysis on the positioning of the Muslim Brotherhood in current Egyptian politics.

67 This does not refer only to their appeal to the general public, which should become the subject of detailed studies, but also to the failure of their political initiatives. See for example Abdel-Latif 2004c. It is no coincidence that while analysts condone their pragmatism, they push them more towards the path of reform, demanding gestures which, in the end, can only transform them into something significantly different, on the model of contemporary European Christian Democrats. See for example el-Choubaki 2003, 2004 and Hassan 2004. In a parallel development, a number of Brothers belonging to a younger generation have formed the Centre Party. Schematically, the difference between the new party and the Brotherhood, visualized in generational terms, is that the older generation Brothers regard the *sharī'a* as the unalterable will of God, while the younger ones "admit that their ideas are politically disputable, not divine mandates" (Shahine 2004: 3; Shadid 2002: 254ff).

68 Metzger 1995: 17.

69 A recent Arab League survey describes Yemen as the poorest Middle Eastern country, with an average annual per capita income of US$508 (Willems 2004a: 7).

70 Willems 2004b: 7. Talking about "education" of prisoners, it should be remembered here that a large percentage of people incarcerated in concentration camps located in extra-legal zones (such as the Guantánamo base) are Muslims. At one level, this has brought together many lawyers and political activists in an effort to formulate a legal framework that can assist those trapped in what the admittedly conservative *Financial Times* has called "a legal no-man's land, a system owing more to Kafka than American jurisprudence" (Hilton 2004:W1). For an interesting article on Kafkaesque politics in relation to Islam, see Noumoff 2004:11.

71 Among the latter was Jarāllah 'Umar, the deputy-secretary general of the Yemeni Socialist Party. Most of the Christian victims were related to the American Southern Baptist Church, which has been operating in Yemen for 35 years. Reputedly, the militant group Islamic Army of Aden-Abyan, which had connections with Ussāma bin Lāden and Abū Ḥamza al-Maṣrī, the well-known preacher at Finsbury Park mosque in London, has been training in the area of Ḥuttāt since the 1990s. Several members of the group had been previously in Afghanistan (Whitaker 2003: 22).

72 Mahmoud 1996: 251.
73 With the important exceptions of a 2002 synagogue bombing and a Tunisian economics student at the Autonomous University of Madrid, who participated in the 2004 Madrid bomb attacks.
74 Some of the men were later indicted for the stoning to death of an inebriated man.
75 The ex-Afghan *mujāhid imām* ʿAbd al-Wahāb Raqīqī, one of the leaders of *al-Ṣirāṭ al-Mustaqīm*, "had expressed clear support for the 11 September attacks and hailed Osama Bin Laden as a hero" (Alaoui 2003a: 4).
76 *Middle East International*, 2003a: 20.
77 *Middle East International*, 2003b: 25. It is indicative that the PJD was advised by the Ministry of the Interior not to participate in the march against terrorism that drew up to 25,000 people in Casablanca on May 25, 2003.
78 It was feared that human rights organizations would be lumped together with the PJD (*Middle East International*, 2003c: 20).
79 *Middle East International*, 2003d: 25.
80 Byrne 2003a, 2003b. The Palace won a subsidiary battle, too: PJD MP Muṣṭafā Rāmid, who supports a strict implementation of the *sharīʿa*, stepped down as leader of the party's parliamentary group.
81 Spencer 1996: 93.
82 Ibid.: 101.
83 Cf. Roberts 1991. Still, just like the Tunisian Islamists, the FIS never managed to win over organized labor. That was due to a number of factors that had to do with the manner in which labor unions were organized and with their relationship with the government. See Alexander 2000.
84 See Tuquoi 2001 and Silverstein 2002. Challenging the dominant approach to conspiracy theorizing as a "subaltern truth regime," Silverstein argues

> in general [it] tends to underwrite a general hegemonic process that reproduces both state and oppositional subjects . . . by highlighting certain truisms – that the government and the military are closely related, or that the military benefits from a state of war – and taking them to their logical extremes . . . it confers authority simultaneously to the accuser and the accused (pp. 664–6).

85 Even nature seems to have conspired against the Algerian government. With more than 2,000 dead and 10,000 injured in the devastating May 2003 earthquake, Algerians blamed the government for the poor quality of the apartment blocks which collapsed so easily. Even the Algerian president was forced to flee the area of devastation under a hail of stones and the cries "the authorities are killers" (Alaoui 2003b: 6).
86 See Vandewalle 1997.
87 See Saleh 2003: 23 and Howeidy 2004: 7.
88 In the pre-9/11 days perhaps this was more easily acknowledged. See for example Wright's 1992 article on the subject in the influential *Foreign Affairs*. Despite its ideological conservatism and the objectification of "the West" and "Islam," it can now be read as a premonition of things to come.

89 This view is also espoused by "liberal" analysts in the West. See for example Zakaria (2004: 120), who writes that "[t]he Arab rulers of the Middle East are autocratic, corrupt, and heavy-handed. But they are still more liberal, tolerant, and pluralistic than what would likely replace them." Cf. Asad (2003: 195–200) for a more theoretically robust view on the issue.
90 Sivan 1990a: 39.
91 Husain 1995: 55.
92 Sivan 1990a: 30. On Quṭb's understanding of the *sharīʿa*, see Bœk Simonsen 2003.
93 Sivan 1990a: 31.
94 Ibid.: 42.
95 Ibid.: 43.
96 The quotation is from ʿAbd al-Salām Faraj, ideologue of the group that assassinated President Anwar Sadat in October 1981; mentioned in Sivan 1990a: 20. See Jansen 1986.
97 Milton-Edwards 1999: 194. The internal quotation comes from the *Charter* of HAMAS.
98 Gellner 1993b: 1. Quoted in Milton-Edwards 1999: 194.
99 Ibid.: 196. For the "Islamic essence" that HAMAS sees at the center of the Palestinian cause, see Litvak 1998.
100 Saad-Ghorayeb 2002: 70.
101 Ibid.: 80, 86.
102 Even in the post-9/11 era, the crystal-clear 1990s position held by Jamāʿa al-Islāmiyya that "[t]here will be no dialogue until one side is victorious over the other, or the Islamic regime is established" (Qasim 1997: 318) is definitely chilling. Perphaps predictably, the current position of the organization has changed.
103 Sivan 1990a: esp. ch. 2.
104 In this respect, I disagree with Roy's assertion (2004: 57) that "Osama Bin Laden has lived in a pre-Leninist world."
105 Aretxaga 2001: 149.
106 Jack Goody (2004: 1) argues that for President G.W. Bush, the "War on Terror" has all the characteristics of a "holy war" of the "Judaeo-Christian civilization . . . against Islam."
107 Aretxaga 2001: 141. Cf. Brill on the political nature of the labeling process:

> [t]errorism awakens the inborn human horror of mysterious, malign contact. It can strike anywhere in the guise of anyone. Terrorists are the ideal "unknown," an incomprehensible Other – at once sub- and superhumanly relentless. Like evil itself, they cannot be understood, only labeled. They cannot be persuaded to quit their wickedness, but must be compelled to do so . . . or killed. (2003: 88)

108 Aretxaga 2001: 147.
109 Ibid.: 145.
110 Though certainly this can be true to a certain extent – or false, as we saw in the case of the Egyptian Muslim Brotherhood which eschewed violence after the experience of systematic and long-term repression.
111 Robben and Nordstrom 1995: 2–3.

112 In relation to this, I find interesting Peteet's 1994 article on male gender and rituals of resistance in the Palestinian *intifāḍa*. As she argues,

> [v]iolence has almost diametrically opposed meanings. For one, it is an index of fictionalized fear and image of inferiority of a subject population and is intended to control and dishonor; for the others, it is constitutive of a resistant subjectivity that signals heroism, manhood and access to leadership and authority.

The article does not focus on Islamists, though a large percentage of those who find themselves beaten or imprisoned by the Israeli authorities in the occupied territories are members of Islamist political organizations. Moreover, Peteet's analysis reveals the gendered character of violence, as this assumes different forms upon, and elicits different responses from, male and female bodies.

113 Jean-Klein 2001: 84.

114 Ibid.: 114.

References

Abdallah, Sana. 2004. "Running out of Tolerance." *Al-Ahram Weekly*, Sept. 16–22: 7.

Abdel-Latif, Omayma. 2001. "A Crusade of the Mind." *Al-Ahram Weekly Online*, Sept. 20–26 (issue no. 552). In http://weekly.ahram.org.eg/2001/552/p3fall3htm.

Abdel-Latif, Omayma. 2004a. "Settling for Small Steps." *Al-Ahram Weekly Online*, Jan. 22–28 (issue no. 674). In http://weekly.ahram.org.eg/2004/674/eg5.htm.

Abdel-Latif, Omayma. 2004b. "Resistance lives on." *Al-Ahram Weekly*, May 6–12: 9.

Abdel-Latif, Omayma. 2004c. "Political Rapprochement." *Al-Ahram Weekly*, Aug. 5–11: 1.

Abdel-Latif, Omayma. 2004d. "The Voice of the Ayatollah." *Al-Ahram Weekly*, Sept. 2–8: 2.

Abdullahi, Abdullahi Osman. 1980. "Conceptualisation, Etiology and Treatment of Illness among the Berti People of Northern Darfur, Sudan." Unpublished MA dissertation, Queen's University of Belfast.

Abu-Lughod, L. 1988. *Veiled Sentiments: Honor and Poetry in a Bedouin Society*. Berkeley: University of California Press.

Abu-Lughod, L. 1989. "Zones of Theory in the Anthropology of the Arab World." *Annual Review of Anthropology*, 18: 267–306.

Abu-Lughod, L. 1993. Review of "Boddy, J. 1989. *Wombs and Alien Spirits: Women, Men, and the Zār Cult in Northern Sudan*. Madison: The University of Wisconsin Press." *American Ethnologist*, 20, 2: 425–6.

Abu-Lughod, L. 1998. "The Marriage of Feminism and Islamism in Egypt: Selective Repudiation as a Dynamic of Postcolonial Cultural Dynamics." In Abu-Lughod, L. (ed.). 1998. *Remaking Women: Feminism and Modernity in the Middle East*, pp. 243–69. Princeton, N.J.: Princeton University Press.

Abu-Manneh, Butrus. 1994. "The Islamic Roots of the Gülhane Rescript." *Die Welt des Islams*, 34: 173–203.

Abu-Rabi, Ibrahim, M. 1999. "John Paul II and Islam." In Sherwin, B.L. and Kasimow, H. (eds) *John Paul II and Interreligious Dialogue*, pp. 187–208. New York: Orbis Books.

Abu-Saud, Mahmoud. 1993. "Economics within Transcendence." *Islamica*, 1, 2: 4–9.

Abu-Zahra, N. 2000. "Islamic History, Islamic Identity and the Reform of Islamic Law: The Thought of Husayn Ahmad Amin." In Cooper, J., Nettler, R., and

Mahmoud, M. (eds). *Islam and Modernity: Muslim Intellectuals Respond*, pp. 82–104. London: I.B. Tauris.

El-Affendi, Abdelwahab. 1991. *Turabi's Revolution: Islam and Power in the Sudan.* London: Grey Seal.

Ahmad, Israr. 1986. *Islamic Renaissance: the Real Task Ahead.* London: Ta-ha Publishers.

Ahmad, Khursid. 1995. *Islam and the West.* Delhi: Markazi Maktaba Islami.

Ahmed, Akbar S. 1990. *Discovering Islam: Making Sense of Muslim History and Society.* London: Routledge.

Ahmed, Akbar S. 1992. *Postmodernism and Islam: Predicament and Promise.* London: Routledge.

Ahmed, Akbar S. 1993. *Living Islam: From Samarkand to Stornoway.* London: BBC Books.

Ahmed, Akbar S. and Donnan, H. 1994. "Islam in the Age of Postmodernity." In Ahmed, Akbar S. and Donnan, H. (eds) *Islam, Globalization and Postmodernity*, pp. 1–20. London: Routledge.

Ahmed, Akbar S. and Hart, D. 1984. *Islam in Tribal Societies: From the Atlas to the Indus.* London: Routledge & Kegan Paul.

Ahmed, Akbar S. and Shore, C.N. 1995. "Introduction: Is Anthropology Relevant to the Contemporary World?" In Ahmed, Akbar S. and Shore, C.N. (eds). *The Future of Anthropology: Its Relevance to the Contemporary World*, pp. 12–45. London: Athlone Press.

Al-Ahram Weekly. 2003. "Ramadan in Baghdad," Oct. 30–Nov. 5: 1.

Alaoui, Hassan. 2003a. "Thunderbolt in Casablanca." *Al-Ahram Weekly Online.* May 22–28 (issue no. 639). In http://weekly.ahram.org.eg/2003/639/re4.htm.

Alaoui, Hassan. 2003b. "Death, Destruction and Anger." *Al-Ahram Weekly Online.* May 29–June 4 (issue no. 640). In http://weekly.ahram.org.eg/2003/640/re6.htm.

Alexander, C. 2000. "Opportunities, Organizations, and Ideas: Islamists and Workers in Tunisia and Algeria." *International Journal of Middle East Studies*, 32: 465–90.

Ali, Abdullah Yusuf. 1975. *The Holy Quran: Text, Translation and Commentary.* Leicester: The Islamic Foundation.

Ali, M. n.d. "Who Practices Polygamy?" III&E Brochure Series: no. 13. In http://www.allrecipes.com/cb/w2m/seaspec/holiday/ramadan/default3.asp.

Ali, Tariq. 2002. *The Clash of Fundamentalisms.* London: Verso.

Alvi, Tayyab Urfi (ed.). 1997. *Daily and Occasional Du'a: Arabic Text, Transliteration and Translation.* Delhi: Royal Publishers and Distributors.

Amin, Galal. 2004. "The Middle Way: Middle Egypt is a Curious Mix of the Secular and the Sacred, the New and the Old, the Foreign and the Local." *Al-Ahram Weekly*, Feb. 12–18: 8.

Anderson, B. 1992. *Imagined Communities.* London: Verso.

Anderson, J.N.D. 1968. "Law Reform in Egypt: 1850–1950." In Holt, P.M. (ed.) *Political and Social Change in Egypt: Historical Studies from the Ottoman Conquest to the United Arab Republic*, pp. 209–30. London: Oxford University Press.

Anderson, J.W. 2002. "Internet Islam: New Media of the Islamic Reformation." In Bowen, D.L. and Early, E.E. (eds) *Everyday Life in the Muslim Middle East*, pp. 300–5. Bloomington: Indiana University Press.

Anthony of Sourozh (Metropolitan). 1999a. *Living Prayer.* London: Darton, Longman and Todd.

Anthony of Sourozh (Metropolitan). 1999b. *School for Prayer.* London: Darton, Longman and Todd.

Antoun, R.T. 2000. "Civil Society, Tribal Process, and Change in Jordan: an Anthropological View." *International Journal of Middle East Studies*, 32: 441–63.

Appadurai, A. 1996. "Disjuncture and Difference in the Global Cultural Economy." In Featherstone, M. (ed.) *Global Culture: Nationalism, Globalization and Modernity*, pp. 295–310. London: Sage.

Appadurai, A. 1997. *Modernity at Large: Cultural Dimensions of Globalization.* Minneapolis: University of Minnesota Press.

Aretxaga, B. 2001. "Terror as Thrill: First Thoughts on the 'War on Terrorism.'" *Anthropological Quarterly*, 75, 1: 139–50.

Armbrust, W. 1996. *Mass Culture and Modernism in Egypt.* Cambridge: Cambridge University Press.

Armbrust, W. 2002. "The Riddle of Ramadan: Media, Consumer Culture, and the 'Christmasization' of a Muslim Holiday." In Bowen, D.L. and Early, E.E. (eds) *Everyday Life in the Muslim Middle East*, pp. 335–48. Bloomington: Indiana University Press.

Asad, T. 1986. "The Idea of an Anthropology of Islam." Center for Contemporary Arab Studies Occasional Papers, Washington, DC: Georgetown University.

Asad, T. 1993. *Genealogies of Religion: Discipline and Reasons of Power in Christianity and Islam.* Baltimore: John Hopkins University Press.

Asad, T. 1996. "Modern Power and the Reconfiguration of Religious Traditions: Interviewed by Mahmood, S." *SEHR*, 5, 1: *Contested Polities.* Updated February 27. http://www.stanford.edu/group/SHR/5-1/text/asad.html.

Asad, T. 2003. *Formations of the Secular: Christianity, Islam, Modernity.* Stanford, Calif.: Stanford University Press.

Ashcroft, B. 2001. *Post-Colonial Transformation.* London: Routledge.

Ashkanani, Zubaydah. 1991. "Zar in a Changing World: Kuwait." In Lewis, I.M., al-Safi, Ahmed and Hurreiz, Sayyid (eds) *Women's Medicine: the Zar-Bori Cult in Africa and Beyond*, pp. 219–29. Edinburgh: Edinburgh University Press.

Asir, S. and Fakiq, Mohalhel. 2004. "Foregone Conclusion." *Al-Ahram Weekly*, May 27–June 2: 7.

Auda, Gehad. 1991. "An Uncertain Response: the Islamic Movement in Egypt." In Piscatori, J. (ed.) *Islamic Fundamentalisms and the Gulf Crisis*, pp. 109–30. The Fundamentalism Project. Chicago: American Academy of Arts and Sciences.

Ayoub, M. 1999. "Pope John Paul II and Islam." In Sherwin, B.L. and Kasimow, H. (eds) *John Paul II and Interreligious Dialogue*, pp. 171–86. New York: Orbis Books.

Ayubi, Nazih. 1998. *Political Islam: Religion and Politics in the Arab World.* London: Routledge.

Al-Azmeh, Aziz. 1992. "Barbarians in Arab Eyes." *Past and Present*, 134: 3–18.

Al-Azmeh, Aziz. 1996. *Islams and Modernities.* London: Verso.

Badiou, A. 2003. *Saint Paul: the Foundation of Universalism.* Stanford, Calif.: Stanford University Press.

Badran, M. 1995. *Feminists, Islam, and Nation: Gender and the Making of Modern Egypt.* Princeton, N.J.: Princeton University Press.

Baer, G. 1968. "Social Change in Egypt: 1800–1914." In Holt, P.M. (ed.) *Political and Social Change in Egypt: Historical Studies from the Ottoman Conquest to the United Arab Republic*, pp. 135–61. London: Oxford University Press.

Bakhtiar, L. 1995. *Ramadan: Motivating Believers to Action. An Interfaith Perspective.* Chicago: The Institute for Traditional Psychoethics and Guidance.

Barber, K. 1989. "Interpreting Oríkì as History and as Literature." In Barber, K. and de Moreas Farias, P.F. (eds) *Discourse and its Disguises: the Interpretation of African Oral Texts*, pp. 13–23. Birmingham University African Studies Series 1. Centre of West African Studies. Birmingham: University of Birmingham.

Barth, F. 1992. "Towards Greater Naturalism in Conceptualizing Societies." In Kuper, A. (ed.) *Conceptualizing Society*, pp. 17–33. London: Routledge.

Beaumont, P. 2001. "The Roots of Islamic Anger." *Observer*, Oct. 14: 24.

Begam, Nawab Sultan Jahan. 1980. *Muslim Married Couple.* New Delhi: Awaru Publishing House.

Beinin, J. and Stork, J. (eds). 1997. *Political Islam: Essays from Middle East Report.* London: I.B. Tauris.

Bellér-Hann, I. and Hann, C. 2001. *Turkish Region.* Oxford: James Currey.

Benthall, J. 1999. "Financial Worship: The Quranic Injunction to Alms-giving." *Journal of the Royal Anthropological Society*, 5, 1: 27–42.

Benthall, J. 2002. "Organised Charity in the Arab-Islamic World: a View from the NGOs." In Donan, H. (ed.) *Interpreting Islam*, pp. 150–66. London: Sage.

Berman, P. 2003. *Terror and Liberalism.* New York: W. W. Norton.

Beshir, M.O. 1968. *The Southern Sudan: Background to Conflict.* London: C. Hurst.

Beshir, M.O. 1975. *The Southern Sudan: from Conflict to Peace.* Khartoum: The Khartoum Bookshop.

Bhabha, H. 2000. *The Location of Culture.* London: Routledge.

Binder, L. 1988. *Islamic Liberalism: a Critique of Development Ideologies.* Chicago: University of Chicago Press.

Bjorgo, T. 1997. " 'The Invaders,' 'the Traitors' and 'the Resistance Movement': The Extreme Right's Conceptualisation of Opponents and Self in Scandinavia." In Modood, T. and Werbner, P. (eds) *The Politics of Multiculturalism in the New Europe: Racism, Identity and Community*, pp. 54–72. London: Zed Books.

Blanks, D. (ed.) 1997. *Images of the Other: Europe and the Muslim World before 1700.* Cairo: American University in Cairo Press.

Bledsoe, C.H. and Robey, K.M. 1986. "Arabic Literacy and Secrecy among the Mende of Sierra Leone." *Man*, 22, 2: 202–26.

Bloch, M. 1974. "Symbols, Songs, Dance and Features of Articulation or is Religion an Extreme Form of Authority?" *Archives Européenes de Sociologie*, 15 (1): 55–81.

Bloch, M. 1975. *Political Language and Oratory in Traditional Societies.* New York: Academic Press.

Bloch, M. (ed.) 1984. *Marxist Analyses and Social Anthropology.* ASA Studies, London: Tavistock Publications.

Bloch, M. 1985. *Marxism and Anthropology.* Oxford: Oxford University Press.

Bloch, M. 1986. *From Blessing to Violence: History and Ideology in the Circumcision Ritual of the Merina of Madagascar.* Cambridge: Cambridge University Press.

Bloch, M. 1989. *Ritual, History and Power: Selected Papers in Anthropology.* London: Athlone Press.

Bloch, M. 1992. *Prey into Hunter: the Politics of Religious Experience*. Cambridge: Cambridge University Press.

Boddy, J. 1989. *Wombs and Alien Spirits: Women, Men, and the Zār Cult in Northern Sudan*. Madison: University of Wisconsin Press.

Bœk Simonsen, J. 2003. "Sharia and Sunna in the Qur'an and in the Writings of Sayyid Qutb." In Kastfelt, N. (ed.) *Scriptural Politics: the Bible and the Koran as Political Models in the Middle East and Africa*, pp. 55–65. London: Hurst.

Boland, V. 2004. "Spotlight Falls on Rebuilding Political Links between the US and Turkey." *Financial Times*, June 26–7: 3.

Bouhdiba, Abdelwahab. 1985. *Sexuality in Islam*. London: Routledge & Kegan Paul.

Bowen, D.L. 2002. "Abu Illya and Zakat." In Bowen, D.L. and Early, E.E. (eds) *Everyday Life in the Muslim Middle East*, pp. 262–5. Bloomington: Indiana University Press.

Bowen, J.R. 1989. "*Salat* in Indonesia: the Social Meanings of an Islamic Ritual." *Man*, n.s. 24, 4: 600–19.

Bowie, F. 2003. *The Anthropology of Religion*. Malden, Mass.: Blackwell.

Bowman, G. 1991. "Christian Ideology and the Image of a Holy Land: the Place of Jerusalem Pilgrimage in the various Christianities." In Eade, J. and Sallnow, M.J. (eds) *Contesting the Sacred: the Anthropology of Christian Pilgrimage*, pp. 98–121. London: Routledge.

Brahimi, Abdelhamid. 1996. "The Origin of Islamic Economics." *Islamica*, 2, 3: 3–13.

Braudel, F. 2001. *History of Civilisations*. Athens: MIET (Greek transln).

Brenner, L. (ed.). 1993. *Muslim Identity and Social Change in Sub-Saharan Africa*. London: Hurst.

Brett, M. and Fentress, E. 2002. *The Berbers*. Malden, Mass.: Blackwell.

Brill, L. 2003. "Terrorism, Crowds and Power, and the Dogs of War." *Anthropological Quarterly*, 76, 1: 87–94.

Brown, N.J. 1997. "Sharia and State in the Modern Muslim Middle East." *International Journal of Middle East Studies*, 29: 359–76.

Buaben, Jabal Muhammad. 1996. *Image of the Prophet Muhammad in the West: a Study of Muir, Margoliouth and Watt*. Leicester: The Islamic Foundation.

Buitelaar, M. 1993. *Fasting and Feasting in Morocco*. Oxford: Berg.

Bukhari, Sahih. "Book 7: Rubbing Hands and Feet with Dust (Tayammum)." http://www.usc.edu/dept/MSA/fundamentals/hadithsunnah/bukhari/007.sbt.html.

Bunt, G. 2002. "Studying Islam after 9–11: Reflections and Resources." *PRS-LTSN Journal*, 1, 2: 156–64.

Burton, J. 2001. *An Introduction to the Hadith*. Edinburgh: Edinburgh University Press.

Byrne, E. 2003a. "Women's Rights." *Middle East Report*, Oct. 24: 24.

Byrne, E. 2003b. "Before and After." *Middle East Report*, Nov. 7: 24–6.

Cardini, F. 2001. *Europe and Islam*. Malden, Mass.: Blackwell.

Casanova, J. 1994. *Public Religions in the Modern World*. Chicago: University of Chicago Press.

Caton, S.C. 1990. *Peaks of Yemen I Summon: Poetry as Cultural Practice in a North Yemeni Tribe*. Berkeley: University of California Press.

Chadwick, O. 1995. *The Secularization of the European Mind in the 19th Century*. Cambridge: Cambridge University Press.

Charter of Hamas. http://womeningreen.org/hamas.html.
Chatterjee, P. 1989. "Colonialism, Nationalism, and Colonized Women: the Contest in India." *American Ethnologist*, 16, 4: 622–33.
Chatterjee, P. 1993. *The Nation and its Fragments: Colonial and Postcolonial Histories*. Princeton, N.J.: Princeton University Press.
Childs, P. and Williams, P. 1997. *An Introduction to Post-Colonial Theory*. London: Prentice Hall.
El-Choubaki, Amr. 2003. "Speaking in Tongues." *Al-Ahram Weekly Online*. Nov. 6–12 (issue no. 663). In http://weekly.ahram.org.eg/2003/663/eg1.htm.
El-Choubaki, Amr. 2004. "An Excuse for Inaction." *Al-Ahram Weekly*, Aug. 12–18: 13.
Choueiri, Youssef M. 1996. "The Political Discourse of Contemporary Islamist Movements." In Sidahmed, Abdel Salam and Ehteshami, Anoushiravan (eds) *Islamic Fundamentalism*, pp. 19–33. Boulder, Colo.: Westview Press.
Choueiri, Youssef M. 2000. *Arab Nationalism: a History*. Oxford: Blackwell.
Christmann, A. 2000. "Islamic Scholar and Religious Leader: Shaikh Muhammad Sa'id Ramadan al-Buti." In Cooper, J., Nettler, R., and Mahmoud, M. (eds) *Islam and Modernity: Muslim Intellectuals Respond*, pp. 57–81. London: I.B. Tauris.
Cole, J.R.I. and Kandiyoti, D. 2002. "Nationalism and the Colonial Legacy in the Middle East and Central Asia: Introduction." *International Journal of Middle East Studies*, 34: 189–203.
Colonna, F. 1984. "Cultural Resistance and Religious Legitimacy in Colonial Algeria." In Ahmed, Akbar S. and Hart, D. (eds) *Islam in Tribal Societies: From the Atlas to the Indus*, pp. 106–26. London: Routledge and Kegan Paul.
Combs-Schilling, M.E. 1989. *Sacred Performances: Islam, Sexuality and Sacrifice*. New York: Columbia University Press.
Connerton, P. 1995. *How Societies Remember*. Cambridge: Cambridge University Press.
Constantinides, P. 1972. "Sickness and the Spirits: a Study of the Zar Spirit Possession Cult in the Northern Sudan." Unpublished PhD thesis, University of London.
Constantinides, P. 1977. "Ill at Ease and Sick at Heart: Symbolic Behaviour in a Sudanese Healing Cult." In Lewis, I.M. (ed.) *Symbols and Sentiment*, pp. 63–84. London: Academic Press.
Constantinides, P. 1979. "Women's Spirit Possession and Urban Adaptation in the Muslim Northern Sudan." In Caplan, A.P. and Bujra, J. (eds) *Women United, Women Divided*, pp. 185–205. Bloomington: Indiana University Press.
Constantinides, P. 1991. "The History of Zar in the Sudan: Theories of Origin, Recorded Observation and Oral Tradition." In Lewis, I.M., al-Safi, Ahmed, and Hurreiz, Sayyid (eds) *Women's Medicine: the Zar-Bori Cult in Africa and Beyond*. Edinburgh: Edinburgh University Press.
Cooper, J. 2000. "The Limits of the Sacred: the Epistemology of 'Abd al-Karim Sorousch." In Cooper, J., Nettler, R., and Mahmoud, M. (eds) *Islam and Modernity: Muslim Intellectuals Respond*, pp. 38–56. London: I.B. Tauris.
Coulson, N.J. 2001. *A History of Islamic Law*. Edinburgh: Edinburgh University Press.
Courbage, Y. and Fargues, P. 1996. *Christians and Jews under Islam*. London: I.B. Tauris.
Crapanzano, V. 1981. *The Ḥamadsha: A Study in Moroccan Ethnopsychiatry*. Berkeley: University of California Press.

Cromer, The Earl of. 1908. *Modern Egypt*. London: Macmillan.
Davis, J. 1987. *Libyan Politics: Tribe and Revolution*. London: I.B. Tauris.
Ḍayf Allāh, Muḥammad al-Nūr b. 1985. *Kitāb al-Ṭabaqāt fī Khuṣūṣ al-Awliyā' wa'l-Ṣāliḥīn wa'l-'Ulamā' wa'l-Shu'arā' fī al-Sūdān*. Khartoum: Khartoum University Press.
De Waal, A. and Abdel Salam, A.H. 2004. "Islamism, State Power and *Jihad* in Sudan." In de Waal, A. (ed.) *Islamism and its Enemies in the Horn of Africa*, pp. 71–113. London: Hurst.
Dekmejian, R.H. 1988. "Islamic Revival: Catalysts, Categories, and Consequences." In Hunter, S.T. (ed.) *The Politics of Islamic Revivalism: Diversity and Unity*, pp. 3–19. Bloomington: Indiana University Press.
Delaney, C. 1990. "The Hajj: Sacred and Secular." *American Ethnologist*, 17, 3: 513–30.
Delaney, C. 1991. *The Seed and the Soil: Gender and Cosmology in Turkish Village Society*. Berkeley: University of California Press.
Deng, F.M. 1973. *Dynamics of Identification: a Basis for National Integration in the Sudan*. Khartoum: Khartoum University Press.
Deng, F.M. 1995. *War of Visions: Conflict of Identities in the Sudan*. Washington DC: The Brookings Institute.
El-Din, Gamal Essam. 2004a. "Shura Turnaround." *Al-Ahram Weekly*, June 24–30: 2.
El-Din, Gamal Essam. 2004b. "Deyar launches 'Umra via Egypt' Programme." *Al-Ahram Weekly*, July 15–21: 3.
Dinmore, G. 2000. "Khatami set to run for Second Term." *Financial Times*, March 12: 2.
Douglas, M. 1985. *Purity and Danger: an Analysis of the Concepts of Pollution and Taboo*. London: Ark Paperbacks.
Doumato, E.A. 2003. "Manning the Barricades: Islam according to Saudi Arabia's School Texts." *Middle East Journal*, 57, 2: 230–47.
Dubish, J. 1995. *In a Different Place: Pilgrimage, Gender and Politics at a Greek Island Shrine*. Princeton, N.J.: Princeton University Press.
Dwyer, K. 1991. *Arab Voices: The Human Rights Debate in the Middle East*. Berkeley: University of California Press.
Eade, J. and Sallnow, M.J. (eds). 1991. *Contesting the Sacred: the Anthropology of Christian Pilgrimage*. London: Routledge.
Early, E.A. 1993. *Baladi Women of Cairo: Playing with an Egg and a Stone*. Cairo: American University in Cairo Press.
Eco, U. 2001. "The Roots of the Conflict." *Saturday Review: The Guardian*, Oct. 13: 2.
Economist (The). 2000. "Arab Intifada: the Armchair Version." Dec. 16: 48–9.
Economist (The). 2001. "Welcome to the Old Kuwait." March 3: 41–2.
Eickelman, D. 1976. *Moroccan Islam: Tradition and Society in a Pilgrimage Center*. Austin: University of Texas Press.
Eickelman, D. 1982a. "The Study of Islam in Local Contexts." *Contribution to Asian Studies*, 17: 1–16.
Eickelman, D. 1982b. *Knowledge and Power in Morocco: the Education of a Twentieth Century Notable*. Princeton, N.J.: Princeton University Press.
Eickelman, D. 1987. "Changing Interpretations of Islamic Movements." In Roff, W.R. (ed.) *Islam and the Political Economy of Meaning: Comparative Studies of Muslim Discourse*, pp. 13–30. Berkeley: University of California Press.

Eickelman, D. 1989. *The Middle East: An Anthropological Perspective*. Englewood Cliffs, N.J.: Prentice Hall.
Eickelman, D.F. 1992. "Mass Higher Education and the Religious Imagination in Contemporary Arab Societies." *American Ethnologist*, 19, 4: 643–55.
Eickelman, D.F. 2002. "Inside the Islamic Reformation." In Bowen, D.L. and Early, E.E. (eds) *Everyday Life in the Muslim Middle East*, pp. 246–56. Bloomington: Indiana University Press.
Eickelman, D.F. and Anderson, J.W. 1997. "Print, Islam, and the Prospects for Civic Pluralism: New Religious Writings and their Audiences." *Journal of Islamic Studies*, 8 (1): 43–62.
Eickelman, D.F. and Anderson, J.W. 1999. "Redefining Muslim Space." In Eickelman, D.F. and Anderson, J.W. (eds) *New Media in the Muslim World: The Emerging Public Sphere*, pp. 1–18. Bloomington: Indiana University Press.
Eickelman, D.F. and Piscatori, J. 1996. *Muslim Politics*. Princeton, N.J.: Princeton University Press.
Enayat, H. 1982. *Modern Islamic Political Thought*. Austin: University of Texas Press.
Esposito, J.L. 1992. *Islam: the Straight Path*. Oxford: Oxford University Press.
Esposito, J.L. 1993. *The Islamic Threat: Myth or Reality*. Oxford: Oxford University Press.
Esposito, J.L. 1997. "Political Islam and Gulf Security." In Esposito, J. (ed.) *Political Islam: Revolution, Radicalism, or Reform?*, pp. 53–74. Boulder, Colo.: Lynne Rienner.
Esposito, J.L. and Piscatori, J.P. 1991. "Democratization and Islam." *Middle East Journal*, 45, 3: 427–40.
Esposito, J.L. and Voll, J.O. 2001. *Makers of Contemporary Islam*. Oxford: Oxford University Press.
Evans-Pritchard, E.E. 1965. *Theories of Primitive Religion*. Oxford: Clarendon Press.
Evans-Pritchard, E.E. 1971. *The Azande: History and Political Institutions*. Oxford: Clarendon Press.
Ezzat, Dina. 2004. "Documenting Gender Bias." *Al-Ahram Weekly*, June 24–30: 20.
Fakih, Mohalhel. 2004. "The Limits of Loyalty." *Al-Ahram Weekly*, Sept. 9–15: 5.
Faure, B. 1996. *Chan Insights and Oversights: an Epistemological Critique of the Chan Tradition*. Princeton, N.J.: Princeton University Press.
Featherstone, M. 1996. "Global Culture: an Introduction." In Featherstone, M. (ed.) *Global Culture: Nationalism, Globalization and Modernity*, pp. 1–14. London: Sage.
Ferchiou, S. 1991. "The Possession Cults of Tunisia: a Religious System functioning as a System of Reference and a Social Field for Performing Actions." In Lewis, I.M., al-Safi, Ahmed, and Hurreiz, Sayyid (eds) *Women's Medicine: the Zar-Bori Cult in Africa and Beyond*, pp. 209–18. Edinburgh: Edinburgh University Press.
Finnegan, R. 1992. *Oral Traditions and the Verbal Arts: a Guide to Research Practices*. London: Routledge.
Firth, R. 1981. "Engagement and Detachment: Reflections on Applying Social Anthropology to Social Affairs." *Human Organization*, 40: 193–201.
Fischer, M.J. and Abedi, M. 1990. *Debating Muslims: Cultural Dialogues in Postmodernity and Tradition*. Madison: University of Wisconsin Press.
Fisk, R. 2001a. "Bush is walking into a Trap." *Independent on Sunday*, Sept. 16: 21.
Fisk, R. 2001b. "Promises, Promises." *Independent: Wednesday Review*, Oct. 17: 1.
Fisk, R. 2002. "A Strange Kind of Freedom." *Independent*, July 9: 17.

Fitzgerald, M.L. 1999. "Pope John Paul II and Interreligious Dialogue: a Catholic Assessment." In Sherwin, B.L. and Kasimow, H. (eds) *John Paul II and Interreligious Dialogue*, pp. 209–22. New York: Orbis Books.

Flores, A. 1997. "Secularism, Integralism, and Political Islam: the Egyptian Debate." In Beinin, J. and Stork, J. (eds) *Political Islam: Essays from Middle East Report*, pp. 83–94. London: I.B. Tauris.

Florofsky, G. 1972. *Bible, Church, Tradition: an Eastern Orthodox View*. Belmont, Mass.: Norland Publishing Company.

Fluehr-Lobban, C. (ed.). 2001. *Against Islamic Extremism: the Writings of Muhammad Sai'id al-'Ashmawy*. Cainesville: University Press of Florida.

Fokas, E. 2004. "The Role of Religion in National–EU Relations: the Cases of Greece and Turkey." Unpublished PhD thesis, University of London.

Freedland, J. 2001. "We can't do it by Bombing." *G2: The Guardian Europe*, Oct. 19: 2–5.

Friedman, J. 1996. "Being in the World: Globalization and Localization." In Featherstone, M. (ed.) *Global Culture: Nationalism, Globalization and Modernity*, pp. 311–28. London: Sage.

Gad, Emad. 2004. "Middle-Class Militancy." *Al-Ahram Weekly*, Sept. 2–8: 13.

Gaffney, P.D. 1994. *The Prophet's Pulpit: Islamic Preaching in Contemporary Egypt*. Berkeley: University of California Press.

Geertz, C. 1971. *Islam Observed: Religious Development in Morocco and Indonesia*. Chicago: University of Chicago Press.

Gefou-Madianou, D. 1999. *Culture and Ethnography: from Ethnographic Realism to Cultural Criticism*. Athens: Ellinika Grammata (in Greek).

Gellner, D.N. 2003. *Anthropology of Buddhism and Hinduism*. New Delhi: Oxford University Press.

Gellner, E. 1985. *Muslim Society*. Cambridge: Cambridge University Press.

Gellner, E. 1987. *Culture, Identity and Politics*. Cambridge: Cambridge University Press.

Gellner, E. 1993a. *Postmodernism, Reason and Religion*. London: Routledge.

Gellner, E. 1993b. *Nations and Nationalism*. Oxford: Blackwell.

George, A. 2003. *Syria: neither Bread nor Freedom*. London: Zed Books.

Gibb, H.A.R. 1947. *Modern Trends in Islam*. Chicago: University of Chicago Press.

Giddens, A. 1990. *The Consequences of Modernity*. Cambridge: Polity Press.

Giddens, A. 1991. *Modernity and Self-Identity*. Cambridge: Polity Press.

Gilsenan, M. 1973. *Saint and Sufi in Modern Egypt: an Essay in the Sociology of Religion*. Oxford: Clarendon Press.

Gilsenan, M. 1990. *Recognizing Islam*. London: I.B. Tauris.

Glassman, J. 1991. "The Bondsman's New Clothes: the Contradictory Consciousness of Slave Resistance on the Swahili Coast." *Journal of African History*, 32: 277–312.

Goddard, H. 2000. "Christian–Muslim Relations: a Look Backwards and a Look Forwards." *Islam and Christian–Muslim Relations*, 11, 2: 195–212.

Golberg, E. 1991. "Smashing Idols and the State: the Protestant Ethic and Egyptian Sunni Tradition." *Comparative Studies in Society and History*, 33: 3–35.

Göle, N. "Islamism and Secularism in Turkey." http://www.umich.edu/~iinet/journal/vol2no2/v2n2_Islamism_and_Secularism_in_Turkey.html.

Goody, J. 1977 (1995). *The Domestication of the Savage Mind*. Cambridge: Cambridge University Press.

Goody, J. 2004. *Islam in Europe*. Cambridge: Polity Press.

Gramsci, A. 1973. *Historical Materialism: Notes from the Prison I*. Athens: Oddyseas (Greek translation).

Greenwood, S. 2003. "Jordan's 'New Bargain': the Political Economy of Regime Security." *Middle East Journal*, 57, 2: 247–69.

Griffith, S.H. 1992. *Arabic Christianity in the Monasteries of Ninth Century Palestine*. Aldershot: Variorum.

Gumbel, A. 2001. "Americans wake up to Ignorance." *The Monday Review: The Independent*, Oct. 15: 7.

Gupta, A. and Ferguson, J. 1992. "Beyond 'Culture': Space, Identity, and the Politics of Difference." *Cultural Anthropology*, 7, 1: 6–23.

Ḥadīth: *EI*.

Ḥadjdj: *EI*.

Haeri, S. 1998. "Freeing Islam from the Taliban." *Al-Ahram Weekly*, Oct. 1–7: 7.

Halawi, Jailan. 2004a. "Deadly Negligence." *Al-Ahram Weekly*, June 17–23: 2.

Halawi, Jailan. 2004b. "Militants arrested." *Al-Ahram Weekly*, July 29–Aug. 4: 2.

Hale, S. 1996. *Gender Politics in Sudan: Islamism, Socialism and the State*. Boulder, Colo.: Westview Press.

Hale, S. 1997. "The Women of Sudan's National Islamic Front." In Beinin, J. and Stork, J. (eds) *Political Islam: Essays from Middle East Report*, pp. 234–49. London: I.B. Tauris.

Hallaq, W. 1984. "Was the Gate of Ijtihad Closed?" *International Journal of Middle East Studies*, 16: 3–41.

Hallaq, W.B. 1997. *A History of Islamic Legal Theories: an Introduction to Sunni Usul al-Fiqh*. Cambridge: Cambridge University Press.

Halliday, F. 1996. *Islam and the Myth of Confrontation: Religion and Politics in the Middle East*. London: I.B. Tauris.

Hamidullah, Muhammad. 1986. "Relations of Muslims with Non-Muslims." *Journal of the Institute of Muslim Minority Affairs*, 7, 1: 7–12.

Hammami, R. 1997. "From Immodesty to Collaboration: Hamas, the Women's Movement, and National Identity in the Intifada." In Beinin, J. and Stork, J. (eds) *Political Islam: Essays from Middle East Report*, pp. 194–210. London: I.B. Tauris.

Hammoudi, A. 1993. *The Victim and its Masks: an Essay on Sacrifice and Masquerade in the Maghreb*. Chicago: University of Chicago Press.

Hann, C. 1996. "Introduction: Political Society and Civil Anthropology." In Hann, C. and Dunn, E. (eds) *Civil Society: Challenging Western Models*, pp. 1–26. London: Routledge.

Hannerz, U. 1987. "The World in Creolization." *Africa*, 57 (4): 546–59.

Hannerz, U. 1992. *Cultural Complexity: Studies in the Social Organization of Meaning*. New York: Columbia University Press.

Hargey, T. 1981. "The Suppression of Slavery in the Sudan: 1893–1939." Unpublished PhD dissertation, Northwestern University, Evanston.

Hassan, Ammar Ali. 2004. "The Islamist Perspective." *Al-Ahram Weekly*, May 20–6: 12.

Hefner, R.W. 1997. "Islam in an Era of Nation-States: Politics and Religious Renewal in Muslim Southeast Asia." In Hefner, R.W. and Horvatich, P. (eds) *Islam in an Era of Nation-States: Politics and Religious Renewal in Muslim Southeast Asia*, pp. 4–41. Honolulu: University of Hawaii Press.

Helmy, Taher. 2004. "Empowering the People." *Al-Ahram Weekly*, Sept. 2–8: 5.

Hensher, P. 2001. "Let's be Honest: We need to Impose our Imperial Rule on Afghanistan." *The Wednesday Review: The Independent*, Oct. 17: 4.

Hill, R. 1959. *Egypt in the Sudan*. Oxford: Oxford University Press.

Hill, R. and Hogg, P. 1995. *A Black Corps d'Élite: an Egyptian Sudanese Conscript Battalion with the French Army in Mexico, 1863–1867, and its Survivors in Subsequent African History*. East Lansing: Michigan State University.

Hilton, I. 2004. "Held in Contempt." *FTWeekend*, Aug. 28–9: W1–W2.

Hinnebusch, R.A. 1996. "State and Islamism in Syria." In Sidahmed, Abdel Salam and Ehteshami, Anoushiravan (eds) *Islamic Fundamentalism*, pp. 199–214. Boulder, Colo.: Westview Press.

Hirschkind, C. 2001a. "The Ethics of Listening: Cassette-Sermon Audition in Contemporary Egypt." *American Ethnologist*, 28, 3: 623–49.

Hirschkind, C. 2001b. "Civic Virtue and Religious Reason: an Islamic Counterpublic." *Cultural Anthropology*, 16, 1: 3–34.

Hirschkind, C. and Mahmood, S. 2002. "Feminism, the Taliban, and Politics of Counter-Insurgency." *Anthropological Quarterly*, 75, 2: 339–54.

Hitti, P.K. 1991. *History of the Arabs*. London: Macmillan.

Hizb ut-Tahrir. 1989. *Khilafah is the Answer*. London: al-Khilafa Publications.

Hizb ut-Tahrir. 1996. *Hizb ut-Tahrir*. London: al-Khilafa Publications.

Hizb ut-Tahrir. n.d. *The Road to Victory*. London: al-Khilafa Publications.

Hobsbawm, E.J. 1995. *Nations and Nationalism since 1780: Programme, Myth, Reality*. Cambridge: Cambridge University Press.

Hobsbawm, E. and Ranger, T. (eds). 1993. *The Invention of Tradition*. Cambridge: Cambridge University Press.

Hodgkin, E. 1990. "Islamism and Islamic Research in Africa." *Islam et Sociétés au Sud du Sahara*, 4: 73–130.

Hodgson, M.G.S. 1977. *The Venture of Islam: Conscience and History in a World Civilization*. Chicago: Chicago University Press.

Holland, G. 2001. "Cartoon Villain." *G2: The Guardian Europe*, Oct. 19: 5.

Holt, P.M. 1977. *The Mahdist State in the Sudan, 1881–1898: A Study of its Origins, Development and Overthrow*. Oxford: Oxford University Press.

Holy, L. 1991. *Religion and Custom in a Muslim Society: the Berti of Sudan*. Cambridge: Cambridge University Press.

Hoodfar, H. 1997. "Devices and Desires: Population Policy and Gender Roles in the Islamic Republic." In Beinin, J. and Stork, J. (eds) *Political Islam: Essays from Middle East Report*, pp. 220–33. London: I.B. Tauris.

Hopko, T. 1984. *The Orthodox Faith. Vol. IV: Spirituality*. The Department of Religious Education. New York: The Orthodox Church in America.

Horton, R. 1967. "African Traditional Thought and Western Science." *Africa*, 31, 50–71: 155–87.

Hourani, A. 1989. *Arabic Thought in the Libearal Age 1798–1939*. Cambridge: Cambridge University Press.

Hourani, A. 1991. *Islam in European Thought*. Cambridge: Cambridge University Press.
Hourani, A. 1993. "Introduction." In Hourani, A., Khouri, P.S., and Wilson, M.C. (eds) *The Modern Middle East*, pp. 1–20. London: I.B. Tauris.
Houtsenen, J. 1994. "Traditional Qur'anic Education in a Southern Moroccan Village." *International Journal of Middle East Studies*, 26: 489–500.
Howeidy, Amira. 2004. "Taking Algeria." *Al-Ahram Weekly*, April 15–21: 7.
Howell, S. 1986. "Formal Speech Acts as one Discourse." *Man*, 21: 79–101.
http://weekly.ahram.org.eg/
http://www.csis.org/islam/
http://www.holidays.net/ramadan/story.htm
http://www.isd.usc.edu/~~jnawaj/ISLAM/PILLARS/FastFiqh.html
http://www.islamknowledge.com/Jumah.htm
http://www.islamknowledge.com/unity_amongst_muslims.htm
http://www.muslimedia.com/archives/special98/hajj2.htm
http://www.muslimedia.com/archives/special-edition/hajj/hajj1.htm
http://www.muslimedia.com/archives/special-edition/hajj/hajj2.htm
http://www.newadvent.org/cathen/15006b.htm
http://www.news.bbc.co.uk/go/pr/fr/-1/hi/world/europe/3840133.stm
http://www.news.bbc.co.uk/go/pr/fr/-/1/hi/world/middle_east/4199363.stm
http://www.news.bbc.co.uk/go/pr/fr/-1/hi/world/europe/3840133.stm
http://www.qss.org/articles/ramadan/toc.html
http://www.submission.org/ramadan.html
http://www.taleban.com/
http://www.ummah.org.uk/ikhwan/index.html
http://www.ummah.org.uk/ramadhan/
http://www.ummah.org.uk/ramadhan/ikhwan/index.html
Huntington, S. 1993. "The Clash of Civilizations." *Foreign Affairs*, Summer: 22–49.
Hurreiz, S. 1991. "*Zar* as a Ritual Psychodrama: from Cult to Club." In Lewis, I.M., al-Safi, Ahmed, and Hurreiz, Sayyid (eds) *Women's Medicine: the Zar-Bori Cult in Africa and Beyond*, pp. 147–55. Edinburgh: Edinburgh University Press.
Husain, Mir Zohair. 1995. *Global Islamic Politics*. New York: HarperCollins College Publishers.
Ibn Khaldūn. 1986. *The Muqaddimah: an Introduction to History*. London: Routledge and Kegan Paul.
Idjtihād: *EI*.
'Ilm al-kalām: *EI*.
Inalcik, H. 1995. *The Ottoman Empire: the Classical Era, 1300–1600*. Athens: Alexandria (Greek translation).
Inalcik, H. and Quataert, D. 1996. *An Economic and Social History of the Ottoman Empire, 1300–1914*. Cambridge: Cambridge University Press.
Iqbal, Zubair and Mirakhor, Abbas. 1987. *Islamic Banking*. Washington DC: International Monetary Fund.
Iṣlāḥ: *EI*.
Ismail, S. 1998. "Confronting the Other: Identity Culture, Politics, and Conservative Islamism in Egypt." *International Journal of Middle East Studies*, 30: 199–225.
Issa, Abdu Ghalib Ahmad. 1996a. *Prayer in Islam*. Khartoum: Dar El-Nil.

Issa, Abdu Ghalib Ahmad. 1996b. *Zakat in Islam*. Khartoum: Dar El-Nil.
Ivy, M. 1995. *Discourses of the Vanishing: Modernity, Phantasm, Japan*. Chicago: University of Chicago Press.
Jameelah, Maryam. 1990. *Islam and Orientalism*. Lahore: Muhammad Yusuf Khan and Sons.
James, W. 1988. "Perceptions from an African Slave Frontier." In Archer, L. (ed.) *Slavery and Other Forms of Unfree Labour*, pp. 130–42. London: Routledge.
Jansen, G. 1995. "Countering Denigration." *Middle East International*, Feb. 3: 10–1.
Jansen, J.J.G. 1986. *The Neglected Duty: the Creed of Sadat's Assassins and Islamic Resurgence in the Middle East*. New York: Macmillan.
Jansen, W. 1987. *Women without Men*. Leiden: E.J. Brill.
Jean-Klein, I. 2001. "Nationalism and Resistance: the Two Faces of Everyday Activism in Palestine during the Intifada." *Cultural Anthropology*, 16 (1): 83–126.
Jenkins, G. 2003. "Muslim Democrats in Turkey?" *Survival*, 45, 1: 45–66.
Johnson, D.H. 2003. *The Root Causes of Sudan's Civil Wars*. Oxford: James Currey.
Jok, J.M. 2001. *War and Slavery in Sudan*. Philadelphia: University of Pennsylvania Press.
Kalyvas, S. 2003. "Unsecular Politics and Religious Mobilisation." In Kselman, T. and Buttigieg, J. (eds) *European Christian Democracy: Historical Legacies and Comparative Perspectives*, pp. 293–320. Notre Dame, Ind.: University of Notre Dame Press.
Kandiyoti, D. 1992. "Women, Islam and the State: a Comparative Approach." In Cole, J.R. (ed.) *Comparing Muslim Societies: Knowledge and the State in a World Civilization*, pp. 237–60. Ann Arbor: University of Michigan Press.
Kapteijns, L. 1985. *Mahdist Faith and Sudanic Tradition: the History of the Masalit Sultanate, 1870–1930*. London: KPI Publications.
Karam, A.M. 1998. *Women, Islamisms and the State: Contemporary Feminisms in Egypt*. Houndmills: Macmillan Press.
Karpat, K.H. 2001. *The Politicization of Islam: Reconstructing Identity, State, Faith, and Community in the Late Ottoman State*. Oxford: Oxford University Press.
Karrar, Ali Salih. 1992. *The Sufi Brotherhoods in the Sudan*. London: Hurst.
Al-Karsani, Awad al-Sid. 1985a. "The Tijaniyya Order in the Western Sudan: a Case Study of Three Centres, al-Fasher, an-Nahud and Khursi." Unpublished PhD thesis, University of Khartoum.
Al-Karsani, Awad al-Sid. 1985b. "The Majdhubiyya Tariqa: its Doctrine, Organization and Politics." In Daly, M.W. (ed.) *al-Majdhubiyya and al-Mikashfiyya: Two Sufi Tariqas in the Sudan*. Khartoum and London: Graduate College, University of Khartoum.
Kassam, Karim Aly. 1993. "Integration of Islam in Young Ottoman Thought, Part I." *Islamica*, 1, 3, 10: 10–14.
Kassam, Karim Aly. 1994. "Integration of Islam in Young Ottoman Thought, Part II." *Islamica*, 1, 4: 15–21.
Kennedy, J.G. 1967. "Nubian Zar Ceremonies as Psychotherapy." *Human Organisation*, 26 (4): 186–94.
Kenyon, S.M. 1991a. *Five Women of Sennar: Culture and Change in Central Sudan*. Oxford: Clarendon Press.
Kenyon, S.M. 1991b. "The Story of a Tin Box: *Zar* in the Sudanese Town of Sennar." In Lewis, I.M., al-Safi, Ahmed, and Hurreiz, Sayyid (eds) *Women's Medicine: the Zar-Bori Cult in Africa and Beyond*, pp. 100–17. Edinburgh: Edinburgh University Press.

Kepel, G. 1995. *The Revenge of God: the Resurgence of Islam, Christianity and Judaism in the Modern World*. Cambridge: Polity Press.
Kepel, G. 1997. *Allah in the West: Islamic Movements in America and Europe*. Cambridge: Polity Press.
Khalil, Nevine. 1998. "Building Anti-terrorism Consensus." *Al-Ahram Weekly*, Sept. 24–30: 2.
Khalil, Nevine. 2004. "Education System due for an Overhaul." *Al-Ahram Weekly*, May 6–12: 2.
Khan, Maulana Wahiduddin. 1997. *Islam and Modern Challenges*. New Delhi: Goodword Books.
Khuṭba: *EI*.
Klein, F.A. 1985. *The Religion of Islam*. London: Curzon Press.
Krämer, G. 1996. "The Integration of the Integrists: a Comparative Study of Egypt, Jordan and Tunisia." In Salame, G. (ed.) *Democracy without Democrats: The Renewal of Politics in the Muslim World*, pp. 200–26. London: I.B. Tauris.
Krämer, G. 1997. "Islamist Notions of Democracy." In Beinin, J. and Stork, J. (eds) *Political Islam: Essays from Middle East Report*, pp. 71–82. London: I.B. Tauris.
Kuper, A. (ed.). 1992. *Conceptualizing Society*. London: Routledge.
al-Kur'ān: *EI*.
Kyrtatas, D. 1987. *The Social Structure of the Early Christian Communities*. London: Verso.
Lamya, L. n.d. "Islamic Traditions and the Feminist Movement: Confrontation or Cooperation." http//www.albany.edu/~ha4934/feminism.html.
Lawrence, B. 1990. *Defenders of God: the Fundamentalist Revolt against the Modern Age*. London: I.B. Tauris.
Leach, E. 1964. *The Political System of Highland Burma*. London: Athlone Press.
Lebrecht, N. 2004. "Fighting the Extremists." *Evening Standard*, July 9: 13.
Leca, J. 1996. "Democratization in the Arab World: Uncertainty, Vulnerability and Legitimacy. A Tentative Conceptualization and some Hypotheses." In Salame, G. (ed.) *Democracy without Democrats: The Renewal of Politics in the Muslim World*, pp. 48–83. London: I.B. Tauris.
Lechner, F. 1990. "Fundamentalism Revisited." In Robbins, T. and Anthony, D. (eds) *In Gods we Trust*, pp. 77–97. New Brunswick, N.J.: Transaction.
Lesch, A.M. 1998. *Sudan: Contested National Identities*. Bloomington: Indiana University Press.
Levi Strauss, C. 1966. *The Savage Mind*. London: Weidenfeld and Nicolson.
Levtzion, N. 2000. "Islam in the Bilad al-Sudan to 1800." In Levtzion, N. and Pouwels, R.L. (eds) *The History of Islam in Africa*, pp. 63–91. Oxford: James Currey.
Levy-Bruhl, L. 1926. *How Natives Think*. London: Unwin Brothers.
Lewis, B. 1981. *The Muslim Discovery of Europe*. New York: W.W. Norton.
Lewis, B. 1990. *Race and Slavery in the Middle East: an Historical Enquiry*. Oxford: Oxford University Press.
Lewis, B. 1991. *The Political Language of Islam*. Chicago: University of Chicago Press.
Lewis, B. 2003a. *What Went Wrong?: the Clash between Islam and Modernity in the Middle East*. New York: Perennial.
Lewis, B. 2003b. *The Crisis of Islam: Holy War and Unholy Terror*. New York: Modern Library.

Lewis, I.M. 1984. "Sufism in Somaliland: a Study in Tribal Islam." In Ahmed, Akbar S. and Hart, D. (eds) *Islam in Tribal Societies: From the Atlas to the Indus*, pp. 127–68. London: Routledge and Kegan Paul.

Lewis, I.M. 1986. *Religion in Context: Cults and Charisma*. Cambridge: Cambridge University Press.

Lewis, I.M. 1989. *Ecstatic Religion: a Study of Shamanism and Spirit Possession*. London: Routledge.

Lewis, I.M. 1990. "Spirits at the House of Childbirth." *The Times Literary Supplement*, June 1–7: 590.

Lewis, I.M. 1998. *Saints and Somalis: Popular Islam in a Clan-based Society*. Lawrenceville, N.J.: Red Sea Press.

Lewis, I.M. 1999. *Arguments with Ethnography: Comparative Approaches to History, Politics and Religion*. London: Athlone Press.

Lewis, I.M., al-Safi, Ahmed, and Hurreiz, Sayyid (eds). 1991. *Women's Medicine: the Zar-Bori Cult in Africa and Beyond*. Edinburgh: Edinburgh University Press.

Lind, M. 2001. "Fundamental Flaws." *Observer*, Nov. 11: 21.

Lindholm, C. 2002. "Kissing Cousins: Anthropologists on Islam." In Donnan, H. (ed.) *Interpreting Islam*, pp. 110–29. London: Sage.

Litvak, M. 1998. "The Islamization of the Palestinian–Israeli Conflict: the Case of Hamas." *Middle Eastern Studies*, 34, 1: 148–63.

Loomba, A. 1998. *Colonialism/Postcolonialism*. London: Routledge.

MacIntyre, A. 1967. *Secularization and Moral Change*. Oxford: Oxford University Press.

MacIntyre, A. 2003. *After Virtue*. London: Duckworth.

MacLeod, A.E. 1992. *Accommodating Protest: Working Women, the New Veiling, and Change in Cairo*. Cairo: American University in Cairo Press.

MacLeod, A.E. 1996. "Transforming Women's Identity: the Intersection of Household and Workplace in Cairo." In Singerman, D. and Hoodfar, H. (eds) *Development, Change, and Gender in Cairo: a View from the Household*, pp. 27–50. Bloomington: Indiana University Press.

Magnuson, K. 1987. "Islamic Reform in Contemporary Tunisia: A Comparative Ethnographic Study." Unpublished PhD thesis in Anthropology, Brown University.

Al-Mahdi, Sadiq. 1983. "Islam: Society and Change." In Esposito, J.L. (ed.) *Voices of Resurgent Islam*, pp. 230–40. Oxford: Oxford University Press.

Mahmood, S. 2001. "Feminist Theory, Embodiment, and the Docile Agent: Some Reflections on the Egyptian Islamic Revival." *Cultural Anthropology*, 16, 2: 202–36.

Mahmoud, Muhammad. 1996. "Women and Islamism: the Case of Rashid al-Ghannusi of Tunisia." In Sidahmed, Abdel Salam and Ehteshami, Anoushiravan (eds) *Islamic Fundamentalism*, pp. 249–65. Boulder, Colo.: Westview Press.

Makris, G.P. 2000. *Changing Masters: Spirit Possession and Identity Construction among Descendants of Slaves and Other Subordinates in the Sudan*. Evanston, Ill.: Northwestern University Press.

Marcus, G.E. and Fischer, M.M.J. 1986. *Anthropology as Cultural Critique: an Experimental Moment in the Human Sciences*. Chicago: University of Chicago Press.

Mardin, S. 1989. *Religion and Social Change in Modern Turkey: the Case of Bediüzzaman Said Nursi*. New York: State University of New York Press.

Masdjid: *EI*.

Maududi, Mawlana Abul A'la, 1992. *West versus Islam*. Delhi: Markazi Maktaba Islami.

Mauss, M. 1979. *The Gift*. Athens: Kastaniotis (Greek translation).

Mauss, M. 2003. *On Prayer*. New York: Durkheim Press, Bergham Books.

McHugh, N. 1994. Holy Men of the Blue Nile. Evanston, Ill.: Northwestern University Press.

Medani, Khalid. 1997. "Funding Fundamentalism: The Political Economy of an Islamic State." In Beinin, J. and Stork, J. (eds) *Political Islam: Essays from Middle East Report*, pp. 166–77. London: I.B. Tauris.

El-Menshawy, Mustafa. 2004. "Re-engineering Religious Education." *Al-Ahram Weekly*, Aug. 19–25: 3.

Mernissi, F. 1975. *Beyond the Veil: Male–Female Dynamics in a Modern Muslim Society*. Cambridge, Mass.: Shenkman.

Mernissi, F. 1988. "Muslim Women and Fundamentalism." *MERIP Middle East Report*, 18, 4: 8–11.

Messick, B. 1986. "The Mufti, the Text and the World: Legal Interpretation in Yemen." *Man*, n.s. 21: 102–19.

Messick, B. 1993. *The Calligraphic State: Textual Domination and History in a Muslim Society*. Berkeley: University of California Press.

Metcalf, B.D. 1996. "Two Fatwas on Hajj in British India." In Masud, Muhammad Khalid, Messick, B., and Powers, D.S. (eds) *Islamic Legal Interpretation: Muftis and their Fatwas*, pp. 184–92. Cambridge, Mass.: Harvard University Press.

Metzger, A. 1995. "Islamists set the Social and Political Agenda in Egypt." *Middle East International*, Jan. 20: 16–17.

Michel, T. 1985. "The Rights of Non-Muslims in Islam: An Opening Statement." *Journal of the Institute of Muslim Minority Affairs*, 7, 1: 7–20.

Michel, T. 1992. "Christian–Muslim Dialogue in a Changing World." *Theology Digest*, 39: 303–20.

Middle East International (anonymous correspondent). 2003a. "Bombers on Trial." July 25: 19–20.

Middle East International (anonymous correspondent). 2003b. "Darkening Skies." May 30: 24–6.

Middle East International (anonymous correspondent). 2003c. "Aftershock." June 13: 19–20.

Middle East International (anonymous correspondent). 2003d. "High Ground." Sept. 26: 25–6.

Milton-Edwards, B. 1991. "A Temporary Alliance with the Crown: the Islamic Response in Jordan." In Piscatori, J. (ed.) *Islamic Fundamentalism and the Gulf Crisis*, pp. 88–108. The Fundamentalism Project. Chicago: American Academy of Arts and Sciences.

Milton-Edwards, B. 1999. *Islamic Politics in Palestine*. London: I.B. Tauris.

Mishal, S. and Sela, A. 2000. *The Palestinian Hamas: Vision, Violence, and Coexistence*. New York: Columbia University Press.

Mitchell, T. 1991. *Colonising Egypt*. Berkeley: University of California Press.

Modood, T. 1997. "The Politics of Multiculturalism in the New Europe." In Modood, T. and Werbner, P. (eds) *The Politics of Multiculturalism in the New Europe: Racism, Identity and Community*, pp. 1–25. London: Zed Books.

Moltman, J. 2002. *Theology of Hope*. London: SCM Press.

Morini, A. 1984. *Pilgrimage in the Hindu Tradition*. Delhi: Oxford University Press.

Morris, B. 1998. *Anthropological Studies of Religion: an Introductory Text*. Cambridge: Cambridge University Press.

Morsy, S. 1991. "Spirit Possession in Egyptian Ethnomedicine: Origins, Comparison, and Historical Specificity." In Lewis, I.M., al-Safi, Ahmed, and Hurreiz, Sayyid (eds) *Women's Medicine: the Zar-Bori Cult in Africa and Beyond*, pp. 189–208. Edinburgh: Edinburgh University Press.

Moustafa, T. 2000. "Conflict and Cooperation between the State and Religious Institutions in Contemporary Egypt." *International Journal of Middle East Studies*, 32: 3–22.

al-Munājjib, Muḥammad Ṣāliḥ. n.d. "Seventy Issues relating to Fasting." In http:www.Islam-QA.com/Books/Seyam/English.shtml1#introduction.

Al-Nabaḥānī, Taqī al-Dīn. 1998. *The Islamic State*. London: al-Khilafah Publications.

Nafie, Reem. 2004. "Big Brother Blocks Brotherhood Site." *Al-Ahram Weekly*, Sept. 9–15, p. 2.

Al-Naqar, U. 1972. *The Pilgrimage Tradition in West Africa*. Khartoum: Khartoum University Press.

Nasr, Seyyed Hossein. 1992. "Oral Transmision and the Book in Islamic Education: The Spoken and the Written Word." *Journal of Islamic Studies*, 3, 1: 1–14.

Nasseef, Abdulla Omar. 1986. "Muslim–Christian Relations: The Muslim Approach." *Journal of the Institute of Muslim Minority Affairs*, 7, 1: 27–31.

Natvig, R. 1988. "Liminal Rites and female symbolism in the Egyptian Zar Possession Cult." *Numen*, 35: 57–68.

Natvig, R. 1991. "Some Notes on the History of Zar in Egypt." In Lewis, I.M., al-Safi, Ahmed, and Hurreiz, Sayyid (eds) *Women's Medicine: the Zar-Bori Cult in Africa and Beyond*, pp. 178–88. Edinburgh: Edinburgh University Press.

Navaro-Yashin, Y. 2002. *Faces of the State: Secularism and Public Life in Turkey*. Princeton, N.J.: Princeton University Press.

Nelson, C. and Altorki, S. (eds) 1998. *Arab Regional Women's Studies Workshop*. Cairo Papers in Social Science, 20, 3.

Nielsen, J. 1995a. *Muslims in Western Europe*. Edinburgh: Edinburgh University Press.

Nielsen, J. 1995b. "Christian–Muslim Relations in Western Europe." *Islamochristiana*, 21: 121–31.

Nkrumah, Gamal. 2002. "Tables turn on Turabi." *Al-Ahram Weekly*, June 24–30: 8.

Nordenstan, T. 1968. *Sudanese Ethics*. Uppsala: Scandinavian Institute of African Studies.

Norton, R.A. 1995. *Civil Society in the Middle East*, vol. i. Leiden: E.J. Brill.

Norton, R.A. 1996. *Civil Society in the Middle East*, vol. ii. Leiden: E.J. Brill.

Noumoff, S.J. 2004. "Be Very Afraid." *Al-Ahram Weekly*, Sept. 9–15: 11.

O'Fahey, R.S. 1973. "Saints and Sulṭāns: the Role of Muslim Holy Men in the Keira Sultanate of Dār Fūr." In Brett, M. (ed.) *Northern Africa: Islam and Modernization*. London: Frank Cass.

O'Fahey, R.S. 1990. *Enigmatic Saint: Ahmad Ibn Idris and the Idrisi Tradition*. London: Hurst.

O'Mahony, A. 1993. "Christianity in the Holy Land: the Historical Background." *The Month*, second n.s., 26, 12: 469–76.

O'Mahony, A. 1996. "Between Islam and Christendom: The Ethiopian Community in Jerusalem Before 1517." *Medieval Encounters: Jewish, Christian and Muslim Culture in Confluence and Dialogue*, 2, 2: 140–54.

O'Mahony, A. (ed.). 1999. *Palestinian Christians: Religion, Politics and Society in the Holy Land*. London: Melisende.

O'Mahony, A. 2001. "Islam in Europe." *The Way: Contemporary Christian Spirituality*, 41: 122–35.

Ong, W.J. 1982 (1997). *Orality and Literacy*. Panepistimiakes Heraclion: Ekdosis Kritis (Greek translation).

Parry, J. 1985. "The Brahmanical Tradition and the Technology of the Intellect." In Overing, J. (ed.) *Reason and Morality*, pp. 200–25. London: Tavistock Publications.

Parsons, T. 1966. *Societies: Evolutionary and Comparative Perspectives*. Englewood Cliffs, N.J.: Prentice Hall.

Pearson, M.N. 2000. "The Indian Ocean and the Red Sea." In Levtzion, N. and Pouwels, R.L. (eds) *The History of Islam in Africa*, pp. 37–59. Oxford: James Currey.

Perry, G.E. 1992. *The Middle East: Fourteen Islamic Centuries*. Englewood Cliffs, N.J.: Prentice Hall.

Peteet, J. 1994. "Male Gender and Rituals of Resistance in the Palestinian *Intifada*: a Cultural Politics of Violence." *American Ethnologist*, 21(1): 31–49.

Pfeifer, K. 1997. "Is there an Islamic Economics?" In Beinin, J. and Stork, J. (eds) *Political Islam: Essays from Middle East Report*, pp. 154–65. London: I.B. Tauris.

Pipes, D. 2002. *In the Path of God: Islam and Political Power*. Somerset, N.J.: Transaction Publishers.

Pipes, D. 2003. *Militant Islam reaches America*. New York: W.W. Norton.

Piscatori, J. 1991. "Religion and Realpolitic: Islamic Responses to the Gulf War." In Piscatori, J. (ed.) *Islamic Fundamentalisms and the Gulf Crisis*, pp. 1–27. The Fundamentalism Project. Chicago: American Academy of Arts and Sciences.

Piscatori, J. 2000. *Islam, Islamists, and the Electoral Principle in the Middle East*. Leiden: ISIM.

Al-Qaradāwī, Y. 1992. *Priorities of the Islamic Movement in the Coming Phase*. Cairo: Dar al-Nashr.

Al-Qaradāwī, Y. 1995. *Islamic Awakening: Between Rejection and Extremism*. Herndon: International Institute of Islamic Thought.

Qasim, Talaat Fuad. 1997. "What does the Gama'a Islamiyya Want?" In Beinin, J. and Stork, J. (eds) *Political Islam: Essays from Middle East Report*, pp. 314–26. London: I.B. Tauris.

Quataert, D. 2001. *The Ottoman Empire, 1700–1922*. Cambridge: Cambridge University Press.

Rahman, Fazlur. 1964. "Riba and Interest." *Islamic Studies*, 3, 4: 6–8.

Rahman, Fazlur. 1984. *Islam and Modernity: Transformation of an Intellectual Tradition*. Chicago: University of Chicago Press.

Rahman, Fazlur. 1986. "Non-Muslim Minorities in an Islamic State." *Journal of the Institute of Muslim Minority Affairs*, 7, 1: 13–24.

Rashid, A. 1999. "The Taliban: Exporting Extremism." *Foreign Affairs*, 78, 6: 22–35.

Rashid, A. 2001. *Taliban: Militant Islam, Oil, and Fundamentalism in Central Asia*. New Haven: Yale University Press.

Rayner, S.E. 1991. *The Theory of Contracts in Islamic Law.* London: Graham and Trotman.

Reinhart, A.K. 1996. "When Women went to Mosques: al-Aydini on the Duration of Assessments." In Masud, Muhammad Khalid, Messick, B., and Powers, D.S. (eds) *Islamic Legal Interpretation: Muftis and their Fatwas*, pp. 116–28. Cambridge: Harvard University Press.

Rey, P.P. 1971. *Colonialisme, Neo-Colonialisme et Transition au Capitalisme.* Paris: Maspero.

Robben, A.C.G.M. and Nordsrom, C. 1995. "The Anthropology and Ethnography of Violence and Sociopolitical Conflict." In Robben, A.C.G.M. and Nordstrom, C. (eds) *Fieldwork under Fire: Contemporary Studies of Violence and Survival*, pp. 1–21. Berkeley: University of California Press.

Roberts, H. 1991. "A Trial of Strength: Algerian Islamism." In Piscatori, J. (ed.) *Islamic Fundamentalisms and the Gulf Crisis*, pp. 131–54. The Fundamentalism Project. Chicago: American Academy of Arts and Sciences.

Robertson, R. 1992. *Globalization.* London: Sage.

Rodinson, M. 1966 [1980]. *Islam and Capitalism.* Athens: Kalvos (Greek translation).

Rodinson, M. 1976. *Mohammed.* London: Pelican.

Roff, W.R. 1985. "Pilgrimage and the History of Religions: Theoretical Approaches to the Hajj." In Martin, R.C. (ed.) *Approaches to Islam in Religious Studies.* Tucson: University of Arizona Press.

Roff, W.R. (ed.) 1987. *Islam and the Political Economy of Meaning: Comparative Studies of Muslim Discourse.* Berkeley: University of California Press.

Roy, O. 1994. *The Failure of Political Islam.* London: I.B. Tauris.

Roy, O. 2004. *Globalised Islam: the Search for a New Ummah.* London: Hurst.

Saad-Ghorayeb, A. 2002. *Hizbu'llah: Politics, Religion.* London: Pluto Press.

Said, E. 1991. *Orientalism.* London: Penguin.

Saktanber, A. 1994. "Becoming the 'Other' as a Muslim in Turkey: Turkish Women vs. Islamist Women." *New Perspectives on Turkey*, Fall 11: 99–134.

Saktanber, A. 2002. *Living Islam: Women, Religion, and the Politicization of Culture in Turkey.* London: I.B. Tauris.

Ṣalāt: *EI.*

Saleh, Heba. 2003. "FIS Figures freed." *Middle East Report*, July 11: 22–3.

Samatar, Said S. (ed.). 1992. *In the Shadow of Conquest: Islam in Colonial Northeast Africa.* Trenton, N.J.: Red Sea Press.

Sardar, Z. 1998. *Postmodernism and the Other: the New Imperialism of Western Culture.* London: Pluto Press.

El-Sayed, Afaf Loufti. 1968. "The Ulama in Egypt during the Early Nineteenth Century." In Hold, P.M. (ed.) *Political and Social Change in Egypt: Historical Studies from the Ottoman Conquest to the United Arab Republic*, pp. 264–80. London: Oxford University Press.

Schacht, J. 1982. *An Introduction to Islamic Law.* Oxford: Oxford University Press.

Schimmel, A. 1975. *Mystical Dimensions of Islam.* Chapel Hill: University of North Carolina Press.

Schmemann, A. 1995. *For the Life of the World: Sacraments and Orthodoxy.* Crestwood, N.Y.: St Vladimir's Seminary Press.

Scott, J.C. 1985. *Weapons of the Weak: Everyday Forms of Peasant Resistance.* New Haven: Yale University Press.

Scott, J.C. 1990. *Domination and the Arts of Resistance*. New Haven: Yale University Press.

Seesemann, R. 2002. "Sufi Leaders and Social Welfare: Two Examples from the Sudan." In Weiss, H. (ed.) *Social Welfare in Muslim Societies in Africa*, pp. 98–117. Stockholm: Nordiska Afrikainstitutet.

Sennett, R. 2002. "They Mean Well: the American Flight from Politics into Faith." *Times Literary Supplement*, June 7: 6–8.

Shadid, A. 2002. *Legacy of the Prophet: Despots, Democrats, and the New Politics of Islam*. Boulder, Colo.: Westview Press.

Shahine, Gihan. 2004. "The Brotherhood's Latest Challenge." *Al-Ahram Weekly*, June 3–9: 3.

Shakry, O. 1998. "Schooled Mothers and Structured Play: Child-rearing in Turn-of-the-Century Egypt." In Abu-Lughod, L. (ed.) *Remaking Women: Feminism and Modernity in the Middle East*, pp. 126–70. Princeton, N.J.: Princeton University Press.

Shankland, D. 1999. *Islam and Society in Turkey*. Huntingdon: The Eothen Press.

Sharī'a: *EI*.

Shaw, R. and Stewart, C. 1994. "Introduction: Problematizing Syncretism." In Stewart, C. and Shaw, R. (eds) *Syncretism/Anti-Syncretism: The Politics of Religious Synthesis*, pp. 1–26. London: Routledge.

El-Shayyal, Gamal el-Din. 1968. "Some Aspects of Intellectual and Social Life in Eighteenth-century Egypt." In Holt, P.M. (ed.) *Political and Social Change in Egypt: Historical Studies from the Ottoman Conquest to the United Arab Republic*, pp. 117–32. London: Oxford University Press.

Shepard, W.E. 1996. "Muhammad Sa'id al-'Ashmawi and the Application of the Shari'a in Egypt." *International Journal of Middle East Studies*, 28: 39–58.

Sidahmed, Abdel Salam. 1996. "Sudan: Ideology and Pragmatism." In Sidahmed, Abdel Salam and Ehteshami, Anoushiravan (eds) *Islamic Fundamentalism*, pp. 179–98. Boulder, Colo.: Westview Press.

Silverstein, P.A. 2002. "An Excess of Truth: Violence, Conspiracy Theorizing and the Algerian Civil War." *Anthropological Quarterly*, 75, 4: 643–74.

Singerman, D. 1995. *Avenues of Participation: Family, Politics, and Networks in Urban Quarters of Cairo*. Princeton, N.J.: Princeton University Press.

Singerman, D. and Hoodfar, H. (eds). 1996. *Development, Change, and Gender in Cairo: a View from the Household*. Bloomington: Indiana University Press.

Sivan, E. 1989. "Sunni Radicalism in the Middle East and the Iranian Revolution." *International Journal of Middle East Studies*, 21: 1–30.

Sivan, E. 1990a. *Radical Islam*. New Haven, Conn.: Yale University Press.

Sivan, E. 1990b. "Islamic Radicalism: Sunni and Shi'ite." In Sivan, E. and Froiedman, M. (eds) *Religious Radicalism and Politics in the Middle East*, pp. 39–75. Albany: State University of New York Press.

Smith, A. 1991. *National Identity*. Athens: Oddyseas (Greek translation 2000).

Smith, A. 1996. "Towards a Global Culture?" In Featherstone, M. (ed.) *Global Culture: Nationalism, Globalization and Modernity*, pp. 171–91. London: Sage.

Sorūsh, Abdolkarim. 2000. *Reason, Freedom, and Democracy in Islam*. Oxford: Oxford University Press.

Spencer, C. 1996. "The Roots and Future of Islamism in Algeria." In Sidahmed, Abdel Salam and Ehteshami, Anoushiravan (eds) *Islamic Fundamentalism*, pp. 93–107. Boulder, Colo.: Westview Press.

Starrett, G. 1995a. "The Hexis of Interpretation: Islam and the Body in the Egyptian Popular School." *American Ethnologist*, 22(4): 953–69.

Starrett, G. 1995b. "The Political Economy of Religious Commodities in Cairo." *American Anthropologist*, 97, 1: 51–68.

Starrett, G. 1996. "The Margins of Print: Children's Religious Literature in Egypt." *Journal of the Royal Anthropological Institute*, 2, 1: 117–39.

Starrett, G. 1997. "The Anthropology of Islam." In Glazier, S.D. (ed.) *Anthropology of Religion: a Handbook*, pp. 279–303. Westport, Conn.: Praeger.

Starrett, G. 1998. *Putting Islam to Work: Education, Politics, and Religious Transformation in Egypt*. Berkeley: University of California Press.

Stern, J. 2000. "Pakistan's Jihad Culture." *Foreign Affairs*, Nov./Dec., 79, 6: 115–26.

Stiansen, E. 1999. "Islamic Banking in the Sudan: Aspects of the Laws and the Debate." In Stiansen, E. and Guyer, J.I. (eds) *Credit, Currencies and Culture: African Financial Institutions in Historical Perspective*, pp. 100–17. Stockholm: Nordiska Afrikainstitutet.

Stiansen, E. 2003. "*al-Islām huwa al-ḥāl*: The Qur'an and Contemporary Islamic Finance." In Kastfelt, N. (ed.) *Scriptural Politics: the Bible and the Koran as Political Models in the Middle East and Africa*, pp. 66–95. London: Hurst.

Stork, J. 1997. "Gender and Civil Society." In Beinin, J. and Stork, J. (eds) *Political Islam: Essays from Middle East Report*, pp. 64–70. London: I.B. Tauris.

Strathern, M. (ed.). 2000. *Audit Cultures: Anthropological Studies in Accountability, Ethics and the Academy*. London: Routledge.

Taji-Farouki, Suha. 1996a. "Islamic State Theories and Contemporary Realities." In Sidahmed, Abdel Salam and Ehteshami, Anoushiravan (eds) *Islamic Fundamentalism*, pp. 35–50. Boulder, Colo.: Westview Press.

Taji-Farouki, Suha. 1996b. *A Fundamental Quest: Hizb al-Tahrir and the Search for the Islamic Caliphate*. London: Grey Seal.

Tambiah, S. 1985. *Culture, Thought and Social Action*. Cambridge, Mass.: Harvard University Press.

Tapper, N. and Tapper, R. 1987. "The Birth of the Prophet: Ritual and Gender in Turkish Islam." *Man*, n.s., 22: 69–92.

Tapper, R. 1984. "Holier than Thou: Islam in Three Tribal Societies." In Ahmed, Akbar S. and Hart, D. (eds) *Islam in Tribal Societies: From the Atlas to the Indus*, pp. 244–65. London: Routledge and Kegan Paul.

Tapper, R. (ed.). 1991. *Islam in Modern Turkey: Religion, Politics and Literature in a Secular State*. London: I.B. Tauris.

Tawḥīd: *EI*.

Taylor, C. 1998. "Modes of Secularism." In Bhargava, R. (ed.) *Secularism and its Critics*. Delhi: Oxford University Press.

Terray, E. 1984. "Classes and Class Consciousness in the Abron Kingdom of Gyaman." In Bloch, M. (ed.) *Marxist Analyses and Social Anthropology*, pp. 85–135. London: Tavistock Publications.

Thomassen, E. and Radtke, B. 1993. *The Letters of Ahmad Ibn Idris*. London: Hurst.

Thomson, D. 2001. "The Disaster Movie made Flesh and Blood." *Independent on Sunday*, Sept. 16: 20.

Tonkin, E. 1992. *Narrating our Pasts: the Social Construction of Oral History*. Cambridge: Cambridge University Press.

Toprak, B. 1993. "The Religious Right." In Hourani, A., Khouri, P.S., and Wilson, M.C. (eds) *The Modern Middle East*, pp. 625–42. London: I.B. Tauris.

Triaud, J.L. 2000. "Islam in Africa and French Colonial Rule." In Levtzion, N. and Pouwels, R.L. (eds) *The History of Islam in Africa*, pp. 169–87. Athens: Ohio University Press.

Trimingham, J.S. 1983. *Islam in the Sudan*. London: Frank Cass.

Tuquoi, J.-P. 2001. "Algerian Army Fighting a 'Dirty War.'" *Guardian Weekly*, Feb. 15–21: 29.

Turabi, Hassan. 1983. "The Islamic State." In Esposito, J.L. (ed.) *Voices of Resurgent Islam*, pp. 241–51. Oxford: Oxford University Press.

Turabi, Hassan (Abdullah al-). 1993. "Islam as a Pan-National Movement and Nation States: An Islamic Doctrine of Human Association." *Islamica*, 1, 2: 10–15.

al-Turabi, Hasan. 1995. "Civilizations at Odds. Special Hasan Turabi: 'as-sahwsh,' the Islamic Awakening, a New Islamic Wave." In http://www.msaosu@magnus.acs.ohio-state.edu, Wed., April, 26, 07:42:44.

Turner, B.S. 1978. *Weber and Islam*. London: Routledge and Kegan Paul.

Turner, V. 1974. *Drama, Fields, and Metaphors*. Ithaca, N.Y.: Cornell University Press.

Turner, V. 1976. "Ritual, Tribal and Catholic." *Worship*, 50(6): 504–5.

Turner, V. 1989. *The Ritual Process: Structure and Anti-Structure*. Ithaca, N.Y.: Cornell University Press.

Turner, V. 2002 [1969]. "Liminality and Communitas." In Lambek, M. (ed.) *A Reader in the Anthropology of Religion*, pp. 358–74. Malden, Mass.: Blackwell.

Turner, V. and Turner, E. 1978. *Image and Pilgrimage in Christian Culture*. New York: Columbia University Press.

Vandewalle, D. 1997. "Islam in Algeria: Religion, Culture, and Opposition in a Rentier State." In Esposito, J.L. (ed.) *Political Islam: Revolution, Radicalism, or Reform?*, pp. 33–51. Boulder, Colo.: Rienner.

Vansina, J. 1985. *Oral Tradition as History*. London: James Currey.

Varisco, D.M. 1995. "Metaphors and Sacred History: the Genealogy of Muhammad and the Arab 'Tribe.'" *Anthropological Quarterly*, 68, 3: 139–56.

Vatikiotis, P.J. 1980. *The History of Modern Egypt from Muhammad Ali to Mubarak*. London: Weidenfeld Paperbacks. (Greek translation 2000)

Vatin, J.C. 1987. "Seduction and Sedition: Islamic Polemical Discourses in the Maghreb." In Roff, W.R. (ed.) *Islam and the Political Economy of Meaning: Comparative Studies of Muslim Discourse*, pp. 160–79. Berkeley: University of California Press.

Vitalis, R. 1997. "Introduction to Part Two." In Beinin, J. and Stork, J. (eds) *Political Islam: Essays from Middle East Report*, pp. 97–102. London: I.B. Tauris.

Voll, J. 1979. "The Sudanese Mahdi: Frontier Fundamentalism." *International Journal of Middle Eastern Studies*, 10: 145–66.

Voll, J. 1982a. "Wahhabism and Mahdist: Alternative Styles of Islamic Renewals." *Arab Studies Quarterly*, 4, 1 & 2, pp. 110–26.

Voll, J.O. 1982b. *Islam: Continuity and Change in the Modern World*. Boulder, Colo.: Westview Press.

Voll, J.O. 1983. "Renewal and Reform in Islamic History: Tajdid and Islah." In Esposito, J.L. (ed.) *Voices of Resurgent Islam*, pp. 32–47. Oxford: Oxford University Press.
Voll, J.O. 1997. "Relations among Islamist Groups." In Esposito, J.L. (ed.) *Political Islam: Revolution, Radicalism, or Reform?*, pp. 231–47. Boulder: Lynne Rienner.
von Rad, G. 1965. *The Message of the Prophets*. San Francisco: Harper Collins.
Waqf: *EI*.
Warburg, G. 1971. "Religious Policy in the Northern Sudan: Ulama and Sufism 1899–1918." *Asian and African Studies*, viii, special number: 89–119.
Warburg, G. 1990. "The Sharia in the Sudan: Implementation and Repercussions, 1983–1989." *The Middle East Journal*, 44, 4: 624–37.
Ware, T. 1964. *The Orthodox Church*. London: Pelican.
Waterbury, J. 1994. "Democracy without Democrats? The Potential for Political Liberalization in the Middle East." In Ghassan Salamé (ed.) *Democracy without Democrats? The Renewal of Politics in the Muslim World*, pp. 23–47. London: I.B. Tauris.
Waters, M. 1995. *Globalization*. London: Routledge.
Watson, H. 1994. "Women and the Veil: Personal Responses to Global Process." In Ahmed, Akbar S. and Donnan, H. (eds) *Islam, Globalization and Postmodernity*, pp. 141–59. London: Routledge.
Watt, W.M. 1953. *Muhammad at Mecca*. Oxford: Oxford University Press.
Watt, W.M. 1956. *Muhammad at Medina*. Oxford: Oxford University Press.
Watt, W.M. 1961. *Muhammad: Prophet and Statesman*. Oxford: Oxford University Press.
Watt, W.M. 1991. *Muslim–Christian Encounters: Perceptions and Misperceptions*. London: Routledge.
Watt, W.M. 1994. *The Influence of Islam on Medieval Europe*. Edinburgh: Edinburgh University Press.
Watt, W.M. and Bell, R. 1990. *Introduction to the Qur'an*. Edinburgh: Edinburgh University Press.
Waugh, P. 2004. "Fury at Visit of the Race-Hate Cleric." *Evening Standard*, July 7: 5.
Weber, M. 1964a. *The Theory of Social and Economic Organization*. New York: Free Press.
Weber, M. 1964b. *The Sociology of Religion*. Boston: Beacon Press.
Weiss, H. 2002. "*Zakāt* and the Question of Social Welfare: an Introductory Essay on Islamic Economics and its Implications for Social Welfare." In Weiss, H. (ed.) *Social Welfare in Muslim Societies in Africa*, pp. 7–38. Stockholm: Nordiska Afrikainstitutet.
Wheatcroft, G. 2001. "Idealising the Other Side." *Guardian*, Oct. 19: 8.
Whitaker, B. 2003. "Islamic Army Revived." *Middle East International*, July 11: 22.
Whitaker, B. 2005. "Saudis use Hajj to call on Muslims to shun Militants." *Guardian*, Jan. 21: 10.
Wiktorowicz, Q. 2000. "The Salafi Movement in Jordan." *International Journal of Middle Eastern Studies*, 32: 219–40.
Wiktorowicz, Q. 2001. *The Management of Islamic Activism: Salafis, the Muslim Brotherhood, and State Power in Jordan*. New York: State University of New York Press.
Willems, P. 2004a. "To Riches or Ruin?" *Al-Ahram Weekly*, May 20–26: 7.
Willems, P. 2004b. "New Trial, Fresh Clashes." *Al-Ahram Weekly*, July 15–21: 7.
Williams, P. and Chrisman, L. (eds). 1994. *Colonial Discourse and Post-Colonial Theory: a Reader*. New York: Prentice Hall/HarvesterWheatsheaf.
Wolfe, M. 1994. *The Hadj: a Pilgrimage to Mecca*. London: Secker and Warburg.

Wright, R. 1992. "Islam, Democracy and the West." *Foreign Affairs*, Summer: 131–45.

Al-Yafai, Faisal. 2004. "Muslim Cleric defends Line on Bombers." *Guardian Weekly*, July 16–22: 8.

Yamba, C.B. 1995. *Permanent Pilgrims: the Role of Pilgrimage in the Lives of West African Muslims in Sudan*. Edinburgh: Edinburgh University Press.

Yapp, M.E. 1987. *The Making of the Modern Near East, 1792–1923*. London: Longman.

Young, W.C. 1993. "The Ka'ba, Gender, and the Rites of Pilgrimage." *International Journal of Middle East Studies*, 25: 285–300.

Zakaria, F. 2004. *The Future of Freedom: Illiberal Democracy at Home and Abroad*. New York: W.W. Norton.

Zakāt: *EI*.

Zaman, M.Q. 2002. *The Ulama in Contemporary Islam: Custodians of Change*. Princeton, N.J.: Princeton University Press.

Zeghal, M. 1999. "Religion and Politics in Egypt: the Ulema of al-Azhar, Radical Islam, and the State (1952–94)." *International Journal of Middle East Studies*, 31: 371–99.

Zižek, S. 2002. *Welcome to the Desert of the Real*. London: Verso.

Zižek, S. 2003. *The Puppet and the Dwarf: the Perverse Core of Christianity*. Cambridge, Mass.: MIT Press.

Zubaida, S. 1993. *Islam, the People and the State: Political Ideas and Movements in the Middle East*. London: I.B. Tauris.

Zubaida, S. 1997. "Religion, the State, and Democracy: Contrasting Conceptions of Society in Egypt." In Beinin, J. and Stork, J. (eds) *Political Islam: Essays from Middle East Report*, pp. 51–63. London: I.B. Tauris.

Zubaida, S. 2002. "The Fragments Imagine the Nation: the Case of Iraq." *International Journal of Middle Eastern Studies*, 34: 205–15.

Zürcher, E.J. 1997. *Turkey: a Modern History*. London: I.B. Tauris.

Index